Humanism and Good Books
in Sixteenth-Century England

Humanism and Good Books in Sixteenth-Century England

KATHERINE C. LITTLE

OXFORD
UNIVERSITY PRESS

Great Clarendon Street, Oxford, OX2 6DP,
United Kingdom

Oxford University Press is a department of the University of Oxford.
It furthers the University's objective of excellence in research, scholarship,
and education by publishing worldwide. Oxford is a registered trade mark of
Oxford University Press in the UK and in certain other countries

© Katherine C. Little 2023

The moral rights of the author have been asserted

All rights reserved. No part of this publication may be reproduced, stored in
a retrieval system, or transmitted, in any form or by any means, without the
prior permission in writing of Oxford University Press, or as expressly permitted
by law, by licence or under terms agreed with the appropriate reprographics
rights organization. Enquiries concerning reproduction outside the scope of the
above should be sent to the Rights Department, Oxford University Press, at the
address above

You must not circulate this work in any other form
and you must impose this same condition on any acquirer

Published in the United States of America by Oxford University Press
198 Madison Avenue, New York, NY 10016, United States of America

British Library Cataloguing in Publication Data

Data available

Library of Congress Control Number: 2022947755

ISBN 978–0–19–288319–3

DOI: 10.1093/oso/9780192883193.001.0001

Printed and bound by
CPI Group (UK) Ltd, Croydon, CR0 4YY

Links to third party websites are provided by Oxford in good faith and
for information only. Oxford disclaims any responsibility for the materials
contained in any third party website referenced in this work.

Acknowledgments

The many years I spent writing this book coincided with my daughters' elementary school education and also with the most recent crisis of the humanities, that is, the shrinking of the academic discipline of English in terms of enrollment and faculty positions. Both contexts provided me with opportunities to discuss the value of books with different kinds of people, including teachers, fellow-parents, fellow-academics, and my many students. I have learned a great deal from all of these conversations, and I am immensely grateful for them.

Writing these acknowledgments near the end of 2022, almost three years after the start of the COVID-19 pandemic, makes me realize just how lucky I was to be able to attend conferences and chat with people in person especially at the beginning of this project. I thank audiences at the Medieval Congress in Kalamazoo, Michigan (2013, 2014, 2017); at the Sixth International *Piers Plowman* Society Conference in Seattle (2015); and at the New Chaucer Society Conferences in London (2016) and in Toronto (2018) for asking questions and making comments that opened up new ways of seeing. Both before and during the pandemic, I have been fortunate in having friends who are always willing to offer feedback and support. For their kindness and generosity, both in general and in the particular act of reading drafts and providing comments on portions of the book, I thank Candace Barrington, Lisa Lampert-Weissig, and Eva von Contzen. Our friendship and collaboration on our journal, *New Chaucer Studies: Pedagogy & Profession*, have been truly sustaining. I am also grateful to Jennifer Bosson for countless conversations about the ideas in this book and the challenges of academic life more generally as well as for being a great friend. Thanks to Teresa Toulouse for lovely lunches and thought-provoking discussions that helped orient me as I began this book.

The University of Colorado Boulder has provided welcome financial support for this project in a variety of ways. I was able to hire summer research assistants to compile resources on morality plays and humanism, and I thank Melanie Stein Lo and Mikhaila Redovian for their helpful work. A year's release from teaching allowed me to complete the first draft of this book, and I thank the University of Colorado for funding a semester sabbatical and the Center for Humanities and the Arts at CU-Boulder for a Faculty Fellowship.

For assistance in bringing this book to its final version I thank the two anonymous reviewers for their perceptive readings, concrete suggestions, and pointed questions and my editor at Oxford University Press, Ellie Collins, who shepherded this project through the process. I am also grateful to Nick Bromley for care in copyediting and to Aimee Wright and Raja Dharmaraj for helping turn this project into a book.

vi ACKNOWLEDGMENTS

Last but certainly not least, thanks to my parents and stepparents for their many kindnesses and to my family—Paul, Charlotte, and Daisy—you light up my life!

I gratefully acknowledge permission to reprint revised portions of the following essays: "What Spenser Took from Chaucer: Worldly Vanity in *The Ruines of Time* and *Troilus and Criseyde*" © 2016 Johns Hopkins University Press (which appeared in *ELH*, Volume 83, Issue 2, July 2016, pages 431–55); "Renaissance Secularism Revised: The Case of the Prodigal Son" © 2021 Johns Hopkins University Press (which appeared in *ELH*, Volume 88, Issue 3, September 2021, pages 579–603); and "What Is Everyman?" © 2018 Northwestern University Press (which appeared in *Renaissance Drama*, Volume 46, Issue 1, pages 1–23, doi: 10.1086/697173).

A note on translations: In order to make this book more accessible to non-specialists, I have translated all of the Middle English quotations. I have also glossed any oddly spelled or unfamiliar words in the quotations in Early Modern English.

Contents

Introduction: Reading Is Good for You	1
1. The New, the Medieval, and the Renaissance	15
2. Humanism and the Morality Play	37
3. Humanist Moral Fusion: Terence and the Prodigal Son	68
4. The Uses of Good Literature	88
5. Good Literature [*bonae litterae*] and the Good	109
6. Horatian *Dulce et Utile* as Poisonous Reading	132
7. Worldly Vanity and George Gascoigne	155
8. Edmund Spenser's *Contemptus Mundi*	170
Afterword: Confidence and Doubt	199
Works Cited	204
Index	221

Introduction

Reading Is Good for You

Sir Thomas More has long been seen as a herald of novelty, as an origin for the English Renaissance.[1] Much of this novelty can be attributed to his humanism—his deep commitment to celebrating, imitating, and reviving the classical legacy, what Francesco Petrarch called the *studia humanitatis*.[2] More's humanism is on full display in one of his lesser-known works: a biography of arguably the most influential Italian humanist, Pico della Mirandola, that he translated into English as *The Life of Pico della Mirandola* (1510; 1525).[3] More describes Pico as a paradigmatically Renaissance man, anticipating the judgment of later historians: Pico is not only recognized as "chief Orator and Poet," a phrase that evokes the ancient Roman rhetorician Cicero, but is also praised for his mastery of the classical legacy, his "study in humanity."[4] At the same time, More follows his source in framing Pico's humanism within a traditional, Christian, penitential trajectory. Pico, who was "an excellent [and] knowledgeable man in all disciplines and virtuous in his living," ends in "the dark fire of Purgatory," where his "venial offences are cleansed."[5] Even more interestingly, More locates Pico's virtue and knowledge, his identifiably Ciceronian ideal, in a mirror.[6] In an opening letter to his friend, the nun, Joyce Leigh, More writes, Pico "was to all them that aspire to honor a true spectacle in

---

[1] Sir Thomas More is the important origin for the Renaissance in Stephen Greenblatt, *Renaissance Self-Fashioning: From More to Shakespeare* (Chicago: University of Chicago Press, 1980), 11–73, and David Norbrook, *Poetry and Politics in the English Renaissance* (London: Routledge, 1984), 18–31.

[2] Petrarch took the term *studia humanitatis* from Cicero's *Pro Archia*, and it is roughly analogous to how the term humanism is being used in this study: the recovery, celebration, and imitation of the classical legacy. See Michael D. Reeve, "Classical Scholarship," in *The Cambridge Companion to Renaissance Humanism*, ed. Jill Kraye (Cambridge: Cambridge University Press, 2004), 20–46.

[3] On this text, see Robert Cummings, "The Province of Verse: Sir Thomas More's Twelve Rules of John Picus Earle of Mirandula," in *Elizabethan Translation and Literary Culture*, ed. Gabriela Schmidt (Berlin: Walter de Gruyter, 2013), 201–226; and Stanford Lehmberg, "Sir Thomas More's Life of Pico della Mirandola," *Studies in the Renaissance* 3 (1956): 61–74. Lehmberg notes that Pico is a figure of fusion (63).

[4] Pico della Mirandola, *Here is conteyned the lyfe of Iohan Picus erle of Myrandula a grete lorde of Italy an excellent connynge man in all sciences, and verteous of lyuynge* (London, 1525) STC 19898, A4v, image 5. Spelling modernized. For accounts of Pico's importance to the history of the Renaissance, see Tony Davies, *Humanism*, 2nd ed. (London: Routledge, 2008), 94–104; Arthur F. Kinney, *Humanist Poetics: Thought, Rhetoric, and Fiction in Sixteenth-Century England* (Amherst, MA: University of Massachusetts Press, 1986), 4–6; and Jennifer Summit, "Renaissance Humanism and the Future of the Humanities," *Literature Compass* 9.10 (2012): 666.

[5] Pico, *The Life*, first quotation from the title and second from C3r, image 15.

[6] On the Ciceronian ideal, see Quentin Skinner, *The Foundations of Modern Political Thought, Volume 1: The Renaissance* (Cambridge: Cambridge University Press, 1978), 1: 84–94 and Paul Oskar Kristeller, *The Classics and Renaissance Thought* (Cambridge, MA: Harvard University Press, for

---

Humanism and Good Books in Sixteenth-Century England. Katherine C. Little, Oxford University Press.
© Katherine C. Little (2023). DOI: 10.1093/oso/9780192883193.003.0001

2 HUMANISM AND GOOD BOOKS IN SIXTEENTH-CENTURY ENGLAND

whose mode of being they might behold, as in a clear, polished mirror, in what points true honor consists ... [his] marvelous knowledge and excellent virtue my rude learning is unable to express sufficiently."[7] The mirror is a familiar figure for a book, one that was used throughout the Middle Ages to encourage readers to reflect on their behavior, to consider whether they have been good or bad according to what they have read. Typical is the use of the mirror by the English poet John Lydgate in his long poem *The Fall of Princes* (c.1431–38):

> Olde exaumples off pryncis that haue fall,
> Ther remembraunce off newe brouht to mynde,
> May been a merour to estatis all,
> How thei in vertu shal remedies fynde
> Teschewe vices ...

[Ancient stories of princes that have fallen, their remembrance newly brought to mind, may be a mirror to all estates, how they shall find remedies in virtue to avoid vices].[8]

Readers of Lydgate's poem should use the stories of the princes as guidelines for their future behavior, just as readers of More's book should model themselves after Pico.

As this brief account should suggest, More's *Life of Pico* fuses together, at times rather strangely, what one might call the humanist—excellent, virtuous, and *studia humanitatis* [study of humanity]—with what one might call the medieval— mirrors, sins, and explicit directives to readers to behold and amend. With this fusion of disparate languages, the text advertises its transitional status; it belongs to both the Middle Ages and the Renaissance. More is certainly aware of the distinctiveness of Pico's life, even of humanism itself, and yet he does not insist on novelty, preferring instead to insert Pico into a traditional, recognizably medieval, moral frame.

Although Pico's *Life* has not played much of a role in literary histories of England, it offers insight into the transition from medieval to Renaissance, or to use

---

Oberlin College, 1955). Kristeller writes, "the combination of eloquence and wisdom" comes from Cicero and "pervades so much Renaissance literature" (*Classics and Renaissance Thought*, 19).

[7] Pico, *The Life*, A3v, image 4, lightly translated.

[8] John Lydgate, *The Fall of Princes*, 4 vols., ed. Henry Bergen (London: Oxford University Press, 1924–27), Part 1: Bk 2.22–26. For a survey of medieval mirrors that emphasizes the moral and didactic focus, see Herbert Grabes, *The Mutable Glass: Mirror-imagery in Titles and Texts of the Middle Ages and English Renaissance*, trans. Gordon Collier (Cambridge: Cambridge University Press, 1982), 23–30. A notable contemporary example can be found in the Dutch play, *Den Spyeghel der Salicheyt van Elckerlijc* [*The Mirror of Everyman's Salvation*] (1496; 1501), which is perhaps most well-known as the source for the morality play *Everyman* (printed c. 1510–25): "Seer uut ghelesen,/ Merct desen spieghel [Very honorable audience/ mark this mirror]" (*Elckerlijc*, in *Everyman and its Dutch Original, Elckerlijc*, ed. Clifford Davidson, Martin W. Walsh, and Ton J. Broos [Kalamazoo, MI: Medieval Institute Publications, 2007], lines 871–72).

a term more recently favored, the early modern period, whose advent, at least for England, has long been located in the sixteenth century.[9] As *The Life of Pico* should suggest, this transition from medieval to Renaissance was far from abrupt: it consisted of fusions and continuities, of attempts to bridge old and new within the bounds of a single text. Moreover, in its framing, its explicit directions to readers, More's book reveals not only what made this particular book possible but also what made the transition possible. That is, it approaches writing and reading through a defined mindset, that books should be morally useful. What both Pico, as a model humanist, and the medieval penitential mirror share is the idea that reading books is good for you; it is instructive in virtue and vice or in virtue and excellence; it can shape readers in how to act, think, and feel.[10] In other words, Pico's "study in humanity," his reading of the classical legacy or of what would now be called literature, is a broad "learning" that includes moral education. That moral education, oriented as it is around the classical legacy, is entirely continuous with other kinds of moral education, such as that found in penitential treatises. Such a perspective is not unique to More, but a vital way of thinking about writing and reading in this transitional period, as will be demonstrated here.

Morality as Cultural Context

To treat morality as a cultural context for reading and writing is to approach it as a set of discourses, with, therefore, all the potential for ambiguity and instability associated with other kinds of discourses, such as literature. Morality is not human behavior itself—there is no such thing as a virtue or a sin empirically speaking— but, rather, ideas about human behavior, whether it is good or bad according to certain guidelines or rules that are themselves rarely homogeneous. Morality cannot therefore be treated as external to a text, as a kind of identifiable experience

---

[9] When the Renaissance or early modern period began in England is a fraught question, because texts written in the sixteenth-century cannot be placed in a simple developmental trajectory, and because identifiably "medieval" concerns persisted throughout the period. James Simpson discusses the difficulty of periodizing in *The Oxford English Literary History, Volume 2, 1350–1547: Reform and Cultural Revolution* (Oxford: Oxford University Press, 2002), e.g., 1–6.

[10] The moral aspect of humanism is widely noted, and it is fundamental to humanist education. See, for example, Anthony Grafton and Lisa Jardine, *From Humanism to the Humanities: Education and the Liberal Arts in Fifteenth- and Sixteenth-Century Europe* (Cambridge, MA: Harvard University Press, 1986), 33, 122–57. At the same time, moral interests tend to be neglected by literary scholars. As Ian Green notes, scholars have tended to "marginalize or offer a narrow account of the ethical dimension of the humanist educational programme" (*Humanism and Protestantism in Early Modern English Education* [Burlington, VT: Ashgate, 2009], 22). For Jeff Dolven, for example, humanist teaching is a form, a poetics, and the content of the morality is largely irrelevant (*Scenes of Instruction in Renaissance Romance* [Chicago: University of Chicago Press, 2007], 1–14). Indeed, much work on humanism is predicated on an opposition between the moral (or didactic) and the literary, a point to which I will return in Chapter 1.

4 HUMANISM AND GOOD BOOKS IN SIXTEENTH-CENTURY ENGLAND

that precedes or is distinct from the writing about it.[11] In brief, morality is "textueel [bookish]" in exactly the way that Geoffrey Chaucer's Manciple explains in the late-fourteenth-century *Canterbury Tales*. At the end of his story about the crow, the Manciple offers a moral lesson, apparently drawn from the biblical book of Proverbs:

> Daun Salomon, as wise clerkes seyn,
> Techeth a man to kepen his tonge weel.
> But, as I seyde, I am noght textueel

[Lord Solomon, as wise scholars say, teaches a man to hold his tongue. But, as I said, I am not bookish].[12]

As the word "textueel [bookish]" underlines, morality often appears in terms of rules or "precepts," that are drawn from a particular text, such as the Book of Proverbs, for the Manciple, or from Aristotle's *Nicomachean Ethics* or Cicero's *De Officiis*, for many humanists.[13] Morality could also be found in imaginative writings, in plays and poetry, such as the Roman comedies of Terence or Virgil's *Aeneid*. These are the "good letters of humanity" that the Dutch theologian Erasmus of Rotterdam famously and influentially describes in his writings, claiming in *A Complaint of Peace* (1517) that they could shape readers in a "faultless" life, because "an education in classical literature makes humans human [*bonae litterae reddunt homines*]."[14] Because it can be found in many different kinds of sources (or books), morality is importantly varied, even as it claims homogeneity or universality, what "a man," as in all men, should do according to the Manciple.

---

[11] Historico-contextualist approaches tend to reinforce a binary between literature, on the one hand, and the world of politics or human experience, on the other, even as they try to see negotiations between these entities. For example, in *Renaissance Self-Fashioning*, Greenblatt reads Sir Thomas More's translation of the *Life of Pico della Mirandola* in terms of More's own "guilt feelings," and not in terms of the penitential tradition to which this text so obviously belongs (51). See Christopher Cannon on the difficulty or, perhaps, futility of drawing a boundary between the "experiential knowledge" gained through reading books and that gained through other actions ("Reading Knowledge," *PMLA* 30.3 [2015], 714).

[12] Geoffrey Chaucer, *Manciple's Tale*, in *The Riverside Chaucer*, 3rd ed., ed. Larry Benson (Boston: Houghton Mifflin, 1987), 9.314–16. All references to Chaucer's works will be to this edition.

[13] The sixteenth-century translation of Aristotle's *Ethics* uses the term "precepts": Aristotle, *The ethiques of Aristotle, that is to saye, preceptes of good behauoute* (London, 1547) STC 754.

[14] The first two quotations come from the English translation of Erasmus's *Adagia* printed in 1534. See Erasmus, *Bellum Erasmi* (London, 1534) STC 10449, image 40 [p. 39 r of original]. The last one comes from his *Querela pacis* in *Opera Omnia Desiderii Erasmi Roterodami*, ed. O. Herding (Amsterdam: North Holland, 1974), 4: 628D; and *A Complaint of Peace*, ed. A. H. T. Levi, trans. Betty Radice in *Collected Works of Erasmus* (*CWE*) 84 vols. (Toronto: University of Toronto Press, 1974–), Vol. 27 (1986): 289–322. In a sixteenth-century English translation, the phrase appears in his discussion of learning as "Good letters make men": "I wyll conuey my selfe to the companye of eruditie and learnyd men. Good letters make men. But Philosophy more than men. Diuinitie maketh them godes" (*The complaint of peace. Wryten in Latyn, by the famous clerke, Erasmus Roterodamus. And nuely translated into Englyshe by Thomas Paynell* [London, 1559] STC 10466, B2v; image 11). On the importance of this phrase, *bonae litterae*, for Erasmus, see Brian Cummings, "Erasmus and the Invention of Literature," *Erasmus Yearbook* 33 (2013): 22–54; and Grafton and Jardine, *From Humanism*, 124–49.

INTRODUCTION 5

Morality is also appropriable, even free-floating.[15] The Manciple is not a clergyman, and yet he refers to the Bible, claiming for himself some of the authority that goes along with it. Even when morality is associated with a particular institution, such as the school or the church, it is not merely an unproblematic location of ideology, a simple vector through which the institution attempts to control people. For that reason, moral discourses cannot be reduced to or equated with social, economic, and political forces.[16] Moral discourses circulate both within institutions and outside of their control, and they are as interpretable, constructed, and capable of being manipulated as the realm of poetry, *bonae litterae*, and prose narratives, the kinds of sixteenth-century texts that have come to be considered literature or literary in the twentieth and twenty-first centuries.[17]

In addition to, or perhaps, as a result of, its bookishness, the language of morality is also conservative in the true sense of that term: it changes very slowly, accreting and adapting. While new words and concepts are added, and others can and do fade, they are rarely precipitously cut off. People in the twenty-first century, for example, still speak of greed, even though very few of them would describe it in specifically Christian terms, as a violation of God's commandments, whereby the greedy "do wrong to Jesus Christ."[18] As *The Life of Pico* demonstrates, More describes Pico's morality, the rightness and wrongness of his behavior, at least in part within the traditional language of sins and purgatory even as he acknowledges the newer language of "excellence." Morality is, in other words, a context for writing that requires a diachronic approach. There is no clear dividing line, in More's text or in those of his contemporaries, between one, older, language of good

---

[15] See similarly, Chaucer's description of his *Tale of Melibee*:

> As thus, though that I telle somwhat moore
> Of proverbes than ye han herd bifoore
> Comprehended in this litel tretys heere,
> To enforce with th' effect of my mateere;
> And though I nat the same wordes seye
> As ye han herd, yet to yow alle I preye
> Blameth me nat; for, as in my sentence (Chaucer, Interruption to *Tale of Sir Thopas*, 7.955–61).

[16] Explicitly moral arguments around literature that circulated in the sixteenth century have been influentially read as ideological. See, for example, Catherine Bates, *On Not Defending Poetry: Defence and Indefensibility in Sidney's Defence of Poesy* (Oxford: Oxford University Press, 2017); Richard Halpern, *The Poetics of Primitive Accumulation: English Renaissance Culture and the Genealogy of Capital* (Ithaca, NY: Cornell University Press, 1991); and Robert Matz, *Defending Literature in Early Modern England: Renaissance Literary Theory in Social Context* (New York: Cambridge University Press, 2000). While morality can certainly express ideology, it would be a mistake to see it as entirely explained by economic and political forces. Readers continue to find books useful for their behavior in ways that also complicate ideology or the status quo. See further discussion in Chapter 1.

[17] The history of the literary canon is a history of the different moral and ideological terminology used to describe some of the same texts. See John Guillory, *Cultural Capital: The Problem of Literary Canon Formation* (Chicago: University of Chicago Press, 1993), ix. See also his survey of the canon debates, 3–82.

[18] Chaucer, *Parson's Tale*, 10.744.

and bad behavior and another, newer one; using morality as a context requires an attunement to particular changes over time.

Accretiveness will be the term used here to refer to this kind of fusion, not only additions, but also occlusions and subtractions, all of which make drawing clear boundaries between medieval and Renaissance difficult. Perhaps the most obvious sign of this accretiveness is that moral discourses defy easy distinctions between secular and religious. Morality is obviously not the same thing as religion, by which one should understand the beliefs people hold and the practices they engage in. It can (and does) present itself at times as secular in the original sense of the word, as "worldly," since it deals with human behavior in the world. One can say that lying is wrong, using Aesop's fable about the boy who cried wolf, without invoking any reference to faith in God or the requirements of faith. The moral of that story, in William Caxton's translation (1484), makes this potential secularism clear: "For men bileue not lyghtly hym whiche is known for a lyer [Men do not easily believe one who is known to be a liar]."[19] Similarly, the sixteenth-century flourishing of interest in moral philosophy, the pagan, classical ethics found in Cicero's *De Officiis* and Aristotle's *Nicomachean Ethics*, could be (and has been) read in terms of its secularism, or at least its independence from Christianity. As one of the foremost scholars of humanism, Paul Oskar Kristeller, notes, "the existence of this large body of moral literature written by humanists and popularizers, and of the still larger body of humanist learning and literature, is in itself a significant historical phenomenon. We are confronted with a vast body of secular learning, nourished from ancient sources and contemporary experience and basically independent of, though not entirely unrelated to, the medieval traditions."[20]

It would be a mistake to insist too much on the secularism of humanist morality, as Kristeller's cautious approach to "independence" might suggest. The history of moral discourses is long and at times complicated, but the fact of its accretiveness in both the Middle Ages and the early modern period is also obvious.[21] The language of morality, of the rightness and wrongness of human behavior, emerged out of an ongoing conversation between classical and Christian writings. In the

[19] *Here begynneth the book of the subtyl historyes and fables of Esope whiche were translated out of Frensshe in to Englysshe by wylliam Caxton at westmynstre in the yere of oure Lorde M. CCCC. Lxxxiij* (London, 1484) STC 175, C2r, image 96.

[20] Paul O. Kristeller, "Humanism and Moral Philosophy," in *Renaissance Humanism: Foundations, Forms and Legacy*, 3 vols., ed. Albert Rabil, Jr. (Philadelphia: University of Pennsylvania Press, 1988), 3:273.

[21] On the relationship between classical and Christian ideas of morality in this period, I have been influenced by the following: Charles F. Briggs, "Moral Philosophy and Wisdom Literature," in *The Oxford History of Classical Reception in English Literature: Volume 1: 800-1558*, ed. Rita Copeland (Oxford: Oxford University Press, 2016), 1:299–321; Jennifer Herdt, *Putting on Virtue: The Legacy of the Splendid Vices* (Chicago: University of Chicago Press, 2008) and "Introduction," *Journal of Medieval and Early Modern Studies* 42 (2012): 1–12; Alasdair MacIntyre, *After Virtue*, 2nd ed. (Notre Dame, IN: University of Notre Dame, 1984), 165–80; and John Marenbon, *Pagans and Philosophers: The Problem of Paganism from Augustine to Leibniz* (Princeton, NJ: Princeton University Press, 2015).

INTRODUCTION 7

penitential tradition, discussions of sin and virtue make use of pagan, classical philosophers, such as Aristotle, together with Christian authorities and the Bible. Chaucer's late fourteenth-century *Parson's Tale*, which is a translation and combination of popular, late medieval penitential manuals, demonstrates this fusion: "After Pride will I speak of the foul sin of Envy, which is, as by the word of the Philosopher (Aristotle), 'sorrow of another man's prosperity'; and according to the word of Saint Augustine, it is 'Sorrow of other men's well-being, and joy of other men's harm.'"[22] For Chaucer, as for many authors, there is nothing disjunctive or odd about setting Aristotle and Augustine together in the same sentence.

Such accretiveness is also a hallmark of Renaissance humanism. Even as humanist authors read, imitated, excerpted, and translated more pagan, classical texts than their medieval forebears, they continued to combine, or even conflate, the language of pagan, classical authors, such as Cicero, Plato, and Aristotle, with the language of Christian behavior, drawn from the Bible, penitential traditions, and other kinds of devotional or exegetical writings. Indeed, much of the output of Erasmus of Rotterdam, which is massive by any measure, could be described in terms of such fusion.[23] In one of his most popular and influential works, *The Education of a Christian Prince* (1516), Erasmus explains that children need "to absorb both Christian principles and also literature that is of sound quality [*honestas literas*] and conducive to the welfare of the state ... Such is the power of education, as Plato has written, that a man who has been correctly brought up emerges as a kind of divine creature."[24] For Erasmus, Plato is entirely compatible with "Christian principles," and pagan, classical literature—here *honestas literas*—is both honored for its quality and honorable in and of itself, or virtuous.

In England, during the initial flourishing of humanism in the first part of the sixteenth century, authors were fully aware of the possibilities: fusing pagan and Christian moral languages, adapting medieval texts, and offering new approaches and, at times, new texts. William Baldwin, most famous as one of the authors of the *Mirror for Magistrates* (1559), re-worked a medieval version of classical moral philosophy, *The Dictes and Sayings of the Philosophers*, titling it *A Treatise of Morall Phylosophie* (1547).[25] The change in title aligns Baldwin's version more closely with the classical legacy, specifically with Aristotle's *Nicomachean Ethics*, which was translated into English and printed in the same year, 1547, as *The*

---

[22] Chaucer, *Parson's Tale*, 10.485.

[23] See Grafton and Jardine, *From Humanism*, 124–49.

[24] Erasmus, *The Education of a Christian Prince*, trans. Neil M. Cheshire and Michael J. Heath in *CWE* Vol. 27 (1986): 259. Latin quotation taken from *Institutio Principis Christiani*, in *Opera Omnia* 4-1: 188.

[25] William Baldwin, *A treatise of morall phylosophie contaynyng the sayinges of the wyse. Gathered and Englyshed by Wylliam Baldwyn* (London, 1547) STC 1253. This book was extremely popular (R. W. Maslen, "William Baldwin and the Tudor Imagination," in *The Oxford Handbook of Tudor Literature, 1485–1603*, ed. Mike Pincombe and Cathy Shrank [Oxford: Oxford University Press, 2009], 291–306). On its medievalism, see Curt F. Buehler, "A Survival from the Middle Ages: William Baldwin's Use of the 'Dictes and Sayings,'" *Speculum* 23 (1948): 76–80.

8 HUMANISM AND GOOD BOOKS IN SIXTEENTH-CENTURY ENGLAND

Ethiques of Aristotle, a guide for "good behavior."[26] In his treatise, Baldwin extends the brief account of paganism that he found in the medieval version, drawing the reader's attention to the potential contradiction between classical and Christian: "For although (Good Reader) that philosophy is not to be compared with the most holy scriptures, yet is it not utterly to be despised."[27] Even though moral philosophy is not biblical, it is nevertheless useful: "Moral philosophy may well be called that part of god's law, which gives commandment of outward behavior: which differs from the gospel, in as much as the gospel promises remission of sins, reconciling to God, and the gift of the holy ghost, and of eternal life, for Christs sake."[28] Even as Baldwin distinguishes between classical and Christian, he acknowledges their shared interest in shaping behavior, through commandments and law.

This accretiveness, of classical and Christian, of medieval and humanist, persists across the sixteenth century, linking pre- and post-Reformation moral discourses.[29] To be sure, the language of Christian behavior changed, as, for example, penitential manuals, like Chaucer's *Parson's Tale*, faded from view. And yet, the moral language around "the study of humanity," or what would now be called literature, remained constant, likely because of the tie to educational settings. That is, given the uniform dependence on the classical legacy in grammar schools and universities, there tended to be general agreement about the moral value of classical texts, their ongoing usefulness in teaching about good and bad behavior, however defined.[30] Such continuity is evident in the popularity and influence of Erasmus, who stands for the moral value of literature throughout the sixteenth century, across the divide of the Reformation or Reformations. Erasmus appears at the origin of English, humanist education, praised for his learning and instrumental in writing the book known as *Lily's Latin Grammar,* which shaped grammar school education throughout the sixteenth century.[31] Later, both Roger Ascham, noted mid-sixteenth-century Protestant tutor, and Thomas Lodge, Elizabethan defender

---

[26] Aristotle, *The ethiques of Aristotle*, F4v, spelling modernized.

[27] Baldwin, *A treatise*, image 5, spelling modernized. In the medieval version, the author only mentions pagans at the beginning: "And in especial by cause of the holsome and swete saynges of the paynems whyche is a glorious fayr myrrour to alle good cristen people to beholde and vnderstonde" (Abu al-Wafa' Mubashshir ibn Fatik, *Here endeth the book named the dictes or sayengis of the philosophres* [London, 1477] STC 6826, image 2).

[28] Baldwin, *A treatise*, image 6.

[29] There are those who see the Reformation as an important rupture. See Paul Cefalu, *Moral Identity in Early Modern English Literature* (Cambridge: Cambridge University Press, 2000) and Brian Cummings, *The Literary Culture of the Reformation: Grammar and Grace* (Oxford: Oxford University Press, 2002). Without denying these important shifts, one can still acknowledge that rupture has been overstated.

[30] Education changed a great deal during the first part of the sixteenth century, but there were important continuities with the late Middle Ages, at least in terms of the value assigned to the classical legacy. See, for example, Nicholas Orme, *Education and Society in Medieval and Renaissance England* (London: Hambledon Press, 1989), 16–17, and Joan Simon, *Education and Society in Tudor England* (Cambridge: Cambridge University Press, 1966), 57–60.

[31] William Lily, *Lily's Grammar of Latin in English: An Introduction of the Eyght Partes of Speche and the Construction of the Same*, ed. Hedwig Gwosdek (Oxford: Oxford University Press, 2013), 83.

of poetry, invoke Erasmus on the moral benefit of reading classical poetry. In his educational treatise, *The Scholemaster* (1570), Ascham describes Erasmus as "the honor of learning of all our time," and therefore an authority for teaching wisdom through study of the classical legacy.[32] Similarly, in his "Defense of Poetry, Music, and Stage Plays" (1579), Lodge uses Erasmus to defend poetry for its moral instructiveness: "Erasmus will make that [i.e. poetry] the pathway to knowledge."[33] For Lodge, Erasmian ideas about *bonae litterae*, the good of classical literature, are still entirely relevant.

Morality and Literary History

With its accretiveness and conservatism, morality suggests an approach to the transition between medieval and early modern, to sixteenth-century literary history, that is as interested in continuities as disruptions, as aware of the fusions as of the novelty informing "the study of humanity," or humanism. This book offers that literary history, arguing that morality can help explain literary production in this period, not only because moral concerns informed individual texts but also because they helped construct an idea of literature. From this perspective, sixteenth-century texts can be seen as participants in a series of ongoing conversations about what literature, whether classical texts or poetry or even stories, should do to and for readers. These conversations involve past texts and authors, whether classical or medieval, and a wide variety of participants: texts that have come to be seen as canonical as well as those at the margins, texts that remain much studied today, and those that have been largely neglected by literary critics.

The first part of the book explores the emergence of humanism, the way in which this literary movement intersected with and transformed what had come before. Chapter 1 is in some ways a continuation of the introduction, a survey of the transition between medieval and humanist, in terms of ideas about literature. It reexamines familiar claims for humanist novelty, claims that depend on opposing humanist to medieval: that humanists offered not only a new approach to the classical inheritance but also a new idea of literary value, as, for example, eloquence. By resituating medieval and humanist texts in relation to each other, my chapter shows medieval texts to be more complex in their approach to value, and humanist texts to be less new than is often assumed. The real novelty of humanism is not its attention to literary value per se but its standardization of the certain link between literary and moral value, in the conflation found in the Erasmian term, "good letters [*bonae litterae*]."

---

[32] Roger Ascham, *The Scholemaster*, in *English Works*, ed. William Aldis Wright (Cambridge: Cambridge University Press, 1904), 215.

[33] Thomas Lodge, "Defence of Poetry, Music, and Stage Plays," in *Elizabethan Critical Essays*, 2 vols., ed. George Gregory Smith (Oxford: Clarendon Press, 1904), 1:66.

The humanist interest in morality was not merely theoretical, it also informed their literary experimentations: the new and newly revised genres that appeared in the first part of the sixteenth century. These are the subject of Chapters 2 through 5. Perhaps the most obvious evidence of humanist moral interest is the morality play, and the second chapter takes up the flourishing of this genre in the early part of the sixteenth century. Assigning the morality play to humanism may seem surprising, since these plays are typically understood as medieval. This dating, or rather, mis-dating, has long reinforced the division between medieval and Renaissance literature, in which medieval texts are characterized by their Christian morality and Renaissance texts by their increasing independence or secularism. The great majority of morality plays, including specifically Christian morality plays, belong, however, to the first part of the sixteenth century. These plays thus not only coincide with the emergence of humanism but also offer insight into it, as I argue, using two cases from the early sixteenth century: the extremely popular play *Everyman*, which was printed at least four times between c. 1510 and 1535, and *Mundus et Infans* (1522).

To refocus humanism around its moral interests is also to revise our understanding of perhaps its most foundational aspect—the reclaiming of the classical legacy, most typically through some form of imitation. Classical imitation has long been understood as signaling the independence identified by Kristeller, even a kind of proto-secularism. From this perspective, embracing and imitating classical texts, appreciating them on their own terms, would seem to mark out a new space for literature and literary value, one that is free of the Christian moral values that had previously been assigned to these texts. Classical imitation in this period was not, however, as independent as it might appear to be. The humanist desire to fuse classical texts to a largely Christian morality shaped one of the most popular kinds of classical imitation in this period: the Christian Terence tradition. Although now largely forgotten, this tradition was extremely influential during the sixteenth century and central to the humanist educational program. Written first in Latin and then in the vernacular, these plays were ubiquitous in Europe and England, and they show the productive fusion of classical texts within Christian moral frameworks, such as the prodigal son. In the third chapter, I use the popular, Latin, humanist play *Acolastus* (1529) and its quasi-official, English translation by John Palsgrave (1540) as a case study for this kind of fusion. Even as the play embraces the goals of Erasmian humanism, in which classical texts teach Christian morals, it also demonstrates an ambivalence about this project. That is, it writes a particularly Christian sense of loss, through the parable of the prodigal son, into its *imitatio*.

Although humanists presented morality as a stabilizing value for literature, it was, as the example of *Acolastus* should suggest, problematic. Indeed, that the classical legacy might not match Christian morality exactly or might even be opposed to it is not a phenomenon unique to *Acolastus* but one found throughout humanist texts.[34] It is typical to view this mismatch or opposition largely positively, as a sign of the independence of literary value for humanists or even, more polemically, by those who embrace Jacob Burckhardt's idea of the Renaissance, as their casting off of veils, dreams, primitivism, and rigid Christian meanings.[35] While there can be no doubt that these mismatches and oppositions were generative, they also carried with them the potential to limit the very values, the good, that these authors claimed to support.

Such limiting appears in one of the most influential humanist texts in England, Sir Thomas Elyot's *Boke of the Governor* (1531), the subject of Chapter 4. This text, at first glance, follows the kind of fusion popularized by Erasmus's *Education of a Christian Prince*, combining Christian principles and classical literature to educate readers morally and politically, to train them to work for what Erasmus calls "the welfare of the state." Elyot's fusion is, on closer look, less an attempt to harmonize the two traditions, and also less an embrace of the independence of the classical legacy, than it is an attempt to limit Christian morality. In his treatise, Elyot uses classical texts and influences ideologically, to contain and disarm familiar Christian virtues, such as charity and patience. Such containment is newly necessary, given Elyot's immediate historical context: fears about socially radical ideas circulating in the Reformation. By the 1520s, some of the ideas associated with Erasmus—access to scripture, condemnations of pagan tyranny—could (and for some did) look like the kind of egalitarianism or collectivism associated with the Anabaptists, the radical Reformers of the sixteenth century. Elyot limits the Erasmian possibilities: in his treatise classical texts provide an alternative and more oppressive set of guidelines for good and bad behavior.

The destabilizing potential of the humanist project—of that confident link between classical texts and Christian morality—receives more sustained attention in a mid-sixteenth-century play by John Phillip, *The Play of Patient Grissell* (c. 1558–61), as I discuss in Chapter 5. This play, which also seems to stem from an educational environment, meditates on the new, heightened, moral status of classical texts by returning to a familiar medieval form, the *exemplum*, and a familiar medieval character, Patient Griselda. In exploring the *exemplum* as a form, the relationship that form encodes between moral and story, it shows how the humanist project is not only or even primarily a new direction, a freeing of classical texts from Christian language, but, rather, alters both moral discourses, the classical and the Christian.

---

[34] Contradictions were inherent in the humanist educational program: this was a "bicultural situation in which Christian and pagan elements existed in an often uneasy symbiosis" (Ann Moss, "Humanist Education," in *The Cambridge History of Literary Criticism: vol. 3: The Renaissance*, ed. Glyn P. Norton [Cambridge: Cambridge University Press, 1999], 3:145).

[35] Jacob Burckhardt *Civilization of the Renaissance in Italy*, trans. S. G. C. Middlemore (London: Sonnenschein, 1904), 129. Greenblatt and more recently Richard Strier quote Jacob Burckhardt approvingly in *Renaissance Self-Fashioning*, 1, and *The Unrepentant Renaissance: From Petrarch to Shakespeare to Milton* (Chicago: University of Chicago Press, 2011), 2, respectively.

12 HUMANISM AND GOOD BOOKS IN SIXTEENTH-CENTURY ENGLAND

Phillip's play, appearing in the middle part of the sixteenth century, is a harbinger that humanist confidence in the moral goodness, even greatness, of literary texts, must and would inevitably fade. And the latter part of the sixteenth century sees the dissipation of humanist confidence, the dissolution of the "graft[ing of] piety onto *litterae*, that Erasmus made both influential and successful."[36] As the titles of both Lodge's "Defense of Poetry, Music, and Stage Plays" and Sir Philip Sidney's more famous *Defense of Poesy* [*An Apology for Poetry*] (1595) should suggest, poetry needed to be defended, its value stabilized, or re-stabilized, on moral grounds, despite and also because of the bold claims made by humanists. Indeed, a retreat from humanism, especially from its morally didactic aspects, is thought to characterize the literature of the Elizabethan period more generally.[37] This retreat or backlash has been influentially described by Richard Helgerson in his study *The Elizabethan Prodigals*. For Helgerson, the flourishing of Elizabethan writing was motivated by a generational conflict, specifically around morality: the authors' rebelled against the moral advice given by their humanist "fathers" and then repented.[38]

And yet, despite their ambivalence about, even rejection of, humanism, late sixteenth-century writers were not in any position to discard the link between literature and morality, to imagine a literature free of morality. They had inherited a framework, from both the much-admired classical tradition, whether Horace's *dulce et utile* or Cicero's wisdom and eloquence, and their medieval ancestors, such as Geoffrey Chaucer and John Gower, that required them to think about and even defend the morality of their writings. As a result, the emergence of doubt, which characterized the literary production of the generation following the humanists, did not cause these authors to abandon morality, but instead drove them to look for other models, namely by returning to pre-humanist, or medieval, authors and traditions.

Chapters 6–8 explore three of the most prolific authors in the Elizabethan period—George Gascoigne, Robert Greene, and Edmund Spenser—in terms of both doubt in and alternatives to humanism. Each of these authors raises doubts about humanist certainty, the good of the *bonae litterae*, and imagines a moral model—"worldly vanity"—that can accommodate and contain the potential moral dangers of the classical legacy and of literature more generally. This moral model acknowledges the instability of literature's moral impact (its moral value) and therefore allows and even encourages the investigation of what humanists have

---

[36] Grafton and Jardine note, "in spite of there being no explicit link between the influential textbooks of Latin eloquence and any moral or devotional meta-system, Erasmus's extremely public personality ... and the letters conveniently available to 'gloss' a work like the *De Copia* enable the Erasmus scholar to graft piety onto *litterae*" (*From Humanism*, 139–40).

[37] For a full account, see the beginning of Chapter 6.

[38] See Richard Helgerson, *The Elizabethan Prodigals* (Berkeley, CA: University of California Press, 1977). Jeff Dolven's opposition between romance and humanism (didacticism) is quite similar to Helgerson's; see his *Scenes of Instruction*.

suppressed—that reading might be bad for you. "Worldly vanity" is the pessimistic medieval *contemptus mundi* tradition in which all earthly things, including, of course, literature, are a waste of time or harmful. Chapter 6 outlines this Elizabethan trajectory, from humanist confidence, to the dissipation of confidence, and then to "worldly vanity." It begins with Sir Philip Sidney's *An Apology for Poetry* as an example of humanist confidence, demonstrating the way in which humanism successfully defined and defended poetry as morally useful at least in part by repressing contradictions between classical texts and Christian morality, the destabilizing potential that inheres in the humanist project. These contradictions had a medieval signature, so to speak, in that they had also preoccupied medieval authors, such as Chaucer. Robert Greene's treatise *Vision Written at the Instant of his death* (1592) demonstrates a fairly typical Elizabethan retreat from humanist confidence and, ultimately, retreat from the idea of *bonae litterae* or literature itself. It returns to Sidney's repressed, invoking Chaucer and his *Canterbury Tales* to call humanist claims for moral usefulness into question, and ultimately, to advocate for turning away from literature (or writing) as a "worldly vanity."

George Gascoigne and Edmund Spenser also offer versions of this trajectory through doubt and into the solution offered by "worldly vanity." Chapter 7 takes up two of George Gascoigne's final works, a moral play *The Glasse of Governement* (1575) and a devotional treatise, *The Droome of Doomesday* (1576). Read together, these texts pessimistically abandon humanism and its moral claims. First, Gascoigne re-imagines an influential humanist mode, the Christian Terence tradition, in his play, *The Glasse*, emptying out its confident claims for the moral value of classical texts. He then turns to the *contemptus mundi* tradition, translating Lotario dei Segni's *De Miseria Condicionis Humane* (c. 1195) as "The View of Worldly Vanities" in *The Droome*, countering the humanist emphasis on virtue with a medieval focus on sin. Like Greene, Gascoigne is not convinced that literature uniformly inculcates in virtue, and he ultimately advocates what he describes as a Chaucerian pathway, of turning away from writing.

While both Greene and Gascoigne question the moral value of reading and writing, Spenser's exploration of moral value is more hopeful, as demonstrated in the eighth and final chapter. In his poetry collection, *The Complaints* (1591), Spenser uses Chaucer both to critique and to remedy the idea of literature that he has inherited from the humanists. First, he portrays the deleterious effect of humanist imitation, its emotional attachment to the past, and then he imagines literature working morally again, as a Christian social corrective. As is fitting for the most Chaucerian of the Elizabethans, Spenser approaches literary invention as inextricably tied to moral questions, and this tie inspires him as much as it causes him concern.

Each of the authors discussed in this study, whether categorized as medieval or Renaissance, understood that almost all texts, the great and the trivial, the delightful and the didactic, the solemn and the ribald, raise questions for readers that are recognizably moral: about how they should act in their lives, about what they should do, think, and believe, about whether they agree or disagree with the behaviors reflected in or encouraged by texts. These concerns not only tie the sixteenth century closely to the Middle Ages, they also reach across into our own time.

1

The New, the Medieval, and the Renaissance

Renaissance humanists famously offered a new approach to poetry, defining themselves against their medieval predecessors.[1] As Sir Philip Sidney writes in *An Apology for Poetry* (c. 1581; printed 1595), the medieval poet Geoffrey Chaucer belongs to a "misty time" in contrast to Sidney himself, who lives in a "clear age."[2] Sidney's clear-sightedness can be understood not merely as new for his own time but as modern, the origin of a twentieth-century sensibility about poetry, even literature more broadly. Indeed, humanist treatises on poetry have long been viewed as a precursor to modern literary criticism. In Bernard Weinberg's influential study, *A History of Literary Criticism in the Italian Renaissance*, he argues that the Renaissance was a "crucial point in the history of Western literary criticism, that point at which the doctrines of classical antiquity were transformed into something new and different, which in turn became the basis of modern literary criticism."[3] Weinberg summarizes this modern approach through the fifteenth-century Italian humanist Guarino Guarini, who offers "a theory of poetry as an independent art, subordinated neither to the rational disciplines nor to the ethical sciences and achieving its own special ends by following principles that are specifically its own."[4] In this familiar perspective, which developed at the end of the twentieth-century, it is only with humanism that one sees a distinct sense of the literary, as "independent art." The modern sense of the literary is, therefore, a sense that originated in the Renaissance, developing in opposition to medieval traditions, which were thought to have subordinated poetry to other kinds of values.[5]

---

[1] Francesco Petrarch famously considered himself new, defining himself against the "dark ages." Such claims must be taken with a grain of salt; Petrarch also imitated his medieval predecessors. See, for example, John Freccero, "The Fig Tree and the Laurel: Petrarch's Poetics," *Diacritics* 5.1 (1975): 34–40.

[2] Sir Philip Sidney, *An Apology for Poetry, or The Defence of Poesy*, 3rd ed., ed. Geoffrey Shepherd, rev. R. W. Maslen (New York: Palgrave Press, 2002), 110. Hereafter all references to this text will appear parenthetically.

[3] Bernard Weinberg, *A History of Literary Criticism in the Italian Renaissance*, 2 vols. (Chicago: University of Chicago Press, 1961), 1: 39.

[4] Weinberg, *A History of Literary Criticism*, 1:30.

[5] On the role of twentieth-century literary criticism in defining literature, see John Guillory, "The Location of Literature," in *A Companion to Literary Theory*, ed. David H. Richter (Oxford: Wiley-Blackwell, 2018), 151–64; and E. D. Hirsch, Jr., "Two Traditions of Literary Evaluation," in *Literary Theory and Criticism: Festschrift Presented to René Wellek in Honor of his Eightieth Birthday*, ed. Joseph P. Strelka (New York: Peter Lang, 1984), 283–98. On the difficulty of reconciling medieval texts with

---

Humanism and Good Books in Sixteenth-Century England. Katherine C. Little, Oxford University Press.
© Katherine C. Little (2023). DOI: 10.1093/oso/9780192883193.003.0002

16 HUMANISM AND GOOD BOOKS IN SIXTEENTH-CENTURY ENGLAND

In Thomas M. Greene's *The Light in Troy: Imitation and Discovery in Renaissance Poetry*, he explains this shift from a medieval to a modern idea of literature: Renaissance poetry defines itself by rejecting the medieval, the "security" of its "enduring, predetermined values," and embracing the instability and slipperiness of language itself.[6] Briefly put, a modern idea of literature begins with a series of related shifts, from medieval to Renaissance, from simple to complex, from subordination to independence. These shifts are, importantly, although often implicitly, moral: from "ethical sciences" and "predetermined values" to art and ambiguity. What makes literature literary is, in this perspective, its independence from the kind of overt moral content associated with medieval literature.

The dominance, even the rightness, of this modern idea of literature—that what makes literature literary is its art and, relatedly, its non-utility, its ambiguity, its independence from morality—has recently come into question. Perhaps the most well-known challenge is that offered in Rita Felski's manifesto *Uses of Literature*, in which she finds that scholars have "a single-minded fixation on the merits of irony, ambiguity, and indeterminacy that leaves it mystified by other structures of value."[7] Felski then outlines a different set of values oriented around readerly uses: recognition, enchantment, knowledge, and shock. All of these uses are moral, at least as that term is being used in this book: they have to do with the capacity of a text to shape readers' behavior, thoughts, and feelings in ways that are (or can be) evaluated as good or bad, that align with values that readers hold in the world outside the text. In so far as books are or continue to be useful for readers, literature, as a category, may not be as independent from the "ethical sciences" as some scholars have made it out to be.[8]

Although Felski does not concern herself either with early modern texts or with earlier ideas about literature, the reassessment that she advocates would necessarily have consequences for the link with which this chapter began, between early modern and modern. That is, if "modern literary criticism" has narrowed the idea of literature by eliding usefulness, then it has done so at least in part by misrepresenting the origins of that idea—in Renaissance humanism.

---

modern ideas of literature, see John Dagenais, *The Ethics of Reading in Manuscript Culture: Glossing the "Libro de buen amor"* (Princeton, NJ: Princeton University Press, 1994), e.g. 10.

[6] Thomas M. Greene, *The Light in Troy: Imitation and Discovery in Renaissance Poetry* (New Haven, CT: Yale University Press, 1982), 30. Joel Altman similarly considers moral ambivalence to be fundamental to "the plays we really cherish," and he comes up with a clear boundary between the demonstrative (plays that tell) and the explorative (plays that show) in *The Tudor Play of Mind: Rhetorical Inquiry and the Development of Elizabethan Drama* (Berkeley, CA: University of California Press, 1978), e.g. 13–30. In a review of Altman's book, G. K. Hunter trenchantly observes, "it is hard not to notice behind the particular felicities of *The Tudor Play of Mind* the recurrent modernist taste for a nonethical language of literary appreciation" (G. K. Hunter, "Elizabethan Drama on the High Wire," *The Sewanee Review* 88.1 [1980]: 105).

[7] Rita Felski, *Uses of Literature* (Malden, MA: Wiley-Blackwell, 2008), 21.

[8] Tobin Siebers also argues for the moral purpose of literature, anticipating Felski to a certain degree, by criticizing scholars for their narrow focus, their disdain for the common reader. See his *Morals and Stories* (New York: Columbia University Press, 1992).

Indeed, it is worth returning to the foundational distinction that twentieth-century literary criticism made, between medieval and Renaissance, and asking some of the same questions again: did humanists have not only a new but a modern idea about the value of literature? Or, to borrow Sidney's language, did humanists see poetry more clearly than medieval authors? The answer is both yes and no. Humanists theorized poetry and eloquent writing in great detail, defining and justifying as Sidney did, creating a more unified idea of literature than had existed previously. At the same time, that idea is not entirely modern, in the sense defined above, because humanists were as interested as their medieval forebears in usefulness, in the capacity of literature to move, teach, and delight. For that reason, their sense of the literary was not independent of morality, those "predetermined values," nor was it oriented around art. Humanist novelty is thus not, on closer look, exactly what or, more properly, where, it is often assumed to be, in a realm of the distinctly literary.

Humanists do not so much rupture or separate from past approaches to value as adapt and alter them, offering a new version of an old concern: the moral usefulness of literature. Read against their medieval predecessors, humanists, somewhat surprisingly, put more, and not less, emphasis on moral value. Where medieval authors recognized that literature, as in the classical legacy, *can* be good for readers, humanist authors thought it *was* without question the best thing. This chapter will trace this shift, from medieval to humanist, using classicism as the most familiar site for ideas about literature to play out.

My revisions to Renaissance (or early modern) novelty will not be surprising to medievalists, who have long understood the complexity of the works they study. It is nevertheless necessary to lay the foundation for the following chapters, to bridge the divide by putting sixteenth-century authors into direct conversation with their predecessors.

The Medieval

Medieval authors, at least in England, do not present nor are they guided by an idea of good literature, or even of poetry, that matches the treatises created by the humanists and their successors. However much medieval authors may have defended poetry, they did not write "defences" of it, and the apparent novelty of the titles given to Sidney's treatise, *Defence of Poesy* or *An Apology for Poetry* can (and does) stand in for a more general novelty of literary interests in the sixteenth century.[9] It is certainly possible to find medieval theories of and treatises on poetry, as

---

[9] See Barbara Kiefer Lewalski, who begins an essay with the claim that Sidney's "emphasis on poetry's power to move to virtuous action and especially to political virtue seems to indicate a new direction in Early Modern poetics" ("How Poetry Moves Readers: Sidney, Spenser, and Milton,"

18 HUMANISM AND GOOD BOOKS IN SIXTEENTH-CENTURY ENGLAND

well as statements about "letters" in various places. After all, classical poems, such as Virgil's *Aeneid*, were an important part of education in this period, and many of the same writings that inspired Renaissance theorists, such as Horace's *Ars Poetica*, were known and discussed.[10] It is, however, also fair to conclude that part of what makes English medieval literature distinct is precisely its lack of a coherent idea of itself. As the editors of the medieval volume of *The Cambridge History of Literary Criticism* recognize, "literature did not occupy a privileged space" in the Middle Ages and that there is an "otherness" to "medieval textuality."[11] Such a point has also been argued more recently by Christopher Cannon in *The Grounds of English Literature*. For Cannon, the Middle Ages is a time of "boldness and experimentation" made possible by the absence of "a general idea of literature."[12] What one might call the untheorized, decentralized, even baggy, nature of writing in this period is also true of statements about moral usefulness, which was an important value assigned to literature. In this section, I refer to two kinds of value: the literary value, which is understood here as elements inherent to texts, such as plot, character, meter, language, subject matter; and moral value, which is understood here as the effect on the reader's behavior, thoughts, and feelings, what Felski calls uses for the reader. I demonstrate that for medieval readers and authors this relationship between literary and moral value was problematic and at times in tension, as is apparent in their treatment of the classical legacy.

At first glance, my claim for medieval heterogeneity might be surprising. It is a commonplace that medieval classicism is Christianizing in its approach, in that it subordinates pagan texts to what one might call Christian messaging or uses for a Christian reader. In this familiar perspective, medieval authors both interpreted and re-wrote classical texts to fit a relatively homogeneous or clearly defined Christian morality. Evidence for this perspective can be found in the *Ovid moralisé* (1309–1320), a French text that intersperses stories from Ovid's *Metamorphoses* with lengthy moralizing exegeses. The author begins with the claim that "All scriptures and writings, be they good or evil, [are] written for our profit and doctrine, the good to the end [for the purpose] to take example by them to do well, and the

---

University of Toronto Quarterly 80.3 [2011]: 756). Lewalski's claim is representative of the way in which novelty is a reflex for early modern scholars: something about the early modern period is new, but no evidence is provided.

[10] For a discussion of Horace in the Middle Ages, see Rita Copeland, "Horace's *Ars poetica* in the Medieval Classroom and Beyond: the Horizons of Ancient Precept," in *Answerable Style: The Idea of the Literary in Medieval England*, ed. Andrew Galloway and Frank Grady (Columbus: Ohio State University Press, 2013), 15–33; Vincent Gillespie, "The Study of Classical Authors," in *The Cambridge History of Literary Criticism, Volume 2: The Middle Ages* (hereafter *CHLC 2*), ed. Alastair Minnis and Ian Johnson (Cambridge: Cambridge University Press, 2005): 2:162–69; D. H. Green, *The Beginnings of Medieval Romance: Fact and Fiction, 1150–1220* (Cambridge: Cambridge University Press, 2008), 28–34; and Glending Olson, *Literature as Recreation in the Later Middle Ages* (Ithaca, NY: Cornell University Press, 1982), 19–38.

[11] Alastair Minnis and Ian Johnson, "Introduction," *CHLC 2*, 3.

[12] Christopher Cannon, *The Grounds of English Literature* (Oxford: Oxford University Press, 2005), 172.

THE NEW, THE MEDIEVAL, AND THE RENAISSANCE   19

evil to the end [for the purpose] that we should keep and abstain us to do evil."[13] The author's allusion to Romans 15:4— "what things soever were written were written for our learning"—places Ovid in the service of Christian teaching.[14] In England, John Gower's adaptations of Ovid in the *Confessio Amantis* (1390) follow a similar model: the seven capital sins provide a moralizing rubric into which a character who is called the Confessor inserts the stories he tells Amans, the character he is advising. Before beginning the story of Narcissus, the Confessor claims, "It may to him noght wel betide/ Which useth thilke vice of Pride [Bad things will happen to the person who is proud]," and links Ovid's story to the moral of avoiding pride:

> And for thin enformacion,
> That thou this vice as I thee rede
> Eschuie schalt, a tale I rede,
> Which fell whilom be daies olde,
> So as the clerk Ovide tolde

[And to instruct you in how you should avoid this vice, as I am advising you, I offer you a story that happened in the olden days, just as Ovid told it].[15]

In its attention to the shaping, "enformacion," of the reader, this passage shows the way in which usefulness was the driving force behind medieval classicism: the applicability of the story to Amans is more important than the text of Ovid's poem, its particular details or even its cultural importance. Indeed, the tale exists outside of Ovid, as a tale that he "told" that was, perhaps, also told by someone else.

In its yoking of pagan texts to a Christian, moral discourse of "vice," Gower's poem matches more theoretical discussions of the classical legacy that can be found in the medieval commentary tradition. These are prologues to classical texts, such as Bernard Silvestris' commentary on Virgil's *Aeneid* (c. 1150), which guide the reader in how to interpret it. For the authors in the commentary tradition, classical texts are valuable as containers of wisdom, a wisdom that is explicitly linked to Christianity.[16] For that reason, and despite their paganism, these texts

---

[13] I am quoting from William Caxton's translation, which he completed in 1480. See *The Book of Ovyde Named Methamorphose*, ed. Richard Moll (Toronto: PIMS, 2013), 75.

[14] "Quaecumque enim scripta sunt ad nostram doctrinam scripta sunt, ut per patientiam et consolationem scripturarum spem habeamus [For what things soever were written were written for our learning, that, through patience and the comfort of the scriptures, we might have hope]" (Romans 15:4 in *The Vulgate Bible: Douay-Rheims Translation*, 6 vols., ed. Swift Edgar and Angela M. Kinney [Cambridge, MA: Harvard University Press, 2010–13], 6:852–53).

[15] John Gower, *Confessio Amantis*, 3 vols., ed. Russell A. Peck with Latin Translations by Andrew Galloway (Kalamazoo, MI: Medieval Institute Publications, 2005–13), 1: Book 1.2265–66, 2270–74.

[16] In their guide, *Medieval Literary Theory and Criticism, c. 1100–c. 1375, The Commentary Tradition* (New York: Oxford University Press, 1988), A. J. Minnis and A. B. Scott argue that the medieval commentary tradition is where one finds medieval ideas about literature, and they further note the emphasis on ethics in this tradition (1, 13).

20 HUMANISM AND GOOD BOOKS IN SIXTEENTH-CENTURY ENGLAND

have the capacity to transform readers morally, or "inform" them as Gower would have it. The *Aeneid* is valuable for its "impressive examples and precepts [*excogitationes*] for adhering more closely to what is honorable and shunning that which is unlawful."[17] Such texts can train readers, giving them "the knowledge of how to act properly."[18]

Insisting on the moral usefulness of poetry means that medieval authors see the individual texts as subordinate to specific moral meanings, and, perhaps more importantly, understand the category of literature (or to use their own terms "writings" and "tales") as itself subordinate to the domain of morality or, more properly, moral philosophy. Indeed, some scholars have argued that the idea of literature in this period was, in fact, ethics.[19] The moral usefulness of a text for its readers was often its most important aspect, and it guided the approach to all texts, whether poetry or philosophy, whether pagan or Christian. At the opening of *The Governance of Kings and Princes* [*De Regimine Principum*] (1277–80), which is a work of political philosophy greatly indebted to Aristotle's writings, Giles of Rome theorizes this approach. I quote from the late fourteenth-century English translation made by John Trevisa: "For it is iwrete ii Ethicorum, we taketh moral work, that is to say highe and derke work, nou[gh]t by cause of contemplacioun nother for to be konnyng, bote for to be good. Thanne the ende and the entent in this sciens is nou[gh]t knowleche bote work and doing, nother sothnes but profit of godenesse [as is written in the second book of Aristotle's *Nicomachean Ethics*, we undertake moral work (study), that is to say elevated and mysterious study, neither for the purpose of contemplation nor for gaining knowledge but in order to be good. For the purpose and the intent of this science (ethics) is not knowledge but work and action; not truth but goodness]."[20] Giles of Rome locates the value, the "profit" of classical works, in their use by readers; classical works such as Aristotle's *Ethics* are most important not for the knowledge they contain but for their effect on the reader's behavior, their future actions. This familiar focus on attaching a Christian, moral message, to pagan, classical texts, has sometimes been described by scholars as static Christian dogmatism or primitive anachronism.[21] A less polemical approach would see the moralizing rather differently, as part of "the common

---

[17] Bernard Silvester, "Commentary on the *Aeneid*," in *Medieval Literary Theory*, 152.

[18] Silvester, "Commentary," in *Medieval Literary Theory*, 152.

[19] See Judson Boyce Allen, *The Ethical Poetic of the Later Middle Ages: A Decorum of Convenient Distinction* (Toronto: University of Toronto Press, 1982), 5–6; A. J. Minnis, *Medieval Theory of Authorship: Scholastic Literary Attitudes in the Later Middle Ages* (London: Scholar Press, 1984), 25; and Eleanor Johnson, *Practicing Literary Theory in the Middle Ages: Ethics and the Mixed Form in Chaucer, Gower, Usk, and Hoccleve* (Chicago: University of Chicago Press, 2013), 1–12. Gillespie also notes the way in which poetry was seen "as moral philosophy" in "The Study," *CHLC 2*, 147.

[20] *The Governance of Kings and Princes: John Trevisa's Middle English Translation of the De Regimine Principum of Aegidius Romanus*, ed. David C. Fowler, Charles F. Briggs, Paul G. Remley (London: Routledge, 1997), 6–7. I have used the extract from Giles of Rome in *Medieval Literary Theory* to make my translation smoother (249).

[21] E.g. Greene, *Light in Troy*, 40.

interest in the affective force of all literature," as Vincent Gillespie describes it, in his overview to late medieval classicism, or, indeed, an interest in usefulness, the applicability of texts to readers.[22]

The apparently moralizing approach to literature is not, however, the whole story of medieval classicism. Most obviously, medieval authors demonstrate a rather varied approach to classical texts: some thought the texts were valuable only in so far as they accorded with Christianity; others thought the texts were mainly valuable on their own terms; and some had more conflicted views.[23] As John Marenbon has argued in his recent study, *Pagans and Philosophers: The Problem of Paganism from Augustine to Leibniz*, the debate over the value of classical texts was a defining aspect of intellectual life in the Middle Ages. Writers provided a range of responses to the central "problem of paganism:" how could pagans be both "moral, intellectual, and cultural heroes" and also be pagans?[24]

Even more important, as far as this study is concerned, is the medieval sense of the incommensurability of the two traditions, the Christian and the classical, and, therefore, a sense that literary and moral value could be distinct, that a text might be variously and even contradictorily useful. I hasten to add that a distinctly literary value was not, for medieval authors, the desirable achievement that it seems to be for those scholars who have characterized medieval moralizing as a sign of innocence and the lack of sophistication.[25] Understanding classical texts on their own terms was not necessarily a means of celebrating those texts, as it sometimes was for Renaissance humanists, but instead tended to make medieval authors very anxious. Medieval thinkers preserve a caution about pagan, classical texts at the same time that they understand them as valuable. In other words, these thinkers understand that reading some good texts can be bad for you.

Medieval authors were, in this way, faced with a particularly interesting problem of value: that texts were simultaneously good, when evaluated in terms of their literary aspects and, more often, cultural importance, and bad, when evaluated in terms of their morality, or usefulness for readers in shaping their future conduct or teaching them the right ways of being and thinking in the world. One might consider the status of Ovid in the Middle Ages and, indeed, well into the Renaissance: Ovid's works were described as both moral and immoral, as both authoritative and as inappropriate.[26] The morality of his poetry could be defended, as the *Ovide moralisé* makes clear, but as any reader of Ovid's *Metamorphoses* will know,

---

[22] Gillespie, "The Study," 145.

[23] John Marenbon devotes his study to examining the variation in Christian approaches to classical texts: he divides the thirteenth-century responses to Aristotle, for example, into three different categories: unity, selective rejection, and limited relativism (*Pagans and Philosophers: The Problem of Paganism from Augustine to Leibniz* [Princeton, NJ: Princeton University Press, 2015], 138–42). See also the essays collected in *CHLC 2* and the texts collected in *Medieval Literary Theory*.

[24] Marenbon, *Pagans and Philosophers*, 1, 3.

[25] Greene, *Light in Troy*, 30.

[26] See, for example, Gillespie, "The Study," 186–206.

22   HUMANISM AND GOOD BOOKS IN SIXTEENTH-CENTURY ENGLAND

the text does not itself contain Christian moral language, any language that advertises itself as having to do with good or bad behavior, or even any explicit statements about usefulness. While one author, like Gower, might insert Ovid's stories into such language, in his case the seven sins, others, like Chaucer, did not, maybe could not. Indeed, Chaucer draws attention to the contradictions around Ovidian moralizing in his *Wife of Bath's Tale*, when the Wife incorrectly retells the story of King Midas to support her claim that women cannot keep secrets:

> Heere may ye se, thogh we a tyme abyde,
> Yet out it moot; we kan no conseil hyde.
> The remenant of the tale if ye wol heere,
> Redeth Ovyde, and ther ye may it leere

[Here you may see that the secret must come out, even though we might delay for a time; we cannot keep our counsel. If you want to hear the rest of the tale, read Ovid, and you may learn of it there].[27]

The Wife's claim—"we [women] cannot keep our counsel"—may not be a conventional moral, but it certainly acts like one. It is a lesson about the badness of human, or in this case women's, behavior. The moral is not in Ovid, and, therefore, reflects the self-interest of the speaker, who is here standing for a reader of Ovid. Ovid can be harnessed to many different moral uses precisely because his text does not contain anything as clearly defined as the "it" to which the Wife refers. While the medieval Ovidian tradition is far too rich to discuss in any detail here, it is enough to note that, viewed in its entirety, it works to preserve the idea or the phenomenon of contradiction, in the simple fact that medieval authors not only themselves used Ovid in differing and sometimes contrasting ways but also offered Ovid as useful to their readers or not useful to their readers in differing and contrasting ways.

An illuminating analogue to the contradictory uses and, therefore, value of classical texts in the Middle Ages can be found in twenty-first century America, in discussions about the canon of American literature. Texts or movies that have long been understood as "good," as in culturally important or skillfully made, can also be seen as harmful to the reader.[28] Something foundational might also be seen as inappropriate, to borrow the terms used here for the Ovidian tradition. For example, in a profile of Toni Morrison in the magazine *The New Yorker*, Hilton Als describes her encounter in junior high school with Mark Twain's *Huckleberry*

---

[27] Geoffrey Chaucer, *The Wife of Bath's Tale*, in *The Riverside Chaucer*, 3rd ed., ed. Larry D. Benson (Boston: Houghton Mifflin, 1987), 3.979–82. Hereafter all references to Chaucer's works will be to this edition and will appear parenthetically.

[28] In "Two Traditions," Hirsch notes the strange way in which literary texts are, in the late twentieth century, assigned "intrinsic" literary value, as if their value is independent of the viewer or reader.

Finn, once an unquestioned classic of American literature: "It provoked a feeling I can only describe now as muffled rage, as though appreciation of the work required my complicity in and sanction of something shaming."[29] For Morrison, and likely others, *Huckleberry Finn* has at least two opposing values that cannot be easily reconciled: on the one hand, there is the literary value, her "appreciation of the work" on its own terms, and, on the other hand, the moral value, being complicit in "something shaming." It might be useful as a literary model, but it can never be useful as a set of moral guidelines, as applicable to the life of this reader.

Such a distinction, between literary and moral value, in the Middle Ages may not be immediately obvious. Many medieval authors can, at times, sound like humanists, in discussing the profit of reading, for example. They do not, however, consciously theorize and standardize their approaches. What one might call a non-theorized approach is apparent in their treatment of one of the most influential, classical works of "literary criticism"—Horace's *Ars Poetica*. In a much-quoted passage Horace states that poetry both instructs and delights and poetry is both sweet and useful: "poetry aims at both instruction and pleasure [aut prodesse volunt aut delectare poetae]" and the best poetry "combine[s] the *utile* with the *dulce* [Omne tulit punctum qui miscuit utile dulci]."[30]

Although medieval authors were familiar with Horace's text, they did not make it the centerpiece of their idea of literature, in so far as they had one. They did not use the *Ars* as a manifesto for the "moral and philosophical status" of poetry nor did they insist on the particular combination of sweetness and usefulness.[31] Instead, authors used Horace as a practical guide to composition.[32] More importantly, they tended to underline that the functions of poetry are distinct—it can instruct or delight, thus preserving the "or's" (*aut*) that Horace uses.[33] Aesop, for example, shows us that "the role of poets is either to be useful or to give pleasure."[34] These distinctions persist throughout the Middle Ages, famously appearing in John Gower's initial remarks on his tale collection, the *Confessio Amantis*. He describes his "bok [book]" as "Somwhat of lust, somwhat of lore," thus indicating the separateness of these categories.[35] Similar oppositions appear in Geoffrey Chaucer's *Canterbury Tales*, in the warning not to make "ernest" of "game" in the Prologue to the *Miller's Tale* or in the discussions of whether the Pardoner

---

[29] Hilton Als, "Ghosts in the House" (2003), *The New Yorker*, July 27, 2020, 33.

[30] The Latin lines come from Horace, *Ars Poetica* (Los Altos, CA: Packard Humanities Institute, 1991), lines 333 and 343; online at https://latin.packhum.org/loc/893/6/0#0. The translation comes from Horace, *Satires. Epistles. The Art of Poetry*, trans. H. Rushton Fairclough, Loeb Classical Library 194 (Cambridge, MA: Harvard University Press, 1926), 447.

[31] See, Copeland, "Horace's *Ars poetica*," 16, 30. See further, Gillespie, "The Study," 162–69; Green, *Beginnings of Medieval Romance*, 28–34; and Olson, *Literature as Recreation*, 19–38.

[32] See Copeland, "Horace's *Ars poetica*," and "Arts of Poetry," *CHLC* 2, 42–67.

[33] Green, *Beginnings of Medieval Romance*, 28.

[34] Conrad of Hirsau, *Dialogue on the Authors*, in *Medieval Literary Theory*, 47. On the "polarization" of these categories, see Olson, *Literature as Recreation*, 22–35

[35] Gower, *Confessio Amantis*, 1: Prol. 18–19.

24 HUMANISM AND GOOD BOOKS IN SIXTEENTH-CENTURY ENGLAND

should tell a "myrie [merry] tale" or "moral thing," in the Introduction to Chaucer's *Pardoner's Tale* (1.3186; 6.316, 6.325). Even when some version of lust and lore, or delight and usefulness, is applied to the same text, the terms still suggest separate frames of reference, as two topics or two levels of allegory.[36] At the end of the *General Prologue* to Chaucer's *Canterbury Tales*, the Host describes the stories that would win the storytelling contest as "tales of best sentence and moost solaas [tales containing the most moral wisdom and the most pleasure]" (1.798). This phrase simultaneously offers the Horatian link of teaching and delighting and also underlines the potential variety of, even distinctions between, tales. The degree to which one tale can contain both sentence and solace is ambiguous, since the plural, "tales," might suggest that some tales have only one quality and some the other. Similarly, in a medieval commentary on Statius's *Thebaid*, the delight is in the covering and the instruction at the center: under "the alluring cover of a poetic fiction" poets "have inserted a set of moral precepts."[37] That statement indicates at least a conceptual if not a practical distinction between the good of a poetic fiction, in that it is alluring and therefore skillfully done, and the good of the moral precepts.

This medieval gap between the literary value, on the one hand, and the moral value, on the other, is closely associated with Augustine, perhaps the most influential interpreter and reader of classical texts in the Middle Ages.[38] In *De Doctrina Christiana* (c. 396–97), Augustine famously confronts the classical inheritance, describing these valuable texts in terms of "Egyptian gold," drawing on Exodus 3:22 and 12:35–36:[39]

> Just as the Egyptians had not only idols and grave burdens which the people of Israel detested and avoided, so also they had vases and ornaments of gold and silver and clothing which the Israelites took with them secretly when they fled, as if to put them to a better use ... In the same way all the teachings of the pagans contain not only simulated and superstitious imaginings and grave burdens of unnecessary labor, which each one of us leaving the society of pagans under the leadership of Christ ought to abominate and avoid, but also liberal disciplines more suited to the uses of truth, and some most useful precepts concerning morals. Even some truths concerning the worship of one God are discovered among them. These are, as it were, their gold and silver, which they did not

[36] Or, this division can be found in the two styles of the *prosimetrum*: prose (useful) and verse (delight), as discussed by Johnson, *Practicing Literary Theory*, 5.

[37] Olson, *Literature as Recreation*, 22.

[38] Marenbon discusses Augustine's foundational role in the "problem of paganism" (*Pagans and Philosophers*, 19, 34–41).

[39] On the importance of this passage as a "moral justification" of the classical legacy, see Edmund Campion, "Defences of Classical Learning in St. Augustine's *De Doctrina Christiana* and Erasmus's *Antibarbari*," *History of European Ideas* 4.4 (1983): 467–71; and *A Dictionary of Biblical Tradition*, ed. David Lyle Jeffrey (Grand Rapids, MI: W. B. Eerdmans, 1992), 226–27. The phrase "moral justification" comes from Campion, 467.

THE NEW, THE MEDIEVAL, AND THE RENAISSANCE   25

institute themselves but dug up from certain mines of divine Providence, which is everywhere infused, and perversely and injuriously abused in the worship of demons.[40]

Augustine underlines the value of these pagan texts by describing them as decorative objects—the ornaments, vases, and clothing. Such objects work well as a metaphor for texts because their craftsmanship is as important in making them beautiful as the material from which they are made. The problem is that these beautiful objects contain many different elements, including both the bad, "superstitious imaginings," and the good, the "useful precepts" that can be separated out. In his focus on use and abuse of the very same objects, Augustine raises the possibility that the moral value of any text is not stable and also not the same as its beauty. The usefulness of poetry will depend on who is reading, whether Egyptians or Israelites, and not only on the elements internal to the text. The very same book might be an idol for one reader and a vase for another, or a pleasure cruise for one reader and a voyage home for another, to stay with the metaphors of *De Doctrina*.[41] In focusing on the usefulness of a text, as distinct from its literary value, Augustine assigns power to readers, who can make of a text what they will. As Rita Copeland has argued, Augustine's writings "give reading and interpretation a new status ... transfer[ring] responsibility for making meaning from the writer to the reader."[42]

The sense of a gap between literary and moral value, implicit in Augustine's "Egyptian gold," persists alongside the confidence that is more typically described as medieval, that is, the yoking of the classical legacy to Christian messaging, as apparent in the moralized Ovid and in Gower's *Confessio*. It also persists alongside a view that is more commonly associated with Renaissance humanism: that classical texts can be valued on their own terms, as literary, without reference to a moral value, whether Christian or otherwise. The entanglement of these ideas about literary and moral value is powerfully explored at the end of Geoffrey Chaucer's *Troilus and Criseyde* (c. 1382–87), perhaps the most well-known response to the classical legacy in medieval England.[43] I begin with the moment that the speaker addresses his book, as he nears the end of his story:

> Go litel bok, go litel myn tragedye,
> Ther God thi makere yet, er that he dye,

---

[40] Saint Augustine, *On Christian Doctrine*, trans. D. W. Robertson Jr. (New York: Macmillan, 1958), 75. See also D. W. Robertson's discussion of this passage and its influence on other medieval authors in *A Preface to Chaucer: Studies in Medieval Perspectives* (Princeton, NJ: Princeton University Press, 1962), 340–41.

[41] Augustine's famous remarks about reading as a voyage appear in *On Christian Doctrine*, 9–10.

[42] Copeland, *Rhetoric*, 158.

[43] I am drawing on some of the ideas published in my essay, "What Spenser Took from Chaucer: Worldly Vanity in *The Ruines of Time* and *Troilus and Criseyde*," *ELH* 83 (2016): 431–55.

26 HUMANISM AND GOOD BOOKS IN SIXTEENTH-CENTURY ENGLAND

> So sende myght to make in som comedye!
> But litel book, no making thow n'envie,
> But subgit be to alle poesye;
> And kis the steppes where as thow seest pace
> Virgile, Ovide, Omer, Lucan, and Stace

[Go little book; go my little tragedy. May God send your maker (the poet) power to write some comedy before he dies. But, little book, do not contend with any poem, but be subject to all poetry; and kiss the steps where you see Virgil, Ovid, Homer, Lucan, and Statius pass] (5.1786–92).

This much-quoted passage is undoubtedly humanist, in that it shows Chaucer's love of the classical tradition and his desire to imitate it. Chaucer even adapts a recognizable metaphor for imitation—as following on foot, referring to the authors' walking (they "pace") up the steps. His book is, by implication, following these great books, even while kissing the steps, to demonstrate his subservience and adoration. To be sure, Chaucer does link his poem to the Christian God, and his comments about turning from tragedy to comedy hint at a moral difference between the pagan world of tragedy and the Christian world of comedy. Despite this muted hint of morality, there is no sense that the speaker or Chaucer finds the paganism of Virgil or the other authors he mentions problematic for readers (and users) of his poem; the tone is one of reverence.

The speaker moves on from this praise of the classical legacy to Christian moral messaging in a manner familiar from many medieval texts. When the narrator ends with Troilus's story, an end emphasized by the repetition of "Swich fyn [Such an end]" at the beginning of each line, he turns to the moral lesson:

> Repeyreth hom fro worldly vanyte,
> And of youre herte up casteth the visage
> To thilke God that after his ymage
> Yow made, and thynketh al nys but a faire,
> This world that passeth soone as floures faire

[Return home from worldly vanity and cast the face of your heart to the same God who made you in his image, and think that everything is but a fair, that is, this world that passes as quickly as do the beautiful flowers] (5.1837–41).

In offering a moral lesson, Chaucer suggests that this story can be useful in shaping the future, Christian behavior of his readers: the audience should love Jesus, "the which that right for love/ Upon a crois, oure soules for to beye,/ First starf [who first died, for love, upon the cross, to buy our souls]" (5.1842–44). Like Gower, Chaucer suggests that reading his poem will "form" his readers: they will be moved

THE NEW, THE MEDIEVAL, AND THE RENAISSANCE   27

by the story to give up the things of this world and change the way that they think about it. And yet, the link between the pagan story and the Christian moral, its usefulness, is not at all confident. In fact, it causes the narrator to experience a great amount of anxiety, or to have, as E. Talbot Donaldson famously noted, a "nervous breakdown in poetry."[44]

Part of the problem, a sign of the breakdown, is that the speaker does not seem to be able to use this Christian moral to end the poem. Instead, he returns to the Trojan world in order to underline the gap between the paganism of the classical legacy and the Christian present. He condemns paganism in definite terms:

> Lo, here of payens corsed olde rites!
> Lo, here, what alle hire goodes may availle!
> Lo, here, thise wrecched worldes appetites!
> Lo here, the fyn and guerdoun for travaille
> Of Jove, Appollo, of Mars, of swich rascaille!
> Lo, here the forme of olde clerkis speche
> In poetrie, if ye hire bokes seche.

[Oh, behold pagans' cursed old rites! Oh, behold what help all of their goods did! Oh, behold the wretched appetites of the world! Oh, behold the end and reward for this labor of Jove, Apollo, of Mars, and of such rascals! Oh, behold the style of old clerks' speech, in poetry, if you look at their books] (5.1849–55).[45]

It is worth noting the way in which the stanza marks the gap between classical and Christian morality exactly at the point where a reader might expect a smooth transition, from the "alluring" poetic fiction to the moral precepts hidden underneath.[46] Here the speaker's evaluation of classical texts contrasts markedly with the reverence of kissing the steps. The "forme of olde clerkis speche/ In poetrie" is exactly parallel with their paganism, "payens corsed olde rites." In sum, classical poetry is problematic for a Christian audience because it tells the stories of "appetites" and other kinds of bad behavior, what the "rascaille" do, and it might not, therefore, be useful as moral guidelines.

Chaucer's *Troilus and Criseyde* is, of course, remarkable for many reasons, not least because it makes it impossible to draw a firm boundary between medieval

---

[44] E. T. Donaldson, *Speaking of Chaucer* (New York: W. W. Norton, 1970), 91.

[45] There is no parallel to this passage in Chaucer's source, Boccaccio's *Il Filostrato*. See the parallel text edition: Geoffrey Chaucer, *Troilus and Criseyde with Facing-page Il Filostrato*, ed. Stephen A. Barney (New York: W. W. Norton & Co., 2006), 424–425.

[46] A. J. Minnis has argued that Chaucer's pagan poems depict pagans according to "sophisticated contemporary notions about what pagan antiquity was like," namely determinism (*Chaucer and Pagan Antiquity* [Cambridge: D. S. Brewer, 1982], 2). See also Jamie C. Fumo, The *Legacy of Apollo: Antiquity, Authority, and Chaucerian Poetics* (Toronto: University of Toronto Press, 2010), which approaches Chaucer's imitation of classical texts through Apollo, and argues for a kind of proto-humanism.

28 HUMANISM AND GOOD BOOKS IN SIXTEENTH-CENTURY ENGLAND

"diachronic innocence" and Renaissance "historicity," or medieval values and modern ambiguity.[47] In its complicated response to the classical legacy, its exploration of what it means to be a self, and its self-consciousness about writing, it refuses the kinds of homogeneity that scholars once assigned to the Middle Ages. The poem simply cannot serve as a backdrop against which those attributes emerge newly in the Renaissance. The temptation to highlight its singularity, to see it as an exceptional and therefore in some ways non-medieval poem should nevertheless be resisted. Chaucer's moral breakdown at the end of *Troilus and Criseyde* fits with the moral explorations found in his other works and in the work of his contemporaries. Indeed, Chaucer confronts the morality of his writing throughout his career, attempting to come to terms with the "lust" and "lore" that Gower also explores in his *Confessio*.[48] The Retraction that Chaucer appends to the end of the *Canterbury Tales* is perhaps the most obvious evidence of such concerns. At first glance, the morality looks straightforward: the Retraction is an attempt to divide his works into the opposed categories of "lust," for which he repents, and "lore," which he would like to preserve. And yet, the Retraction is ambiguous in its aims: it is and is not an apology for poetry. Chaucer begins with what looks like a sweeping and wholehearted defense: "And if ther be any thyng that displese hem, I preye hem also that they arrette it to the defaute of myn unkonnynge and nat to my wyl, that wolde ful fayn have seyd bettre if I hadde had konnynge./ For oure book seith, 'Al that is writen is writen for our doctrine,' and that is myn entente [And if there be any thing that displeases them, I pray also that they blame it on the fault of my lack of wit and not on my will that would much prefer to have said better if I had had knowledge. For our book says, 'All that is written is written for our doctrine,' and that is my intent]" (10.1082–83). The biblical passage Chaucer quotes is Romans 15:4, which was also used to defend Ovid, as discussed above.[49] In this way, Chaucer's statement is recognizable as a defense of morally problematic poetry, one that was developed in relation to classical texts in the commentary tradition.

Chaucer does not, however, spend much time defending his own poetry or any other writings on moral grounds. He does not invoke the register of profit, as do the authors in the commentary tradition or the adapters of Ovid. Instead, he goes on to reject, somewhat contradictorily, a number of his works, dividing his texts into two categories. First, a grouping that he labels, "enditynges of

---

[47] A point made effectively and influentially by Lee Patterson in *Chaucer and the Subject of History* (Madison, WI: University of Wisconsin, 1991), 84–164.

[48] On the intersections between Chaucer's works and contemporary moral discourses, see Alcuin Blamires, *Chaucer, Ethics, and Gender* (Oxford: Oxford University Press, 2006).

[49] On its use in the writings of Ranulph Higden, a monk of the early fourteenth-century, and in medieval commentaries on Ovid, see Minnis, *Medieval Theory*, 203–6 and Copeland, *Rhetoric*, 109–10. Both associate this justification with *compilatio*; nevertheless, the readerly focus is clear: "Ralph Higden cited Romans xv.4 in defence of his juxtaposition of pagan and Christian *auctoritas*," and "the onus is therefore placed on the discriminating reader" (*Medieval Theory*, 203).

worldly vanitees [compositions of worldly vanities]," which includes "the tales of Caunterbury, thilke that sownen into synne [the tales of Canterbury, those that encourage sin]," and, second, a grouping he does not assign a label to, which is a list of devotional and moral works: "the translacion of Boece de Consolacione, and othere bookes of legendes of seintes, and omelies and moralitee, and devocioun [the translation of Boethius's *Consolation* and other books of legends of saints, and homilies and morality and devotion]." This division is, of course, motivated by the moral content of the works, "lust" and "lore." It would, however, be a mistake to think that content alone determines the value, or that his two categories are equally stable. Instead, in his focus on the effects on the reader, Chaucer matches Augustine's categories of use and abuse. The devotional and moral works can be used, and that is clear from the description, which matches the Augustinian perspective on the kinds of usefulness found in pagan classical texts: "useful precepts concerning morals" and "some truths concerning the worship of one God." The other works might, however, encourage abuse, in that they potentially "sownen [encourage or incite]" sin. In reading, the *Miller's Tale*, for example, readers might find themselves "entangled in a perverse sweetness" and "wandering from God," to use Augustine's language.[50] Perhaps more importantly, Chaucer's Retraction contains some uncertainty about how to evaluate the individual tales of the *Canterbury Tales*, which are only partially or ambiguously retracted. He thus allows for the possibility that a particular text, one that is not explicitly Christian in content and analogous therefore to pagan, classical texts, may vary in its effects or usefulness: leading one reader astray and training another in virtue.

In imagining the moral effect of his texts on Christian readers, Chaucer resembles not only Gower, whose *Confessio* is organized around the sins, but also his contemporary William Langland, who offers a moving meditation on the value of writing in his late fourteenth-century dream vision, *Piers Plowman* (c. 1377–1379). Langland describes a conversation that occurs in a dream between the first-person speaker and the allegorical figure, Ymaginatif, who personifies the image-making faculty within the mind, the creative capacity that is responsible for the poem he is writing. In this conversation, Ymaginatif castigates the dreamer for writing his book:

And thow medlest thee with makynges—and myghtest go seye thi Sauter,
And bidde for hem that yyveth thee breed; for ther are bokes ynowe
To telle men what Dowel is, Dobet and Dobest bothe,
And prechours to preve what it is, of many a peire freres.'

---

[50] Augustine, *On Christian Doctrine*, 9–10.

30 HUMANISM AND GOOD BOOKS IN SIXTEENTH-CENTURY ENGLAND

[And you mess around with writing poetry when you could be saying your Psalms and praying for those that give you bread; because there are enough books to tell people what it means to live a good life (to Do-well, Do-better, and Do-best) and preachers, of many a pair of friars, to explain it].[51]

For Langland, there is no independent realm of "makyng," a common term for writing, including the writing of poetry, no poem that does not also confront morality, or what people should do, which is here described in terms of the triad of Do-well, Do-better and Do-best. The anxiety is that no writing can be justified as morally useful within a Christian framework. As both Chaucer and Langland demonstrate, the "makynge" or "enditying" of literature was as much motivated by exploring discourses of morality, the language of what people should do, think, and feel, as by the attempt to imagine a realm of "poesye" independent of such discourses.

The New

Renaissance humanists recovered, imitated, and celebrated far more of the classical inheritance than most medieval authors, such as Chaucer or Gower, were able to do or were interested in doing. They also wrote treatises on poetry and justified poetry in their educational treatises in ways that their medieval predecessors did not. Such a flourishing of interest has led scholars to claim that humanists had a new idea of poetry, or literature, as distinctively literary, or as "an independent art" guided by its own principles, as described above. This sense of "rupture" and "rift" between the medieval and the Renaissance has tended to dominate accounts of poetry and literary production more broadly.[52] For most scholars of sixteenth-century literature, there is a clearly defined "realm of the 'early modern,' which is somehow always already there."[53]

Approaching Renaissance humanism as a rupture with the medieval, however, occludes the way in which an important part of its novelty emerged from the same concerns that motivated medieval thinkers: how to make sense of the classical inheritance in a Christian culture, how to describe the value of poetry and of imaginative texts, whether from the classical past or their own present. While humanists praised eloquence more fully and were more invested in imitating the classical

---

[51] William Langland, *The Vision of Piers Plowman: A Complete Edition of the B-Text*, ed. A. V. C. Schmidt (London: J. M. Dent & Sons, 1987), 12.16–19.

[52] The word "rupture" is taken from Greene, *Light in Troy*, 3 and "rift" from Glyn P. Norton, "Introduction," in *The Cambridge History of Literary Criticism, Volume 3: The Renaissance* (hereafter *CHLC 3*), ed. Norton (Cambridge: Cambridge University Press, 1999), 3:2.

[53] Richard Halpern, *The Poetics of Primitive Accumulation: English Renaissance Culture and the Genealogy of Capital*. (Ithaca, NY: Cornell University Press, 1991), 12. Halpern is describing the impact of New Historicism, which has focused attention on the immediate historical context.

legacy than their medieval forebears, they followed those medieval forebears in understanding classical texts as morally instructive, useful in shaping Christian behavior. Perhaps the most well-known purveyor of this approach was Erasmus of Rotterdam.[54] In his book of proverbs, the *Adages*, Erasmus vastly increased the classical knowledge available to readers in its many different editions (1500–36).[55] In explaining the "usefulness" of proverbs near the opening, Erasmus insists on their relation to "philosophy," by which he means moral philosophy. After quoting a proverb found in Plato's *Gorgias*: "it is preferable to receive an injury than to inflict one," he relates the proverb back to Christianity: "What doctrine was ever produced by the philosophers more salutary as a principle of life or close to the Christian religion?"[56]

Aside from his more detailed knowledge of the classical inheritance, Erasmus sounds very similar to the medieval traditions out of which he emerges: the "doctrine" and "principles" of pagan philosophers and of Christian religion can be brought together. Similarly, Sir Thomas More, friend of Erasmus, famously defended the study of Greek at Oxford in 1518 with the claim that reading "sound learning [bonas literas]," "prepares the soul for virtues [animam ad virtutem praeparat]."[57] Such justifications would have been recognizable to medieval authors, who defended pagan texts as profitable for the reader, as Giles of Rome explains in his praise of Aristotle's *Ethics*. There is a sense that the classical pagan texts are indebted to the same, that is, Christian, wisdom at their heart, the gold dug from God's mines in Augustine's description in *De Doctrina*. As the insistence on Christian morality, whether Erasmus's "principle[s] of life" or More's virtues, makes clear, the humanists influential in early sixteenth-century England were not motivated by any love of the secular, the worldly as opposed to the Christian, even if, paradoxically, their appreciation of these pagan texts for their Christian usefulness may have ultimately led to appreciation on secular grounds.[58]

At the same time, humanists provided a new answer to the usefulness of pagan, classical texts by confidently linking literary and moral value: good, as in wellwritten literature, is good, as in morally instructive, for the reader. In other words, they theorized and codified the bagginess and hesitancy of medieval approaches

---

[54] One could also point to Philipp Melanchthon and Johannes Sturm, humanists who combined classical learning with Christian piety, and whose ideas were widely circulated in England (Ian Green, *Humanism and Protestantism in Early Modern English Education* [Burlington, VT: Ashgate, 2009], 12, 51).

[55] Margaret Mann Phillips, *The "Adages" of Erasmus: A Study with Translations* (Cambridge: Cambridge University Press, 1964), ix.

[56] Erasmus of Rotterdam, *Adages*, notes by R. A. B. Mynors, trans. Margaret Mann Phillips, *Collected Works of Erasmus* (*CWE*) 84 vols. (Toronto: University of Toronto Press, 1974–), Vol.31 (1982):14.

[57] Thomas More, "Letter to Oxford," in *The Complete Works of St. Thomas More*, 15 vols. (New Haven, CT: Yale University Press, 1963–97), 15: 133, 138.

[58] See Ada Palmer, "Humanist Lives of Classical Philosophers and the Idea of Renaissance Secularization: Virtue, Rhetoric, and the Orthodox Sources of Unbelief," *Renaissance Quarterly* 70.3 (2017): 935–976.

32   HUMANISM AND GOOD BOOKS IN SIXTEENTH-CENTURY ENGLAND

into one much-repeated idea: the best poetry is sweet and useful; writing should combine eloquence and wisdom.[59] As Anthony Grafton and Lisa Jardine note, in *From Humanism to the Humanities*, humanists "consistently make the identity of humanist eloquence and moral integrity—right living—automatic and self-evident."[60] This new link has its roots in classical texts: Horace's *Ars Poetica*, Aristotle's *Poetics*, and Cicero's later writings on rhetoric, such as the *De Oratore*. Humanist thinkers made these ideas their own by categorizing poetry as rhetoric and by claiming that poetry consistently has a moral purpose—to persuade readers to right action.[61] Given the importance of this link between literary and moral value to the humanists, a reader might be surprised by the casualness of Horace's original formulation of teaching and delighting. The link appears within a passage of the *Ars* that goes into detail about what makes a poem bad or good. I cite at some length to give a sense of the context from which humanists derived their formula:

> The first essential is wisdom. This you can cultivate by study of the philosophers, and when you have first learned from them valuable lessons of life, you should apply yourself to life itself, and then your personages will speak like real living beings. Sometimes striking passages and characters properly portrayed commend a mediocre play better than do verses which lack substance, mere trifles, however melodious.
>
> The Greeks had genius, eloquence, and ambition; the Romans are too practical, even in their elementary schooling. How can we expect a people thus trained to develop poets? Poetry aims at both instruction and pleasure. In your didactic passages, be not long-winded; in your fiction, avoid extravagance. Combine the *utile* with the *dulce*, for only thus will you produce a book that will sell, and enjoy a wide and lasting fame.[62]

It is worth noting that the perspective here is above all practical: about what authors should do when they write poetry. While Horace suggests that a poet should offer morality in the wisdom and the "lessons of life" learned from philosophers, he is as interested in directing the author to write realistic dialogue for his characters. The brief theoretical observation about the nature of poetry, to provide "instruction and pleasure" or "things of profit/ and pleasaunce [pleasure]," as rendered in an English translation printed in 1567, is followed by tips on how a

---

[59] On the novelty of the link, see Robert Matz, *Defending Literature in Early Modern England: Renaissance Literary Theory in Social Context* (New York: Cambridge University Press, 2000), especially 1–23, and Shepherd, "Introduction," *An Apology*, 21.

[60] Anthony Grafton and Lisa Jardine, *From Humanism to the Humanities: Education and the Liberal Arts in Fifteenth- and Sixteenth-Century Europe* (Cambridge, MA: Harvard University Press, 1986), 33.

[61] The literary interests of Renaissance humanists vis-à-vis the rediscovery of these classical treatises on poetry and rhetoric are well-attested. See, for example, *CHLC 3*, 1–22, 66–76, 77–87. Weinberg's *History of Literary Criticism in the Italian Renaissance* is still relevant in this regard.

[62] Horace, *Satires. Epistles. The Art of Poetry*, p. 447, lines 309–46.

THE NEW, THE MEDIEVAL, AND THE RENAISSANCE   33

writer achieves that duality.[63] Horace leaves the content of the didacticism open. The line that circulates so widely—the "dulce and utile" or "delectable style" and "good counsel," in the sixteenth-century translation—is rather anticlimactic or at least not very concerned with morality in its original context.[64] The measure of the best poetry for Horace is not that it "prepares the soul for virtue," as More would have it, but that people buy it and the poet becomes famous.

It would be difficult to underestimate the importance of Horace's *Ars* for human-ist thinkers, as Weinberg's massive collection of Italian treatises, *A History of Literary Criticism in the Italian Renaissance*, amply demonstrates.[65] Horace helped humanists outline a heightened status for poetry: renewed attention to his trea-tise provided a more confident language to describe the moral purpose of reading classical texts that permeated the culture. In brief, Horace's text became a "metadis-course," to borrow Rita Copeland's helpful term.[66] The effects can be found simply everywhere. In his popular educational treatise, *On the Method of Study* (1511), Erasmus describes the fusion of profit and pleasure, instruction and delight, with a compelling metaphor of a fountain: "traditionally almost all knowledge of things is to be sought in the Greek authors. For in short whence can one draw a draught so pure, so easy, and so delightful as from the very fountain-head."[67] For Erasmus the knowledge found in the classics, the Greek authors, is inextrica-ble from the beauty of the texts. Water is both obviously useful and, in the pure state described here, also "delightful." His choice of metaphor contrasts starkly with the vases and clothing that Augustine describes in his *De Doctrina*: water is complete unto itself; there is no need to strip away the decorations, no need to melt down the gold; there is only the easy motion of drinking.

Erasmus's confidence in the natural and at times divine link between wisdom and eloquence in pagan, classical texts was not, at first, ubiquitous, at least in Eng-land. John Colet, noted Christian humanist and educator, was cautious about the texts assigned to students at St. Paul's, a school he founded on Erasmian princi-ples in 1509. In his statutes for the school, Colet invokes the familiar Ciceronian ideal to describe what will be taught: "authors who have joined wisdom with pure chaste eloquence." His humanism cannot be doubted, since he is adamant that students read "literature" not "blotterature"; literature is, as he explains, "the true Latin tongue" used by Virgil and Terence, and "blotterature," unspecified later corruptions written in Latin, presumably some of the texts used in medieval

---

[63] *Horace his arte of poetry, pistles, and satyrs* (London, 1567) STC 13797, B3r, image 17. Spelling modernized.

[64] *Horace his arte*, B3v, image 18.

[65] Weinberg, *History of Literary Criticism*, 1:71.

[66] Copeland, "Horace's *Ars Poetica*," 18.

[67] Erasmus, *On the Method of Study*, ed. Craig R. Thompson, trans. Brian McGregor, *CWE*, Vol. 24 (1978): 671.

34   HUMANISM AND GOOD BOOKS IN SIXTEENTH-CENTURY ENGLAND

schools.[68] At the same time, however, he makes it clear that he aligns the good of "good literature," with Christianity: "I would they were taught always in good literature both in Latin and Greek, and good authors such as have the very Roman eloquence joined with wisdom, especially Christian authors that wrote their wisdom with clean and chaste Latin either in verse or in prose, for my intent is that this school will increase knowledge and worship of God and our lord Jesus Christ and the good Christian life and manners in the children."[69] Colet embraces the classical inheritance for its beauty—the pure and chaste Latin—but his embrace is not unqualified. For Colet, good is still linked to Christianity, since even the pagan authors are being used to train the children in Christian morality, in "life and manners."

Debates about the increased access to classical texts in the first part of the sixteenth century underline the use-abuse framework within which readers still approached the classical inheritance, a framework that I've been calling Augustinian. For these Englishmen, pagan, classical texts were not secular; they were pagan and, therefore, potentially dangerous, or not useful, to their Christian readers, in precisely the way that Augustine imagined. That is, they were capable of being abused. The concern about abuse apparently motivated the attack made by the Bishop of London on the "good literature" assigned at St. Paul's, John Colet's humanist school. He describes that school as "a temple of idolatry," thus suggesting that reading Greek authors is spiritually, and also, therefore, morally, dangerous for a Christian audience.[70] His concern was that children would be inculcated in pagan not Christian values. Even Thomas More, who defends the study of ancient Greek, does so in primarily Augustinian terms, implicitly acknowledging that these writings initially belonged to the wrong people and were, therefore, subject to abuse. Those who read Greek authors are "despoiling the women of Egypt to grace their own queen [spoliatis videlicet Aegyptis mulieribus in reginae cultum]."[71] Those who read Greek are the Israelites of the biblical book of Exodus, stealing the beautiful clothes and vases from the pagans and putting them to better use.

By the middle of the sixteenth-century, explicit concerns about the abuse of pagan texts, the idolatry that Augustine imagined, disappear from educational treatises and theorizations of poetry. Instead, a new set of certainties begins to

---

[68] John Colet, "Statutes of St. Paul's School (1518)," in Joseph Hirst Lupton, *A Life of John Colet: With an Appendix of Some of his English Writings* (London: George Bell and Sons, 1887), 280; spelling modernized.

[69] Colet, "Statutes," 279; spelling modernized. On Colet's school, see James P. Carley and Ágnes Juhász-Ormsby, "Survey of Henrician Humanism," in *The Oxford History of Classical Reception in English Literature: Volume 1: 800–1558*, ed. Rita Copeland (Oxford: Oxford University Press, 2016), 1: 518–19; James McConica, *English Humanists and Reformation Politics under Henry VIII and Edward VI* (Oxford: Clarendon Press, 1965), 46–49; and Joan Simon, *Education and Society in Tudor England* (Cambridge: Cambridge University Press, 1966), 73–80.

[70] Simon, *Education and Society*, 78.

[71] More, "Letter to Oxford," in *Works*, 15:140.

govern the relationship between the reader and the classical text: writing, often poetry specifically, would be uniformly viewed as rhetoric, as a means of persuading readers to good and bad behavior.[72] Humanists used Horatian and Ciceronian views to assert that classical texts were undeniably the best way to teach morality, transforming a medieval mix of possibility and doubt into a party line: "the best" poetry (or literature) is marked by the inextricable link of wisdom and eloquence or sweetness and usefulness. In his Erasmian treatise on education, *The Scholemaster* (printed 1570, but written earlier), Roger Ascham writes:

> Againe, behold on the other side, how Gods wisdome hath wrought [has worked], that of *Academici* and *Peripatetici,* those that were wisest in iudgement of matters and purest in vttering their myndes, the first and chiefest [highest ranking], that wrote most and best, in either tong, as *Plato* and *Aristotle* in Greek, *Tullie* [Cicero] in Latin.[73]

For Ascham, "wisest" and "purest" are parallel with "first and chiefest" and "most and best." The purity of Cicero's Latin is also a moral purity: what is delightful is also wise. In this approach, the reader is almost irrelevant; as long as readers read the "best" authors they will be certain to gain the correct lesson. Such a clear sense of the text as good, as *bonae litterae*, reduces, even erases, some of the anxiety or ambivalence that might have collected around readers' responses to classical texts, such as Ovid's *Metamorphoses*. While readers are central to this rhetorical understanding of literature—after all, who is being persuaded, if not the reader?—they are also passive, the objects on which the text works.[74] Readers are not workers in the creation of meaning, deciding which texts were useful or not useful, as they were imagined in Chaucer's Retraction or at the end of *Troilus and Criseyde*. Instead of being used or abused by readers, as in the Augustinian formulation, texts use or abuse readers, persuading them and shaping them.

This humanist certainty—in the link between literary and moral value—became so common in the sixteenth century as to seem entirely natural. Humanist terminology standardizes an idea of poetry, or writing, and of its value through frequent repetition: eloquence and wisdom, the best poetry, sweetness and usefulness, *bonae litterae*, and good literature. The success of these terms is apparent not just in their ubiquity vis-à-vis the classical legacy, but also in their use for all kinds of writing. That is, sixteenth-century authors begin to position their own literary production explicitly in terms of *bonae litterae*—their texts are both good,

---

[72] The shift to understanding literature as rhetoric is well attested. See the "Introduction," in *CHLC* 3:1–22 and Victoria Kahn, *Rhetoric, Prudence, and Skepticism in the Renaissance* (Ithaca, NY: Cornell University Press, 1985), 29–54. As Kahn rightly points out, this shift is a moral shift as much as it is a disciplinary one: it signals that "we are best persuaded to ethical praxis by the rhetorical practice of literature" (*Rhetoric, Prudence*, 9). See also Markku Peltonen, "Virtues in Elizabethan and Early Stuart Grammar Schools," *Journal of Medieval and Early Modern Studies* 42 (2012): 157–179.

[73] Roger Ascham, *The Scholemaster* in *English Works*, ed. William Aldis Wright (Cambridge: Cambridge University Press, 1904), 266.

[74] In rhetoric, the reader is "the object of the text's impact," as nicely put by Nicholas Cronk in "Aristotle, Horace, and Longinus: The Conception of Reader Response," in *CHLC 3*, 204.

36 HUMANISM AND GOOD BOOKS IN SIXTEENTH-CENTURY ENGLAND

as in well-written, and good for the reader, as in morally instructive. In *The Palace of Pleasure* (1566), William Painter collects a variety of "histories" and "novelles," written by "diverse good and commendable authors," such as the Roman historian Livy and the Italian poet Boccaccio.[75] Such a description takes up the humanist approach to the classical legacy, *bonae litterae*, and applies it to a range of authors. Boccaccio, for example, is as good and commendable as Livy, because his works similarly demonstrate skilled writing and moral instructiveness. Moreover, Painter opens his collection with a letter to the reader in which he describes the contents in clearly Horatian terms, as "both profitable and pleasant."[76] He goes on to explain what he means by those terms: the stories will be profitable in that they instruct in virtue and vice, "disclosing" or "revealing" both "good desert" and "misery;" and they will be pleasant because they entertain, "recreating" and "refreshing."[77] At first glance, Painter's use of these terms recalls Gower's "lust" and "lore" or Chaucer's "ernest" and "game." On closer look, however, Painter understands these terms as linked within the text in ways that Gower and Chaucer do not. The two goods of eloquence and wisdom are inseparable, found in the same tales. Even Painter's pleasantness is at least in part moral, since it is precisely the "delectable"-ness that gives the stories the capacity to cleanse the readers of their sins: "the angry and choleric [will be] purged."[78] As importantly, it is the text, and not the reader, that controls the usefulness. The text will purge readers of their sins; they do not need to turn away from the poem to Jesus as does the reader of Chaucer's *Troilus and Criseyde*.

From the perspective of Painter and Ascham and their contemporaries, there is no poetry, or history or novels, or even writing, without morality. Texts provide the principles of good living or show the vanity of the world or prepare the soul in virtue or demonstrate the harm of sin. In this way, sixteenth-century authors resemble the medieval authors Gower, Chaucer, and Langland, for whom there was no poetry, or making, without morality. At the same time, the later authors redefined the relationship between the value of texts, the literary and the moral, insisting that they were inextricably linked: reading good literature was good for you, without exception, for every reader. Such a claim was both bold and new, and it had to be shored up and defended against the messiness and contradictions around writing that these thinkers inherited and with which they themselves were faced. This work of inventing, reconciling, and repressing motivated many authors in the first part of the sixteenth century, as the next chapters will explore.

---

[75] William Painter, *The Palace of Pleasure Beautified, adorned and well furnished, with Pleasaunt Histories and excellent Nouelles, selected out of diuers good and commendable Authors* (London, 1566) STC 19121. On this text, see Arthur F. Kinney, *Humanist Poetics: Thought, Rhetoric, and Fiction in Sixteenth-century England* (Amherst, MA: University of Massachusetts Press, 1986), 212.

[76] Painter, *Palace*, image 12.

[77] Painter, *Palace*, image 12; image 13.

[78] Painter, *Palace*, image 13.

2
Humanism and the Morality Play

At the end of Henry Medwall's play, *Fulgens and Lucrece* (printed c. 1512), a character known only as "B" insists upon the moral usefulness of literature, invoking the familiar Horatian claim about its capacity to delight and to teach:

> That all the substaunce of this play
> Was done specially therfore
> Not onely to make folke myrth and game,
> But that suche as be gentilmen of name
> May be somewhat movyd
> By this example for to eschew
> The wey of vyce and favour vertue.[1]

Medwall was not alone in thinking of a play as a vehicle for moral instruction; the first part of the sixteenth century in England saw a rapid increase in plays explicitly interested in providing audience members with "examples" of what they should or should not do. According to the tally in Alfred Harbage's *Annals of English Drama*, the heyday of moral plays belongs to the period 1495–1530, for which he collected evidence for almost three times as many moral plays as in the entire Middle Ages.[2] Despite this relatively sudden popularity, moral plays, or morality plays, have long been understood as a medieval genre. This debt is perhaps most obvious in guides and handbooks to drama, such as John Watkins' essay on the essential "conservatism" of the medieval plays and Tudor interludes in *The Cambridge History of Medieval English Literature*.[3] Even studies that understand

---

[1] Henry Medwall, *Fulgens and Lucrece*, in *The Plays of Henry Medwall*, ed. Alan H. Nelson (Cambridge: D. S. Brewer, 1980), lines 897–903.

[2] In the *Annals of English Drama: 975–1700*, Alfred Harbage, uses the term "moral interlude" for plays post-dating 1495, and identifies seventeen such plays between 1495 and 1550 (*Annals of English Drama: 975–1700*, rev. Samuel Schoenbaum [London: Methuen & Co., 1964], 16–31). It is worth noting, though, that the "moral interlude" dated 1495 (Henry Medwall's *Nature*) was not printed until c. 1530. If one adds the thirteen plays classified as "anti-Catholic moral interlude" and "political moral" that belong in this time frame, then the total of moral plays grows to thirty. That the "morality play" is more of a sixteenth-century than a medieval genre is noted by Pamela M. King, "Morality Plays," in *The Cambridge Companion to Medieval English Theatre*, ed. Richard Beadle (Cambridge: Cambridge University Press, 1994), 240; and Howard B. Norland, *Drama in Early Tudor Britain* (Lincoln, NE: University of Nebraska Press, 1995), 38. Scholars typically refer only to five medieval morality plays, as shall be discussed below.

[3] John Watkins, "The Allegorical Theatre: Moralities, Interludes, and Protestant Drama," in *The Cambridge History of Medieval English Literature*, ed. David Wallace (Cambridge: Cambridge University Press, 1999), 767–92.

Humanism and Good Books in Sixteenth-Century England. Katherine C. Little, Oxford University Press.
© Katherine C. Little (2023). DOI: 10.1093/oso/9780192883193.003.0003

38 HUMANISM AND GOOD BOOKS IN SIXTEENTH-CENTURY ENGLAND

the moral interests of humanist drama, such as Joel Altman's, *The Tudor Play of Mind: Rhetorical Inquiry and the Development of Elizabethan Drama*, and Kent Cartwright's *Theatre and Humanism: English Drama in the Sixteenth Century*, still rely on a backdrop of a medieval morality play.[4] The dominant perspective seems to be that morality is something old and boring, inherited from the medieval plays that will be cast off as drama develops toward the ambiguities and complexities of Shakespeare.[5]

Such an approach does a disservice to both the sixteenth-century and the medieval plays, yoking them together in an evolutionary development that is almost entirely illusory.[6] Very few "medieval morality plays" exist and those that do survive do not share much of their morality with the sixteenth-century plays. To read this relationship as causal is to misread the plays and the cultural context more generally. This chapter takes the rather sudden popularity of the moral interlude in the sixteenth-century at face value, as evidence of a new awareness and attention to moral instruction, the desire to move men to avoid vice and favor virtue through the example of a text (or play), a goal that Medwall succinctly describes.[7] I argue that the morality play as a distinct form emerges as a symptom and product of humanism, generated as a more resolutely and self-consciously text-based approach to morality intersected with pre-existing penitential and devotional discourses. My argument will follow three stages. First, I deconstruct the genre of the "medieval morality play," to show the relative uselessness of this category. Second, I

---

[4] Joel B. Altman, *The Tudor Play of Mind: Rhetorical Inquiry and the Development of Elizabethan Drama* (Berkeley, CA: University of California Press, 1978), 25, 27; Kent Cartwright, *Theatre and Humanism: English Drama in the Sixteenth Century* (Cambridge: Cambridge University Press, 1999), 9, 12–14, 49–74.

[5] There are several refreshing accounts of medieval plays that emphasize their diversity and ambiguity over the unified didacticism that scholars of the Renaissance tend to ascribe to them. See, for example, Sarah Beckwith, "Language Goes on Holiday: English Allegorical Drama and the Virtue Tradition," *Journal of Medieval and Early Modern Studies* 42 (2012): 107–30 and Claire Sponsler, *Drama and Resistance: Bodies, Goods, and Theatricality in Late Medieval England* (Minneapolis, MN: University of Minnesota Press, 1997), 75–103. For two studies that emphasize the on-going sixteenth-century interest in the morality play, see Joerg O. Fichte, "New Wine in Old Bottles: The Protestant Adaptation of the Morality Play," *Anglia: Zeitschrift fur Englische Philologie* 110 (1992): 65–84 and Ineke Murakami, *Moral Play and Counterpublic: Transformations in Moral Drama, 1465–1599* (New York: Routledge, 2011).

[6] Despite the insightful discussion in the introduction to *The Oxford Handbook of Tudor Drama*, in which the editors survey the variety of Tudor drama and note the absence of any evolutionary developments, the individual essays tend to replicate the developmental model at least as far as the morality plays are concerned. See Thomas Betteridge and Greg Walker, "'When Lyberte Ruled': Tudor Drama 1485–1603," in *The Oxford Handbook of Tudor Drama*, ed. Betteridge and Walker (Oxford: Oxford University Press, 2012), 1–17, and the later mentions of morality plays in Andrew Hadfield, "The Summoning of *Everyman*," 93; Jane Griffiths, "*Lusty Juventus*," 262; and Eleanor Rycroft, "Morality, Theatricality, and Masculinity in *The Interlude of Youth* and *Hick Scorner*," 466. An older example of the developmental model would be that of Bernard Spivack in *Shakespeare and the Allegory of Evil: The History of a Metaphor in Relation to his Major Villains* (New York: Columbia University Press, 1958), which describes the morality play as a coherent tradition that precedes the "secular revolution of the Renaissance" (59; see more fully 60–95).

[7] K. Cartwright notes that learning "saturates" sixteenth-century drama, although he is less interested in specifically moral instruction (*Theatre and Humanism*, 50).

examine the emergence of a humanist morality, a concern with text-based precepts that dominates the educational environment, in which many sixteenth-century discussions of right and wrong behavior took place. Third, I explore the way in which two early sixteenth-century plays, *Everyman* and *Mundus et Infans*, which are typically and incorrectly described as "medieval morality plays," enact the intersection of pre-humanist and humanist discourses, the accretiveness described in my introduction. These plays transform a baggy, penitential, devotional, and didactic mode, one that is not exclusively dramatic, into a dramatic form with a more clearly defined approach to human behavior, to morality as such. From this revised perspective, one can see that the newest aspect of the humanist plays is precisely what has been mistakenly described as their medieval inheritance—their moral certainty.

There is no such Thing as a Medieval Morality Play

Standard reference works and anthologies have long included a genre called the morality play: it is "an immensely popular form of vernacular medieval drama" concerned with "stories of temptation, fall and regeneration."[8] Despite the ubiquity of this category, most medieval scholars acknowledge problems with it: very few plays matching this definition or aspects of it survive. There are only five so-called medieval morality plays in English, *Pride of Life* (c. 1350), *Castle of Perseverance* (c. 1400–25), *Wisdom* (c. 1465–70), *Mankind* (c. 1465–70), and *Everyman* (c. 1510), all of which are so different from each other that it is very difficult to generate a uniform definition. Insisting on their relationship has produced some influential mis-readings, perhaps the most durable being that *Everyman* is "quintessential" for this form, as a recent entry in *The Oxford Encyclopedia of British Literature* attests.[9] *Everyman* has, in fact, very little in common with the other plays, whether in terms of its content or its date, which locates its considerable popularity in the sixteenth-century.[10] Confidence in the morality genre seems entirely misplaced when one contrasts it with other medieval dramatic forms, such as biblical plays, for which there is a fair amount of surviving evidence and also a coherent and consistent content: four complete or near complete cycles, a few

---

[8] See John Coldewey, "Morality Plays," in *The Oxford Encyclopedia of British Literature*, ed. David Scott Kastan (Oxford: Oxford University Press, 2006), doi: 10.1093/acref/9780195169218.001.0001; Watkins, "The Allegorical Theatre," 767; and Andrew Hadfield, "The Summoning of *Everyman*," 93.

[9] Coldewey, "Morality Plays."

[10] On the print history, see Clifford Davidson, Martin W. Walsh, and Ton J. Broos, "Introduction," in *Everyman and its Dutch Original, Elckerlijc* (Kalamazoo, MI: Medieval Institute Publications, 2007); Hadfield, "Summoning," William Kuskin, *Symbolic Caxton: Literary Culture and Print Capitalism* (Notre Dame, IN: University of Notre Dame Press, 2008), 285–97; and David Mills, "Anglo-Dutch Theatre: Problems and Possibilities," *Medieval English Theatre* 18 (1996): 85–98.

40 HUMANISM AND GOOD BOOKS IN SIXTEENTH-CENTURY ENGLAND

singular plays, such as *Abraham and Isaac*, and records for performances of others, such as nativity pageants.[11]

The main argument for the morality genre is not, interestingly enough, based on much evidence from the Middle Ages, nor is it based on the idea that medieval audiences and authors had a concept of a morality play, but, rather, on the insistence by scholars of the sixteenth century that there had to be such a genre to explain the interest in morality in the sixteenth-century plays. As Pamela King writes in *The Cambridge Companion to Medieval English Theatre*, "the identification of the genre has been retrospective and depends largely on the perceived influence of these plays on the more abundantly surviving Tudor interlude."[12] Indeed, editors of the sixteenth-century plays have long asserted that the humanist interest in morality is inherited despite lacking any evidence of direct influence. For example, in his edition of the plays of Henry Medwall, Alan Nelson notes that "*Nature* has deep roots in native professional morality."[13] David Bevington takes a similar approach in his anthology of early plays, *Medieval Drama*, arguing that humanist drama "borrowed morality conventions."[14] Some medievalists have even obligingly speculated a host of missing morality plays, burned in the Reformation, to make up for the fact that so few plays survive, although, in doing so, they directly contradict another, and fairly dominant, view that morality plays were particularly adaptable to Reformation sensibilities, perhaps more so than other forms of medieval drama.[15] As will become apparent in the discussion of *Mundus et Infans* below, there is nothing to suggest that humanist drama is necessarily or specifically indebted to earlier drama as opposed to qualities more generally prevalent in the visual arts and in other kinds of writing circulating at this time.[16]

---

[11] John Wasson has argued that morality plays were never popular, surveying the records to show that there is "not a single recorded performance" of a morality play in the Middle Ages, in "The Morality Play: Ancestor of Elizabethan Drama?," *Comparative Drama* 13 (1979): 214 and 210–22. See also his survey of parish records from the 1520s in "'The End of an Era: Parish Drama in England from 1520 to the Dissolution,'" *Research Opportunities in Renaissance Drama* 31 (1992): 70–78. Such a perspective matches with my own investigation of the data in Harbage, *Annals*. Our generic terms are part of the problem, a point made persuasively by Lawrence M. Clopper, *Drama, Play, and Game: English Festive Culture in the Medieval and Early Modern Period* (Chicago: University of Chicago Press, 2001), 3–19.

[12] King, "Morality Plays," 240. See, similarly, the editors for the TEAMS edition of *Everyman*, Davidson, Walsh, and Broos, who note that "with the lack of evidence concerning moralities prior to the Reformation in England we cannot be sure that there ever was a recognizable genre until the sixteenth century." For a brief claim that there is evidence of missing morality plays, see Jessica Brantley, "Middle English Drama Beyond the Cycle Plays," *Literature Compass* 10.4 (2013): 331–42.

[13] *The Plays of Henry Medwall*, 23–24.

[14] David Bevington, *Medieval Drama* (Boston: Houghton Mifflin, 1975), 967.

[15] Bevington introduces the morality plays in his anthology as "more adaptable to new ideologies and social conditions during the sixteenth century than ... other kinds of drama" (*Medieval Drama*, 791). See similarly, Fichte, "New Wine in Old Bottles" and Norland, *Drama in Early Tudor Britain*, 40. Such accounts directly contradict that of John Coldewey, who claims that many plays have been lost: "Although only five complete or partial texts of English morality plays survived the book burnings of the Reformation, references to them are widespread in town and parish records, and many later plays self-consciously make use of morality play conventions" ("Morality Plays").

[16] Nelson makes this observation but holds on to the idea of direct influence (*Plays of Henry Medwall*, 24). The editors to *Mundus et Infans* also note the relationship between the play and "conventions"

HUMANISM AND THE MORALITY PLAY   41

Despite being grouped together as "morality plays," the medieval plays do not share any kind of coherence about morality—human behavior evaluated in terms of right and wrong—and that is what is significant about them. To begin with, morality is an entirely unhelpful term to describe these plays as a genre, partly because it is anachronistic. This term is first used to indicate a genre in the eighteenth century, and it reflects the mindset of a later period, a belief in evolutionary development that has characterized much of the history of drama. *The Oxford English Dictionary* dates the earliest use to 1765, in the work of Thomas Percy, who claims, in *The Reliques of Ancient English Poetry*, that something called a morality play developed into later, recognizably dramatic genres: "The writers of these Moralities were upon the very threshold of real Tragedy and Comedy."[17] "Morality" is likely an effective term because it has allowed scholars to group and distinguish plays at the very same time: morality is the larger category that includes both religious and secular, both medieval and humanist. This is Bevington's perspective, and it is typical: "When we turn from the morality plays of the fifteenth century to humanist plays of the early sixteenth century, we turn from a primarily religious drama to one that is often concerned with issues of politics, social change, law, and education."[18] Such a perspective is, however, misguided, since it flattens out and obscures the actual content of the medieval plays. It is worth noting that the medieval plays themselves do not use the word moral in any of the forms current in Middle English ("moral" or "moralitee").[19]

If the medieval plays do not think of themselves as "moral," then what are they? Their approach to human behavior, the realm of morality, can be described more accurately as penitential and devotional in that the plays draw on a wide range of Christian discourses for describing human action and the meaning of human action. In other words, the plays imagine a space where individual conduct in this world (the realm of the moral) is intermixed with beliefs about God (the realm of the religious). As the common definition of such plays makes clear—"the progress of a representative human soul through life, depicting temptations, inner struggles, initial failures, and ultimate triumph"—they are indebted to the language of lay instruction, of sins and virtue, the sacraments, the doctrine of salvation.[20] It is their interest in examining sin and virtue, terms easily mapped onto wrong and right, that has led scholars to describe them as morally instructive, along the lines of Medwall's play. After all, they do include "examples" for viewers to follow, to

---

in religious literature and art (*The Worlde and the Chylde*, ed. Clifford Davidson and Peter Happé [Kalamazoo, MI: Medieval Institute Publications, 1999], 8).

[17] *OED* s.v. "morality."

[18] Bevington, *Medieval Drama*, 967.

[19] See for example the notes to *Mankind*, ed. Kathleen Ashley and Gerard NeCastro (Kalamazoo, MI: Medieval Institute Publications, 2010).

[20] Coldewey, "Morality Plays." See also Bevington who defines the genre as "the dramatization of a spiritual crisis in the life of a representative mankind figure in which his spiritual struggle is portrayed as a conflict between personified abstractions representing good and evil" (*Medieval Drama*, 792).

42   HUMANISM AND GOOD BOOKS IN SIXTEENTH-CENTURY ENGLAND

borrow Medwall's language. And yet to see them as simply morally didactic, or even as offering both mirth, on the one hand, and guidance in virtue and vice, on the other, as in Medwall's phrasing, would be misguided. Their instruction is quite idiosyncratic, varying a great deal, from the massively comprehensive *Castle* to the sophistication of *Wisdom* to the funny and irreverent *Mankind*. More importantly, their instruction is not limited to human behavior: they are as interested in exploring the why, of accepted beliefs and practices (the more properly religious), as they are in the what, as in what to do and what to think (the moral). In his thoughtful remarks on the morality genre, John Cartwright suggests a more useful definition than the one typically on offer: they are plays of ideas, "mini-polemics" concerned with presenting and analyzing an argument.[21]

A survey of the discourses that scholars have lumped under the term morality for the medieval plays is beyond the scope of this chapter. It is possible, however, to investigate something of what the medieval plays tell us about human behavior and right and wrong, that is, the domain of morality, in a way that will necessarily put them in conversation with the sixteenth-century plays. Each of the identifiably medieval plays, except *Pride of Life*, which is missing its ending, concludes with a kind of directive or lesson that resembles the end of Medwall's play, quoted at the opening of this chapter: that seeing this play is supposed to teach the audience how to follow virtue and avoid vice. Such a directive, or lesson, is commonly called a "moral," and this meaning of moral was available to medieval audiences, as the end of Geoffrey Chaucer's *Nun's Priest's Tale* makes clear: "Taketh the moralite, goode men [Take the morality, good men]."[22] One might ask what kind of moral—as in what kind of lesson—do the medieval plays offer at their ends, in order to ask what kind of morality this is. I confine my examples to three of the so-called medieval morality plays, *Castle*, *Wisdom*, and *Mankind*, because *Pride* is missing its ending and *Everyman* will be discussed further below.

Of the three plays, *Castle* offers the clearest directive to the audience about what to do; or, rather, it offers two. At the end of the play God appears on stage to offer his final judgment and then comes out of his role to speak, as an actor, to the audience:

> And they that wel do in this werld, here welthe schal awake;
> In hevene they schal heynyd [be] in bounté and blis;
> And they that evil do, they schul to helle-lake
> In bitter balys to be brent: my jugement it is.
> My vertus in hevene thanne schal thei qwake.
> Ther is no wyth in this world that may skape this.

---

[21] J. Cartwright, "The Morality Play: Dead End or Main Street?," *Medieval English Theatre* 18 (1996): 8; and more fully, 3–14.

[22] Geoffrey Chaucer, *The Nun's Priest's Tale*, in *The Riverside Chaucer*, 3rd ed., ed. Larry D. Benson (Boston: Houghton Mifflin, 1987), 7.3440.

All men example hereat may take
To maintein the goode and mendyn her mis.
Thus endyth oure gamys.
To save you fro sinninge
Evyr at the beginninge
Thynke on youre last endnge!
Te Deum laudamus!

[And they that do well in this world, their wealth shall grow;
In Heaven they shall be exalted in virtue and bliss;
And they that do evil, they shall go to the pit of Hell
To be burnt in bitter pain: it is my judgment.
Then shall they quake before my power in Heaven.
There is no person in this world that may escape this.
All men may take example here-at
To cherish the good and amend their sins.
Thus end our games.
To save you from sinning
Always at the beginning
Think on your last ending!
Oh God, we praise you.][23]

In the last five lines, the speaker offers an explicit command to the audience: the play's end should cause the audience to think of another kind of end, the "last ending," of Judgment Day, when they will be called to account. Such a lesson sounds, at first glance, quite prescriptive, especially when coupled with God's earlier command that everyone should take example from the play to be good and correct sin. On closer look, though, this moral does not provide any kind of certainty or even consciousness that this is the main (or only) lesson of the play. It leaves the link between "games" and the audience's future "thinking" entirely implicit, through the repetition of the word "end" instead of any obvious grammatical construction. More importantly, the word "Think" is meditative, reflective, and open-ended, leaving the audience to determine, as they would when reading a penitential manual or hearing a sermon, what is, in fact most helpful. Finally, the play's confidence in its instruction is unmediated: it is confidence in God's teaching, not confidence in the capacity of a text (or a play) to instruct in virtue, as one sees in B's comment at the end of Medwall's play. God speaks, referring to familiar teaching about the works of mercy, telling the audience what they must do to be saved.

---

[23] *The Castle of Perseverance*, in *Medieval Drama*, ed. Bevington, lines 3637–49. Hereafter references will appear parenthetically.

44 HUMANISM AND GOOD BOOKS IN SIXTEENTH-CENTURY ENGLAND

As much as this play contains a lesson about avoiding vice and following virtue, God's speech, which directly precedes the command, indicates a far more ambitious goal, and that is to describe why the audience should do it—in order to be saved. In this way, the play is as much an answer to those asking "how shall I be saved" as it is to those asking "how should I act?" The former is not exclusively a moral question, and to describe it as such separates it from the frame in which the author of *Castle* understands the language of human behavior, of sins and virtues, and that is God's relationship to humankind.

Mankind offers an even-more contemplative and reflective moral lesson than *Castle,* one that refuses to detail the kinds of actions humans should embrace or avoid. At the end of the play, after Mankind departs, Mercy turns to the audience:

> Wyrschep[f]yll sofereyns, I have do my propirté:
> Mankind is deliveryd by my faverall patrocinye.
> God preserve hym fro all wyckyd captivité
> And send hym grace hys sensuall condicions to mortifye!
> Now for His love that for us receivyd His humanité,
> Serche your condicions wyth dew examinacion!
> Thinke and remembyr the world is but a vanité,
> As it is provyd daly by d[i]verse transmutacion.
> Mankend is wrechyd, he hath sufficyent prove.
> Therefore God [grant] yow all *per suam misericordiam*
> That ye may be pley-ferys with the angell[ys] above,
> And have to your porcyon *vitam eternam. Amen!*
>
> [Worshipful sovereigns, I have done my duty:
> Mankind is delivered by my favorable protection.
> God preserve him from all wicked captivity
> And send him grace to destroy his sensual habits!
> Now for the love of him who became human for us,
> Search your habits with due examination.
> Think and remember that the world is but a vanity
> As it is proved daily by its diverse transmutation.
> Mankind is wretched; he has been sufficiently tested.
> Therefore God grant you all through his mercy
> That you may be companions of the angels above
> And have life eternal as your inheritance.
> Amen!].[24]

All of the recommended actions are here internal and open-ended: audiences should examine their consciences, think, and remember. The point of such activity is also clear—salvation. Only by thinking and remembering will people be able to

---

[24] *Mankind,* in *Medieval Drama,* ed. Bevington, lines 899–914.

deserve eternal life. The lesson for Mankind is not so much about his behavior, what he should feel or do, but about recognizing his state—wretchedness. His lesson will never be completed but is an ongoing process of evaluating when he is in captivity or delighting in his "sensual habits."

The play *Wisdom* is simultaneously the least and the most morally directive, offering a kind of paradox suitable for the most intellectual and contemplative of the plays. At its end, Anima (the soul) comes to "Solomon's conclusion," learning what wisdom is. Then, the character Wisdom appears to speak the final lines, which are directed to the audience:

> The tru son of ryghtusnes,
> Wyche that ys Our Lorde Jhesu,
> Shall sprynge in hem that drede hys meknes.
> Nowe ye mut every soule renewe
> In grace, and vycys to eschew.
> Ande so to ende wyth perfeccyon,
> That the doctryne of Wysdom we may sew:
> *Sapiencia Patris*, graunt that for hys passyon! AMEN!
>
> [The true son of righteousness,
> That is, our Lord Jesus,
> Must rise in them that fear his meekness.
> Now you must renew every soul
> In grace and eschew vices
> And so to end with perfection
> So that we may follow the doctrine of Wisdom:
> Bestow upon us, through his passion, the Wisdom of the Father!
> AMEN!][25]

On the one hand, the lines sound quite similar to Medwall's clearly defined instruction: the audience ("you") should renew their souls and avoid sin. On the other hand, such an action is not an end in itself. Avoiding sin (and renewing grace) will enable the audience to do something far more open-ended, to follow the "doctrine of Wisdom." This doctrine is not only open-ended; it is directly associated with the life of monastic contemplation, or alignment with God through "perfection." The slippage between the speaking voice who is directing the audience and the "you" or "we," who will follow those directives, parallels the slippage between Jesus and "them." All of the thoughts and actions are only possible because of Jesus's "passion"; there is no human behavior or thinking that does not spring from Jesus or lead back to him.

---

[25] *Wisdom*, in *Two Moral Interludes: The Pride of Life and Wisdom*, ed. David Klausner (Kalamazoo, MI: Medieval Institute Publications, 2008), lines 1150–65.

To draw attention to the potential for contemplation at the end of each of these plays is to shift the emphasis away from the prescriptiveness typically associated with the term "morality." "Morality" in the medieval plays has, of course, long been understood as referring to their penitential concerns, as it is in some of the broad definitions with which I began. Penitence and morality are not, however, interchangeable, nor is one the subset of the other. In so far as they converge around actions, both direct humans in what they should do—confess their sins and be forgiven—and both share a clarity of right and wrong, virtues and vices. And yet, penitence is also part of a much larger set of discourses that cannot be described in terms of morality, discourses concerning interior states of mind and emotions, the necessity of salvation, and stories about other sinners or about Jesus's actions. While all of the medieval plays portray or describe confession and what one should or should not do, their final directive is to think and remember. Even the language of sin is to a certain degree open and flexible: the sins themselves show how difficult it is to recognize sin or how easy it is to fall prey to sin. In this broad goal of thinking and remembering, the plays resemble the images, Books of Hours, and penitential manuals circulating in the later Middle Ages, all of which were not didactic in a limited prescriptive manner—what to do to avoid sin—but also aids to devotion and contemplation—what it means to be sinful and ask for mercy.[26]

Humanist Morality

If what has been called morality in the medieval plays is less a monolith than a complex and heterogeneous accretion of penitential and devotional discourses, then the morality of humanist writers was, in contrast, far more clearly defined as morality, as self-consciously text-based lessons about human behavior for action in this world.[27] It is important to note that this morality is still identifiably Christian. The shift to morality as such was not a conscious process of de-Christianization or of secularization, and it is a mistake to see the morality plays as developing by secularizing religious material. After all, many of the recognizably humanist plays, such as Medwall's *Nature,* are as explicitly Christian as the medieval ones. Rather, this is a shift from understanding drama in penitential and devotional terms, a larger category that includes moral didacticism, to

---

[26] On the plays' relationship to and imbrication in wider religious culture, see especially Gail McMurray Gibson, *The Theater of Devotion: East Anglian Drama and Society in the Late Middle Ages* (Chicago: University of Chicago Press, 1989) and Jessica Brantley, *Reading in the Wilderness: Private Devotion and Public Performances in Late Medieval England* (Chicago: University of Chicago Press, 2007). On the specific relationship between plays and iconography, see Clifford Davidson, *Visualizing the Moral Life: Medieval Iconography and the Macro Morality Plays* (New York: AMS Press, 1989).

[27] Altman's category, the plays of inquiry, can describe all moral drama in this period, including those he dismisses as plays that merely show: "the play functioned as media of intellectual and emotional exploration" and "the experience of the play was the thing" (*Tudor Play of Mind*, 6).

understanding it as primarily or importantly didactic, in the manner of Medwall's "B." Such a shift was made possible by humanism's new, or new-ish attention to the specifics of instruction: using texts to locate clearly identifiable lessons about good and bad behavior. As the many celebrations of *bonae litterae* make clear, goodness was an expected outcome of reading the right kinds of books.

Humanist authors did not merely insist that virtue could be acquired via reading and teaching, they also offered distinctive methods for doing so. One of the most pervasive methods in educational settings involved locating the lesson, or sentence, or maxim that the reader could take away from the text.[28] Erasmian humanism is closely associated with, even indistinguishable from, the notebook, a process of collecting sayings and quotations that fit with conventional and Christian, morality.[29] This method can be found everywhere in Erasmus's writings, which circulated widely in England. For example, his book of proverbs, the *Adages*, which appeared in many different editions (1500–36), became a popular and influential resource, a repository of sayings taken from their original texts and offered as digestible portions of wisdom.[30]

Erasmus offers eloquent testimony to how this method works in another of his influential works, *On the Method of Study* (1511): the reader must assimilate and imprint the message. He writes, "You will write some brief but pithy sayings such as aphorisms, proverbs, and maxims at the beginning and ending of your books; others you will inscribe on rings and drinking cups; others you will paint on doors and walls or even in the glass of a window so that what may aid learning is constantly before the eye."[31] This passage demonstrates the thingness of moral meanings, the

---

[28] As C. S. Lewis long ago remarked, humanists wanted wisdom "at an easier rate" and so they "turned naturally to that kind of 'philosophy' or 'moral constancy' which embodies itself in striking attitudes, anecdotes, and epigrams" (C. S. Lewis, *Oxford History of English Literature, Volume 3: English Literature in the Sixteenth Century: Excluding Drama* [Oxford: Oxford University Press, 1954], 53). On this aspect of humanist pedagogy, see Rebecca Bushnell, *A Culture of Teaching: Early Modern Humanism in Theory and Practice* (Ithaca, NY: Cornell University Press, 1996), 132; Mary Thomas Crane, *Framing Authority: Sayings, Self, and Society in Sixteenth-Century England* (Princeton, NJ: Princeton University Press, 1993), 6; Jeff Dolven, *Scenes of Instruction in Renaissance Romance* (Chicago: University of Chicago Press, 2007), 101–4; Eugene Kintgen, *Reading in Tudor England* (Pittsburgh, PA: University of Pittsburgh Press, 1996), 34–37; and Peter Mack, *Elizabethan Rhetoric: Theory and Practice* (Cambridge: Cambridge University Press, 2002), 2, 20–22.

[29] Crane, *Framing Authority*, 15; Anthony Grafton and Lisa Jardine, *From Humanism to the Humanities: Education and the Liberal Arts in Fifteenth- and Sixteenth-Century Europe* (Cambridge, MA: Harvard University Press, 1986), 136; Paul Oskar Kristeller, "Humanism and Moral Philosophy," in *Renaissance Humanism: Foundations, Forms and Legacy*, 3 vols., ed. Albert Rabil, Jr. (Philadelphia: University of Pennsylvania Press, 1988), 3: 281; and Ann Moss, *Printed Commonplace Books and the Structuring of Renaissance Thought* (Oxford: Clarendon Press, 1996), 101–15.

[30] Margaret Mann Phillips, *The "Adages" of Erasmus: A Study with Translations* (Cambridge: Cambridge University Press, 1964), ix.

[31] *On the Method of Study*, ed. Craig R. Thompson, trans. Brian McGregor, *Collected Works of Erasmus* (*CWE*) 84 vols. (Toronto: University of Toronto Press, 1974–), Vol. 24 (1978): 671. See similarly the more familiar passage in *The Education of a Christian Prince*: "But it is not enough just to hand out the sort of maxims which warn him off evil things and summon him to the good. No, they must be fixed in his mind, pressed in, and rammed home. And they must be kept fresh in the memory in all sorts of ways: sometimes in a moral maxim, sometimes in a parable, sometimes by an analogy, sometimes by

48 HUMANISM AND GOOD BOOKS IN SIXTEENTH-CENTURY ENGLAND

sententiae or sentences in the rings and drinking cups, the assumption that moral instruction can best be delivered as isolated and discrete units that the reader can possess. This sense of the thingness or materiality of sentences pervades humanist writing.[32] In an influential work of English Erasmianism, Sir Thomas Elyot's *The Boke of the Governour* (1531), the author describes a reading plan for children that is directly concerned with finding "sentences" "contained" in books, as if a reader could pull out a series of valuable objects from Horace that they could then carry around with them: "let us bring in Horace, in whom is contained much variety of learning and quickness of sentence."[33] Such an approach to morality, the wisdom in texts, is often described in terms of digesting or harvesting or collecting pollen as bees do, a mode familiar from humanist writings on *copia*.[34] In viewing the sentence as fruit or as an object, the reader dislodges morality, the sentence or the wisdom, from its larger discursive context. Such an approach prioritizes usefulness: it subordinates all texts, no matter the provenance, to the idea of the wisdom that can be grasped from a text.

The first part of the sixteenth century in England was characterized by an immense increase in books characterized by this Erasmian method, most notably commonplace books, educational treatises, and grammar books. This is not to say that these books were entirely new or even consistently humanist, and it is worth noting their continuity with medieval grammar books and *florilegia*.[35] They nevertheless mark an important shift, when the capacity of texts to teach morality became an explicit and extended topic of concern. This shift was due to the massive number of new books available, the recovery of the classics, and the new sense that classical authors were in and of themselves valuable.

The grammar books that flourished in the early sixteenth-century show this Erasmian method at work: one learned right conduct just as and at the same time as one learned Latin by memorizing and assimilating worthy sayings and bits of wisdom, or, to use a word much favored in this time, precepts. An early and well-known English humanist, John Colet, wrote a Latin grammar for his students, the *Aeditio* (1527), which combined religious instruction, such as the Articles of Faith, with more general rules for behavior—"precepts of living"—and instruction in grammar.[36] In reading this text, the students would understand the fundamental

---

a live example, an epigram, or a proverb; they must be carved on rings, painted in pictures, inscribed on prizes, and presented in any other way that a child of his age enjoys" (*The Education of a Christian Prince*, trans. Neil M. Cheshire and Michael J. Heath, CWE, Vol. 27 [1986]: 201).

[32] Bushnell, *A Culture of Teaching*, 133; Crane, *Framing Authority*, 34.

[33] Thomas Elyot, *A Critical Edition of Sir Thomas Elyot's The Boke Named the Governour*, ed. Donald W. Rude (New York: Garland Press, 1992), 46; Crane, *Framing Authority*, 52.

[34] Bushnell, *A Culture of Teaching*, 120; Crane, *Framing Authority*, 57–64; Moss, *Printed Commonplace Books*, 12–15, 51–52.

[35] Crane, *Framing Authority*, 77–92; Moss, *Printed Commonplace Books*, 24–50; Nicholas Orme, *Education and Society in Medieval and Renaissance England* (London: Hambledon Press, 1989), 17.

[36] John Colet, *Ioannis Coleti theologi, olim decani diui Pauli, aeditio. una cum quibusdam G. Lilij Grammatices rudimentis, G. Lilij epigramma* (Antwerp, 1527) STC 5542, A3v.

humanist directive that learning wisdom and learning eloquence (Latin) are not only aligned but require some of the same tools, opening the container of the text. Such an approach also informs the Latin grammar textbook that was used throughout the sixteenth century and beyond, *A Short Introduction of Grammar*, otherwise known as *Lily's Latin Grammar*, which builds on and modifies Colet's *Aeditio*. Most obviously, the authors open their book with "rules" and "precepts" for using it, thus implicitly tying linguistic and moral rules together.[37] In addition, many of the Latin sentences that are used to illustrate grammatical points contain bits of wisdom. That is, the authors illustrate a moral fact (or truth) and a linguistic fact at the same time. After a rule about the operations of the verb to be [*sum*], the following sentence appears as an example, "*Orantis est nihil nisi coelestia cogitare*," with the translation, "It is the duty of a man that is saying his prayers to have his mind on nothing but heavenly things."[38] Even more importantly, the authors explicitly frame Latin learning as an education in Christian wisdom. In the opening address to the reader, they describe an assignment in which students would translate Psalms, Proverbs or Ecclesiastes from English into Latin.[39] Each of those biblical books is famous for containing wisdom, often in the form of a precept.

In emphasizing the precept-orientation of humanist Latin instruction, its interest in moral lessons, I aim to correct an imbalance in some of the scholarship. Much has been made of the literary and performative elements of the new, humanist instruction. Indeed the assumption seems to be that humanists rejected rote, rule-following in favor of more creative or at least more thoughtful exercises, usually around some form of imitation.[40] In the words of the most popular grammar book, the student of Latin should learn every part of speech, "not by rote but by reason" and should be knowledgeable "in the understanding of the thing" and not only in "rehearsing of the words."[41] The sense is that older instruction was more limited in its appreciation of the classical text, but the newer, humanist instruction, aimed higher, to understanding it on its own terms. Such educational practices have been understood as extremely generative for sixteenth-century literary production, in that they provided new literary and, especially dramatic, models: debates between two different parties or opportunities to impersonate characters.[42] It is also the case, however, that humanists did not abandon moral

---

[37] William Lily and John Colet, *A Short Introduction of Grammar, 1549* (Menston, UK: Scolar Press, 1970). Learning of "rules" at A3r and "preceptes" in Appendix 1 (unpaginated).

[38] *A Short Introduction*, D2v; spelling modernized.

[39] *A Short Introduction*, A3v.

[40] See, for example, Richard Halpern, *The Poetics of Primitive Accumulation: English Renaissance Culture and the Genealogy of Capital* (Ithaca, NY: Cornell University Press, 1991), 44–45.

[41] *A Short Introduction*, A3r.

[42] See, for example, Lynn Enterline, *Shakespeare's Schoolroom: Rhetoric, Discipline, Emotion* (Philadelphia: University of Pennsylvania Press, 2012), 9–32; Arthur F. Kinney, *Humanist Poetics: Thought, Rhetoric, and Fiction in Sixteenth-Century England* (Amherst, MA: University of Massachusetts Press, 1986), 3–38; Mack, *Elizabethan Rhetoric*, 47; and Paul Sullivan, "Playing the Lord: Tudor *Vulgaria* and the Rehearsal of Ambition," *ELH* 75 (2008): 181–82.

50 HUMANISM AND GOOD BOOKS IN SIXTEENTH-CENTURY ENGLAND

lessons, whether in terms of precepts or of rule-following, as indicated throughout this section. After all, imitation and precepts are not mutually exclusive, and the grammar books amply demonstrate their coexistence. The wisdom that was contained in the classical text was as important as the eloquence (or style) that the text modeled.

The Morality of *Everyman*

In locating guides for behavior in classical and other kinds of texts, educational treatises and grammar books helped to generate what one might call a more consciously text-based or bookish morality. That is, the Erasmian method trained students not only to find moral lessons in texts but to understand books as containers of morals. This approach is both dramatized and solidified in the early-sixteenth-century plays, as is nicely demonstrated in *Everyman*.[43] In describing *Everyman* as importantly novel, I deviate from the long-standing tradition in which it is not only assigned to the Middle Ages but understood as "quintessential" or conventional for that period. Although this tradition seems to flourish only in anthologies and reference works, it is influential enough to spend some time here highlighting two of the main reasons why *Everyman* is not medieval, but, instead, a form new to sixteenth-century humanism.

The most obvious evidence for considering *Everyman* as contemporary with and a response to humanism comes from the dates. It was printed four different times in the first part of the sixteenth century, c. 1510–25, 1525–30, 1528–29, 1530–35, and quite possibly more.[44] Although there is a very long tradition of dating the play to c. 1495, there is no evidence to support this early date.[45] No manuscripts survive, and the Dutch play on which *Everyman* is based was probably not printed until shortly before 1496.[46] Even if *Everyman* had been written before the sixteenth century, its popularity coincided exactly with the plays that are typically considered within a Tudor and/or humanist milieu, such as John Skelton's *Magnificence* (printed c. 1529) and Henry Medwall's *Nature* (printed c. 1530).[47] The so-called morality plays that can be securely dated to the fourteenth and fifteenth centuries and are, therefore, called "medieval," do not, in contrast, provide any evidence for popularity or of a larger literary tradition. Three of the

---

[43] Scholars have been more interested in the tension between precepts and experience, arguing that this tension is new and distinct in the sixteenth-century. See, for example, Cartwright, *Theatre and Humanism*, 14–15; and Richard Helgerson, *The Elizabethan Prodigals* (Berkeley, CA: University of California Press, 1977), 1, 16–43.

[44] Davidson et al., "Introduction;" Kuskin, *Symbolic Caxton*, 289.

[45] *Medieval Drama*, 939; Harbage, *Annals*, 16.

[46] Davidson, et al., "Introduction."

[47] Altman, *Tudor Play of Mind*, 26; Peter Happé, "'Pullyshyd and Fresshe is your Ornacy': Madness and the Fall of Skelton's *Magnyfycence*," in *The Oxford Handbook of Tudor Drama*, 484; and *Plays of Henry Medwall*, 3.

four plays that survive are unique copies: *Pride of Life* (c. 1350), *The Castle of Perseverance* (c. 1400–25), and *Mankind* (c. 1465–70). One play, *Wisdom* (c. 1465–70), exists in two manuscripts, but it is thought that one is a copy of the other.[48]

Second, and more importantly, *Everyman* has a new generic consciousness that has specifically to do with morality.[49] At the opening of the play, the Messenger says:

> I pray you all gyve your audyence
> And here [hear] this matter with reverence,
> By fygure a morall playe.
> *The Somonyng of Everyman* called it is
> That of our lyves and endynge shewes
> How transytory we be all daye.[50]

It might come as a shock to most readers that *Everyman* is the only one of the group known as medieval morality plays that uses the word "moral." This self-naming is significant: none of the other medieval plays demonstrates the kind of generic self-reflexivity found in *Everyman*. Only two, *Castle* and *Pride*, explicitly name the play with a generic term: both use the term "game" in places where one would expect generic identification, at the end and beginning, respectively (*Castle*, 3645).[51] Relatedly, characters within *Mankind* also use the term "game" to refer to their actions within the play.[52] "Game" does not have any moral connotations, nor is it an exclusively dramatic term. It is broadly performative, linked to oral traditions, and often used for festivities, for the Christmas activities at the court of King Arthur in the late fourteenth-century poem, *Sir Gawain and the Green Knight*, or for performances on holidays, such as the Corpus Christi plays.[53] It is, to speak somewhat reductively, very medieval in the way that it links various kinds of public recreations together in one category.

Everyman's new generic self-consciousness connects it instead to its sixteenth-century contemporaries. Those plays that are moral are typically described on the title page with the word "interlude" usually with a qualifier. Although it is true that the term interlude appears in the Middle Ages, in the *Interludium de Clerico et Puella* (c. 1300), it was used relatively rarely, and it was not used at

---

[48] "Introduction," in *Two Moral Interludes*.

[49] David Mills explores the self-consciousness in relation to performance through the "metaphoric" use of drama. See his "The Theaters of *Everyman*," in *From Page to Performance: Essays in Early English Drama* ed. John A. Alford (East Lansing, MI: Michigan State University Press, 1995), 127–49.

[50] *Everyman and its Dutch Original, Elckerlijc*, ed. Davidson, Walsh, and Broos; lines 1–6. Hereafter all references to this play will appear parenthetically.

[51] *The Pride of Life*, line 16.

[52] *Mankind*, lines 417, 591; Katie Normington, *Medieval English Drama: Performance and Spectatorship* (Cambridge: Polity Press, 2009), 124.

[53] *MED* s.v. "game;" Clopper, *Drama, Play, and Game*, 12–13 and John Coldewey, "Plays and Play," *Research Opportunities in Renaissance Drama* 28 (1985): 181–88.

52 HUMANISM AND GOOD BOOKS IN SIXTEENTH-CENTURY ENGLAND

all in the four medieval plays typically grouped with *Everyman*.[54] And yet, it begins to be the term of choice for title pages of plays in the sixteenth century. It evokes a Latinate, and therefore, writerly sensibility as well as a printed not oral context.[55] More importantly, it lends itself to the kinds of distinctions that the Middle English "game" does not. Henry Medwall's *Nature* is described on the title page as a "goodly interlude," a phrase that certainly suggests a morality play, or a play concerned with right behavior, since "goodly" can mean virtuous.[56] A similar phrase appears on the title page of *Mundus et Infans* (1522): a "proper new Interlude."[57] "Proper" has similar connotations to "goodly" and "moral"—right and correct.

As the phrase "moral play" suggests, *Everyman* thematizes something called morality that most scholars have been happy to accept without question or to group together with the penitential and devotional concerns of earlier plays.[58] But one should press more closely on this term, because it is a new term for drama.[59] "Moral" is used once at the beginning of *Everyman* in the speech quoted above, and it appears on the title page and in the colophon. In the opening speech, the primary meaning of moral is lesson, because after describing the play as moral, the messenger provides an entirely conventional lesson that can be found in any number of texts: life is transitory. The play does not merely present a moral, it is at its heart interested in exploring a moral as a rule: the play shows not only that Death comes to everyone (life is transitory) but also what one must do in the face of that rule. Near the end of the play, Everyman has learned a lesson about what is and is not transitory, and at that point, he offers himself as an example of that lesson:

> Take example all ye that this do here [hear] or se [see]
> How they that I loved best do forsake me
> Excepte my Good Dedes that bydeth [remain] truly (*Everyman*, 867–69).

---

[54] Nicholas Davis, "The Meaning of the Word 'Interlude,'" *Medieval English Theatre* 6 (1984): 5–15; Jean-Paul Debax, "Complicity and Hierarchy: a Tentative Definition of the Interlude Genus," in *Interludes and Early Modern Society: Studies in Gender, Power and Theatricality*, ed. Peter Happé and Wim Hüsken (Leiden: Brill, 2007), 23–42; *MED* s.v. "enterlude." Clopper's account of this term, which includes musical performances as well as what we think of as plays, refers almost exclusively to sixteenth-century records (*Drama, Play, and Game*, 17–18).

[55] Debax, "Complicity and Hierarchy," 28.

[56] Medwall, *Nature*, 92.

[57] *Mundus et Infans*, in *Three Late Medieval Morality Plays*, 108. Hereafter all references to this text will appear parenthetically.

[58] David Bevington, *From Mankind to Marlowe: Growth of Structure in the Popular Drama of Tudor England* (Cambridge, MA: Harvard University Press, 1962), 9–10; Robert Potter, *The English Morality Play: Origins, History and Influence of a Dramatic Tradition* (London: Routledge & Kegan Paul, 1975), 34; Watkins, "Allegorical Theatre," 767.

[59] *MED* s.v. "moral."

Good Deeds responds: "All erthly thynge is but vanyté" (*Everyman*, 870), an allusion to "All is vanity" of Ecclesiastes 1.2 and a repetition of the initial rule about the transitoriness of life, now with greater strength, because it has been demonstrated by an example.[60] Finally, as if to underscore the importance of lessons, the play ends with a Doctor, a figure of authority, who offers a series of final directives to the audience:

> This memoryall men may have in mynde.
> Ye herers [hearers] take it of worth olde and yonge
> And forsake Pryde, for he deceyveth you in the ende,
> And remembre Beautye, Fyve Wyttes, Strength, and Discression.
> They all at the last do Everyman forsake,
> Save his Good Dedes, there dothe he take.
> But beware, for and they be small
> Before God, he hath no helpe at all.
> None excuse may be there for Everyman.
> Alas, how shall he do than?
> For after deth amendes may no man make,
> For than Mercy and Petye [Pity] doeth hym forsake
> If his rekenynge be not clere whan he do cume [come].
> God wyll saye, "*Ite maledicti in ignem eternum*" [Go, wicked ones,
> into eternal fire].
> And he that hath his accounte hole and sounde
> Hye [High] in Heven he shall be crounde [crowned],
> Unto the whiche place God brynge us all thether
> That we may lyve, body and soule togyther.
> Therto helpe, the Trynytye,
> Say ye for saynte charytye,
> Amen (*Everyman*, 902–21).

The Doctor begins with a directive resembling those in the earlier plays, to keep this play in mind, and then reduces and defines it by suggesting specific actions and terminology: to give up Pride and to embrace Discretion. It is significant that in one of the surviving editions of the play, "memorial" is altered to "moral." In some ways, moral makes more sense for the rest of the speech, which is in every way concerned with what Everyman should do and not so much with the reasons behind it (*Everyman*, note to 902).

---

[60] In one of the four surviving printed editions, the Doctor begins the final speech of the play with the following statement: "This moral men may have in mind" (*Everyman*, in *Three Late Medieval Morality Plays*, line 902). In the other three editions, the line reads, "This memoryall men may have in mynde" (902; see note). This mistake or emendation indicates that the printer (or someone) understands "moral" in the terms I'm outlining here—an explicit and digestible lesson.

As these lessons demonstrate, *Everyman* offers much conventional thinking as digestible "sentences." It is not so much interested in whether precepts work, as some of the later humanist plays may be, as it is in the idea of precepts themselves. This new emphasis for drama is evident in the large number of proverbs of which many operate as moral rules.[61] Most important are the two that are repeated at the beginning and end of the play: promise is duty or debt (*Everyman*, 248 & 821), and a friend in need is a friend indeed (*Everyman*, 229 & 854). The fundamental aspect of proverbs is that they circulate relatively free of context; insofar as they refer to right behavior, they do not tend to describe that behavior in terms of religious practices, such as penance, or beliefs.[62] They are certainly compatible with religious beliefs and practices, but they do not require knowledge of them. One can be a good friend without being Christian, as Cicero's much quoted *De Amicitia* indicates. Even when *Everyman* includes elements of penitential discourses, it tends to gesture towards them; it does not dramatize them. For example, at the opening, God states that people are sinful, using the seven sins, which are, of course, central to penitential handbooks, sermons, and devotional treatises:

> They use the Seven Deedly Synnes dampnable,
> As Pryde, Covetyse, Wrathe, and Lechery
> Now in the worlde be made commendable [praiseworthy],
> And thus they leve of [depart from] aungeles, the hevenly company.
> Everyman lyveth so after his owne pleasure,
> And yet of theyr lyfe they be not sure (*Everyman*, 36–41).

Despite the familiar use of sins, the passage also makes clear that the sins will not carry much moral weight in the play. Sin is not used here to describe the wrong behavior of Everyman, who lives instead "after his own pleasure," and the seven sins do not appear again in the play proper. The play is far more interested in imagining and dramatizing the lack of certainty about the transitoriness of life (its opening moral) than it is in the sins.

Given that the play's explicit moral involves death, as in, flowers fade and life is transitory, it should come as no surprise that the figure of Death is closely

---

[61] B. J. Whiting finds eight proverbs and eight sententious remarks (*Proverbs in the Earlier English Drama: With Illustrations from Contemporary French Plays* [Cambridge, MA: Harvard University Press, 1938], 92). By my count, Lester identifies eleven throughout his edition of *Everyman* in *Three Late Medieval Morality Plays*, and the editors of the TEAMS *Everyman* identify eighteen in their notes.

[62] *Mankind* also includes a large number of proverbs, but they are not the only text-based discourse of human behavior, since the play also includes many more biblical allusions than *Everyman*. John Skelton's play *Magnificence*, also early sixteenth century, is more similar to *Everyman* in that it explores from the opening a single proverb "Measure is treasure" (Happé, "Pullyshyd and Fresshe," 485) and has "an unusually large proportion of miscellaneous proverbial phrases" (Whiting, *Proverbs*, 85). Similarly, K. Cartwright has argued that John Heywood's *The Foure PP* "grapples with the dilemma of explaining life proverbially while presenting it complexly" (*Theatre and Humanism*, 26).

associated with the precept-oriented morality. That is, Death not only makes the audience think about Death as an experience—am I ready to die?—but also makes the audience think about Death as a series of rules or as a condition by which those rules can exist—because I will die, I must get ready to give an account. Death's first words in the play refer us to God's orders:

> Almyghty God, I am here at your wyll
> Your commaundemente to fulfyll (*Everyman*, 64–65).

The main sense here is that Death will follow God's orders, but there is also the sense, given the common usage of commandment in the phrase the Ten Commandments, that Death will enforce God's rules for behavior. Indeed, the overarching lesson of the play about the transitoriness of life only has force because people do die. The play makes this association between Death and rules clear at the opening of the play. Everyman has a nitpicky argument with Death about the reckoning God has asked for because he does not know who this character is, other than a messenger of God. After Death identifies himself, Everyman says, "O, Deth, thou cummest whan I had thee leest in mynde" (*Everyman*, 115), an exclamation with the force of a rule. Death comes to most people as a surprise. Indeed, Everyman does not understand his relationship with God in terms of rules, things he must do or not do, until Death appears. It is not enough for Death to say, as he first does, "Hast thou thy Maker forget [forgotten]?" (*Everyman*, 86); Everyman simply has no idea what it means to remember God. He does understand, however, once he speaks with Death that he must "amend" (*Everyman*, 174).

Such a focus on precepts as distinct and digestible guides for behavior reifies them in the same way as the aphorisms on the rings and cups described by Erasmus in *On the Method of Study*. After detailing the moral about transitoriness, in the opening speech, the Messenger says,

> This matter is wonderous precyous,
> But the intente of it is more gracious [grace-filled]
> And swete [sweet] to bere awaye.
> This story sayeth: man in the begynnynge,
> Loke well and take good hede to the endynge,
> Be you never so gaye.
> Ye thynke synne in the begynnynge full swete
> Whiche in the ende causeth thy soule to wepe
> Whan the body lyeth in claye.
> Here shall you se how Felawshyp and Jolyté [Joy]
> Bothe, Strengthe, Pleasure, and Beauté,
> Wyll vade [fade] from thee as floure in Maye (*Everyman*, 7–18).

56 HUMANISM AND GOOD BOOKS IN SIXTEENTH-CENTURY ENGLAND

With his reference to "matter" and "story," the Messenger asserts a kind of solidity to the truths the play shows, to conventional wisdom itself. These truths—that life is transitory, that pleasures fade—are something that the viewers can hold and "bear away," in the same way that they would hold a cup or ring. The goal of the play is to have the viewer recognize ("Look well") these to be true.

Moreover, the emphasis on showing and looking and seeing reveals the play to be an image, a mirror, in which the viewers should find themselves, a sense that is clearer in the original title of the Dutch play: *Den Spyeghel der Salicheyt van Elckerlijc* [*The Mirror of Everyman's Salvation*]. *Everyman's* mirror is only implicit, but it nevertheless underlines the bookishness of the play. The play is a mirror just as a book is a mirror, containing the image of virtue. That same mirror is also, of course, found in Sir Thomas More's translation of the biography of Pico della Mirandola, as discussed in the introduction.

This play not only insists on precepts, it also demonstrates an optimism about their power, their forceful effect on *Everyman*. The audience watches Everyman learn the truth of precepts that are so familiar as to have lost their meaning, to remind him of what he has forgotten, that is, God. The conversations that Everyman has with the allegorical characters consistently draw attention to the visceral realization of an accepted truth. For example, Everyman laments the suddenness of Death in a way that positions him vis-à-vis a proverb:

> Alas, shall I have no longer respyte?
> I may saye Deth geveth no warnynge;
> To thynke on thee it maketh my herte secke [sick] (*Everyman*,
> 131–33).

This is not so much the lesson itself (Death comes when you least expect it!) as it is the individual encounter with that lesson, underlined in the framing of the statement with "I may say." As this passage demonstrates, what is important is not merely the expression of conventional wisdom as rules but the effect of those rules on human characters. Similarly, the long conversation between Everyman and Fellowship consists of a series of proverbs: a friend in need is a friend indeed (*Everyman*, 229, 254, 284); a story about a friend who accompanies his friend to hell (*Everyman*, 232); and promise is duty (*Everyman*, 248). Each of these sayings about friendship would have been familiar, whether from the story of Barlam and Iosaphat or the widely read and cited treatise on friendship by Cicero.[63] Everyman realizes the truth of each of these, and he ends with "my herte is sore" (*Everyman*, 299), emphasizing that what has been external (all those sayings) now matters to him, and the meaning has penetrated his consciousness. Even the names of allegorical figures, whether Fellowship or Kindred, have a kind of proverbial status,

---

[63] John Conley, "The Doctrine of Friendship in *Everyman*," *Speculum* 44 (1969): 374–82.

because they echo the common moral dilemmas that face each individual: is a good friend one who agrees with everything I say or one who challenges me when I make mistakes? Should my family help me in every circumstance? If the whole point of proverbs is that people must apply them to their own experience, then the play shows exactly how that works: Everyman (and through him the audience) encounters all the conditions that make the proverbs about dying true.[64] One does not need to die to learn the truth of the saying death comes suddenly; instead, one can watch Everyman die.

This precept-oriented morality dominates the play's Christianity, its devotional and even doctrinal content. Such a statement should hardly be surprising since a single moral about life's transitoriness organizes the play, and all of the other Christian doctrine, about Jesus's suffering to redeem people (*Everyman*, 30–34), for example, is subordinated to it. But it is worth noting that such an approach to Christian teachings distinguishes it from the other medieval plays, which are far more varied in their focus. Indeed, the morality shifts the emphasis of Christian teaching in an "unusual" and "atypical" direction—toward Good Deeds and away from a more expected penitential language.[65] There is a very Erasmian piety at work in the play, a sense of doing the right thing while living in the world.[66] Indeed, in *Everyman*, good deeds, not the sins and virtues of the penitential tradition, generate the self-knowledge Everyman needs to be saved.[67] When Everyman realizes that he has been abandoned by his friends, kinsmen, and his goods, he calls on Good Deeds,

> Good Dedes, I praye you helpe me in this nede,
> Or els I am forever damned indede.
> Therfore helpe me to make my rekenynge
> Before the Redemer of all thynge
> That Kynge is and was and ever shall (*Everyman*, 509–13).

Good Deeds then brings him to the character, Knowledge and says:

> I have a syster that shall with you also
> Called Knowlege, which shall with you abyde
> To helpe you to make that dredfull [frightening] rekenynge
> (*Everyman*, 519–21).

---

[64] Alastair Fowler, *Kinds of Literature: An Introduction to the Theory of Genres and Modes* (Cambridge, MA: Harvard University Press, 1982), 73.

[65] Hadfield, "Summoning," 100.

[66] Erasmus's interest in "individual Christian conduct" and "personal and undogmatic religion" are well established. For the former, see A. G. Dickens and Whitney R. D. Jones, *Erasmus the Reformer* (London: Reed International Books, 1994), 290 and for the latter, see James McConica, *English Humanists and Reformation Politics under Henry VIII and Edward VI* (Oxford: Clarendon Press, 1965), 262.

[67] On the importance of Good Deeds in this play see William Munson, "Knowing and Doing in *Everyman*," *Chaucer Review* 19 (1985): 252–71 and V. A. Kolve, *Everyman* and the Parable of the Talents," in *The Medieval Drama*, ed. Sandro Sticca (Albany, NY: SUNY Press, 1972), 78–79.

The sisterly relation suggests not only that Good Deeds and Knowledge are the same kind of idea, necessary to Everyman's understanding of himself, but also that they are equally important in his progress toward his goal. When placed alongside Good Deeds, the thingness of knowledge is emphasized. Knowledge (what one knows) is something a person can possess, the wisdom found in books, for example (n 520).[68] It is worth noting that making knowledge a thing, as this playwright does, limits its potential, and more active, meanings. Knowledge often carries with it penitential connotations at this time through the verb, "knowlechyng" [acknowledging], which is a common word for the act of confessing. Even more strikingly, the allegorical figure Knowledge is somewhat peripheral to Everyman's process of learning, which occurs primarily through Good Deeds.

What links Good Deeds to precepts in the play is that both are things that refer to (or require) an action. That is, Good Deeds is presented as a figure parallel to Goods and therefore a kind of thing, but her name also includes with it an action, or the memory of action. From a pre-Reformation perspective, both precepts and deeds similarly insist on the efficacy of human action in this world: one must follow rules, and this means doing good deeds. Indeed, this alignment is expressed in the allegorical figure of Good Deeds in that she fulfills two of the important precepts at the end of the play. First she repeats one of the rules that caused Everyman so much anguish when he applied it mistakenly to Fellowship: "Thou shalte fynde me a good frende at need" (*Everyman*, 854). Now this proverb helps Everyman instead of hurts him, because it is applied properly. Then, she repeats the explicit moral about life's transitoriness with which the play began: "All erthly thynge is but vanyté" (*Everyman*, 870). Good Deeds is not an "earthly thing," but another kind of thing, and, as such, will not fade away.

One might contrast the morality of *Everyman*—learning precepts and doing deeds—with that found in *The Castle of Perseverance*, which is, in some ways, a dramatized penitential handbook. Although *Castle* provides a similar moral lesson about considering one's end, as quoted above, the play is more interested in sin than in rules. Of course, sins can also be described in terms of rules (do not be greedy!), but that is not how this play works. Instead, a great deal of the play dramatizes the interactions of sins and their remedies, as allegorical figures, with the main character. Given that the language of sin is a language of what one feels as much as what one does, it should come as no surprise that the play communicates an explicit interest in what happens inside. At the opening, the messenger says,

> The case of oure cominge, you to declare,
> Every man in himself forsothe he it may finde

[The reason for our being here, which we declare to you, Is something that every man may find in himself truly] (*Castle*, 14–15).

---

[68] See also *Everyman*, in *Three Late Medieval Morality Plays*, p. 5 n520; *MED* s.v. "knoulechinge."

The contrast with *Everyman* is striking. In *Castle,* the mirror is inside each individual: every man *has* a mirror. It is not external to people as it is in *Everyman*: Everyman *is* a mirror (for everyone else). The emphasis on the interior—"in himself"—in *Castle* makes sense, because the play offers viewers a *psychomachia,* the battle between the sins and virtues, or the good and bad angels, happening inside the individual. Humanum Genus's failure is a failure to see his behavior as wrong, and it is not a failure to understand the lessons he has been told all of his life. For this reason, the conversations that Humanum Genus has with the other allegorical characters in *Castle* do not reveal a painful struggle to learn. Instead, Humanun Genus knows immediately who and what they are. For example, during a long speech, Death goes to Humanum Genus and hits him with a dart; Humanum Genus immediately reacts:

> A Deth, Deth, drye is thy drifte
> Ded is my desteny

[Oh, Death, Death, your power is hard; Death is my destiny] (*Castle,* 2843–44).

The repetition of Death and dead indicate the surety of the knowledge: this is what death is, the suffering and dying that Humanum Genus goes on to detail.

To re-orient *Everyman* away from *Castle* and toward the influence of humanism is to set aside the long-standing scholarly assumption that it is a product of a homogenized and unchanging medieval Christianity. Its explicit concern with morality as a discourse of sentences or maxims marks its difference from earlier discourses of penance or contemplation, which position morality—how to behave—in relation to Christian belief and practice. As the first play to call itself a "moral play," *Everyman* tells us something about the emergence of the genre at the moment when morality as such, that is a morality gained (or harvested) from texts, both classical and Christian, becomes a subject for discussion. The humanist grammars and treatises discussed above indicate why this might have been the case—the desire to train readers to appropriate a large number of non-Christian (i.e. classical) texts into discussions of right behavior. Although *Everyman* does not, of course, take up classical texts, the play offers insight into what it means to approach morality in relation to books, as part of a changing textual environment.

The Morality of *Mundus et Infans*

To re-locate *Everyman* in the early sixteenth century is to tie it more closely to the morality plays, such as Medwall's, that are more typically associated with humanism and to understand the morality play within its cultural moment. *Everyman* is not the only moral play that has been mis-categorized, as I shall suggest with my

60 HUMANISM AND GOOD BOOKS IN SIXTEENTH-CENTURY ENGLAND

next case study, *Mundus et Infans*. Like *Everyman*, this play belongs to the early sixteenth century: it was printed in 1522 by Wynkyn de Worde. It is, on the face of it, a more medieval play than *Everyman*, since its primary source is a fifteenth-century poem, "The Mirror of the Periods of Man's Life" (c. 1430).[69] In adapting a medieval, penitential poem to a recognizably "moral play," the author offers particular insight into the cultural shift described here—the development of a text-based, precept-oriented morality in and around humanism.[70]

As this play is not very well known, a brief plot summary might be in order. The plot of *Mundus* fits nicely into the trajectory traditionally associated with the morality play: a representative human figure first gives himself over to sin, corrects himself, gives into sin again, and then finally repents.[71] *Mundus* begins with Infans, whose name changes as he ages. He decides to serve the World, as he matures into a teenager (Wanton) and young man (Love-Lust-Liking). As a man (Manhood), he encounters Conscience for the first time and is told about the importance of "coveting" good and staying away from Folly, a figure for sin. Despite this warning, he joins Folly. Manhood's name changes again, to Shame, but it is only when he ages (and becomes Age), that he begins to sorrow for his sins. Conscience returns, bringing Perseverance, who changes Manhood's name yet again to Repentance and tells him what he needs to know to be saved: a veritable catalogue of pastoral instruction including "shrift of mouth," the Five Wits, the Twelve Articles at great length, and a brief mention of the Ten Commandments.

There is no question that this play is deeply invested in and informed by the same Christian teaching to which the medieval plays, such as *Castle*, and the source poem are indebted. One can trace the language of sin and repentance far more easily in *Mundus* than in the so-called quintessentially medieval play *Everyman*. Although the seven sins do not appear as characters, they function as such, since Mundus refers to them as the seven kings that follow him (170–83). In addition, the protagonist's repentance consists of lamenting his sins and embracing the practices of the church: contrition and "shrift" as described by the character

---

[69] Its most recent editors, Davidson and Happé, consider it within a medieval, devotional context (*The Worlde and the Chylde*, 1–34). Potter and Lester group it with *Everyman* and *Mankind* (Potter, *English Morality Play*, 44–46; *Three Late Medieval Morality Plays*, xi–xxxvii). Harbage, however, uses the term "moral interlude," thereby distinguishing it from *Everyman* and *Mankind*, which are called "morality," and linking it instead with Medwall's *Nature* and Skelton's *Magnificence* (Harbage, *Annals*, 10–11, 16–17, 18–19, 20–21). In a more recent study by Jane Griffiths, it is considered alongside plays about youths, a sixteenth-century phenomenon ("*Lusty Juventus*," in *The Oxford Handbook of Tudor Drama*, 264, 266)

[70] On the play's relation to its source, see Henry Noble MacCracken, "A Source of *Mundus Et Infans*," *PMLA* 23 (1908): 486–96 at 488. See more briefly the introduction to *The Worlde and the Chylde*, 6–8.

[71] In transforming a medieval poem into a play, this author follows Henry Medwall, whether consciously or not. Henry Medwall's *Nature*, which is typically dated to c. 1490 and printed c. 1530, adapts a poem thought to have been written by John Lydgate (*Plays of Henry Medwall*, 2–3, 28). The editor, Nelson, notes *Nature's* relationship to a medieval poem "Reson and Sensuallyte," which he attributes to John Lydgate (2), and which is now known as *The Assembly of the Gods*. See Jane Chance, "Introduction," in *The Assembly of the Gods*, ed. Jane Chance (Kalamazoo, MI: Medieval Institute, 1999).

Perseverance (849–80). At the same time, however, the play's treatment of human behavior is new, in that it is far more explicit than the poem, or any of the medieval plays, in treating behavior in terms of rules about what one should or should not do. In other words, it has a precept-oriented approach, similar to that in *Everyman*. The contrast between play and source poem was long ago noted by Henry Noble MacCracken in terms of the greater artistry of the poem: he describes the poem as a "highly finished and artistic production" and "a more poetic work than the morality."[72]

The play's precept-oriented morality is most apparent in the huge chunks of pastoral instruction that appear as dialogue. In Conscience's first encounter with Manhood, he tells Manhood how to do good by listing the Ten Commandments:

> Manhood, ye must love God above all thing;
> His name in idleness ye may not ming [mention];
> Keep your holy day from worldly doing [activity]
> Your father and mother worship aye [always];
> Covet ye to slay no man;
> Ne do no lechery with no woman;
> Your neighbours good take not by no way;
> And all false witnesse ye must denay;
> Neither ye must not covet no man's wife,
> Nor no good that him belieth [belongs].
> This covetise shall keep you out of strife.
> These ben [are] the commandmentes ten;
> Manhood, and [if] ye these commandments keep
> Heaven bliss I you behete [promise],
> For Christ's commandments are full sweet,
> And full necessary to all men (*Mundus*, 425–40).

This speech plays on the word "covet," altering a word that Manhood knows very well from its original associations with sin—he has followed "King Covetousness"—to new associations with the good. There is therefore an echo of medieval pastoral instruction, in which knowing sin is closely connected to knowing virtue, and vice versa. Despite this one bit of word play, the speech can be taken as an example of MacCracken's point about the lack of artistry. It is entirely straightforward and useful, as if it had been cribbed from any number of textual sources: a grammar book or guide to conduct or a catechism. Similarly, the character Perseverance's penultimate speech consists of a list of the Twelve Articles of the Faith and then a brief reminder of the importance of the Ten Commandments (*Mundus*, 901–56). At fifty-five lines, this speech is the longest in the entire

---

[72] MacCracken, "A Source," 488.

62 HUMANISM AND GOOD BOOKS IN SIXTEENTH-CENTURY ENGLAND

play with only two others given by the protagonist, as Manhood and then Age, that even come close, at fifty-one lines (*Mundus*, 237–87) and forty-four lines (*Mundus*, 763–806), respectively. Like Conscience's speech regarding the Ten Commandments, it is purely informational and could just as easily be found in a more overtly didactic text, such as John Colet's grammatical treatise, the *Aeditio* (1527), which prefaces its Latin instruction with the Twelve Articles, the Seven Sacraments, a description of charity, and other rules for behavior.[73]

The concreteness of this morality, the clear definition of these precepts, is most noticeable when the play is read against its source poem, "The Mirror of the Periods," which takes a more imaginative and less rule-oriented approach to the same language of sin and repentance. First and most obviously, the poem is a dream vision, in which an "I" witnesses the progress of the child and his conversation with particular allegorical figures. In mediating the vision, the "I" provides a mixed perspective: the tone is bleak, because the world is harsh, but there is sympathy for the child. In addition, the characters are not so strident or insistent. This more complex and potentially ambiguous approach to morality, to right and wrong human behavior, is at least in part due to the greater variety of both good and bad characters: the seven sins, the remedies for sin, a good and a bad angel, youth and age, Conscience, and some of the virtues. The play, in contrast, only has five speaking parts: the World, the Child (who changes his name frequently but is the same character), Folly, Conscience, and Perseverance.

While there is no question that "The Mirror of the Periods" offers moral positions, in so far as some of the characters are recognizably bad, and others recognizably good, its morality is less precept-oriented and more dialogic. The extended conversations suggest that morality is not so much a matter of following explicit instructions as it is a constant struggle to interpret life experience within the categories that one has been given. In "The Mirror," each of the seven sins appears as a character who tells the child, when he becomes, man, what he should do, the kinds of actions associated with that sin. For example, Gluttony commands him "loue thi wombe [love thy belly]."[74] Hence the dominance of the character, Conscience, in the poem, who is a figure for that part of the individual who must make choices between good and bad. There is very big difference between showing an audience how to evaluate experience in terms of Wrath and Patience—should one hit back if one is beaten?—and merely providing them with a list of sins and virtues.

The meditative function of the source poem is worth highlighting, since it resembles the medieval plays discussed above. The "Mirror" offers an opportunity to think about what it means to confront the moral dangers of the World in the

---

[73] Colet, *Aeditio*, A2r–A4r.

[74] "The Mirror of the Periods of Man's Life," in *Hymns to the Virgin and Christ*, ed. Frederick James Furnivall (London: Kegan Paul, Trench, Trübner, 1867), line 193. Hereafter all references to this poem will appear parenthetically.

language of the penitential tradition, sin and repentance. The poem presents the conditions out of which an individual must approach the world, and it therefore begins with a description of the child's birth, and not with the World speaking, as does the play. The child is utterly alone in the "wildirnesse" ("Mirror," 14), and although two angels take this child "in gouernaunce," the child seems to be unaware of them. The first character who speaks to the child is the World, and it is difficult to see what is wrong with what it says, especially when we remember that the child is "al alone" ("Mirror," 13). The World tells the child that "thou schuldist deie for hunger and coolde/ But y lente meete and clothe to thee [you would have died of hunger and cold if I had not given you food and clothes]" ("Mirror," 19–20). Such a statement is true, and for that reason, the World is persuasive. The World has power and money and the child does not. In emphasizing the child's vulnerability and offering him what he needs to survive, the World shows the impossibility of avoiding worldly concerns. The child must accept these necessities, but in doing so, he agrees to serve the World. In this way, the poem describes the same kind of question explored at length in many medieval works, including William Langland's late fourteenth-century dream vision, *Piers Plowman*: how can one live in the world without sin?

Such a complex view of sin necessarily produces a complex view of repentance, which emerges as the result of a conversation between virtue figures—Hope and Faith—and the more ambiguously moralized figures—Manhood and the World. Just as Manhood shifts in his meaning, so does the World, who becomes an agent of Repentance. The World responds to Hope and Faith, the figures who have come to save Manhood, asserting that he will repay "hise dettis" and help him feel contrite: "I wole waissche awey that feendis write/ With sorowe of herte and teer of yghe [I will, with sorrow of heart and tear of eye, wash away what fiends have written]" ("Mirror," 617, 621–22). The World also invokes "the comaundementis" the "seuene werkis of mercy," and the "crede" as the "keies" that will let Manhood into heaven (629–32). This shift in meaning, of the relationship between Manhood and World, makes its own kind of sense, since repentance must happen in this world before it is too late. Although the poem thus borrows its terminology and its language from penitential handbooks, none of the characters sounds like talking penitential handbooks, as do the characters in the play version. In addition, the explicit didacticism appears only here, at the end of the poem, as the focus shifts to the reader. These are the rules for living in the world the right way, in accordance with Christian teaching, and their presence here, along with contrition, show the conditions out of which those rules emerge: they are resources for addressing the moral dangers of living in the world.

In the play, in contrast, the language of sin and repentance is much reduced. Sins tend to operate as a meta-discourse, in that they draw attention to their status as words used in various contexts, whether accepted knowledge or rules for behavior. In other words, the play uses the traditional language of sin but does not

64 HUMANISM AND GOOD BOOKS IN SIXTEENTH-CENTURY ENGLAND

spend much time exploring what the words mean. The seven capital sins, the most familiar language of sin, appear only cursorily, when the character Mundus gives a list:

> For seven kings suen [follow] me,
> Both by day and night:
> One of them is the king of Pride;
> The king of Envy, doughty [valiant] in deed (*Mundus*, 170–73).

Allegorizing the sins as kings who follow the World is only slightly more complicated than baldly stating that the world is characterized by sins. Indeed, this account of sin provides no information of what the sins, such as Envy, actually entail, nor does the play go on to dramatize the actions or feelings or experience to which these words, the seven sins, typically refer.[75]

This meta-discourse is most apparent in the central sin figure, Folly. Part of this meta-discursiveness has to do with Folly's novelty. As an unconventional sin, he points to a far narrower and more recent textual tradition than, say, Pride, which can be found simply everywhere in many kinds of writings, dramas, sermons, and visual arts. Folly gestures toward Sebastian Brant's *Das Narrenschiff* (1494), which was translated into English as *The Ship of Fools* (1509) by Alexander Barclay, and toward Erasmus's *Praise of Folly* (1511).[76] Perhaps more importantly, Folly is meta-discursive because he is less a sin per se than an idea about sin: that all sin is foolish or unwise. As such, he is a kind of guarantee of sin's existence, of the necessity of behaving virtuously and of repenting, in much the same manner as Death in *Everyman*. Just as Death proves the rule that all life is transitory, Folly proves that people should not succumb to the seven sins. In his first appearance, Folly demonstrates the precept-oriented morality at work. Before Folly appears, Conscience warns Manhood about why one should behave well, should avoid evil company and act charitably, and that is to preserve oneself from folly. In other words, Conscience offers a rule to guide Manhood's behavior:

> Sir, keep you [yourself] in charity,
> And from all evil company
> For doubt [fear] of folly doing (*Mundus*, 454–56).

---

[75] There is not a great deal of scholarship on *Mundus*, and the little there is tends to focus on its allegorical characters, as compared, whether implicitly or explicitly to later plays. See Catherine Belsey, *The Subject of Tragedy: Identity and Difference in Renaissance Drama* (London: Methuen, 1985), 18–26 and Joyce E. Peterson, "The Paradox of Disintegrating Form in *Mundus et Infans*," *English Literary Renaissance* 7 (1977), 3–16.

[76] See Erasmus, *Praise of Folly*, trans. Betty Radice, *CWE*, Vol. 27 (1986): 77–153. Erasmus's text was translated into English and printed under the title *The praise of folie* (London, 1549) STC 10500. The editors to *The Worlde and the Chylde* note that "the idea of folly was being developed and exploited in a number of ways" in the early sixteenth century (15).

HUMANISM AND THE MORALITY PLAY 65

Then, after Manhood asks, "Folly? what thing callest thou folly?" (*Mundus*, 457) Conscience explains Folly in terms of the seven capital sins:

> Sir, it is pride, wrath, and envy,
> Sloth, covetise [covetousness], and gluttony
> Lechery the seventh is:
> These seven sins I call folly (*Mundus*, 458–61).

In identifying Folly as a thing, Manhood gives insight into the way in which moral rules work: they name behaviors or feelings that one should or should not do. In establishing behavior (the "keeping" from evil company) as right or wrong, rules clarify and define it, getting rid of muddiness or complications. In this way, the traditional seven sins become things, recognizable however or whenever they appear. Conscience's response reinforces this perspective, because he provides a list of more words, instead of describing the kinds of actions involved in Folly, such as drinking too much wine or stealing money. Sins are, of course, not things at all; they are only names for behaviors and feelings, but, when limited to names or words, they become more similar to things than to feelings or actions. Such a focus on the language of sin as such makes sense because the play is exploring a reorientation of moral perspective: Manhood has previously understood these terms as belonging to a positively connoted category, of beauty and strength, and, after conferring with his Conscience, he must now put them in another, negative, category of evil company and folly.[77] Moral behaviors are more words than actions in this play: we never see pride doing anything, for example, and so the audience is never shown what it is to be proud.

Moral rules also motivate the action of the play, in that both sinning—falling prey to Folly—and repentance—the appearance of Perseverance—are presented in terms of rule-following. Manhood is not tempted by the fun of spending time with Folly, although Folly does provide a vivid account of what he does—hanging out with lawyers, drinking wine in taverns. Instead, Manhood is tempted by changes and challenges to the rules. At first, Manhood resists Folly by repeating Conscience's parting rule: "Peace, man! I may not have thee for thy name/ For thou sayest thy name is both Folly and Shame" (*Mundus*, 640–41). This is an echo of Conscience's, "beware of Folly and Shame" (*Mundus*, 490). It is safe to assume that Manhood recognizes Folly as folly and wants nothing to do with him. And yet, Manhood cannot resist Folly after Folly changes his name, and thereby the application of the rule. Folly redefines himself: "Sir, here in this clout [cloth] I knit Shame,/ And clepe [call] me but proper Folly" (*Mundus*, 642–43). In this way,

---

[77] Jane Griffiths argues persuasively for a self-consciousness about language in the sixteenth-century morality plays that is linked to new (humanist) ideas about the capacity of words to represent things. See "Counterfet Countenance: (Mis)representation and the Challenge to Allegory in Sixteenth-century Morality Plays," *Yearbook of English Studies* 38 (2008): 17–33.

66   HUMANISM AND GOOD BOOKS IN SIXTEENTH-CENTURY ENGLAND

Folly presents Manhood with a challenge to Conscience's rule. "Proper" generates some important ambiguity: the sentence can mean "just call me Folly because
that is the correct term" or "just call me Folly, because Folly is the characteristic
distinctive to me," thus implying that Shame is not; or it could even mean "call
me suitable Folly." The word "proper" often has a moral inflection, since it means
"correct" or "right," and so Folly here implies that he has changed his moral status:
he is not Folly but a proper kind of Folly. However we interpret "proper," his new
name means that Conscience's warning now does not apply to him. With Folly's
help, Manhood has figured out a way to follow Conscience's rule and break it at
the same time. It is tempting to see this exchange as a kind of critique of the effect
of a precept-oriented morality: the way people tend to defend themselves against
the charge of breaking rules is to appeal to a hairsplitting literalism. One could
even imagine a petulant character defending himself to Conscience: "you told me
to beware of Folly and Shame; you didn't say beware of just Folly."

Rule-following also motivates repentance: the play's answer to Folly is the
character Perseverance, who spouts precepts at length, silencing any response
or resistance to those precepts. Perseverance is the only virtue character in the
play and is, like Folly, more of a meta-virtue than the more traditional virtues, of
Patience or Faith. To be sure, Perseverance is also allegorized in the medieval play
Castle, but, as that title makes clear, it is a "place" (1546) where Humanum Genus
can "dwelle" (1547), not a personified character. As a space, Perseverance in *Castle*
refers to a state of mind, and this concept is thereby distinguished from all the allegorical characters, who are forces that act upon Humanum Genus (sins), aspects
of Godly behavior (the virtues), practices one undergoes (Confession), or a part of
him (the Soul). In *Mundus*, in contrast, Perseverance is not a space but a character,
and, more specifically, a figure for precepts, not only because he speaks them, but
because he is the agent of instruction in the play:

> Sirs, Perseverance is my name;
> Conscience born brother that is [brother to Conscience];
> He sente me hither mankind to indoctrine [teach],
> That they should to no vices incline,
> For oft[en] mankind is governed amys [wrongly]
> And through Folly mankind is set in shame.
> Therefore in this presence to Christ I pray,
> Ere that I hence wend [go] away,
> Some good word that I may say
> To borrow [protect] man's soul from blame (*Mundus*, 757–66).

It is worth pausing over the word "indoctrine." The meaning of "indoctrine" is
to teach, and it is a relatively new word at the time the play was written. *The
Oxford English Dictionary* has the first usage at 1450, but other uses date quite

a bit later.[78] One might rephrase Perseverance's speech as follows: "I have been sent by Conscience to teach and to provide guidelines to Mankind in how to be good." But Perseverance is an odd choice for a teacher: in order to persevere in good behavior, after all, one must already know what good behavior entails. Perhaps Perseverance is less a teacher than a reminder. The "good word" he refers to is then the earlier moral lesson: beware of shame and folly. From the perspective of a precept-oriented, humanist morality, the quality of perseverance would certainly be more central than any one virtue, suggesting as it does that one must stick with the rules, or "persevere in goodness," as in the penitential manual that is Chaucer's *Parson's Tale*.[79] From this perspective, the play transforms the complex moral problem of the poem—Manhood trying to decide between sinful and virtuous behavior—to a simple choice between not following rules (Folly) and following rules (Perseverance).

While *Mundus* may be less "poetic" than its source poem, its similarity to *Everyman* should suggest that the changes are as much a result of a more general shift in thinking about morality as they are a one-off, the work of an inferior author. To set these morality plays together and within their proper context, the flourishing of humanism, is to recapture the nuances that have been occluded by the "medieval morality" genre. The plays' specific form of moral didacticism, their rule-orientedness, has long been assigned to their religious, i.e., Christian, content, as if morality and religion were the same thing, or as if religion were essentially synonymous with rules. Such a blurring has led scholars to see a development toward secularization that is not there, to trace lines of influence from *Castle* to *Everyman* to *Fulgens and Lucrece* and then on to Shakespeare. And yet tying morality plays more closely to their particular moment, the first part of the sixteenth-century, means that their vitality can be more fully appreciated. Instead of a stepping-stone, part of a seamless path to other genres, of tragedy and history, they are better understood as self-consuming artifacts, plays that made a certain kind of thinking possible and were made possible by a certain kind of thinking and then, when they had reached their limit, faded away.[80]

---

[78] *OED* s.v. "indoctrine" and *MED* s.v. "endoctrinen."

[79] Chaucer, *Parson's Tale*, 10.1070, 1074.

[80] I am borrowing the term from Stanley Fish, *Self-Consuming Artifacts: The Experience of Seventeenth-Century Literature* (Berkeley, CA: University of California Press, 1972). I have also borrowed my first sub-heading from the title of another book by Stanley Fish, *There's No Such Thing as Free Speech: And It's a Good Thing Too* (Oxford: Oxford University Press, 1994).

3

Humanist Moral Fusion: Terence and the Prodigal Son

Humanism was a literary and cultural movement founded on an embrace of classical texts, on a desire to understand them and appreciate them on their own terms. Perhaps the most recognized mode of humanist embrace and appreciation is the imitation of classical texts.[1] In his treatise, *The Scholemaster* (1570), Roger Ascham includes a long section on imitation, asserting its centrality to humanist education. Only by imitating will students achieve eloquence, the literary greatness assigned to the classical legacy. He explains that "if you would speak as the best and wisest do, you must be conversant, where the best and wisest are."[2] The program he outlines in his treatise is standard: students should read Cicero, Terence, and Livy; they should translate and re-translate them, learning all of their "tools and instruments" and "skill and judgement."[3] In attending to the specific elements that make Cicero a model of eloquence, or "best and wisest," Ascham assesses the literary value of writing, its eloquence or its well-written-ness, to a great degree independently of its moral and religious uses. It is easy to see, based on Ascham's account, the way in which imitation can mark out a space of the distinctly literary. Imitation helped establish a value for skills and eloquence, one that was not obviously subordinate to Christianity, a realm of independence that has been noted by many scholars including Bernard Weinberg and Paul Oskar Kristeller.[4] After

---

[1] In the introduction to the Renaissance volume of *The Cambridge History of Literary Criticism*, the editor, Glyn P. Norton writes, "the predominant poetic issue of the entire period [was] imitation" (*Cambridge History of Literary Criticism: vol. 3: The Renaissance*, ed. Glyn P. Norton [Cambridge: Cambridge University Press, 1999]), 3: 4. That imitation of the classical legacy was immensely generative for authors in the sixteenth century is well attested. See, for example, Colin Burrow, *Imitating Authors: Plato to Futurity* (Oxford: Oxford University Press, 2019); Thomas M. Greene, *The Light in Troy: Imitation and Discovery in Renaissance Poetry* (New Haven, CT: Yale University Press, 1982); and G. W. Pigman, "Versions of Imitation in the Renaissance," *Renaissance Quarterly* 33 (1980): 1–32.

[2] Roger Ascham, *The Scholemaster*, in *English Works*, ed. William Aldis Wright (Cambridge: Cambridge University Press, 1904), 264–65.

[3] Ascham, *The Scholemaster*, 267.

[4] See, e.g. Bernard Weinberg, *A History of Literary Criticism in the Italian Renaissance*, 2 vols. (Chicago: University of Chicago Press, 1961), 1:30 and Paul O. Kristeller, "Humanism and Moral Philosophy," in *Renaissance Humanism: Foundations, Forms and Legacy*, 3 vols., ed. Albert Rabil, Jr. (Philadelphia: University of Pennsylvania Press, 1988), 3:273. None of the studies of classical imitation in the Renaissance—Burrow, *Imitating Authors*, Greene, *Light in Troy*, or Pigman, "Versions"—explores imitation within an explicitly Christian framework, even though both medieval imitators and early humanists were preoccupied with Christian meanings.

Humanism and Good Books in Sixteenth-Century England. Katherine C. Little, Oxford University Press.
© Katherine C. Little (2023). DOI: 10.1093/oso/9780192883193.003.0004

HUMANIST MORAL FUSION: TERENCE AND THE PRODIGAL SON   69

all, Ascham's "best and wisest" are pagan, classical authors, whose "skill" does not refer to Christian teachings in any obvious way.

Such an account of classical imitation in the sixteenth century, as enabling a new realm of literary value, even a secular idea of literature, can, however, only be partial. One of the most popular and pervasive kinds of classical imitation in the Renaissance was not at all secular, as that word is commonly understood, but instead explicitly Christian and moral in its goals. I am referring to a literary tradition called the Christian Terence, the humanist school drama that fused comedy in the style of the Roman author Terence with biblical stories and guides to Christian conduct, most famously around the parable of the prodigal son.[5] These plays were composed in the early to mid-sixteenth century, first in Latin and then in European vernaculars, and they were ubiquitous in educational settings, namely schools and universities.[6] For this reason, it would be difficult to underestimate their influence on readers and writers in this period.[7] Despite their popularity and their apparent influence on the most famous authors of the Renaissance, such as William Shakespeare and Ben Jonson, the plays in this tradition have been mainly dismissed by literary scholars. In so far as they are studied at all, they function as a static backdrop against which the emergence of a resolutely secular Renaissance literature can be charted.[8]

This chapter uses the Christian Terence tradition to offer an alternate history of humanist imitation, and therefore of literary production, that is centrally concerned with Christian morality. My focus will be the most influential and self-consciously literary of these plays: the Latin play *Acolastus* (1529) by Gulielmus Gnapheus, or Willem de Volder, which was printed frequently and widely used in schools across Europe.[9] It had a quasi-official status in England in a dual-language edition of 1540, in which the translator, John Palsgrave, aligns himself

---

[5] The name of this tradition is a back-formation based on Cornelis Schonaeus, *Terentius Christianus, sive Comoediae duae* (London, 1595).

[6] See W. E. D. Atkinson's introduction in Gulielmus Gnapheus, *Acolastus: A Latin Play of the Sixteenth Century* (London, ON: Humanities Departments of the University of Western Ontario, 1964), 1–2, 87; Ervin Beck, "Terence Improved: The Paradigm of the Prodigal Son in English Renaissance Comedy," *Renaissance Drama* 6 (1973): 107–22; Richard Helgerson, *The Elizabethan Prodigals* (Berkeley, CA: University of California Press, 1977), 34–39; Charles Herford, *Studies in the Literary Relations of England and Germany in the Sixteenth Century* (London: Frank Cass and Co, Ltd., 1966), 70–164; John Dover Wilson, "*Euphues* and the Prodigal Son," *The Library* 10.40 (1909): 337–61; Alan R. Young, *The English Prodigal Son Plays: A Theatrical Fashion of the Sixteenth and Seventeenth Centuries* (Salzburg: Universität Salzburg, 1979), 1–78.

[7] A point made long ago by Wilson, "*Euphues*," 341–42.

[8] See Helgerson, *Elizabethan Prodigals*; Ezra Horbury, "Performing Repentance: (In)sincerity in Prodigal Son Drama and the Henry IVs," *Renaissance Studies* 32.4 (2017): 583–601; and Wilson, "*Euphues*."

[9] Atkinson calls *Acolastus* the "most celebrated play in Northern Europe and one of the most frequently printed among all the literary works of its time" (Gnapheus, *Acolastus*, 1). There were 48 editions between 1529 and 1585 (2).

70 HUMANISM AND GOOD BOOKS IN SIXTEENTH-CENTURY ENGLAND

with the plan of King Henry VIII to improve education along humanist lines.[10] *Acolastus* generated many imitations in England, which are still described in terms of a sub-genre called prodigal-son-plays.[11] It was, in other words, a school-play whose influence extended far beyond the school-room into the drama of universities and commercial theater, into the wave of prose fiction beginning with John Lyly's *Euphues: The Anatomy of Wit* (1578), and into the penitential-devotional treatises written by Elizabethan authors, or to borrow Richard Helgerson's term, the "Elizabethan prodigals."[12]

Despite being now largely forgotten, *Acolastus* is an exemplary humanist play: an imitation of Roman comedy that theorizes its own imitation. At the same time, in addition to its classicism, this play also has a Christian goal, similar to *Everyman*, ending as it does with a call for repentance: "We summon all of you who are present here to this same joy, if only you will acknowledge your sins" ["Huc gaudiorum omnes quidem uocamini,/ Qui astatis istic, si modo agnito malo/ Resipiscitis]."[13] It uses a well-known, perhaps the most well-known, story of repentance throughout the Middle Ages and into the sixteenth century: the parable of the prodigal son, Luke 15:11–32. Gnapheus expands the parable around the character types and plot elements that it shares with Roman comedy: the tensions between father and son and the riotous living, which entails drinking and having fun with courtesans. Although the play is interested in repentance, it should not be seen as simply didactic. That is, it does not merely add a lesson about Christian behavior (a moral lesson) onto an imitation of Roman comedy, as the Christian Terence tradition is so often understood as doing.[14] *Acolastus* is an exercise in thinking about the fusion of these traditions and, even as it embraces Roman comedy, it demonstrates a deep ambivalence about the value of the classical heritage for a Christian readership, as I shall argue here. As a genre that emerged out of an identifiable

---

[10] John Palsgrave directs his translation to the king himself, writing "you haue ... wylled one self and vniforme maner of teachinynge all those Grammaticalled ensygnements, to be vsed through out all your hyghnes domynions," and then offers this play in "furtherance of this your noble graces so goodly, and therto so godly and moche fruitefull a purpose" (Gulielmus Gnapheus, *The Comedy of Acolastus, Translated from the Latin of Fullonius by John Palsgrave*, ed. P. L. Carver [London: Humphrey Milford, 1937], 3–4). On Palsgrave's edition, see Jan Bloemendal, "Religion and Latin Drama in the Early Modern Low Countries," *Renaissance Studies* 30 (2016): 542–61; and Ágnes Juhász-Ormsby, "Dramatic Texts in the Tudor Curriculum: John Palsgrave and the Henrician Educational Reforms," *Renaissance Studies* 30.4 (2016): 526–41.

[11] As is made clear in the titles of Beck "Terence Improved: The Paradigm of the Prodigal Son in English Renaissance Comedy;" and Horbury, "Performing Repentance: (In)sincerity in Prodigal Son Drama and the Henry IVs."

[12] On Lyly as prodigal, see Helgerson, *Elizabethan Prodigals*, 58–78.

[13] Gnapheus, *Acolastus*, 203/202. Quotations from *Acolastus* come from Atkinson's edition unless otherwise indicated. Hereafter all references will appear parenthetically with the page number of the English translation followed by the page number of the Latin original.

[14] Patricia Parker understands the "Christian Terence" tradition in terms of "hierarchal incorporation" ("Shakespeare and the Bible: *The Comedy of Errors*," *Recherches Sémiotiques/Semiotic Inquiry* 13.3 [1993]: 67). This view seems fairly typical; see, for example, Helgerson's account of duty, in which Christianity is hierarchical and didactic (*Elizabethan Prodigals*, 16–43).

HUMANIST MORAL FUSION: TERENCE AND THE PRODIGAL SON 71

historical moment—the flourishing of Renaissance humanism—the play offers a cultural model, in which the value of and feelings about, indeed the morality of, classical texts in relation to Christianity can be worked out.[15]

In invoking this term, cultural model, I am drawing on the work of anthropologists on the way cultures think. In his helpful survey, *The Development of Cognitive Anthropology*, Roy D'Andrade writes, "a model consists of an interrelated set of elements which fit together to represent something. Typically one uses a model to reason with or calculate from by mentally manipulating the parts of the model in order to solve some problem."[16] The parallels between a cultural model, also called a schema, on the one hand, and genre, on the other, should be apparent in the description given by another anthropologist, Naomi Quinn, who describes a schema as "a bounded, distinct and unitary representation" that "organize[s] and process[es] experience."[17] Approaching genre, in this case the prodigal-son-play, as a cultural model underlines its usefulness and helps explain why this particular genre emerged at this precise moment in time. As Hans Robert Jauss writes, in an influential essay on genre, "genres are thus neither subjective creations of the author, nor merely retrospective ordering-concepts, but rather primarily social phenomena, which means that they depend on functions in the lived world."[18] In this reading, a genre offers a tool for thinking with, one that structures feelings, experiences, and knowledge for readers so that they can make sense of the world around them.[19]

My discussion will proceed in two parts. In the first part I examine Renaissance classical imitation in terms of the challenge it posed to a Christian readership. By highlighting humanists' attempt to recover classical texts for a still predominantly Christian culture, I revise those accounts of Renaissance humanism that

---

[15] Latin humanist drama flourished in the early part of the sixteenth-century, and the prodigal-son-plays in particular seem to have had a universal appeal in a time of fierce theological debate. See Bloemendal, "Religion and Latin Drama" and Fidel Rädle, "Acolastus – Der Verlorene Sohn: Zwei lateinische Bibeldramen des 16. Jahrhunderts," in *Gattungsinnovation und Motivstruktur*, Teil II, ed. Theodor Wolpers (Göttingen: Vandenhoeck & Ruprecht, 1992), 15–34. On the potential Lutheranism, see Atkinson's introduction in *Acolastus*, 51–67; and Stephen L. Wailes, "Is Gnapheus' Acolastus a Lutheran Play?," in *Semper Idem et Novus: Festschrift for Frank Banta*, ed. Francis Gentry (Göppingen: Kümmerle, 1988), 345–57.

[16] Roy D'Andrade, *The Development of Cognitive Anthropology* (Cambridge: Cambridge University Press, 1995), 151.

[17] Naomi Quinn, "The History of the Cultural Models School Reconsidered: A Paradigm Shift in Cognitive Anthropology," in *A Companion to Cognitive Anthropology*, ed. David B. Kronenfeld et al (Malden, MA: Wiley-Blackwell, 2011), 35.

[18] Hans Robert Jauss, *Toward an Aesthetic of Reception*, trans. Timothy Bahti (Minneapolis, MN: University of Minnesota Press, 1982), 100.

[19] Discussions of genre acknowledge its importance in organizing social and cultural knowledge. See John Frow, "Reproducibles, Rubrics, and Everything You Need: Genre Theory Today," *PMLA* 122.5 (2007): 1633; Frow, *Genre*, 2nd ed. (New York: Routledge, 2015), 2; and Jauss, *Toward an Aesthetic*, 76–109. In describing genre as a tool, I'm indebted to many conversations with Nicola McDonald about romance.

72 HUMANISM AND GOOD BOOKS IN SIXTEENTH-CENTURY ENGLAND

have posited classical imitation as a realm of independence or a means to set Christianity aside.[20] I then turn to the solution that *Acolastus* offers Christian readers of classical texts: it both embraces Roman comedy and demonstrates its moral limitations through the term "prodigality." This Gnaphean solution is deeply ambivalent, conscious of the value of the classical texts as well as the incommensurability of the two traditions, of what is lost in the process of classical imitation.

Classical Imitation in a Christian Culture

Even as humanists praised pagan, classical texts for their eloquence and wisdom, for being "the best and wisest," to borrow Ascham's phrasing, they continued to understand best and wisest in terms of their own Christian culture: the usefulness of these texts for a sixteenth-century Christian morality. This claim, for the Christian moral usefulness of pagan, classical texts, shaped English education thoroughly, and it can be found repeatedly in grammar-books, reading lists at schools such as St. Paul's, and educational treatises. As Ascham's guide, *The Scholemaster,* indicates, all education had both specifically Christian and more general moral goals: "In writing this book, I have had earnest respect to three special pointes, truth of Religion, honesty in living, right order in learning."[21] Such a perspective matches that of Erasmus, for whom Christianity provides a moral rubric within which these classical authors could be safely read, a deeper and primary interpretive framework. As Erasmus writes in his widely-disseminated treatise, *Education of a Christian Prince* (1516), "What must be implanted deeply and before all else in the mind ... is the best possible understanding of Christ."[22]

Reading Terence, or any of the classical great authors, for guidelines for behavior meant training students, and readers more generally, to find the morals in the text. Erasmus details the process for "turn[ing] to philosophy and skillfully bring[ing] out the moral implication of the poets' stories" in his influential treatise on education, *On the Method of Study* (1511).[23] Such an Erasmian approach

---

[20] Greene, *Light in Troy,* 28–53.

[21] Ascham, *Scholemaster,* 180.

[22] *The Education of a Christian Prince,* trans. Neil M. Cheshire and Michael J. Heath in *Collected Works of Erasmus* (*CWE*), 84 vols. (Toronto: University of Toronto Press, 1974–), Vol. 27 (1986): 212.

[23] In *On the Method of Study,* Erasmus describes in detail how a teacher should approach the Roman comedies of Terence, beginning with the literary elements that make Terence a great model, such as "the elegance of his language" and genre, comedy "and its laws." After teachers have offered a comprehensive survey of such elements, they should "turn to philosophy and skillfully bring out the moral implication of the poets' stories" (*On the Method of Study,* ed. Craig R. Thompson, trans. Brian McGregor, *CWE,* Vol. 24 [1978]: 683). On the importance of Terence in this period, see Joel B. Altman, *The Tudor Play of Mind: Rhetorical Inquiry and the Development of Elizabethan Drama* (Berkeley, CA: University of California Press, 1978), 130–47; Micha Lazarus, "The Dramatic Prologues of Alexander Nowell: Accommodating the Classics at 1540s Westminster," *The Review of English Studies* Vol. 69. 288 (2017): 32–55; Robert S. Miola, *Shakespeare and Classical Comedy: The Influence of Plautus and Terence* (Oxford: Clarendon Press, 1994), 3–9; Ursula Potter, "'No Terence phrase: his tyme and myne are

informs the translations and selections from Terence's comedies that were printed in the first part of the sixteenth century as *vulgaria* and *florilegia*. These books provide model translation exercises, in which Latin sentences are followed by their English equivalents. The English humanist, Nicholas Udall, states the purpose on the title page of his *florilegia*: "Flowers for Latin speaking selected and gathered out of Terence, and the same translated in to English, together with the exposition and setting forth as well of such Latin words, as were thought needfull [necessary] to be annoted [annotated], as also of diverse grammatical rules, very profitable [and] necessary for the expedite [unimpeded] knowledge in the Latin tongue: compiled by Nicolas Udall."[24] The moral function of reading Terence is largely implicit in Udall's version, part of the general idea of "profitability." What is implicit becomes clearer, when the excerpts in Udall are compared with the original. The first play in Udall's *Flowers* is the *Andria* [*The Woman of Andros*] (c. 166 B.C.E). Udall renders Terence's Prologue as four disconnected snippets, radically altering its sense by suggesting a moral message that is simply not there in the original. The final snippet is: "*Animum advortite*. Take hede [heed], or sette your myndes hereto and harken[listen]," a familiar appeal to audiences in morality plays, such as *Everyman* and *Mundus et Infans*.[25] What precisely the audience will attend to is left unstated, but Udall has provided a familiar rubric, of priming them for morality, in much the manner that Erasmus had described in *On the Method of Study*.

It is worth nothing that there is nothing in Terence's play or prologue that would suggest moral usefulness, as a mirror of human behavior, as a container of virtue and vices, as moving the audience to act or feel in the right way. In fact, in his prologue to the *Andria*, which Udall has carefully excerpted, Terence offers a version of sweetness and usefulness, or delight and instruction, that defies assimilation into humanist, that is moralized, versions of this Horatian link. For Terence, the pleasure of writing certainly has a usefulness, but not in its moral message to the audience; it is, rather, to "answer the slanders of a malicious old playwright."[26] Moreover, his opening words indicate that the poet's primary duty is, in fact, one of pleasure and not of any kind of usefulness: "When the playwright first turned his mind to writing, he believed that his only problem was to ensure that the plays he

---

twaine': Erasmus, Terence, and Censorship in the Tudor Classroom," in *The Classics in the Medieval and Renaissance Classroom: The Role of Ancient Texts in the Arts Curriculum as Revealed by Surviving Manuscripts and Early Printed Books*, ed. Juanita Feros Ruys, John O. Ward, and Melanie Heyworth (Turnhout: Brepols, 2013), 365–89, and Martine van Elk, "Thou shalt present me as an eunuch to him': Terence in Early Modern England," in *A Companion to Terence*, ed. Antonios Augoustakis and Ariana Traill (Hoboken, NJ: Blackwell, 2013), 410–28.

[24] Ágnes, Juhász-Ormsby, "Nicholas Udall's *Floures for Latin Spekynge*: An Erasmian Textbook," *Humanistica Lovaniensia: Journal of Neo-Latin Studies* 52(2003): 137–158.

[25] Terence, *Floures for Latine spekynge selected and gathered oute of Terence*, trans. Nicholas Udall (London, 1534) STC 23899, A1r, image 13.

[26] Terence, *Andria [The Woman from Andros]*, in *Terence 1. The Woman of Andros. The Self-Tormentor. The Eunuch*, ed. and trans. John Barsby LCL 22 (Cambridge, MA: Harvard University Press, 2001), 1:51.

74   HUMANISM AND GOOD BOOKS IN SIXTEENTH-CENTURY ENGLAND

had created would win the approval of the public."[27] It is hardly surprising that this opening statement is shortened to "*Animum ad scribendum appulit,* [He applied his mind to writing]" in Udall's excerpts.[28]

The need to supply or appropriate Terence for morality appears widely, in both editions of Terence and in accounts of Terence during the first part of the sixteenth-century, and beyond.[29] In the dual language edition of the *Andria* entitled *Terens in English* (1520), the translator disappears Terence's prologue entirely.[30] Instead, he provides one of his own, in which he indicates, in contradiction to Terence, that the poet's duty is in fact moral usefulness. After establishing an English context, in which poets "write about diverse matters in their mother tongue," he offers the familiar models of Gower, Chaucer, and Lydgate.[31] He gives Gower pride of place, since he "first began/ And of morality wrote right craftily," thus implying that what Terence and the English authors have in common is their instructiveness, both in language and in "morality."[32] Such moral re-purposings of Terence are made explicit in Ascham's *Scholemaster,* when he baldly asserts the moral usefulness of reading Terence in a section on how servants can lead youth astray, "corrupt[ing] the best natures."[33] One should "read Terence and Plautus" because these authors provide a useful guide to the dangers of such bad company: "you shall find in those two wise writers, almost in every comedy, no unthrifty man, that is not brought there unto, by the subtle enticement of some lewd servant."[34] Ascham is typical in his rather paradoxical insistence that reading about the bad behavior in Terence's comedies will necessarily lead to condemning that behavior instead of imitating it.

As these texts suggest, humanists were confident that Terence and other classical authors could be harnessed to a morality for their own time. What has been said about Erasmus, that he offered a "package of *bonae litterae* [the classics] and individual piety," is more generally true as an educational goal.[35] Such a package is, of course, deeply contradictory, since the texts known as *bonae litterae,* such as Terence's Roman comedy, contain lots of behaviors that would seem to counter the "good" behavior that was encouraged in sixteenth-century England. Terence's *Andria* is not only about "lewd servants," to borrow Ascham's moralizing, it is also

---

[27] Terence, *Andria,* 51.

[28] Terence, *Floures,* A1r, image 13.

[29] See the prologues transcribed in Lazarus, "The Dramatic Prologues."

[30] *Terens in englysh* (Paris, 1520). See also Terence, *Terence in English: An Early Sixteenth-Century Translation of The Andria,* ed. Meg Twycross (Lancaster: Dept. of English Language and Medieval Literature, University of Lancaster, 1987). This is a dual language edition, in which the Latin is printed in the margins, as a kind of gloss to the English.

[31] *Terens in englysh,* A1r.

[32] *Terens in englysh,* A1r.

[33] Ascham, *The Scholemaster,* 209.

[34] Ascham, *The Scholemaster,* 208.

[35] Anthony Grafton and Lisa Jardine, *From Humanism to the Humanities: Education and the Liberal Arts in Fifteenth- and Sixteenth-Century Europe* (Cambridge, MA: Harvard University Press, 1986), 140. For an overview, see Charles G. Nauert, "Rethinking 'Christian Humanism,'" in *Interpretations of Renaissance Humanism,* ed. Angelo Mazzocco (Leiden: Brill, 2006), 172, 175–80.

HUMANIST MORAL FUSION: TERENCE AND THE PRODIGAL SON   75

about courtesans, premarital sex, pregnancy, trickery, and defying one's father. Humanists were certainly aware of the problems, the contradictions between the details of the classical texts and the morals traditionally applied to them, and their writings are filled with attempts to navigate, smooth over, or distract readers from them. One well-known example is Erasmus's treatment of Virgil's Second Eclogue in *On the Method of Study*. This eclogue is an obviously homoerotic poem and not at all easy to moralize, as Erasmus is well aware, and yet, he insists that the poem has a clear moral about friendship: it is "a symbolic picture of such an ill-formed friendship."[36] As "symbolic" in nature, this moral must be prepared for. To borrow the same terms used by Udall for Terence's plays, the teachers must "set the minds" of their students so that they can "take heed" to the right lesson. Erasmus provides guidance in such an operation: "If, then, he [the teacher] prefaces his remarks in this way, and thereupon shows the passages which indicate the mistaken and boorish affections of Corydon, I believe the minds of his audience will suffer no ill effects, unless someone comes to the work who has already been corrupted. For such a person will have brought his infection with him and will not have acquired it from this activity."[37] Erasmus's claim about the "audience" is telling: the reader "brings" either the right rubric, the "preface," which allows him [Erasmus's reader is likely male] to see that the homoerotic affections are "mistaken," or he brings the wrong one, an "infection" in which these affections are "corrupting." Erasmus knows that the pagan, classical text does not fit the moral world into which he's interpreting it, sixteenth-century, Christian Europe, and yet he values the text so highly that he will mis-interpret it in order to hold onto it.

There can be no question that Erasmus and his fellow humanists appreciated classical texts for many of the reasons that still resonate in the twenty-first century and that are recognizable as literary: the elegance of the writing, the vividness of the characterization, the wisdom about human behavior and emotion. For Udall, as for many of his contemporaries, Terence's Latin is "pure" and "elegant."[38] In insisting, at the same time, on the value of those texts in shaping the behavior of Christian readers, these humanists also posed a challenge to teachers and students: how would this fusion, with its attendant contradictions, play out in the lives of the readers? That is, what would the moral effect of this fusion be, the effect on beliefs and behaviors, as distinct from its effect on the knowledge, language, and style in which students were being instructed?

Acolastus and Ambivalence

The answers to these questions can be found in Gnapheus's play *Acolastus*, which upholds the central Erasmian premise, that classical texts not only align with

[36] Erasmus, *On the Method of Study, CWE,* Vol. 24 (1978): 686.
[37] Erasmus, *On the Method of Study, CWE,* Vol. 24 (1978): 686–87.
[38] Terence, *Floures,* image 4, unpaginated prefatory material.

76 HUMANISM AND GOOD BOOKS IN SIXTEENTH-CENTURY ENGLAND

Christian teaching but can train students in virtuous, Christian behavior.[39] The fact that Gnapheus's play is one of a group of plays that combine Christian teaching with Roman comedy and tragedy, all of which emerged at the same time and, largely independently of each other, suggests that the interest in fusing these traditions was widely shared, and that it emerged because classical texts were being offered as models for behavior, not only models for eloquence.[40] After all, plays in the Christian Terence tradition, and humanist school drama more generally, are simultaneously language-exercises, teaching students good, classical Latin, and training in behavior, in the right, and often specifically Christian, ways of thinking and acting. As John Dover Wilson long ago noted, "a remarkable series of dramas were produced" in the sixteenth century that allowed "the treasures of the Latin language" to be taught while preserving the teacher's "ethical function."[41] As crucial as the fusion of the two traditions, is the dramatic form: this is a play, and as such, it suggests that the fusion of values must be enacted in the lives of readers as opposed to merely described or implied, as it is in the educational treatises, or worked out on paper, in sonnet sequences or epic poetry. The play is, as mentioned above, a cultural model or schema, in which the readers' experience of pagan, classical texts can be accommodated within a Christian life. *Acolastus* and similar plays educate students in the classics and, at the same time, in the appropriate feelings to have about such an education.

Despite its popularity and broad influence, *Acolastus* is more often invoked than discussed at any length. A brief summary may, for that reason, be in order. The play opens with a father, Pelargus, who discusses his concerns about his disobedient son, Acolastus, with his friend Eubulus. Eubulus advises Pelargus to provide his son his freedom by giving him the money he requests. After receiving his inheritance, Acolastus falls in with a bad crowd, including parasites and courtesans, and ultimately loses everything, including the clothes off his back. During this period of riotous living, Pelargus continues to worry about his son, in many conversations with Eubulus. After he has lost everything, Acolastus despairs but ultimately realizes his faults and returns home. In the end the father and son are reunited.

As this brief summary makes clear, *Acolastus* looks, at first glance, like a simple case of fusion, in which Roman comedy is made didactic, enlisted to support

---

[39] On Erasmus's influence see Atkinson's introduction to *Acolastus,* 51–81 and Carver's notes in *The Comedy of Acolastus*, e.g. 197 n23, 201n32, 271 n150. See also Bloemendal, "Religion and Latin Drama;" Juhász-Ormsby, "Dramatic Texts;" and Young, *English Prodigal Son Plays*, 14–16.

[40] In the early to mid-sixteenth century, a number of Dutch and German playwrights began writing plays that combined classical drama and Christian stories. There is general agreement on the novelty of the plays, their large number, and their influence across Europe. See, for example, Herford, *Studies*, 84–85; Miola, *Shakespeare and Classical Comedy*, 8; and James A. Parente, Jr, "Drama," in *The Encyclopedia of the Reformation*, ed. Hans J. Hillebrand (Oxford: Oxford University Press, 1996), doi: 9780195064933. Two different playwrights, George Macropedius and Gnapheus, independently came up with the idea of combining Roman comedy and the parable of the prodigal son. Macropedius's play, titled *Asotus*, was printed 1537 but probably written earlier.

[41] Wilson, "*Euphues,*" 338.

a Christian moral about the importance of repentance. In his opening Epistle, Gnapheus asserts the compatibility of classical and Christian in recognizably humanist language, and his theory of comedy could serve as an example of the Erasmian mode in action. There can be no question that Gnapheus values classical texts on their own terms. After lamenting the state of poetry with his surprise that "the art of comedy should be so neglected [demiror poesim comicam sic iacere neglectam]" during his own time, he underlines the importance of imitating well-known classical authors; and he quotes Cicero and Horace on what a comedy should be or do (85/84). He then explains his understanding of the proper subject matter of comedy, which also matches the classical tradition: "For the plots of comedies are drawn from the middle state of life, and demand a corresponding style, so that it is not at all difficult for a writer who has observed and reflected upon the characters and habits of human society to render them with decorum [Nam ut comoediarum argumenta e media hominum uita petuntur, ita et tractari facile possunt ob stili mediocritatem dicam an facilitate, potissimum ab iis, qui hominum ingenia, mores et uitam sic habent meditate, ut pro decoro queant exprimere]" (85/84). Gnapheus's account of comedy makes perfect sense as part of a humanist conversation about the imitation of classical texts, and his "break[ing] the ice" and "try [ing] out" his "comic Muse" lead one to believe that his play will be a recognizable attempt at imitation (85/84). The logic is clear: comedy now is not done right (or at all), according to the classical definitions and authors, and "therefore [autem], I will try my hand at doing it right" (85/84). In his comments on comedy, Gnapheus reveals his appreciation of literary elements—of art, of style and decorum (the style appropriate to a certain topic), of characterization. His imitation is, in other words, motivated by an appreciation of classical texts that he shares with many other humanist authors.

Placing such a high value of the literary, on the elements of classical comedy, does not lead Gnapheus down the same path as other authors whose imitations are now more widely read. He does not lament the ruins of the Roman past or try to repair or restore them, in the vein of a Francesco Petrarch or a Joachim du Bellay or even an Edmund Spenser, whose complicated relationship to the Roman past is discussed in the final chapter. Rather, he appropriates classical comedy for its Christian uses.[42] Indeed, he is not at all nostalgic for the Roman past, since he describes his own time in terms of "men of outstanding ability [who] sedulously cultivate and bring to perfection all branches of knowledge [qui omne disciplinarum genus tractent, uersent et excolant]" (85/84). Perhaps his confidence comes from his desire to appropriate instead of return to Roman comedy. After invoking the comic muse (Thalia), Gnapheus writes, "I have taken from Holy Scripture a story which I thought was suited to comic treatment—except that here

---

[42] Greene, *Light in Troy*, 81–146; 220–41. His focus on ruins has been taken up recently by Andrew Hui, *The Poetics of Ruins in Renaissance Literature* (New York: Fordham University Press, 2017).

78 HUMANISM AND GOOD BOOKS IN SIXTEENTH-CENTURY ENGLAND

and there it involves outcries more appropriate to tragedy, and thus transgresses those laws of comedy handed down to us by Horace. However, I considered it a less serious crime to defy him than to depart from the meaning and the dignity of the subject matter. For I preferred to respect the claims of religion than to observe some principle of literary decorum [Argumentum delegi ex sacris, quod in comoediae formam cogi posse iudicarem, praeterquam quod hic res subinde in nimis Tragicas exeat exclamationes idque praeter comicas illas leges, quas nobis tradidit Flaccus. Quod quidem crimen leuis esse duxim quam a sensu et rei dignitate recedere. Malui enim pietatis respectui quam litteraturae decoro alicubi seruire]" (85/84). For Gnapheus, the Roman "rules" of poetry are generative for his own writing, much as they are for other, perhaps more well-known, Renaissance imitators, such as Sir Philip Sidney. At the same time, however, his Epistle indicates that he is rather more concerned about the incommensurability of the two traditions, that Roman literary traditions can only approximate the scriptural story, than he is with the rupture between his own time and a past Roman greatness.

If the Epistle hints at a problem with Erasmian compatibility, a gap between the classical and the Christian, the play seeks to resolve it by clearly subordinating the classical texts to a Christian story.[43] While such subordination should be familiar from defenses of Terence—he is moral and therefore appropriate reading for Christians—Gnapheus's subordination is less a defense than a contradictory mixture of embrace and implicit condemnation. That is, even as Gnapheus uses Terence, he does so by framing this pagan, classical tradition in terms of the sin of prodigality and, therefore, as ultimately immoral. In this play, the Erasmian mode of compatibility fails: pagan classical texts do not lead toward Christian morality; they lead away from it. This movement is most apparent at the level of plot, in which the Christian moral, the repentance, reverses the mainstays of Roman comedy, which include the sons' triumph over fathers; marriage and sex; and trickery.[44] In Gnapheus's play, the father wins out over the son; the trickery leads to despair; and there are no marriages.

As a result, even as Gnapheus celebrates and embraces classical comedy, he also shows the moral danger of reading classical texts. For Gnapheus, classical texts are both a resource for representing temptations, the son's disobedience and the tavern scenes, which are borrowed from Terence, and are themselves a temptation that must ultimately be rejected or at least controlled. In other words, the prodigality in the play is an intensely literary prodigality, a wandering through the pleasures of immoral texts, as much as through the pleasures of sex or gaming or drinking. Acolastus's problem, his disobedience, seems to stem as much from having read too many of the wrong kind of books as from desiring the wrong kinds of things.

---

[43] As Young notes, the play "does not completely solve the problem of adapting a Christian story to a classical setting" (*English Prodigal Son Plays*, 77).

[44] On this play's inversion of the values of Roman comedy, see Atkinson's introduction to *Acolastus*, 26; Beck, "Terence Improved," 110–11; and Young, *English Prodigal Son Plays*, 59.

Most obviously, there's the main character's name, Acolastus, which locates the particular nature of his sinfulness, indeed his very identity, in a classical text.[45] The name Acolastus is likely taken from Aristotle's *Nicomachean Ethics*, a modification of *acolastia* or prodigality.[46] In Aristotle's *Ethics,* prodigality is an extreme against which the virtue of liberality is defined. It is a very specific kind of sin or vice, having to do with ruining oneself through the spending or "wasting" of money. As Aristotle writes, "prodigality and meanness are excesses and defects with regard to wealth; and meanness we always impute to those who care more than they ought for wealth, but we sometimes apply the word 'prodigality' in a complex sense; for we call those men prodigals who are incontinent and spend money on self-indulgence. Hence also they are thought the poorest characters; for they combine more vices than one. Therefore the application of the word to them is not its proper use; for a 'prodigal' means a man who has a single evil quality, that of wasting his substance; since a prodigal is one who is being ruined by his own fault, and the wasting of substance is thought to be a sort of ruining of oneself, life being held to depend on possession of substance."[47] In linking the comedic scenes drawn from Terence—gaming, drinking, spending money on courtesans—with the sin of prodigality, the "wasting" and "ruining of oneself" in the *Ethics*, Gnapheus ensures that we see Acolastus in richly allusive terms drawn from the classical tradition. Indeed, the characters in the prodigal scenes, the parasites and courtesans, are not only drawn from Terence, they refer to Terence as an author, invoking the name of one of his characters, "Terence's Gnatho" (123/122; 121/120).[48]

Even more compelling is the way in which the name Acolastus marks its distance from the biblical parable from which this character was taken. At a certain point in the play, we learn that the son's name is not actually Acolastus. Acolastus tells his friend that he has been named "Acolastus" by his friend Philautus, that he has another "virtuous name [frugi nomine]" given by his father, a name that we never learn (107/106). Given that the son in the biblical parable is also nameless, this absent name of virtue recalls the biblical text: the character has replaced his biblical identity, of namelessness, with another, drawn from the classical tradition.

---

[45] Young notes that the play introduces a "prudential ethic" around prodigality that doesn't exactly fit with the biblical story, a morality organized around not wasting money (*English Prodigal Son Plays*, 24–25).

[46] See Atkinson's introduction to *Acolastus*, 52 and Young, *English Prodigal Son Plays*, 70–72.

[47] Aristotle, *The Nicomachean Ethics*, trans. David Ross, rev. Lesley Brown (Oxford: Oxford University Press, 2009), 60. Aristotle's account of prodigality is much shortened in a mid-sixteenth-century English translation. It nevertheless gives a sense of the prodigal as wasting money: a "Prodigall or a waster, is he that excedeth in geuyng & wanteth in receiuing" (*The ethiques of Aristotle, that is to saye, preceptes of good behauoute and perfighte honestie, now newly translated into English* (London, 1547), D7v, image 31.

[48] Sannio and Syrus are a pimp and his servant in *Acolastus*, named for a pimp and a servant in Terence's *Adelphoe [The Brothers]* (Terence, *Terence II: Phormio, the Mother-in-Law, the Brothers*, ed. and trans. John Barsby LCL 23 [Cambridge, MA: Harvard University Press, 2001], 2:253).

In invoking Aristotle and Terence, Gnapheus revises and alters the traditional approach to the prodigality of the prodigal son, as it had long been depicted in sermons, wall paintings, and biblical exegesis.[49] The character of Acolastus reifies prodigality as a specific kind of sin, having to do with riotous living, the wasting of money, and the embrace of classical texts, whereas in the earlier tradition prodigality is a placeholder for a lot of different kinds of sins, or sinfulness more generally. Indeed, it's worth pointing out that in the exegetical tradition, found in the influential writings of Ambrose and Jerome and then circulated in the *Glossa Ordinaria* (completed c. 1150), the massive medieval collection of biblical exegesis, the prodigal son is a universalized individual sinner, who confesses, does penance, and returns to God; or he represents the Gentiles, and their conversion narrative.[50] This quasi-institutional, penitential meaning is underlined in the link between the terms used in contemporary translations of the Bible and existing penitential discourses. In the Vulgate, the son wastes his money in "*vivendo luxuriose*," which is translated as "living riotously."[51] Both William Tyndale's New Testament (1534) and the Geneva Bible (1560) translate the phrase as "riotous living."[52] In its connection to the word, *luxuria*, the word "luxuriose" can and often does invoke the sin of lechery and therefore the familiar sin rubrics of the penitential tradition through which much morality, as in right and wrong behavior, was discussed during the Middle Ages.[53] "Riot" appears less often in the penitential tradition than forms of the word *luxuria*, but it is nevertheless often linked to an identifiably Christian morality, whether in sermons or in storytelling.[54] Riot is, for example, vividly described in Geoffrey Chaucer's *Pardoner's Tale* (c. 1395) in terms of "glotonye," "luxurie," "hasardrye," and "sweryng."[55] And yet, Gnapheus's play resists these associations between Acolastus's actions, when he has gone astray, and the established language of sin and virtue, the explicitly clerical or pastoral language of human behavior. Rather, Gnapheus wants to mark out a new area of sinfulness to go with a specifically textual kind of temptation.

---

[49] On the iconography of the prodigal son, see Young, *English Prodigal Son Plays*, 27–52. On the popularity of the story in this period, see Pietro Delcorno, *In the Mirror of the Prodigal Son: The Pastoral Uses of a Biblical Narrative (c. 1200–1550)* (Leiden: Brill, 2017), 18–98.

[50] The penitential meaning gained in importance during the late Middle Ages and into the Reformation. Sermons on the prodigal son were often preached in Lent, the season of Christian repentance. For the exegetical tradition, see Delcorno, *In the Mirror*, 18–98 and Stephen L. Wailes, *Medieval Allegories of Jesus' Parables* (Berkeley, CA: University of California Press, 1987), 236–45.

[51] Luke 15:13 in *The Vulgate Bible: Douay-Rheims Translation*, 6 vols., ed. Edgar Swift and Angela M. Kinney (Cambridge, MA: Harvard University Press, 2010–13), 6: 404–5.

[52] Luke 15:13 in *Tyndale's New Testament*, ed. David Daniell (New Haven, CT: Yale University Press, 1989), 117 and in *The Geneva Bible: a Facsimile of the 1560 Edition* (Madison, WI: University of Wisconsin Press, 1969), 36v of the New Testament.

[53] *MED*, s.v. "luxurie."

[54] *MED*, s.v. "riot."

[55] Geoffrey Chaucer, *Pardoner's Tale*, in *The Riverside Chaucer*, 3rd ed., ed. Larry D. Benson (Boston: Houghton Mifflin, 1987), 6.465, 6.484, 6.482, 6.590, 6.631.

HUMANIST MORAL FUSION: TERENCE AND THE PRODIGAL SON   81

As a result, Acolastus's prodigality consists not only of wrong actions, as in drinking and gaming and flirting, but a misdirected sense of right and wrong, or a bad philosophy. The bad crowd that he falls in with describe themselves as "philosophers," in a scene indebted to Terence's *Andria*.[56] Similarly, when Acolastus embraces his life of doing whatever he wants, he claims that "Philautus has taught me the whole system of moral philosophy, and I've got it letter-perfect [Postquam meus Philautus subiecit mihi boni et mali/ Rationes omnes, quas ad unguem teneo]" (129/128).[57] What distinguishes Acolastus from the prodigal son of the parable is that he has generated an alternative system of value, of "good and bad [boni et mali]." In this way, riotousness and disobedience, or material drawn from Terence's plays, appear both as a diversion from the right way, from the path associated with the father, and as an alternative and harmful morality organized around a perverted sense of right and wrong and of sinful self-love, as captured in his friend's name—Philautus. This alternative morality makes use of (and corrupts) familiar humanist commonplaces about heroic virtue. In flattering Acolastus, the Terentian characters praise Acolastus for being "cast in the heroic mould [forma heroic]" with his "manners [mores]," and other qualities demonstrating that he was "born to greatness [Magno te ortum loco arguunt]" (133/132). He has "virtues [virtutes]," which here mean gold. In this way, the play ensures that an implicitly classical idea of virtue is prodigal and, therefore, bad or wrong.

For Gnapheus, the problem is not that Acolastus wants to have fun or follow his own desires, it is that he has abandoned the right book, "the Book of the Law [bibliorum codex]," given to him by his father, "pater mihi relinquebat" and replaced it with the "precepts [praecepta]" "instilled [instillaro]" by Philautus (115/114). The association between prodigality and the seduction of classical learning is not entirely new to this play, although it is certainly much altered. For example, Jerome interpreted the seed pods the son eats, during his time away from his father, as "the songs of the poets, worldly wisdom, and rhetoric [carmina poetarum, saecularis sapientia, rhetoricum pompa verborum]."[58] And yet, part of the point of this parable for the homiletic tradition was that the prodigal's son's rebellion could be read as sinfulness more generally.

The alternative value, and therefore danger, of reading classical texts is represented not only as a temptation to fun (riotous living) but also as a temptation to despair. Comedy gives way to tragedy, when Acolastus, who has lost everything at dice, is stripped of his clothes and cast out. At this low moment, he fails to repent, fails to understand his own role, his own sinfulness. This failure of repentance is described in tragic terms, when Acolastus presents himself as a victim:

---

[56] In his introduction, Atkinson points out the similarities between the two plays (*Acolastus*, 33–37).

[57] Acolastus contrasts Philautus's "dicta" [advice] with his father's advice. Philautus's "dicta" have the same proverbial sound, even if wrong, as the kinds of sayings that would be associated with the right kind of biblical/ pious learning: "Fac tibi/ fidas" (124).

[58] Jerome quoted in Delcorno, *In the Mirror*, 28. Also noted by Helgerson, *Elizabethan Prodigals*, 55.

82 HUMANISM AND GOOD BOOKS IN SIXTEENTH-CENTURY ENGLAND

> I am so encompassed and cast down by circumstances that I know not where
> I am, nor where to go, nor where to begin. I am ruined, I am undone. I who
> was a wealthy monarch have suddenly become a penniless beggar

> [Tam multae res me circumsident Quae me afflictent male, ut, ubi sim, quo
> eam, rei Quid coeptem, nesciam. Perii, interii, miser. Ex rege nummato ampliter
> repente inops Mendicus?]" (179/178).

He underscores his helplessness in pagan terms, by referring to himself as an object
of the other forces, which surround him and afflict him ("me") and by appealing
both to Jupiter and to Nemesis. His second soliloquy, after he has been employed
by the farmer to herd pigs, goes over similar, pagan ground. He laments his
"harsh change of Fortune," details his misery, and contemplates death (189/188).
Although he does not name particular gods, he mentions "the gods," who "have
shown themselves so indifferent to my fate" (191/190). In this way, Acolastus's distance from his father is represented as the distance between a pagan understanding
of the world and a Christian one. Indeed, Acolastus's tragic focus on pagan gods
and fortune contrasts with an earlier speech made by the character Eubulus, which
begins by locating itself in the pagan world of Homer and "gods [deos]" but then
shifts to God, who is very much in charge of people on earth: "it is God alone
who determines how things will turn out [quando exitum future habet Deus in
sua unius manu]" (151/150).

At this point in the play, the literary resources of the classical tradition have
been harnessed to describe disobedience, or the path away from the father, and
the absence of a solution, in Acolastus's despair. Although tragedy interrupts Acolastus's riotous living, and it gives him a vocabulary for rejecting the world and its
temptations, it cannot return him to the father, and it cannot solve the problems
generated by the comedy: his loss of money, his hunger, his isolation. The solution is the return to the father, and a return to the language of repentance in the
parable. This is not only a physical or actual return to his father's house, but also
a return to his language. Gnapheus has associated the father, Pelargus, from the
beginning of the play not only with law, the "bibliorum codex," but also with sin
and repentance. In Pelargus's opening speech, he expresses his concern that his son
will "exchange freedom for bondage to sin" by "foolishly casting off the gentle sway
of his father [Neue seruus peccati euaserit ex libero,/ Patris imperium lene dum
male sanus abicit]" (95/94). Pelargus tells his friend Eubulus that he has warned his
son that "sudden decisions usually bring swift regret [Solent enim subita consilia
ducere/ Secum comitem praesentem paenitentiam]" (101/100). He also advises
his son that if the son lives according to the father's "moral principles" he will not
need to repent: "Fac uiuas moribus, ut qui paenitendum habent/ Nihil" (111/110).
These terms, sin and repentance, which are familiar from the Christian exegesis of

HUMANIST MORAL FUSION: TERENCE AND THE PRODIGAL SON   83

the parable, have been entirely absent during the scenes of Acolastus's prodigality and despair, in which he has specifically rejected penitence: "I shall never repent of treating myself with too much leniency [nulla ut hinc capiar paenitudeine/ Mei, ut mihi ignoscam]" (125/124). In his third soliloquy, however, Acolastus takes over his father's language. He has been lamenting his losses and his miserable existence in the first two soliloquies, and he turns, somewhat abruptly to self-castigation in his third: "Oh, I am tortured in so many ways by the rack of a bad conscience that nowhere can I find peace of mind [Sceleratae mentis carnificina, uah, quibus/ Me excruciate modis, ut nusquam sit locus]" (191/190). Acolastus now knows that what he has done is wrong, or criminal [sceleratus]. He sees before him his sins and feels the pains of hell: "Must I forever be haunted by the sins I have committed [An nunquam desinent oculis meis mala/ Mea et quae admisi turpiter]," and I am "now truly experiencing the torments of [hell] [experior inferos]" (193/192). He also abruptly asks about his father, suggesting that he regrets how he has acted: "what about my father, whom I have wronged in so many ways? [Tum quid dicam de patre, / In quem tot nominibus iniurius fui?]" (193/192). The penitential nature of his speech is perhaps more noticeable in Palsgrave's translation, which refers to his "sinful dedes" and his desire for "forgyueness."[59] At this point in the play, with this speech, Acolastus's pagan, classical story starts to become an identifiably Christian one, and the plot follows the parable until its close: Acolastus returns, and he is embraced by his father.

The play's solution, its abandonment of both comedy and tragedy in favor of repentance, draws our attention to the limits of its classical imitation. After all, Terence's comedies, and Roman comedies more generally, manage to solve the conflicts between sons and fathers without lamentations, repentance, or self-knowledge on the part of any characters, whereas Acolastus most definitely cannot. This same solution, effectively abandoning the classical tradition even while imitating it, seems to have resonated widely. It can even be found in texts that cannot be directly related to Acolastus or the Christian Terence tradition. Indeed, such ambivalence informs the exemplary humanist text mentioned in my introduction, Sir Thomas More's translation of the Life of Pico (1510), which is based on an Italian text of 1496–98. The Life of Pico is a biography of the famous Italian humanist Pico della Mirandola, and it anticipates Acolastus by both celebrating Pico's classicism and also mapping it onto a prodigal trajectory. Pico is clearly established from the outset as a model humanist, whose virtue is tied to his study of classical texts, the "excellent connyng [knowledge]" and "virtuous living" of the title.[60] And yet, classical learning also seems to lead Pico astray, to the same riotous living

---

[59] Gnapheus, The Comedy, 165.
[60] Pico della Mirandola, Here is conteyned the lyfe of Iohan Picus erle of Myrandula a grete lorde of Italy an excellent connynge man in all sciences, and verteous of lyuynge (London, 1525).

84 HUMANISM AND GOOD BOOKS IN SIXTEENTH-CENTURY ENGLAND

as Acolastus: women fall in love with him at least in part because of "his excellent learning," and, as a result, he "was somewhat fallen into wantonness."[61] Pico's prodigality is much briefer, lasting only a few sentences: "after that [the wantonness] ... he drew back his mind flowing in riot and turned to Christ."[62] The text nevertheless demonstrates the same kind of ambivalence about the moral resources of the classical legacy. The virtue Pico learns from all of his classical learning, from his "study of humanity," cannot remedy the sins that he experiences in his life. Although the *Life* fuses the virtue of the classical tradition with the sin and repentance of the penitential tradition, these languages do not overlap or occupy the same space. That is, they appear at different points of the text but not actually together.

Moral Fusion and Loss

In focusing on prodigality, or, rather, the repenting of prodigality, *Acolastus* and, to a certain degree, *The Life of Pico*, both offer a model or schema for negotiating the classical tradition, for recognizing it as a temptation that must be subordinated to Christian meanings and values. In framing the classical tradition within the parable, these works also offer something like an emotional map, a training in ambivalence and contradiction and, at least for *Acolastus*, for loss. The loss-orientation of this play is quite intense, and it reinforces the Christian sensibility of the play. Loss has, of course, long been considered a byproduct of classical imitation; this is the loss of Roman greatness, the rupture that Greene imagines in *The Light in Troy: Imitation and Discovery in Renaissance Poetry*. The desire to repair that loss is thought to drive the imitation of classical authors.[63] But Gnapheus does not mention the loss of the classical past, either in his opening letter or in the play proper. He does not meditate on ruins, as does Edmund Spenser, nor does he spend much time chiding others for not living up to the classical poets, as does Sir Philip Sidney.

It is also important to note that the intensity of loss is particular to the imitation of Terence, or the Christian Terence, and not to Terence's plays themselves. Terence's comedies do not dwell on the emotions of loss even when they are based around losses. They are, after all, comedies, and they focus their attention on the everyday conversations and actions of the characters and not so much on the tragic circumstances that have shaped those characters. Terence's *Andria* gives some important context, since Gnapheus drew upon it in writing *Acolastus*.[64] The

---

[61] Pico della Mirandola, *Lyfe*, A7v–B1r, image 7.
[62] Pico della Mirandola, *Lyfe*, B1r, image 7.
[63] Greene, *Light in Troy*, e.g. 3.
[64] In his introduction, Atkinson notes that both Terence's *Andria* and Gnapheus's *Acolastus* focus on recognition (*Acolastus*, 36).

plot of *Andria* is similarly motivated by a father's loss: in this case, a father's loss of his daughter that happens before the action of the play. Moreover, the play also includes a kind of reunion, when the father learns that he has found his daughter. And yet, loss and reunion are not central to the play, since neither of these events is portrayed. Instead, the play's action concerns a marriage plot in which a young man (Pamphilus) defies the alternative arrangements made by his father in order to marry the young woman (Glycerium) he loves. The recognition scene, in which another father, Chremes, learns of the existence of his long-lost daughter Passibula (the love interest, Glycerium) is not much concerned with Chremes's emotion about his lost daughter. When describing the separation, Chremes emphasizes that he has lost contact with his brother not his daughter: "Then fared [made his way] he to leave my daughter in this place and since that time I never heard of him till now [tum illam hic relinquere est veritus, post illa nunc primum audio quid illo sit factum]."[65] After discovering that his daughter is, in fact, alive, Chremes merely states, "to my daughter now will I go. Cryto come with me for I think that she now knows me not [Propero ad filiam. Eho mecum Crito. Nam illam me haud nosse credo]."[66] And that is that.

Such a matter-of-fact approach to loss does not seem to have escaped notice among readers in the sixteenth century. The sixteenth-century translator of the *Andria*, in *Terens in English*, acknowledges the absence of expected emotion in a long prologue of his own devising. In it, he describes the loss that motivates the play: Chremes's brother Phania brought Passibula/ Glycerium to the "isle of Andro" and

> Soon after this Phania there did die
> Then was Passibula left desolately
> Without any succor of all her friends.[67]

In this way, he ensures that the audience approaches the play with the emotions of loss, or "desolately," that are mainly lacking within it.

In *Acolastus*, Gnapheus uses the story of the prodigal son to imagine not only the loss of parents and children, as suggested in Terence's plays, but also a broader, literary loss: what is lost by imitating, what cannot be represented in the terms borrowed from classical texts, in comedy and tragedy or Horace's ideas of decorum, as described in the Epistle. The loss-orientation of *Acolastus* happens more at the level of plot than in specific passages; nevertheless, it is key to understanding the popularity and influence of this play: why readers and authors found this story so

---

[65] *Terens*, D4r. See also, *Terence in English*, 131. The Latin in *Terens in englysh* differs slightly from the Loeb edition.

[66] *Terens*, D4v; *Terence in English*, 133.

[67] *Terens*, A2r; *Terence in English*, 9. In her introduction, Twycross notes "The English prologue is much more expansive than the Latin summary" (*Terence in English*, 6).

86 HUMANISM AND GOOD BOOKS IN SIXTEENTH-CENTURY ENGLAND

compelling at this particular historical moment. The most obvious meaning of the parable of the prodigal son is not, in fact, his prodigality, but his loss and return. That the story is about loss is underlined in the biblical context: the parable follows two other, briefer parables, about the lost sheep and lost coin, or "groat," to use the word in Tyndale's translation.[68] And, loss is also apparent in the German tradition of both biblical exegesis and prodigal-son-plays: a German play contemporary with *Acolastus* is entitled *De Parabell vam vorlorn Szohn* (1527), the parable of the lost son.[69]

The parable's perspective on loss is taken over in the play and greatly expanded. The simple, material fact of loss in the parables—the sheep is gone; then the groat is gone; then the son is gone—becomes an intense, emotional state, even a trauma. The father's mind is constantly preoccupied with absence: "How great is the anxiety of a father for his absent son, my own experience teaches me. Because my child has been cut off from me I have not a moment's ease of mind, but in my imagination he stays constantly before my eyes [Parentis quanta sit sollicitudo erga absentem filium,/ Ex me disco. Gnatus quia abdicatus est dudum meus/ Non sustinet animus quiescere, quin is sedulo mihi/ Ob oculos, ob mentem uersetur]" (149/148). Moreover, the scenes in which Pelargus describes his anxiety are intermingled with the Terentian scenes of comedy, as if to underline that the loss of the son is the loss into Terentian comedy, the scenes that are "ob oculos," or always before his eyes. These feelings of loss are represented in the play as excessive and wrong. Eubulus, the wise councilor, spends much of the play trying to stop Pelargus from being so sad about his son's disappearance:

> Now all that remains is for me to go back to Pelargus, who sinfully persists in tormenting himself with grief. I know he is waiting, full of anxiety, until I return to his home
>
> [Quid restat, nisi Vt Pelargum repetam, qui curis se afflictat improbis. Nam me, scio, sollicitus expectat, dum ad se redeam domum] (191/190).

This brief scene consists only of this speech, and, immediately after it, Acolastus appears speaking of his own "torture," as quoted above. In this way, Gnapheus links Pelargus's anxiety about loss with Acolastus's despair, as "sinful" or "unreasonable," to borrow Palsgrave's translation.[70]

In addition, the play focuses as much, perhaps more, on the son's experience, representing his riot in terms of loss. In so doing, it introduces a trajectory of

---

[68] Luke 15:1–10 in *Tyndale's New Testament*, 171.
[69] See Burkardt Waldis, *De parabell vam vorlorn Szohn* (Riga, 1527); Herford, *Studies*, 89.
[70] Gnapheus, *The Comedy*, 164.

acquiring and losing that is not necessarily apparent in the parable: the son gets the money from the father, acquires friends, and then loses everything, even hope. The lamentations that precede the son's return to his father ensure that the audience understands the son's experience first as the loss of his material things, and second as the loss of his identity. In his first lament, he repeats the word "lost [periit]" three times in response to questions he poses to himself about his clothes, money, and gold necklace (178/179). In the second lament, he again mentions the loss of his "wealth, good name, friends, honor, what you will [rem, nomen, amicos, gloriam, quid non]" (189/188). Both of these perspectives on loss, the father's and the son's, represent the imitation of classical tradition, the Terentian comedy, as infused by loss. Classical imitation shows the distance the son has travelled from the father and the father's awareness of that distance.

Acolastus repents, returning to his father, as, for that matter, does Pico della Mirandola. The fathers, both literal and figurative, embrace them. And yet, pieces of their past lives remain unassimilated or unfused, as virtues that do not correspond to the penitential tradition or as worldly and emotional attachments, as anxieties and excessive sadness. From this perspective, the act of returning and repenting is darkened by a sense of incompletion. There is, in this way, a sense of incommensurability—of sons and fathers not matching up completely, of the inadequacy of the return. This sense of incommensurability is an important part of humanism, generated and reflected by the popular link between the classical tradition and the story of the prodigal son. The fact that these two traditions, the classical and the Christian, do not match up completely may have been immensely generative, inspiring authors to be innovative, disruptive, and even modern, but the gaps certainly also signaled what would or could be lost.

4

The Uses of Good Literature

Many early humanists, including, perhaps most famously, Erasmus of Rotterdam, were motivated by a desire to fuse classical texts with Christian values or into a Christian moral framework. Despite the pervasiveness of Erasmian fusion, notably in the Christian Terence tradition discussed in the previous chapter, humanism has more often been seen as freeing classical texts from Christianity by asserting their independence or as outlining a new secularism. The kind of independence, or quasi-secularism, that is typically associated with humanism is evident in a popular and influential text, Sir Thomas Elyot's educational treatise, *The Boke of the Governor* (1531). Elyot opens his treatise with a description of its contents—"sayenges of most noble autours (grekes and latynes)" as well as "myn own experience"—and he makes only the vaguest reference to Christian teachings and biblical stories.[1] Indeed, the independence of Elyot's text has been much remarked upon: for many scholars, he provides a "new secular ideal" for governance or a "secularized humanism."[2]

Such independence was generative for writers because it allowed them to think separately from Christianity in ways that are commonly recognized as new for this period.[3] At the same time, as is worth noting, this independence also allowed

---

[1] Sir Thomas Elyot, *A Critical Edition of Sir Thomas Elyot's The Boke Named the Governour*, ed. Donald W. Rude (New York: Garland Press, 1992), 5. Hereafter all references to this work will appear parenthetically. For the popularity of Elyot's treatise, see Robert Matz, *Defending Literature in Early Modern England: Renaissance Literary Theory in Social Context* (New York: Cambridge University Press, 2000), 25.

[2] Quotations from Arthur Ferguson, *The Articulate Citizen and the English Renaissance* (Durham, NC: Duke University Press, 1965), 148 and Matz, *Defending Literature*, 29, respectively. For the ongoing debate over humanist secularism, see the essays collected in *Interpretations of Renaissance Humanism*, ed. Angelo Mazzocco (Leiden: Brill, 2006); and Ada Palmer, "Humanist Lives of Classical Philosophers and the Idea of Renaissance Secularization: Virtue, Rhetoric, and the Orthodox Sources of Unbelief," *Renaissance Quarterly* 70.3 (2017): 935–976.

[3] The novelty and the strangeness of Elyot's treatise are worth emphasizing. Although he is writing in the Mirror for Princes tradition and using conventional ideas and examples, the resulting product is notable for its humanist insistence on classical texts, its attempts at practical utility, and its idiosyncratic propagandizing and self-promotion. About Elyot's debts to Erasmus and humanist ideas more generally, there is no doubt, but there is disagreement about the overall effect. One of the earliest accounts, that of Stanford Lehmberg, finds the organization "peculiar" (*Sir Thomas Elyot: Tudor Humanist* [Austin, TX: University of Texas Press, 1960], 36). Such skepticism about what exactly Elyot is doing in his treatise is echoed by Alistair Fox, who finds the text not at all "practical" (Alistair Fox and John Guy, *Reassessing the Henrician Age: Humanism, Politics and Reform, 1500–1550* [Oxford: Basil Blackwell, 1986], 25). Attempts to assign it some unity of purpose, first by John Major and more recently by Cathy Shrank and Greg Walker are not entirely convincing. Major locates the "unity" in the debts to Plato (*Sir Thomas Elyot and Renaissance Humanism* [Lincoln, NE: University of Nebraska Press, 1964], 4-7). Shrank argues that Elyot puts "love (*caritas*) at the core of his perception of how

---

Humanism and Good Books in Sixteenth-Century England. Katherine C. Little, Oxford University Press.
© Katherine C. Little (2023). DOI: 10.1093/oso/9780192883193.003.0005

authors to think against Christianity. It is this lesser known aspect of Elyot's so-called secularism, this oppositionality, that this chapter will address, arguing that Elyot turns the classical against the Christian, using it to contain and limit what was, during his time, conventional Christian morality.[4] Why Elyot would want to do so, that is, the motive for his oppositionality, can only be understood in terms of his immediate Reformation context: the political consequences of Erasmian ideas (or ideas associated with Erasmus) about Christian education in the first part of the sixteenth century.[5] This chapter will explore Erasmianism first through Erasmus's treatise *The Education of a Christian Prince* (1516), which Elyot used as a model, and then in the wider cultural context before turning to the response Elyot provides in his treatise.

Erasmus as Model

Erasmus dedicated his writings not only to championing the classical legacy as useful but also to exploring its resources in detail. Although he always insists on the ultimate primacy of Christianity—after all, the prince in the title of his famous treatise is being educated as a Christian—many of his discussions of *bonae litterae*, that is, the classical legacy, appreciate it on its own terms. His massively influential treatise, *The Education of a Christian Prince* (hereafter *ECP*) is, for example, a translation and adaptation of one classical text, by the ancient Greek philosopher Isocrates. In attending to the integrity of the text, Erasmus ensures that readers see its value as independent, to a certain degree, from familiar Christianized rubrics of Advice to Princes. As importantly, the *ECP* sets the classical and Christian traditions in parallel from the outset. Both the classical and the Christian are, for Erasmus, unified in their wisdom and can therefore be fused together, effectively as equals. Such an approach appears in his dedicatory letter to Prince Charles, in which he begins by praising wisdom, which is similarly available in Aristotle and Solomon: "Wisdom in itself is a wonderful thing, Charles greatest of princes, and no kind of wisdom is rated more excellent by Aristotle than that which teaches how

civilization operates and comes into being" ("Sir Thomas Elyot and the Bonds in Community," in *The Oxford Handbook of Tudor Literature, 1486-1603*, ed. Mike Pincombe and Shrank [Oxford: Oxford University Press, 2009], 160), a similar point to that made by Greg Walker, who argues that Elyot is interested in "reconciliation, tolerance, and healing" (*Writing under Tyranny: English Literature and the Henrician Reformation* [Oxford: Oxford University Press, 2005], 151).

[4] In noting the ideological effects of humanism, I've been influenced by Anthony Grafton and Lisa Jardine, *From Humanism to the Humanities: Education and the Liberal Arts in Fifteenth- and Sixteenth-Century Europe* (Cambridge, MA: Harvard University Press, 1986), 24.

[5] On Elyot's Erasmianism, see James McConica, who calls the *Boke* "a magisterial statement of the Erasmian educational and political programme" (*English Humanists and Reformation Politics under Henry VIII and Edward VI* [Oxford: Clarendon Press, 1965], 121). Erasmus's influence on Elyot and on humanism in England is well-documented. See Fritz Caspari, *Humanism and the Social Order in Tudor England* (Chicago: University of Chicago Press, 1954), 45-89; Fox and Guy, *Reassessing the Henrician Age*, 9-33; McConica, *English Humanists*, 13-43; and Joan Simon, *Education and Society in Tudor England* (Cambridge: Cambridge University Press, 1966), 102-23.

90 HUMANISM AND GOOD BOOKS IN SIXTEENTH-CENTURY ENGLAND

to be a beneficent prince ... This naturally is the wisdom so much to be desired by princes, the one gift which the young Solomon, highly intelligent as he was, prayed for, despising all else."[6]

Erasmus's attempts to harmonize the traditions by setting them in parallel are not entirely successful, and his treatise introduces contradictions between classical and Christian values.[7] After all, the closer one gets to the details of pagan, classical texts, the harder it is to harmonize them with a Christian value system. Given that the education Erasmus offers is political—education for a Christian prince—these contradictions take on an ideological valence. They threaten the idea of political unity around the prince of the title, even the idea of monarchy itself, by associating Christianity with a kind of anti-hierarchical sensibility, even egalitarianism. As Timothy Hampton notes in his persuasive account of this treatise, "In this [Erasmus's] model of history, Christians are implicitly equals; pagans live in hierarchies."[8]

From the very opening of his treatise, as in the dedicatory letter, Erasmus is concerned that the paganism found in classical texts might somehow interfere with the kind of lessons he desires to offer his readers by supporting tyranny instead of Christian rulership. He is careful to distinguish between the historical context for Isocrates and that of himself and Prince Charles: "[Isocrates] was a sophist, instructing some petty king or rather tyrant, and both were pagans; I am a theologian addressing a renowned and upright prince, Christians both of us" (ECP, 204). The assumption here is that Charles will not be a tyrant because he is Christian. This distinction between the political structures imagined by classical and those of Christian texts appears more forcefully in a direct address to the prince within the treatise: "Whenever you think of yourself as a prince, always remember the fact that you are a *Christian* prince! You should be as different from even the noble pagan princes as a Christian is from a pagan" (ECP, 216). Each of these statements contains an incipient egalitarianism: all Christians are the same when opposed to pagans, who are, however noble, susceptible to tyranny. Moreover, Christianity mitigates the problems associated with monarchy, namely abuses of power. Elsewhere he warns his readers that the terms describing rulership come

---

[6] Erasmus, *The Education of a Christian Prince* (ECP), trans. Neil M. Cheshire and Michael J. Heath in *Collected Works of Erasmus* (CWE), 84 vols. (Toronto: University of Toronto Press, 1974–), Vol. 27 (1986): 203.

[7] The contradictions or tensions between classical and Christian in Erasmus's writings have been much discussed. See Caspari, *Humanism and the Social Order*, 45–89; Fox, *Reassessing*, 28, 35–36; Richard F. Hardin, "The Literary Conventions of Erasmus' *Education of a Christian Prince*: Advice and Aphorism," *Renaissance Quarterly* 35 (1982): 151–163; Timothy Hampton, *Writing from History: The Rhetoric of Exemplarity in Renaissance Literature* (Ithaca, NY: Cornell University Press, 1989), 48–62; and Victoria Kahn, *Rhetoric, Prudence, and Skepticism in the Renaissance* (Ithaca, NY: Cornell University Press, 1985), 89–114. For an alternative viewpoint, which sees in Erasmus "an easy bridging of the gap between Christianity and pagan classicism," see James McConica, *English Humanists*, 34, and more fully 13–43.

[8] Hampton, *Writing from History*, 49, and on the *ECP* more fully, see 48–62.

from a non-Christian tradition: "Always bear in mind that the words 'dominion,' 'imperial authority' ... are pagan terms, not Christian; the 'imperial authority' of Christians is nothing other than administration, benefaction, and guardianship" (*ECP*, 233). Erasmus suggests that a Christian ruler is a kinder one: although a guardian or benefactor typically holds power over his ward or the recipient of his largesse, that power remains implicit and is subordinated to the idea of care. If "dominion" might or might not involve abuse, "benefaction" cannot by definition include it.

It is worth emphasizing that Erasmus's treatise unsettles ideas about the monarchy by attending to the difference between classical and Christian rulership in a genre that traditionally not only links classical and Christian together but also subordinates the classical to the Christian. The genre of Mirror for Princes, or Advice to Princes, that Erasmus inherits is a long and varied literary tradition, and yet is fairly unified in its approach to the classical legacy.[9] Indeed, the most obvious characteristic of Mirrors for Princes is fusion: these texts translate and expound the classical legacy for Christian rulers, as "incitements and inducements to virtue," as John of Salisbury writes in his Prologue to the *Policraticus* (c. 1159).[10] The medieval mode of fusion is not, however, typically the same as Erasmus's— of parallels and harmonizing—but is rather one of subordination and hierarchy, along the lines of the medieval classicism discussed in Chapter 1. All of the stories, whatever their provenance, are subordinated to their lessons; all of the readers are subordinated to the monarch. John Lydgate's early fifteenth-century poem, *The Fall of Princes* offers a representative example of this approach in a familiar passage:

> Olde exaumples off pryncis that haue fall,
> Ther remembraunce off newe brouht to mynde,
> May been a merour to estatis all,
> How thei in vertu shal remedies fynde
> Teschewe vices ...

> [Ancient stories of princes that have fallen, their remembrance
> newly brought to mind, may be a mirror to all estates, how they
> shall find remedies in virtue to avoid vices].[11]

---

[9] The scholarship on medieval Advice to Princes is fairly extensive. For a recent overview of this genre, see Matthew Giancarlo, "Mirror, Mirror: Princely Hermeneutics, Practical Constitutionalism, and the Genres of the English *Fürstenspiegel*," *Exemplaria* 27.1–2 (2015), 35–54. Elyot's debts to the medieval tradition are recognized but not extensively discussed. See Major, *Sir Thomas Elyot*, 39–43 and Walker, *Writing under Tyranny*, 167–77. Walker is convincing in arguing that Elyot is interested in approaching political concerns in terms of "personal morality," an interest he shares with medieval authors (169).

[10] John of Salisbury, *John of Salisbury: Policraticus*, ed. and trans. Cary J. Nederman (Cambridge: Cambridge University Press, 1990), 3.

[11] John Lydgate, *The Fall of Princes*, ed. Henry Bergen, 4 vols. (London: Oxford University Press, 1924–27), Part 1: Bk 2.22–26. Further references will appear parenthetically. Derek Pearsall's brief

92 HUMANISM AND GOOD BOOKS IN SIXTEENTH-CENTURY ENGLAND

Classical and Christian stories about rulers are here unified as "olde exaumples," and they are harnessed to a familiar Christian, moral discourse of virtues and vices. Similarly, all of the readers are made subject to the prince: they are reading a book intended for princes, modelling themselves after the princes, and being reminded that they belong to particular social classes, in the "estatis."

In introducing a contradiction between classical and Christian ideas of ruler-ship, between classical and Christian behaviors, between beneficent and tyranni-cal, Erasmus invents a position from which a reader could potentially question the monarchy itself. Is inherited monarchy the best political structure for Christians? What if the monarch is similar to a pagan tyrant? Erasmus's title even implies that a prince is not necessarily going to act in a Christian manner but needs to be trained to do so. Indeed, a Christian education appears throughout as a kind of remedy for monarchy. Given that in a monarchy people are stuck with the ruler they get, it is best to educate him as well as one can: "But when the prince is born to office, not elected ... then the main hope of getting a good prince hangs on his proper education, which should be managed all the more attentively, so that what has been lost with the right to vote is made up for by the care given to his upbringing" (*ECP*, 206). To be sure, Erasmus, who is critical of monarchy, ends up supporting it—both by directing his text to the Prince and openly praising him. Nevertheless, his distinctions and refinements call into question the presumed naturalness or inevitability of the monarchy. For Erasmus, greater appreciation for the classical tradition produces a finer sense of what Christianity requires of the powerful.

The Erasmian Reformation Context

Erasmus' *ECP* associates Christian behavior with a kind of anti-hierarchical sen-sibility, even egalitarianism, in a manner that is largely implicit and therefore theoretical. Nowhere does Erasmus openly advocate for overthrowing the monar-chy or even for modifying the status quo. Yet, the associations he generates in this educational treatise, between specifically Christian behavior and the ques-tioning of hierarchy, resonated with the calls for access to scripture in his other writings and in the Reformation context more generally. That is, calls for access to scripture could, in the early sixteenth-century, take on social and political ramifi-cations.[12] While Erasmus avoids making any direct connections (and would likely oppose such connections), between access to scripture, on the one hand, and the dismantling of political hierarchy or other kinds of social change, on the other, some of his contemporaries did make those connections. Indeed, views about access to scripture that were very similar to Erasmus's sometimes accompanied

account of the poem and its sources is still useful: *The Routledge History of English Poetry: Volume 1: Old English and Middle English Poetry* (London: Routledge & Kegan Paul, 1977), 230–33.

[12] That humanism could be politically radical, or at least more radical than had been previously assumed, is argued by David Norbrook around Sir Thomas More's *Utopia* in *Poetry and Politics in the English Renaissance* (London: Routledge, 1984), 18–31.

THE USES OF GOOD LITERATURE   93

broader anti-hierarchical sentiments in the Radical Reformation, a term now used to describe Protestant groups, such as the Anabaptists, who desired to abandon or alter established social and political structures. While such a link, between access to scripture and anti-hierarchy or egalitarianism, was certainly not widely shared, it nevertheless seemed to have captured the imaginations of those who feared social unrest, as I shall demonstrate here.[13] In this heated context, traditional aspects of Christian morality, even quite conventional precepts, shifted in meaning and value, at times taking on the sense of political radicalization. This context is vital for understanding Elyot's treatise, and it will be the subject of this section.[14]

During the Reformation, reading the Bible was often described using anti-hierarchical and egalitarian language. It is true that this language is not directly connected to the world outside the text, to actual social hierarchies; Protestants, for the most part, did not abandon hierarchical forms of living or participating in the church. It is also true that reformers were not consistent in their approach, in that they generated other kinds of controls over reading, as made apparent in James Simpson's *Burning to Read: English Fundamentalism and its Reformation Opponents*.[15] There is, nevertheless, a notable rhetoric of inclusiveness and boundary-breaking when it comes to describing access to scripture. Perhaps the most famous instance technically pre-dates the Reformation; it is the much-cited passage in Erasmus's *Paraclesis* (1516), an essay written as a preface to his translation of the New Testament. This treatise circulated independently in England, where it was translated into English by William Roye and printed in 1529, in what appears to be a reforming context, that is, alongside Martin Luther's commentary on 1 Corinthians 7. It is in this text that one finds Erasmus's comments on workers reading the Bible: "I wold to god the plowman wold singe a texte of the scripture at his plowbeme. And that the wever at his lowme with this [the scripture] wold drive away the tediousnes of time."[16] Such a desire assumes that the Bible (and reading it) belongs as much to the plowman and weaver as to the clergy, or to anyone else. To view the Bible in this way is to break down the boundary between those who

[13] One cannot speak of the Reformation as a uniform and homogeneous set of ideas about religious belief and practice or, indeed, about the social and political world. Recently scholars have emphasized the flexibility and fluidity of this period. See the essays collected in *The Beginnings of English Protestantism*, ed. Peter Marshall and Alec Ryrie (Cambridge: Cambridge University Press, 2002). Ethan Shagan also notes both the variety of religious positions and the fact that humanism supported all of them in *Popular Politics and the English Reformation* (Cambridge: Cambridge University Press, 2003), 45.

[14] On the tensions around communism, communal access to scripture, and communal property in Erasmus and Elyot, see David Weil Baker *Divulging Utopia: Radical Humanism in Sixteenth-Century England* (Amherst, MA: University of Massachusetts Press, 1999), 9–10, 22–47, 76–105.

[15] James Simpson, *Burning to Read: English Fundamentalism and its Reformation Opponents* (Cambridge, MA: Belknap Press of Harvard University Press, 2007).

[16] *An exhortation to the diligent studye of scripture, made by Erasmus Roterodamus. And translated in to inglissh* (London: 1529) STC 10493, image 6. The original text is unpaginated; hence the electronic image number. References will appear hereafter parenthetically.

94   HUMANISM AND GOOD BOOKS IN SIXTEENTH-CENTURY ENGLAND

can read and those who cannot. This was at the time not only a spiritual bound-ary, between laity and clergy, but also a social one, which Erasmus underlines by including a plowman, the typical representative of the third estate. While the singing implies that the reading the Bible is fun, a kind of pastime, elsewhere Erasmus makes clear that he is, in fact, concerned with education. At the very opening of the *Paraclesis*, he writes, "I exhorte and entyse *all mortall men* vnto the most holye and holsome studye of Christian wisdome and pure Philosophye" (2, my emphasis). Claims for an egalitarianism of readers appear throughout this treatise in the frequent use of some version of the phrase "all men" (2, 3, 5, 12), "equally" (12), and "common" (5-6) in relation to scripture.

The language of egalitarianism, at least vis-à-vis reading the Bible, was taken up and popularized by reformers everywhere, including in England. William Tyndale, perhaps the most famous advocate for an English Bible, is assigned an Erasmian speech about a ploughboy in *The Acts and Monuments* (1563) of John Foxe: "I defie the Pope and all his lawes, and sayde, if God spare my lyfe ere many yeares, I wyl cause a boye that dryueth þe plough, shall knowe more of the scripture then thou doest."[17] Tyndale may not have actually made this speech, but related statements can be found in what he wrote during his lifetime. In the preface to his treatise, *A path way into the holy scripture* (1536?) Tyndale describes his demand for "every man's" access to scripture: "I do marueyle [wonder] greatly derely beloued in Christ that euer any man shulde repugne [resist] or speke agaynst [the idea that] the scrypture to be hadde [should be available] in euery language and that of euery man."[18] Like Erasmus, Tyndale understands access to the Bible as breaking down boundaries and ending divisions; he is less interested in classical learning than Erasmus, but similarly attuned to the end of clerical dominance. He writes, "In this poynte are the enemyes of Jesu Christ greatly to be reproued which say that the laye people and worldly (for so they call them) ought nat to rede the holy scripture nor for to commen of [discuss] the worde of god as who sayth Christ spake to clerkes [priests] only and shewed them onely the secretes of his father and nat to the vulgare and commen laye people" (49/F8v). The distinction between clergy and laity certainly invokes the social world outside the text, as Tyndale emphasizes with the words "vulgar" and "common." The openness of scripture is therefore imagined in politically resonant terms.

Tyndale, like Erasmus, scrupulously avoids direct discussion of the political effects of open access to the Bible. For this reason, scholars have been interested in distancing him from social radicalism, and they tend to invoke his defense of the

---

[17] John Foxe, *The Unabridged Acts and Monuments Online* [TAMO] (1563 edition) (HRI Online Publications, Sheffield, 2011), 570, http://www.johnfoxe.org. Also quoted in David Daniell, *William Tyndale: A Biography* (New Haven, CT: Yale University Press, 2001), 1, 83. Daniell describes Tyndale's debts to Erasmus, 59–74.

[18] William Tyndale, *A path way into the holy scripture* (London, 1536) STC 24462, A2r/1; electronic image number/ folio number. Hereafter references will appear parenthetically.

political status quo or monarchy in his treatise *On the Obedience of the Christian Man* (1528).[19] It would be a mistake, however, to minimize the threat to hierarchy that others found in such writings. Despite the many assurances made by Tyndale and his contemporaries of their belief in social order and obedience, the perception at the time was that reading the Bible might in fact have disruptive political consequences and even that Erasmus himself was the source of dangerous ideas. One of Henry VIII's ministers, Stephen Gardiner, accused Erasmus of such disruptions in 1547, describing his *Paraphrases*, as "'able to minister occasion to evil men to subvert, with religion, the policy and order of the realm,' by reason of misinterpretation of Scripture on the state of princes."[20]

The connection between some Christian behaviors, such as Bible-reading, and challenges to social and political hierarchy, even egalitarianism, was familiar enough to cause concern, and fear of a particularly Christian social disorder pervades the writing of this time.[21] The same kind of language about reading scripture, used by Erasmus and Tyndale, could be politically directed to attack established institutions of property and government, as apparent in the rhetoric surrounding the German Peasant War of 1524–25 or in the writings of the Anabaptists, a radical sect of Protestants.[22] Whether or not these groups actually practiced social and political egalitarianism or even believed in it is almost irrelevant. Hostile commentators grouped these two kinds of egalitarianism together. For example, in a treatise printed in 1545, John Bale indicates that Anabaptists are marked by their simultaneous collectivism or egalitarianism and their access to the Bible. He concludes a list of the Anabaptists' social beliefs, including "They would have all mens goods in common," with an exclamation about their religious beliefs that almost suggests admiration: "Marry in deed a zeal they have unto the Gospel."[23] Bale's treatise makes clear the way in which various meanings of common, as the vernacular, as the people, as the lower class, and as communication itself, can be conflated.

It may, in the twenty-first century, be easy to distinguish between radical reformers, including the Anabaptists, and their more socially conservative contem-

---

[19] Such a perspective is well-established; see William Clebsch, *England's Earliest Protestants 1520–1535* (New Haven, CT: Yale University Press, 1964), 146–50; and Daniell, *William Tyndale*, 223–49. Thomas Betteridge suggests one of the ways in which scholars have underestimated what I'm calling Tyndale's potential egalitarianism; he links Tyndale's ideas about scriptural access to the Lollards in "William Tyndale and Religious Debate," *Journal of Medieval and Early Modern Studies* 40 (2010): 439–61.

[20] A.G. Dickens and Whitney R. D. Jones, *Erasmus the Reformer* (London: Mandarin Paperbacks, 1995), 75.

[21] Helen C. White, *Social Criticism in Popular Religious Literature of the Sixteenth Century* (New York: The Macmillan Company, 1944), 125. Erasmus was notable for changing his mind: "Before the Reformation broke loose Erasmus had freely stressed that learning confers nobility of mind and character, that this could be acquired by the ordinary man ... But the uprisings in Germany burned deeply into men's minds and the post-Reformation Erasmus proclaimed that princely tyranny was preferable by far to anarchy" (Simon, *Education and Society*, 153).

[22] In the sixteenth century, the Anabaptists and radical reformers were often associated with some form of communism, see White, *Social Criticism*, 120–27; Ferguson, *Articulate Citizen*, 269–70.

[23] John Bale, *A mysterye of inyquyte contayned within the heretycall genealogye of Ponce Pantolabus* (London, 1545) STC 1303, image 61.

96 HUMANISM AND GOOD BOOKS IN SIXTEENTH-CENTURY ENGLAND

poraries, but such distinctions were only just becoming necessary and therefore articulable in the first part of the sixteenth century. In a sermon preached at St. Paul's Cross in 1521 and then printed in 1526, Bishop John Fisher gives a long and detailed account of the dangers of Martin Luther, including the way in which Luther's "mischievous doctrine" has led to "the subversion of that country ... by insurrections among themselves: whereby many piles [buildings], many castles, many strong fortresses have been overthrown."[24] Although Fisher is primarily concerned with identifying heresy and not so much with supporting monarchy or private property, his sermon nevertheless indicates that many in the sixteenth-century associated scripture-reading with politics, with abolishing the hierarchy of kings and governors. Such a perspective also informs Henry VIII's letter in 1530, in which he "announced that he feared the devastating potential of erroneous books to 'perverte and corrupte' the opinions of 'our people,' leading to 'division, contention and debate, in the cheif and principall pointes and articles of our faithe and religion' that could bring about 'the dissolution of our common wealthe' through 'totall confusion and destruction.'"[25] Even those who wanted to defend Bible-reading from charges of social radicalism gave a sense that the two activities had become linked. In Sir Richard Morison's treatise, *A Remedy for Sedition* (1536), which is not, for the most part, concerned with religious dissent, he opines that "If our byshops had done so, we shuld haue sene that preachyng of the gospell, is not the cause of sedition, but rather lacke of preachyng of it."[26] In forestalling the causal link between the Bible and sedition, he certainly suggests that this link is the subject of discussion. These musings on social disorder tend to leave the precise nature of that disorder ambiguous, but there can be no question that the "confusion" and "subversion" concern threats to social and political hierarchy, that they link access to scripture with resistance to established political hierarchy and some form of egalitarianism.

Classical v. Christian in Elyot's *Boke*

When Thomas Elyot wrote his educational treatise, the *Boke of the Governor*, in the first part of the sixteenth century, he was taking up and popularizing Erasmus's humanist educational program, the *bonae litterae* that Erasmus had come to represent. He was also, and importantly, responding to the context in which

---

[24] John Fisher, *A sermon had at Paulis* (London, 1526) STC 10892, H2v. See also *English Works of John Fisher, Bishop of Rochester: Sermons and Other Writings 1520 to 1535*, ed. Cecilia A. Hatt (Oxford: Oxford University Press, 2002), 48–144.

[25] Susan Wabuda, "'A day after doomsday': Cranmer and the Bible Translations of the 1530s," in *The Oxford Handbook of the Bible in Early Modern England, c. 1530–1700*, ed. Kevin Killeen, Helen Smith, and Rachel Willie (Oxford: Oxford University Press, 2015), 30. See further 30–35.

[26] Sir Richard Morison, *A remedy for sedition vvherin are conteyned many thynges, concernyng the true and loyall obeysance, that commens owe vnto their prince and soueraygne lorde the Kynge* (London, 1536) STC (2nd ed.) / 18113.7 E3r, image 19.

Erasmus's treatises and Erasmianism were being read, Reformation debates over access to scripture. Or, to put it more bluntly, Elyot approached humanist education at least in part through the fear articulated by Henry VIII in 1530: social disorder among the people, fed at least in part by books, and their potentially egalitarian messages, threatened the commonwealth. As Elyot writes, "where all thynge is commune, there lacketh ordre: and where ordre lackethe, there all thynge is odiouse, and uncomly" (*Boke*, 19).[27] From this perspective, Elyot's most obvious change to Erasmus's model is also the most telling. His treatise is directed at a new audience, "governors," instead of the prince himself. In other words, the prince does not so much need advice, or the performance of advice, as he needs people to help him keep order, and Elyot's treatise is therefore intended to help create that governing class.

Under such disruptive circumstances, when the language of Christian conduct had become so potentially incendiary, classical texts gained a new ideological usefulness, one that Elyot is interested in exploiting. That new usefulness is their independence from traditions for describing the monarchy, the "old examples" that Lydgate mentions, their independence from the older language of vice and virtue and of human behavior more generally, to which all Christians are equally subjected, no matter their rank, or "estate." Although the goal of Elyot's advice treatise is broadly similar to Erasmus's and even to the medieval tradition of Mirrors for Princes—to support the monarchy—that support is found less in making the best of it, as Erasmus did, or asserting its rightness and universality, as did the medieval traditions, than in shoring it up, actively protecting it from threats. That shoring up means, for Elyot, containing and limiting some of the traditional Christian moral language—especially about virtue—that had, in the new circumstances, taken on radical, or at least disruptive, associations. It is for this reason that Elyot's treatise appears more "pagan" than its forerunners, as indicated in an early study by Stanford Lehmberg.[28] In other words, the "secularized humanism" that Elyot offers is not inevitable, especially given the Erasmian model he used, which is not secular at all; it is, instead, an ideological choice.[29] His shift to secularism, or away from Christian moralizing, is apparent both in terms of the content, since there are many more examples from the classical tradition than stories from the Bible, and in the approach to those stories. Where Erasmus explicitly asserts the harmony of these traditions even as he distinguishes between them, Elyot further disentangles them, assigning the classical tradition a greater independence, and, in some cases, pitting classical against Christian morality.

---

[27] Previous scholars have tended to understand Elyot's aversion to communism primarily as a response to Sir Thomas More's *Utopia*. See, for example, Baker, *Divulging Utopia*, 76–105; Pearl Hogrefe, *The Life and Times of Sir Thomas Elyot, Englishman* (Ames, IA: Iowa State University Press, 1967), 119; and, at great length, Major, *Sir Thomas Elyot*, 109–39.

[28] Lehmberg, *Sir Thomas Elyot*, 77.

[29] Matz, *Defending Literature*, 29. Although scholars accept that Elyot's text is Erasmian, no one has accounted for why Elyot so completely abandons Erasmus's Christianity.

98   HUMANISM AND GOOD BOOKS IN SIXTEENTH-CENTURY ENGLAND

At the center of Elyot's treatise, and, therefore, what is motivating his treatise is the new, distinct class status of the nobility. Whereas Erasmus directed *bonae litterae* to the figure of the prince and to other readers only in relation to that prince, Elyot makes *bonae litterae* the sign of the nobility newly imagined, in service to the king, using the classical legacy to define the behaviors required of this new nobility, to shape them in their role as governors. The hierarchy described in Erasmus's text—the actual monarchy it addresses and what one might call the moral or textual monarchy, of readers modelling themselves after the prince—is thus rewritten to describe another kind of hierarchy, a class of people who gain their special status because of their relationship to the king.

Education, and the virtue it generates, is in a very Erasmian way, the basis of the authority that the nobility have over the people in Elyot's account of the new social order. In this way nobility are given a new identity, a link with the monarch, through their similar educations, as opposed to, say, a link through military service or lineage or custom.[30] Elyot begins his text by imagining that link, the way in which governors become agents of the king: "Sens [since] one mortall man can nat have knowlege of all thynges done in a realme or large dominion, and at one tyme discusse all controversies, refourme all transgressions, and exploite all consultations, concluded as well for outwarde, as inwarde affaires: it is expedient and also needful [necessary], that under the capitall governour be sondry meane authorities, as it were aydyng hym in the distribution of justice in sondry partes of a huge multitude" (*Boke*, 27). These governors, whether the lower (mean) or higher (capital), all share their authority because of education: "I intend to write of *theyr education* and *vertue* in maners, whiche they have in *commune with princes*, in as moche as therby they shall as well by example, as by authoritie ordre well them, which by theyr capitall governour, shall be to theyr rule committed (*Boke*, 27–28, my emphases). In this scheme, each governor serves as an example to those under him, in a manner similar to the monarch in the older, medieval and Erasmian, versions of the Mirror for Princes. The shared education distinguishes the king, or princes, and the governors, on the one hand, from the common people, on the other. Education in classical texts becomes in this system, as has been recognized, a form of "cultural capital."[31] But not only that. Education is a source of virtue, which will also distinguish the nobility from the people. Indeed, it is worth noting that the new identity of the nobility comes at a cost to the people: the word

---

[30] There is general agreement that educating the nobility in the classics was an idea new to the sixteenth-century, and that it had its roots in humanist thinking and writing. See, for example, Caspari, *Humanism and the Social Order*, 145–209; Maria Dowling, *Humanism in the Age of Henry VIII* (London: Croom Helm, 1986), 111–90; Ian Green, *Humanism and Protestantism in Early Modern English Education* (Burlington, VT: Ashgate, 2009), 57, 76; J. H. Hexter, "The Education of the Aristocracy in the Renaissance," *Journal of Modern History* 22 (1950): 1–20; Simon, *Education and Society*, 59–101.

[31] See, for example, Richard Halpern, *The Poetics of Primitive Accumulation: English Renaissance Culture and the Genealogy of Capital* (Ithaca, NY: Cornell University Press, 1991), 15 and Matz, *Defending Literature*, 4–8.

"common" that is used to refer to the king and the nobility both evokes and exiles the people from this newly imagined social order.

Elyot uses the classical legacy, or an education in classical texts, not only to define the nobility as a class in service to the king, but also to moralize this class position, to associate their higher rank with virtue, or "noble vertues." In this way, he reifies and standardizes virtue, engaging in a kind of class essentialism.[32] Nobility was, of course, a contested term in the pre-modern period, because it is at once an idea, and therefore immaterial, and, at the same time, a very material socioeconomic status. In its immateriality, as a virtue, the idea of nobility has the potential to slip away from its socio-economic markers. A compelling account of such slippage can be found in Chaucer's *Wife of Bath's Tale*, which makes use of Dante's *Convivio*.[33] The Wife claims not once but three times that "gentilesse [nobility]" comes from God and is not "descended out of old richesse [riches]," and she is very specific about the way in which that "gentilesse [nobility]" can subvert established estates.[34] The man who does not do "gentil dedes [noble deeds]" is "nat gentil, be he duc or erl/ For vileyns synful dedes make a cherl [not noble, whether he is a duke or earl because a peasant's sinful deeds make him a peasant]."[35] Such a perspective is not exactly politically egalitarian, since it does not advocate altering the social order because some dukes are sinful and some peasants noble. It is, nevertheless, somewhat aligned with a Christian egalitarianism, of all people equally capable of nobility to the extent that all follow God (or are led by him) in graces. One sees a similar approach in Lydgate's poem, *The Fall of Princes*, in which all estates are supposed to look in the mirror of the book and then apply the vices and virtues to themselves. In other words, moral language applies equally to everyone in the limited context of reading that poem.

Elyot takes the idea of nobility, as a virtue that can be independent of social class, and ensures that it does in fact describe social class, that it is a kind of thing that one can have. In a chapter dedicated to the topic "What very [true] nobilitie is," he identifies the error of those who "thinke that nobilitie may in no wyse be but onely wher men can avaunte them [boast] of auncient lignage, an auncient robe, or great possessions" (*Boke*, 121). Such a statement suggests that he locates nobility on the inside, in the "wisedome and vertue" (122) that he identifies in his exemplary figure, Numa Pompilius, an ancient Roman king (on which more below). That this is largely a definition by negatives, what nobility is not, is only

---

[32] Although earlier readers noted Elyot's "aristocratic bias," they tended to understand his views on nobility as generally humanist in nature (Hogrefe, *Life and Times*, 146; Major, *Sir Thomas Elyot*, 49, 23–28). In contrast, Matz describes Elyot as having "an essentialist vision of class," rooted in a love of objects, a perspective with which I'd agree (*Defending Literature*, 54).

[33] Dante Aligheri, *Dante's Convivio*, trans. William Walrond Jackson (Oxford: Clarendon Press, 1909), 190–93.

[34] Geoffrey Chaucer, *The Wife of Bath's Tale*, in *The Riverside Chaucer*, 3rd ed., ed. Larry D. Benson (Boston: Houghton Mifflin, 1987), 3.1117, 3.1129–30, 3.1162, 3.1110.

[35] Chaucer, *Wife of Bath's Tale*, 3.1155, 1157–58.

part of the problem. Elyot wants to preserve the nobility as a real, social class, and he ends up stating that the "ancient robe" itself does confer nobility, only not exactly in the way that it had before, as an external marker. He does so by making it a marker of something internal: "If he have an auncient robe lefte by his auncetor [ancestor]: Let him consider, that if the first owner were of more vertue than he is that succedeth [follows], the robe being worne, it minissheth [lessens] his prayse, to them whiche knowe or have herde of the vertue of him that first owed [owned] it" (*Boke*, 121). The robe mediates between inner and outer in precisely the way that Elyot needs. It is a possession that already belongs to the nobility, a marker of an external class status, but it also provides inner virtue, as a reminder of the virtue of the ancestors.

A nobility that is both a possession (a thing one can have) and an internal identity (virtues) is, of course, not a robe, but a classical education. Instruction in classical texts affects the interior, according to a foundational humanist belief, and, if it is preserved for an already existing group, it ensures that the group, and only that group, can claim "true nobility." Elyot makes this claim explicit early in his text, after his chapters on what texts are best for educating the young: Aesop, Homer, Virgil, Lucan (Chapter 10); Livy, Sallust, Cicero, and others (Chapter 11). He writes, "And here I make an ende of the lernynge and studie wherby noble men may attayne to be worthy to have autoritie in a publike weale" (*Boke*, 54). This claim indicates the role of these texts in shaping the inner virtues that are typically described as noble, and which he here calls "worthy." It also indicates that those virtues have a real, material existence, in the public role that nobility will play, in their authority in the public weal. In this way, classical learning will become the new sign of class status, replacing the lineage, ancient robe, and possessions.

In reimagining the nobility around and through their classical education, Elyot alters the ways in which social order can be imagined and described. He implicitly redefines the role of the clergy, who were traditionally the keepers of the classical legacy, and they are, as a result, mentioned only infrequently. More interestingly, Elyot revises the role of the people, those who are going to be governed by this new and newly educated class, by erasing them. This erasure is made possible by the classically based conceptualizations of social order that Elyot invokes. For example, in his discussion of the body politic, Elyot writes that "inferior governours ... be named of Aristotel his [the prince's] eies, eares, handes, and legges" (*Boke*, 28). While the body is a popular metaphor for a political entity, Elyot's version is quite distinctive. In it, he underlines that the prince and his governors are the same person, as they are in serving as examples to those below them, and he demonstrates that the body politic now consists entirely of those in power. The people are nowhere to be found; perhaps they are implicitly the trunk with the prince the head, but that is not clear from the metaphor.

The image of the body politic, as it appears in any number of late medieval and humanist texts, is typically (and frequently) used to imagine the place of the people

THE USES OF GOOD LITERATURE   101

in relation to other classes. That is, the lower parts of the body are the people, and
they are necessary for the functioning of the body. For example, in *ECP*, Erasmus
writes, "the prince's authority over a people is the same as that of the mind over
the body. The mind has control over the body because it is wiser than the body,
but its control is exercised for the advantage of the body" (233); or "the state is a
kind of body composed of different parts" (237); or "Let him think of his kingdom
as being like some great body of which he himself is a vital part" (254). Similarly,
in his *Fall*, Lydgate compares the prince to the head and the commons to the feet
and legs:

> Hed, armys, bodi, and ther fressh visages,
> Withoute feet or leggis may nat vaile
> To stonde vpriht; for needis thei mut faile.
> And semblabli subiectis in comountees
> Reise up the noblesse off pryncis in ther sees

[Head, arms, body, and their fresh faces cannot stand upright without feet or
legs. Similarly, subjects in communities raise up the nobility of princes on their
thrones] (2.829–33).[36]

In each of these instances the tradition of imagining the monarch is always also
a tradition of imagining the people, however minimal or limited the social and
political role of the people might be. Such an ideology is usefully described by the
term "monarcho-populism," which was coined by James Holstun to describe the
alliance between small landholders and a centralized monarchy.[37] Even when the
metaphor of the body politic is used in a clearly repressive manner, as in the treatise
against sedition by Sir Richard Morison, it reminds readers that all classes are parts
of the body: "A comune welthe is lyke a body, and soo lyke, that it can be resembled
to nothyng so conuenient, as vnto that. Nowe, were it not by your faythe a madde
herynge, [crazy thing to hear], if the fote shuld say, I wyl weare a cappe, with an
ouche [brooch], as the heade dothe."[38] In Morison's view, the idea of the lower
classes' demanding power is ridiculous—a foot wearing a cap!—but their claims
are also thinkable and representable,

Not all accounts of monarchy or hierarchy are the same, and if monarcho-
populism describes earlier perspectives, such as Lydgate's, and potentially
Erasmus's, it does not describe Elyot's. Elyot's text certainly supports both

---

[36] On this passage and its relationship to John of Salisbury's *Policraticus*, see Jennifer Summit, *Memory's Library: Medieval Books in Early Modern England* (Chicago: University of Chicago Press, 2008), 44–45.

[37] Holstun is more interested in the mode of production, or economics, but his idea is also clearly relevant to political ideology. See James Holstun, "The Spider, the Fly, and the Commonwealth: Merrie John Heywood and Agrarian Class Struggle," *ELH* 71.1(2004): 53–88.

[38] Morison, *A Remedy*, B3v, image 8.

monarchy and hierarchy, but it does so not by repressing or subjecting the people, nor by placing them at the foot of the body, but by erasing them. Indeed, that is one of the jobs of this new, educated class—to contain the threat of social disruption, the insurrections that Henry VIII so feared. Elyot makes clear from the very beginning of his text that his humanist educational program arises out of a particular need, the preservation of the commonwealth, and a particular anxiety over the lack of order. What will contain the threat of social disorder, at least on the page, is the classical legacy. Latin terminology and Roman history allow him to imagine a new commonwealth without the people, to rewrite and repress all of the meanings of "common" circulating in his time: the commons (as a Parliamentary unit), the common people, and Christian egalitarianism/ collectivism.[39] He asserts that he favors the term "public weal" over "common weal" or common because the latter implies the kind of egalitarianism associated with the Anabaptists, who were thought to hold all things in common, or were thought to desire to hold all things in common. Elyot explains that "Publike (as Varro saith) is dirivied [derived] of people: whiche in latin is called Populus. Wherfore hit semeth that men have ben longe abused in calling *Rempublicam* a comune weale. As they which do suppose it so to be called for that, that every thinge shulde be to all men in commune without discrepance of any astate or condition" (*Boke*, 15). Latin allows him to make political distinctions between groups and ideas that have become conflated, in his mind dangerously: rewriting the "common good" as the "public good" means preserving social hierarchy, the estates and conditions in the realm. Such distinctions allow him to sever "the people" from the larger political community and reduce them to their baseness and vulgarity: "*Plebs* in English is called the communalitie, which signifieth only the multitude, wherein be contayned the base and vulgare inhabitantes, not advanced to any honour or dignite" (*Boke*, 15–16).

Elyot's interest in Roman history and Latin terms is not just academic, an argument over words. For Elyot social disorder is a real threat, and his attempts to control the English word "common" by translating it into Latin and associating it with the Roman republic, are, in fact, attempts to control the people's political power.[40] The threat of social disorder can be allayed by invoking the Latin terminology, which not only writes the people out of the commonwealth, but also reinforces social classes, the basis for social order. Immediately after contrasting the familiar word—*Res publica*—with a Latin word to indicate governance by the wrong kind of people—*Res plebia*—he writes, "for as moche as Plebs in latin and cominers in englisshe be wordes only made for the discrepance of degrees: wherof procedeth ordre ... [T]ake away ordre from all thynges, what shuld than

---

[39] The strangeness of this opening has not been sufficiently appreciated, although Lehmberg notes in passing that his definition of the commonwealth is "unusual" (*Sir Thomas Elyot*, 40).

[40] Elyot's anxiety about the people is also noted by David Norbrook, "Rehearsing the Plebeians: *Coriolanus* and the Reading of Roman History," in *Shakespeare and the Politics of Commoners: Digesting the New Social History*, ed. Chris Fitter (Oxford: Oxford University Press; 2017), 187–88.

THE USES OF GOOD LITERATURE   103

remayn?" (*Boke*, 16). To which he answers, "*Chaos?*" (*Boke*, 16). Elyot describes a logic by which the breakdown in "words" is also a breakdown in "things," the social structures themselves. Chaos in the word common because of its multiple meanings leads directly to political chaos.

While Elyot offers his classical terminology as a correction of men's long-standing mistakes or the abuse he describes, he is instead providing something entirely new. The Roman term will erase the long history encoded in the English term, the association of various political and social meanings of common around the people that is entirely traditional, part of what James Holstun calls "the medieval social gospel."[41] One can find this "medieval social gospel" in many places including John Lydgate's *Fall*. Lydgate is no less interested than Elyot in preserving hierarchy and monarchy, and yet his use of the term "comountees [community]" indicates that he considers all the "subjects" as member of the community; all are holding up the throne of the ruler (2.832). All readers of Lydgate's *Fall* are subjects, and all can see themselves in the mirror, can read the same book within their estates, can apprehend the same lessons without threatening the existence of their estates.

In rejecting and replacing the medieval social gospel, Elyot is also rejecting the morality associated with it. Indeed, a new social order requires a new idea of virtue, or "noble vertues" (44). It is the classical legacy that will help with this project because it offers a language of virtue, of right and wrong action, that can be independent of Christianity, of the contested debates about what being a Christian might entail. Nobility as an idea is thus seen to arise out of classical history, not, significantly, the story of Adam and Eve. Elyot provides a version of the Golden Age, the myth about a past time in which people did not work nor did they own possessions. This origin story portrays social hierarchy as inevitable but, very significantly, not Christian and not even fated by God: "Fyrst that in the begynnyng whan private possessions and dignite were given by the consent of the people: who than had all thinges in commune, and equalitie in degree and condition" (*Boke*, 120). This little story erases any potential problems that have collected around the story of Adam and Eve, whose stay in Paradise might offer a desirable political model without lordship. Such an egalitarian perspective is pithily rendered in the popular medieval saying: "Whan Adam dalf and Eve span/ Who was then a gentleman?"[42] Elyot's classicized origin story retains the egalitarianism of humanity's origin, but he also rewrites the end of egalitarianism as a conscious choice by the people, not a punishment for sin, as a fall. From this perspective, egalitarianism is neither Christian nor virtuous, but merely a worldly state that has been superseded.

---

[41] Holstun, "The Spider, the Fly," 77.
[42] Paul Freedman, *Images of the Medieval Peasant* (Stanford, CA: Stanford University Press, 1999), 60–66.

104   HUMANISM AND GOOD BOOKS IN SIXTEENTH-CENTURY ENGLAND

Elyot's re-writing of moral guidelines, of vice and virtue, as a response to Christian egalitarianism, is also apparent in the stories he uses to illustrate the idea of nobility, the *exempla*. Like the origin story, these *exempla* both gesture toward and foreclose the radical possibilities circulating at the time. Elyot includes the stories of two Romans, Numa Pompilius and Quintius, who, as, plowmen, respond to the potentially subversive, or at least reformist, English plowmen, who appear from the late-fourteenth through the sixteenth-century and beyond: in anti-enclosure movements, in critiques of corruption in the church and the social world more generally, and in calls for reform of the established church.[43] Those plowmen are virtuous in an explicitly Christian framework: humble, hard-working, and charitable, as Chaucer's portrait of the Plowman in the *General Prologue* to his *Canterbury Tales* or Langland's Piers Plowman, in *Piers Plowman,* both demonstrate. Their virtues can have a socially subversive element, as the peasants in the Peasants' Revolt of 1381 surely understood, because their very existence suggests that virtue is independent of wealth, maybe even inversely correlated with it. Elyot's plowmen, in contrast, possess civic virtues, the same ones that are everywhere linked to nobility but rarely specified beyond the catchall terms of "wisdom and virtue." As a result of their "very nobility," these plowmen are chosen as governors. Such leadership does not result in any changes in the social structure, and they function therefore as figures who will work within the established structures virtuously. They are not the reformist plowmen of the *Piers Plowman* tradition, who would change those established structures, by pulling down fences or getting rid of the friars or demanding the end of serfdom.

On the one hand, Elyot's *exempla* illustrate the very humanist idea that nobility is independent of class structure, since even a plowman can have inner worthiness. On the other hand, they show how the social/ political class not only pre-exists worthiness but also helps create it. That is, the Roman people are already divided into classes—plowmen and Senators—and that class division helps them recognize the behavior appropriate or inappropriate for each class. What Elyot cannot seem to illustrate is his original point: that egalitarianism necessarily leads to a hierarchical class structure because some people have inner worthiness. Neither *exemplum* shows an original egalitarian state, and one could certainly make the argument that the leaders are only chosen because of their class status. As plowmen, they are always already associated with virtuous labor, sanitized as their virtue may be of its Langlandian radicalism. Indeed, the text offers an insightful exploration of how inequality persists. Not because some people are inherently worthier than others but through a selective promotion process. One way of deradicalizing plowmen is to make some of them nobles. Once complicit in the power structure, they will no longer ask for equality for their estate as a whole.

---

[43] On this tradition, see my *Transforming Work: Early Modern Pastoral and Late Medieval Poetry* (Notre Dame, IN: University of Notre Dame Press, 2013), 111–42.

THE USES OF GOOD LITERATURE   105

Elyot uses the classical legacy to contain the radical potential not only of virtuous plowmen figures, but also of familiar Christian virtues, such as charity and patience. Such containment is most notable in Elyot's emphasis on the cardinal virtues: justice, prudence, temperance, and fortitude. The third book is organized around these, and the theological virtues, such as charity, are subordinated to them.[44] Although it would be a mistake to see the cardinal virtues as secular—they had, after all, been fully integrated into Christian writings during the Middle Ages—renewed attention to Cicero's writings during this period had freed them to be Ciceronian and, therefore, pagan or non-Christian again.[45] In modelling his treatise at least in part after Cicero's *De Officiis*, which similarly lists and discusses virtues, Elyot is suggesting the independence of these virtues from Christianity instead of their subordination to or alignment with it. Of the twenty-four chapters about virtue and vice that Elyot includes, the great majority are devoted to the four cardinal virtues, as apparent in their titles: justice (five chapters), fortitude (three chapters), temperance (three chapters), and prudence (one chapter, headed "understanding"). A further three virtues are described as subsets of fortitude: magnanimity, abstinence, and continence. The familiar theological virtues not only receive very little attention, they are also shown to be in the service of the classical tradition: faith receives two chapters, both subordinated to justice; love/ charity is also discussed under justice; and hope receives no attention at all, perhaps unsurprisingly for such a bleak work. Patience, to which three chapters are dedicated, is the only other virtue from an explicitly and recognizably Christian tradition, and it is subordinated to fortitude (*Boke*, 207–11). Such a choice contrasts starkly with the Erasmian harmonies and even more starkly with earlier traditions, in which classical stories are subordinated to Christian virtues and vices, to penitential mirrors, as apparent in Lydgate's poem.

Elyot shows how a specifically classical knowledge should drive morality and the future conduct of readers in his account of justice. He writes, "Knowlege also, as a perfeyte instructrice and maistresse ... declareth by what meane the sayd preceptes of reason and societie may be well understande: and therby justice finally executed. The wordes be these in latine, *Nosce te ipsum*. Whiche is in englysshe, know thy self. This sentence is of olde writars supposed for to be firste spoken by Chilo or some other of the seven auncient Greekes called in latine *Sapientes*"

---

[44] For his sources see Lehmberg, *Sir Thomas Elyot*, 72–94 and Major, *Sir Thomas Elyot*, 140–70. Major notes that Elyot offers "the first complete analysis of the cardinal virtues in modern English" and directly responds to Cicero's *De Officiis*, the dialogues of Plato, and Aristotle's *Ethics* (*Sir Thomas Elyot*, 28). Hogrefe describes his reluctance to include much from the Bible and what appears to be a unique focus on sexual morality (*Life and Times*, 134, 136–40).

[45] There seems to have been a great deal of interest in translating and disseminating Cicero's writings in this period. See *The thre bookes of Tyllyes offyces both in latyne tonge [et] in englysshe, lately translated by Roberte Whytinton poete laureate* (London, 1534) STC 5278 and (London, 1540) STC 5279; and *Marcus Tullius Ciceroes thre bokes of duties to Marcus his sonne, turned out of latine into english, by Nicholas Grimalde* (London, 1556) STC 5281 and (London, 1558) STC 5281.8.

(*Boke*, 182). For Elyot, "precepts," as in moral guidelines, come from reason and society. They can be gained through knowledge of old writers, and they are entirely independent of God's commandments. Even the allegory, of Knowledge as an instructress, ensures that we see wisdom as being conveyed outside the realm of Christianity, where wisdom is, at least for Erasmus, often located.

Such a reframing responds to and rejects the egalitarian or even subversive potential that Elyot finds in some of the Christian virtues as they have traditionally been offered to readers. Simply put, Elyot is afraid that one of the two most basic Christian commandments—love of neighbor—might reinforce the social radicalism that he is desperate to contain. He acknowledges that Christian charity requires a certain degree of egalitarianism: under the heading of charity, he states that the governor must accept the equality of all Christians before God: "all other men be equall unto the[e]" (*Boke*, 183). And yet, that equality has no consequences for social order: the "inferior persone or subjecte aught to consider, that all be it (as I have spoken) he in the substaunce of soule and body be equall with his superior, yet for as moche as the powars and qualities of the soule and body, with the disposition of reason, be nat in every man equall, therfore god ordayned a diversitie or preeminence in degrees to be amonge men" (*Boke*, 184). The repetition of the word "equal" should give one pause: although people are equal in soul and body, as taught by Christianity, they are not equal in their skills; therefore, they are not equal. One might contrast this approach to spiritual equality, of the soul and body, with that of Erasmus, who aligns himself with the prince, as a kind of equal, when he describes them as "Christians both of us" (*ECP*, 204).

In addition, Elyot is careful to distinguish this form of spiritual or Christian equality from its political forms. Anyone interested in linking equality before God to social equality risks anarchy and chaos. Some people "wolde exterminate all superioritie, extincte all governaunce and lawes, and under the coloure of holy scripture, whiche they do violently wraste to their purpose, do endevour them selfs to bryng the life of man in to a confusion inevitable" (*Boke*, 184). That is, holy scripture has been used to call social stratification and hierarchy into question; calls for access to scripture can threaten social division, and scripture itself can provide alternate guidelines for social and political organization, the egalitarianism of Adam and Eve, the equality of Erasmus and his Prince as Christians. In forestalling this vision of social disorder, Elyot provides a clue to what he sees as wrong: charity itself, which he aligns with egalitarianism. He thus links charity to social disorder, implying that this familiar virtue has led to the political problems he sees. Elyot first details the murders, rapes, adulteries that this "confusion" (i.e. equality) would bring, and then finally invokes the word charity in the penultimate sentence of his chapter. At this point, readers have been trained to think of charity as a pipedream, something belonging to angels not men, not a commandment at all: these crimes would of "necessitie ensue: except these evangelicall persones [radical reformers] could perswade God or compelle him to chaunge men to aungels, makinge them all of one disposition and confirminge them all inne form of *charity*" (*Boke*, 185, my emphasis).[46] Loving one's neighbor is considered an impossible demand, requiring people to be "angels," and attempts to insist upon it only result in crime and chaos. In short, Christians are relieved of any obligation to love their neighbors in this world, because bad people, the "evangelical persons," have exploited the idea of charity to create chaos.

That Elyot is redefining virtue to a more narrowly civic and classically inflected meaning should by now be clear: the virtue of the plowman is neither his Christ-like humility nor his work but his wisdom and leadership; charity is not a boundless love for one's neighbor but proper interactions ("society") and social cohesion. Perhaps the most politically significant of these redefinitions concerns patience, which empties it of its broad Christian meaning of suffering, the "vertuous suffraunce" of Chaucer's *Clerk's Tale*, (4.1162), out of fear of detailing forms of political oppression and makes it more narrowly about accepting the status quo. Patience is an identifiably and specifically Christian virtue that has a very long history in the medieval period.[47] That it could still be understood in traditional, i.e. medieval, terms in Elyot's own time is apparent in the persistence of the Griselda story, which will be discussed in the next chapter, and the continued circulation of Lydgate's poem, *The Fall of Princes*, which commends patience in specifically Christian terms. Accounts of this Christian virtue often carry with them political ramifications: patience is typically explored in relation to tyranny, in addition to, or alongside, the private suffering of a Job-like figure. This political aspect is apparent in Lydgate's *Fall*, which includes an account of the three philosophers who are "comendid for ther pacience, [commended for their patience]" because they suffered for "comoun profit [common profit]" (9.2243, 9.2266). Their interest in common profit is opposed to the actions of "tyrants": "Tirauntis hertis this vertu doth appese/ Modefieth ther cruel fell woodnesse [This virtue appeases the hearts of tyrants and modifies their cruel madness]" (9.2357–58). While such stories overtly work for the oppressor, in that they remind readers to suffer and not revolt, they also have a built-in inflammatory potential for the simple fact that one cannot have an account of patience that is not also an account of the abuses committed by those in power.

Elyot, unlike Lydgate, sees the potentially disruptive aspects of patience, fears that its anti-tyrannical capacity might translate into an anti-monarchical capacity. He therefore redirects and contains the meaning of patience around the governors of the title. That is, he locates patience not within the people-ruler relationship, as suggested in Lydgate, but within the governor-ruler relationship. Elyot begins conventionally enough, defining patience as putting a good face on adversity

---

[46] Baker also notes Elyot's concerns with Anabaptists (*Divulging Utopia*, 100–01).

[47] See Ralph Hanna, "Some Commonplaces of Late Medieval Patience Discussions: An Introduction," in *The Triumph of Patience*, ed. Gerald J. Schiffhorst (Orlando, FL: University Presses of Florida, 1978), 65–87 and 1–31.

—"retayninge all wayes glad semblaunt [appearance] in adversitie" (*Boke*, 207)— and offers a familiar account of patience in the face of tyranny in the story of the philosopher Zeno. Zeno is not, however, linked with the people through their love of "common profit," as in Lydgate; he is rather distinguished from them by "wisedome and eloquence," a phrase that makes him, in this text, more of a governor than a philosopher (*Boke*, 207). Even more significantly, this patience has little or nothing to do with Christian martyrdom, the context in which Lydgate places Zeno. Despite a brief mention of "examples of martyrs," Elyot does not compare the various kinds of suffering, and patience is in the end far less Christian than in Lydgate (*Boke*, 207). The word "cruciate," which is used to describe Zeno's torture is a reminder of Jesus's suffering that remains inactive (*Boke*, 207).

Redefined away from its Christian radicalism, patience is a "noble virtue," or a virtue for the nobility: it has to do with the nobility's relationship with the king. In other words, patience is necessary for enduring tyranny as its agent, not enduring tyranny alongside all the other subjects. Elyot thus converts patience from suffering to "governance:" "Pacience ... pertaineth unto interior governaunce, wherby the naturall passions of man be subdued, and malyce of fortune sustayned: for they which be in autoritie, and be occupied about great affaires" (*Boke*, 207–8). Future governors will themselves be in positions of "authority," and they receive the same advice that the tyrant Phalaris received from Zeno: to be temperate in one's passions. In this way, Elyot turns patience from a virtue directly related to rebellion in the story of Zeno to one related to preserving the status quo. How the governor will show his patience is then apparent in the titles to the next two chapters: "Of Pacience in sustayninge wronges and rebukes" and "Of Pacience deserued in repulse or hynderaunce of promocion" (*Boke*, 208, 209). Elyot then provides examples drawn from the classical legacy that detail the patience of governors under a king: Antony, who does not kill the rebel Cassius's children, and Cato who was not chosen as Consul and did not get angry. Patience is still political, but it has shifted from a virtue that reminds readers of their powerlessness—the suffering people undergo at the hands of a tyrant—to one that serves power—suffering because one works for a tyrant.

Elyot's treatise, like many humanist writings, insists that the classical legacy is morally instructive for readers in his own time, for shaping their behavior, thoughts, and feelings. Elyot departs from the tradition he inherited from Erasmus, however, by representing that moral usefulness in terms of its independence from Christianity. In this way, his treatise demonstrates the secularized humanism that many scholars have found in the sixteenth century: when the classical legacy aided writers in imagining something new. And yet, Elyot's view of the classical legacy is neither as celebratory nor as confident in its goals as his Erasmian model, which keeps the two traditions linked together, however contradictorily. Patently ideological and anxious, Elyot's treatise serves instead as a reminder of some of the ugly uses to which the classical legacy has been put—to find new languages for political oppression.

5

Good Literature [*bonae litterae*] and the Good

In the first part of the sixteenth century, humanists developed a new and more theorized approach to literary value, the good of the *bonae litterae*. Celebrated and popular as the idea of *bonae litterae* may have been, it did not erase or supersede previously existing ideas about value, whether of the classical legacy or of poetry and books more generally. After all, even as sixteenth-century English authors translated and imitated classical texts or invented new genres, they continued to read the works of the medieval poets Geoffrey Chaucer and John Lydgate, which were printed throughout the sixteenth century.[1] For this reason, it is more appropriate to see humanism as continuing a conversation with earlier, i.e. medieval, texts and authors, than as entirely new. Understanding the impact of English humanism on writing in this period, means, therefore, reading not only those texts that advertise their humanism, that directly imitate and promote the classical legacy, as do *Acolastus* and Sir Thomas Elyot's *The Boke of the Governor*, but also texts that are more conflicted, that meditate on humanism, especially humanist confidence in *bonae litterae*.

This chapter explores such a reflective and medieval-inflected humanism in a mid-sixteenth-century play, John Phillip's *Play of Patient Grissell* (c. 1558–61), which uses a well-known story based on the patient Griselda who appears in Giovanni Boccaccio's *Decameron* (c.1353) and in Geoffrey Chaucer's *Clerk's Tale* (c. 1380s). It is, of course, not just any story, but an *exemplum*, a short story that illustrates a moral, and not just any *exemplum*, but one that advertises its place in a literary tradition. It was Francesco Petrarch who famously moralized Boccaccio's story about Griselda, and it was Chaucer who translated that moralization into English. As Chaucer writes, at the end of the *Clerk's Tale*, "this storie is seyd [this story is told]"

> But for that every wight, in his degree,
> Sholde be constant in adversitee

[1] On the print history of Chaucer and Lydgate, see Alexandra Gillespie, *Print Culture and the Medieval Author: Chaucer, Lydgate, and their Books, 1473–1557* (Oxford: Oxford University Press, 2006). On Chaucer's reputation in the sixteenth century, see Megan Cook, *The Poet and the Antiquaries: Chaucerian Scholarship and the Rise of Literary History, 1532–1635* (Philadelphia: University of Pennsylvania Press, 2019).

Humanism and Good Books in Sixteenth-Century England. Katherine C. Little, Oxford University Press.
© Katherine C. Little (2023). DOI: 10.1093/oso/9780192883193.003.0006

110   HUMANISM AND GOOD BOOKS IN SIXTEENTH-CENTURY ENGLAND

> As was Grisilde; therfore Petrak writeth
> This storie, which with heigh stile he enditeth

[So that every person, in his estate, should be as constant in adversity as Griselda was; therefore, Petrarch writes this story, which he composed in the high style].[2]

For Chaucer, this story has a moral purpose: it was written "for" the "wight" who reads it, to guide him in his future behavior: being constant in adversity. That moral purpose is fundamental not only to the story itself, but to its reception, or place in the literary tradition, a point Chaucer underlines with his "therefore," which links the purpose to the author, Petrarch. Phillip's adaptation of this story takes up the same concern—the moral value of a literary tradition—but in a new environment, that of humanist education. His play is educational in content, in that it explicitly instructs in virtue, along the lines imagined by sixteenth-century Latin grammar books, such as *Lily's Grammar of Latin in English*, and likely also in context, in that it was written for children to perform.[3] As such, it belongs to the world of the Christian Terence and the Erasmianism discussed in Chapter 3, the fusion of classical and Christian. Although Phillip's play was neither particularly popular nor influential, in contrast to the texts discussed previously in this study, its medievalism is nevertheless significant as a harbinger of the doubts about humanism that will pervade the work of much more popular and influential Elizabethan authors. Indeed, Phillip's play shows how medievalism could function as a response to humanist *bonae litterae*, to help an author imagine how a text might or might not teach and delight or produce noble virtues, the pieties that guided humanist readers of the classical legacy, as I shall argue here.

The Exemplum, Medieval to Humanist

It is no accident that Phillip uses an *exemplum* to explore humanist *bonae litterae*. As brief stories in service of a lesson, *exempla* are famous for tying together the literary and the moral; these are narratives, even well-known narratives, that circulated with explicit guidelines for human behavior. For this reason, they appear in the genres that are most directly concerned with such guidelines: in sermon collections, penitential handbooks, and Mirrors for Princes. For example, Robert Mannyng's penitential handbook, *Handlyng Synne* (c. 1303) collects many stories together under the headings of the seven sins. Mannyng begins by explaining that his text will help readers understand the truth:

---

[2] Geoffrey Chaucer, *Clerk's Prologue*, in *The Riverside Chaucer*, 3rd ed., ed. Larry D. Benson (Boston: Houghton Mifflin, 1987), 4.1142, 4.1145–48. All references to Chaucer's works will appear parenthetically hereafter.

[3] On its dating and its association with the boys' theater companies, see Lee Bliss, "The Renaissance Griselda: A Woman for All Seasons," *Viator* 23 (1992): 304–5 and Ursula Potter "Tales of Patient Griselda and Henry VIII," *Early Theatre* 5.2 (2002): 19.

> Wyþ ofte redyng mayst þou lere.
> þou mayst nou3t wyþ onys redyng
> knowe þe soþe of euery þyng.

[With frequent reading, you may learn. You cannot know the truth of everything by reading only once].[4]

Similarly, in his massive poem of *exempla*, *The Fall of Princes* (c. 1431–38), John Lydgate provides a compelling account of how books will train readers in their actions:

> For what auaileth thexaumples that thei reede,
> To ther reedyng yiff contraire be the deede?
> Cunnyng and deede, who can comprehende,
> In cleer conceites thei be thynges tweyne;
> And yiff cunnyng doth the deede amende,
> Than atwen hem is maad a myhti cheyne,
> A noble thyng, and riht souereyne:
> For thanne off cunnyng the labour is weel spent,
> Whan deede folweth, & bothe been off assent.

[What use are the examples that they read if their actions are contrary to their reading? Knowledge and action are two things for those who can comprehend. And if knowledge corrects, or governs, the deed, then a mighty chain is made between them, which is a noble thing. For the labor of learning is well spent when a deed follows it, and knowledge and deed are in agreement].[5]

Lydgate's "mighty chain" demonstrates that reading is part of a process of connecting knowledge drawn from books to behavior in the world. The usefulness of books lies in their "cunning" and "truth," their applicability to the lives of their readers.

As important as the usefulness of the *exempla* is their association with the classical legacy.[6] They are, in an important sense, the medieval version of *bonae litterae*: texts drawn from the classical legacy that were thought to shape readers or listeners in good behavior and warn them about bad behavior. *Exempla* collections not only made the classical tradition available to authors and readers, they also helped

---

[4] Robert Mannyng, *Handlyng Synne*, ed. Idelle Sullens (Binghamton, NY: Center for Medieval and Renaissance Texts and Studies, 1983), lines 126–28.

[5] John Lydgate, *The Fall of Princes*, 4 vols., ed. Henry Bergen (London: Oxford University Press, 1924–27), Part 1: Bk 2.118–26. Hereafter all references to the text will appear parenthetically.

[6] On the classical exemplum in the Middle Ages, see Larry Scanlon, *Narrative, Authority, and Power: The Medieval Exemplum and the Chaucerian Tradition* (Cambridge: Cambridge University Press, 1994), 81–134.

112   HUMANISM AND GOOD BOOKS IN SIXTEENTH-CENTURY ENGLAND

to ensure a particular approach to that legacy: as morally useful. To be sure, *exempla* were not the only means through which the classical tradition was conveyed, but they were a very popular means. For example, the *Gesta Romanorum* (late thirteenth century), a book of classical and Christian tales compiled in England for the use of preachers, survives in 165 manuscripts.[7] Each of the brief stories in the *Gesta* ends with a moralization, as apparent in the very first story, of Atalanta, which is drawn from Greek mythology. According to the moralization that concludes the brief account, Atalanta represents "the soule of man with whome many deuylles desyren to renne and to dysceyue her thorugh theyr temptacyons [the soul of man, with whom many devils desire to run and whom they desire to deceive through their temptations]."[8] This collection, and the many others like it, certainly values the classical legacy, and it does so by harnessing it to a Christian moral language, of sins and souls, that may not be found in the narrative itself.

In linking classical stories to Christian language, *exempla* seem to support a well-known commonplace about medieval classicism, as discussed in Chapter 1: that medieval authors subordinate classical texts to Christian moral rubrics. Just as Petrarch applied "constancy" to Boccaccio's story of Griselda, the author of the *Gesta Romanorum* applied sin to the story of Atalanta.[9] From this perspective, *exempla* appear to be only partially literary for two main reasons: only one of the parts, the story, is thought to be literary, and also, the moral lesson is thought to be the more important part. For many scholars of *exempla*, the moral discourse is presumed to be the authoritative idea that precedes the story and dominates it. One of the earliest scholars of *exempla*, Jean-Thiébaut Welter, describes the secondariness of the story; authors use *exempla* as an illustration ["par maniére d'illustration"] of doctrine or morality or other kinds of points ["certain points doctrinaux d'ordre dogmatique, moral, mystique, et liturgique"].[10] That is, the points are the core, and the story is the extra. Another theorist of *exempla*, Karl-Heinz Stierle, underlines the inherent duality of *exempla* by using two terms to define them: they consist on the one hand of "systematic discourses," which

---

[7] See *The Early English Versions of the Gesta Romanorum*, ed. Sidney J. H. Herrtage, Early English Text Society Extra Series 33 (London: N. Trübner & Co., 1879; repr. 1962).

[8] *Gesta romanorum* (London, 1510) STC 21286.3, A2v.

[9] The thirteenth-century friar John of Wales compiled two *exempla*-collections, both of which were popular. His *Breviloquium* survives in 150 manuscripts (Jenny Swanson, *John of Wales: A Study of the Works and Ideas of a Thirteenth-Century Friar* [New York: Cambridge University Press, 1989], 61). The extended title of the *Breviloquium* demonstrates the link between classical stories and Christian moral discourses (virtues), a link that was being established or renewed in the thirteenth-century: *Breviloquium de virtutibus antiquorum principum et philosophorum* (Swanson, *John of Wales*, 41–62). See also Charles F. Briggs, "Moral Philosophy and Wisdom Literature," in *The Oxford History of Classical Reception in English Literature: Volume 1: 800–1558*, ed. Rita Copeland (Oxford: Oxford University Press, 2016), 1:302–3.

[10] Jean-Thiébaut Welter, describes "la tendance à employer l'exemplum pour élucider, expliquer ou completer par maniére d'illustration certain points doctrinaux d'ordre dogmatique, moral, mystique, et liturgique" (*L' Exemplum dans la litterature religieuse et didactique du moyen age* [Paris: Occitania, 1927, rept. New York: AMS Press, 1973], 156).

GOOD LITERATURE AND THE GOOD   113

link, of course, to other utilitarian and truth-oriented writings, and, on the other hand, narratives, which are often fictions.[11] Such an approach to the duality of *exempla* can explicitly or implicitly suggest their primitivism and innocence: they are a genre that is only proto-literary, since literature as such only emerges by casting off explicit moral lessons, the systematic discourse. Indeed, Stierle's distinction between narrative and systematic discourse is part of a larger argument about an evolutionary development from *exempla* toward fiction.[12] To borrow the language of twentieth-century literary criticism, *exempla* have not achieved the status of an "independent art," because they remain "subordinated" to the "ethical sciences."[13]

Viewing *exempla* as only incompletely literary, a shoehorning of classical or other stories into Christian morality that does not, by definition respect the independence of the classical text, obscures the nature of the form and cannot explain why it was popular, except to imply that people in the past were primitive and unsophisticated in the kinds of stories that they liked.[14] It is more helpful to view an *exemplum* as a distinct kind of story than it is to view an *exemplum* as an inferior story, one that would have been less (or not at all) moral if its author were more skilled. What is important about the *exemplum* is a that is a story that proves or enacts the truth of a moral point; the story cannot be separated out. For example, it demonstrates that humans are always in danger of being tempted by wrong desires, such as greed, and must outrun them, as in Atalanta. Relatedly, it enacts a cultural belief in the link between texts and morality, what this book has considered as the text-based and discursive aspect of morality: the idea that human behavior in the world is best guided by "cunning [knowledge]," to use Lydgate's word, gained from books. In using the word "enact," I am drawing on the work of Larry Scanlon, in his important study of *exempla*, *Narrative, Power, and Authority: The Medieval Exemplum and the Chaucerian Tradition*, which defines the *exemplum* as a "narrative enactment of cultural authority."[15] Although Scanlon is more interested in the ideological—the power of the Church and monarchy—than the moral—ideas

---

[11] Karl-Heinz Stierle, "Story as Exemplum, Exemplum as Story: On the Pragmatics and Poetics of Narrative Texts," in *New Perspectives in German Literary Criticism: A Collection of Essays*, ed. Richard E. Lange and Victor Amacher, trans. David Henry Wilson (Princeton, NJ: Princeton University Press, 1979), 396.

[12] Stierle, "Story as Exemplum."

[13] Bernard Weinberg, *A History of Literary Criticism in the Italian Renaissance*, 2 vols. (Chicago: University of Chicago Press, 1961), 1: 30.

[14] I have benefitted from the following studies on *exempla*, all of which explore the contradiction between story and lesson: Elizabeth Allen, *False Fables and Exemplary Truth in Later Middle English Literature* (New York: Palgrave Macmillan, 2005), 1–10; Alexander Gelley, *Unruly Examples: On the Rhetoric of Exemplarity* (Stanford, CA: Stanford University Press, 1995), 157; Timothy Hampton, *Writing from History: The Rhetoric of Exemplarity in Renaissance Literature* (Ithaca, NY: Cornell University Press, 1989), 16; John D. Lyons, *Exemplum: the Rhetoric of Example in Early Modern France* (Princeton, NJ: Princeton University, 1990), 9–12; and Tobin Siebers, *Morals and Stories* (New York: Columbia University Press, 1992), 38–55.

[15] Scanlon, *Narrative, Authority, and Power*, 34.

114 HUMANISM AND GOOD BOOKS IN SIXTEENTH-CENTURY ENGLAND

about human behavior—he rightly emphasizes that the two parts of the *exemplum* should be seen as inextricably linked.

This duality, the link between story and moral, is not arbitrary nor is it a primitive or misguided approach to literature that will be discarded in modernity. Rather, it imitates or preempts an interpretive process, thus signaling that part of a story's meaning is always its meaning for a reader. Wanting to find a moral in a story may be, especially for non-professional readers, as common a response to reading as not wanting to find one, to see a text as indeterminate. Indeed, *exempla* distil a process that is widely practiced in educational settings: reading a story and coming up with a meaning that is both generally accepted and applicable to the reader. One can make almost any story into an *exemplum* precisely because this operation is so basic to reading or hearing stories. Instead of seeing *exempla* merely as programmatic illustrations of previously existing lessons, one might, therefore, see them as a conversation and negotiation between discourses, the kinds of bookishness identified by Chaucer's Manciple at the end of the *Manciple's Tale* when he gives his moral. That conversation occurs as much when a reader (or author) identifies stories that were thought to move readers to recognize particular "truths," to borrow Mannyng's term, as when a reader (or author) identifies truths that lend themselves to narrative exposition. From this perspective, the stories are less the sugarcoating of rules about how to behave and more occasions and spaces to think through how to behave, even case-studies for particular ideas about right and wrong behavior.[16] Such an approach is well supported simply by the fact that *exempla* travelled in large groups, offering what Judson Boyce Allen calls a "normative array."[17] It is easy to imagine Petrarch reading Boccaccio and, moved by the story, trying to communicate what he thinks the story is about through the moral. Just as it is easy to imagine Robert Mannyng of Brunne recalling various folktales so that he could effectively illustrate the sin of greed in his *exempla*-collection, *Handlyng Synne.*

Tying classical stories to Christian moral lessons does not necessarily make *exempla* naïve about human behavior or about the capacity of stories to teach. Even as collections of *exempla* insist on the morality of classical or other kinds of stories, they also provide opportunities to reflect on the duality inherent in the form, on the relationship between morals and stories. Such reflections can be found even in the most official, or even propagandistic, *exempla* collections,

---

[16] J. Allan Mitchell approaches *exempla* precisely as casuistry: they provide an opportunity for "moral cognition" as the reader thinks through the relationship between the story and the norm (*Ethics and Exemplary Narrative in Chaucer and Gower* [Woodbridge, UK: Boydell and Brewer, 2004], 1–73). For similar approaches to the practical aspects of *exempla* (as opposed to their use as instruments of control), see Judson Boyce Allen, *The Ethical Poetic of the Later Middle Ages: A Decorum of Convenient Distinction* (Toronto: University of Toronto Press, 1982), 95–106 and Mark Miller, "Displaced Souls, Idle Talk, Spectacular Scenes: *Handlyng Synne* and the Perspective of Agency," *Speculum* 71 (1996): 606–32.

[17] Allen, *Ethical Poetic*, 101.

GOOD LITERATURE AND THE GOOD   115

such as Mannyng's penitential manual, *Handlyng Synne*. They are perhaps most familiar from Chaucer's *Canterbury Tales*, which will be here singled out as a source, if not of the particulars of Phillip's play but of its self-consciousness about the *exemplum* form. Phillip's play would certainly have resonated not only with the *Clerk's Tale* but also with the other *exempla* included in the *Canterbury Tales*, which were very well known at this time, having been printed several times before 1500 and then most influentially as part of Chaucer's *Works* in 1532.[18] Although the success of Chaucer's *exempla* as *exempla* could be said to vary, there is general agreement that in all cases he tends to destabilize the relationship between the story and the moral. The most obvious evidence of this destabilization is the potential irony: each of the stories is voiced by a character who is given reasons for advocating that particular moral. That means that even the good, or unobjectionable, morals, such as "every person should be constant to God" (Clerk) and "the love of money is the root of all evil" (Pardoner), start to seem less authoritative because they are personally motivated.

This discussion will focus on the destabilized moral in Chaucer's *Physician's Tale* as an opportunity to think through classical stories and their applicability to readers, their moral lessons. Although the story originally appears in Livy's *History of Rome*, Chaucer is not very interested in following Livy, since he draws on the version that appears in the thirteenth-century medieval French poem the *Roman de la Rose*, and, even more importantly, affixes a Christian moral lesson. He begins with the source, "Ther was, as telleth Titus Livius [There was, as Livy tells]" (6.1), and then signals the Christian moral at the end: "Heere may men seen how synne hath his merite [Here may men see how sin has its reward]" (6.277). Such a framing, or shoehorning, indicates that Chaucer is not a humanist in the way this term is being used in this book: he is not trying to recover Livy's text on its own terms nor is he particularly interested in celebrating Livy as a moral author. Celebrations of Livy are, of course, typical for sixteenth-century humanists: Livy's *History* was praised by Erasmus in the *Apothegms* (1531), for being a "true mirror" and providing "moral portraits."[19] Despite, or perhaps because of, his non-humanist, as in non-celebratory, approach, Chaucer is aware of the potential contradictions that arise when an author subordinates a classical text to a Christian moral, to guidelines for the reader's behavior in the world outside the story. Simply put, the story does not fit the moral attached to it in that sin and "merit" (reward or punishment) do not coincide: Virginia, the innocent young girl, is brutally killed by her

---

[18] Geoffrey Chaucer, *The workes of Geffray Chaucer newly printed* (London, 1532) STC 5068. See Gillespie, *Print Culture*, 134–42.

[19] On the reading of Livy in humanist schools, see T. W. Baldwin, *William Shakspere's Smalle Latin and Lesse Greeke* (Urbana, IL: University of Illinois Press, 1944), 161 and 325; and Ian Green, *Humanism and Protestantism in Early Modern English Education* (Burlington, VT: Ashgate, 2009), 237–38. For the quotation from Erasmus see *A Companion to Livy*, ed. Bernard Mineo (Chichester, UK: Wiley-Blackwell, 2015), 445.

116 HUMANISM AND GOOD BOOKS IN SIXTEENTH-CENTURY ENGLAND

father, and Apius, the predatory man who brings a false charge against her father in order to rape her, is pardoned not punished.

It is tempting to say that the problem with this story is that it is an *exemplum*, that this is what happens when one applies a moral to a story that cannot support it, as suggested by Anne Middleton in her important reading of this story.[20] Such a view is motivated by a sense that the *exemplum* is only partially literary; that it needs to lose its moral lesson in order to achieve the ambiguity so prized by modern literary criticism. At the same time, one could also note that the story is not moral enough: there is a problem with the way in which its stated moral is applied to the reader. Unlike the Clerk's and Pardoner's moral lessons, which make sense, the Physician's is muddled and its applicability to the reader unclear. To be sure, given the mention of sin and punishment, the Physician seems to be quoting sermons and penitential manuals. On closer look, however, his moral does not actually match those more authoritative instances. Although he uses familiar words—sin, merit, and forsake—he does not use them in the relations and the contexts in which they are typically found. Perhaps most disconcerting is the use of "merit" in relation to sin: "Heere may men seen how synne hath his merite [Here may men see how sin has its reward]" (6.277). Usually, merit is assigned to virtue or to other kinds of good works. In Chaucer's *Parson's Tale*, which is the most helpful context, the word merit (or the related word "meritorious") is used seven times, all in relation to reward for virtuous behavior not as punishment for sin.[21] The discussion of chastity is typical, and especially pertinent in relation to the *Physician's Tale*: "Now comth the remedie agayns Leccherie, and that is generally chastitee and continence, that restryeneth all the desordeynee moevynges that comen of flesshly talentes. And evere the gretter merite shal he han that moost restreyneth the wikkede eschawfynges of the [ardour] of this synne [Now comes the remedy against lechery, and that is generally chastity and continence, which control the discordant desires that come from bodily urges. And the greater merit will go to those that have the most control over the wicked inflaming that this sin causes]" (10.915–16). As this passage might suggest, sin is often discussed in relation to a remedy for it, the virtue to which it is opposed, and it is that virtue that receives merit. Even Chaucer's Pardoner, who claims to be steeped in sin, is nevertheless concerned with curing it, or, at the very least, in viewing it as something that needs a remedy, since he describes Jesus as "leche [leech]" (6.916). To be sure, the positive correlation between merit and virtue is not absolute: the word merit can also

---

[20] Anne Middleton, "The Physician's Tale and Love's Martyrs: 'Ensamples Mo Than Ten' as a Method in the *Canterbury Tales*," *Chaucer Review* 8 (1973): 9–32. Middleton writes, "the *literary* limits of the exemplum are themselves held up for inspection by the reader" and notes "the fundamental *literary* problem of exemplary narrative" ("*The Physician's Tale*," 26, 27, my emphasis).

[21] *Glossarial Concordance to Middle English: The Works of Geoffrey Chaucer and the English Works of John Gower*, Johns Hopkins University, Sheridan Libraries, 2021, https://middleenglish.library.jhu. edu.

GOOD LITERATURE AND THE GOOD   117

be used neutrally, as in people get a reward according to their actions (bad or good).[22] There are, nevertheless, few instances in which merit is used to refer to punishment for sin.

Just as the juxtaposition of merit and sin sits oddly in the context of this story, so does that of sin and forsake: "Forsaketh synne, er synne yow forsake [Abandon sin before sin abandons you]" (6.286). Although this second moral is a popular and conventional saying, it does not function in that expected way, as a warning about repentance, in this instance, since it refers back to the actions of the story, in which no one repents, but some are certainly punished. Its more usual penitential function can be found in the *Parson's Tale*: "And therfore repentant folk, that stynte for to synne and forlete synne er that synne forlete hem, hooly chirche holdeth hem siker of hire savacioun [And, therefore, holy church considers secure the salvation of those who repent, who stop sinning and abandon sin before it abandons them]"(X.93).[23] In its penitential context, the saying's negative, even punitive aspect, is yoked to a positive lesson about repentance. Indeed, the term forsaking often appears in penitential and sermon literature with this positive connotation: rejecting wealth or the world in order to get mercy or live "cleanly."[24] For example, in Proverbs 28:13, forsaking sin leads to mercy: "Qui abscondit scelera sua non dirigetur, qui autem confessus fuerit et reliquerit ea misericordiam consequetur [He that hideth his sins shall not prosper, but he that shall confess and forsake them shall obtain mercy]."[25]

As a kind of false friend, language that looks penitential (and biblical) but does not, in fact, advocate repentance, the moral allows the Physician to appear to be a moral guide but to remain focused on sin. He can engage in a prurient interest in Apius, in his desire to "make hire with hir body synne [make Virginia sin with her body]" (6.138) and describe violence as Christian, both the violence of the father against his daughter and the punishment of the perpetrators. This tension, between the pseudo-Christian world that the Physician creates in and around the *Tale* and Christian teaching outside of it, is also evident earlier in the *Tale*, in another allusion that echoes and transforms a biblical passage. The Physician refers to a bad shepherd who allows violence to be done to his sheep: "Under a shepherde softe and necligent/ The wolf hath many a sheep and lamb torent" [The wolf tears apart many sheep and lambs when a weak and negligent shepherd is in charge] (6.101–3). This phrase inverts the "pastor bonus" of John

---

[22] *MED* s.v. merit. The *MED* offers three related definitions, only the first of which, regarding desert, carries the meaning of punishment. The quotations demonstrate that merit as punishment is rare: out of ninety-nine quotations for this word, only three refer specifically to punishment or sin, and one of those is the quotation from the *Physician's Tale*.

[23] For comments on this saying, see the editorial notes (*Riverside Chaucer*, p. 957 n. 93). For the potential irony of the moral in the *Physician's Tale*, see *Riverside Chaucer*, p. 903–04 nn277–86.

[24] *MED* s.v. "forsake."

[25] *The Vulgate Bible: Douay-Rheims Translation*, 6 vols., ed. Swift Edgar and Angela M. Kinney (Cambridge, MA: Harvard University Press, 2010–13), 3:669–69.

118   HUMANISM AND GOOD BOOKS IN SIXTEENTH-CENTURY ENGLAND

10:11, a foundational moment in which Jesus describes himself as a shepherd, caring for his flock. The Physician does not invoke his bad shepherd to criticize shepherd-priests, implicitly comparing bad shepherds to Jesus, as do many instances of anti-clerical critique. John Gower, for example, laments that "Cristes folde [Christ's sheep pen]" is destroyed because of shepherds who "her wit beware/ Upon the world [direct their attention to the world]" in the opening of his *Confessio Amantis* (1390).[26] In contrast, the Physician's shepherd underscores the violence against the innocent, the same kind of violence one finds in Apius. The Physician's morality is not misguided because he has subordinated classical to Christian, nor is his story problematic because he tries to offer a moral lesson at all. The problem is that he has altered biblical allusions to provide that lesson. In other words, the problem lies with the Physician himself. And, indeed, part of his description in the *General Prologue* is that he does not study the Bible ("His studie was but litel on the Bible" [1.438]). It would seem that Physician's lack of Bible study accounts for his odd emphases, for his sidelining of mercy or Jesus in favor of punishment and bodily harm.

Chaucer's *Physician's Tale*, like all of his *exempla*, is an opportunity to think through the relationship between stories and their moral lessons, their usefulness or value to readers. That this story is drawn from the classical legacy is less important than its form and function. What one might call a Chaucerian or even medieval perspective on the moral usefulness of the classical legacy changed, of course, in the early sixteenth century with humanism. For humanists, the sense of moral usefulness and value certainly persisted, but it was no longer linked so clearly to the form of the *exemplum*. This is not to say that *exempla* disappear entirely. After all, Elyot includes *exempla* in his *Boke of the Governor*. And, yet, moral claims are also, and more frequently, applied to the entirety of the classical legacy, the *bonae litterae*, and therefore to works understood in their wholeness, in which their wholeness is part of the point.[27] As Elyot notes in his educational treatise, the *Boke of the Governor*, "noble Homere" is the source of "all eloquence and lernyng." In reading his books, "the reders *shall* be so all inflamed, that they most fervently *shall* desire and coveite, by the imitation of their vertues, to acquire semblable [similar] glorie."[28] This same confidence in the reader's capacity to gain virtue and the text's capacity to communicate it can be found in Arthur Golding's version of Ovid's *Metamorphoses* (1567). Golding provides the entire text of Ovid,

---

[26] John Gower, *Confessio Amantis*, 3 vols. ed. Russell A. Peck with Latin Translations by Andrew Galloway (Kalamazoo, MI: Medieval Institute Publications, 2005–13), 1: Prologue, 390–95.

[27] Critics before the advent of theory, and the resulting celebration of the slipperiness of language, were more likely to focus on the didacticism of Renaissance texts. See Phillip Salman, "Instruction and Delight in Medieval and Renaissance Criticism," *Renaissance Quarterly* 32 (1979) 303–32; Marion Trousdale, "A Possible Renaissance View of Form," *ELH* 40 (1973): 179–204; and John Wallace, "Examples Are Best Precepts": Readers and Meanings in Seventeenth-Century Poetry," *Critical Inquiry* 1 (1974): 273–290.

[28] Sir Thomas Elyot, *A Critical Edition of Sir Thomas Elyot's The Boke Named the Governour*, ed. Donald W. Rude (New York: Garland Press, 1992), 44; my emphasis.

stripped of its glosses, but he does preface his edition with a clear statement about its moral usefulness:

> all [the stories] are pitthye, apte and playne
> Instructions which import [indicate] the prayse of vertues, and the shame
> Of vices, with the due rewards of eyther of the same.[29]

Golding asserts that Ovid's stories are easily understood as moral, as "plain" in their instructions. That ease is conveyed in the list of the specific lessons: "In Phaetons fable vntoo sight the Poet dooth expresse / The natures of ambition blynd, and youthfull willfulnesse."[30] The similarity between Golding's general moral and Chaucer's Physician's—vices will be punished and virtues rewarded—underlines the important continuity between medieval and Renaissance classicism. Classical texts were still discussable within a traditional and recognizably Christian moral language of virtues and vices and rewards and punishments. At the same time, the forms that the texts take—an edition of Ovid's stories, on the one hand and a story from Livy mediated through another poem, on the other—demonstrate a significant shift: the humanists' greater interest in the classical text as classical text. The change to the form of the classical legacy, the mode in which it would be encountered, necessarily affected the approach to usefulness, how these texts would be applied to the reader or audience.

Phillip's Play

John Phillip's *The Play of Patient Grissell* responds to the greater confidence that humanists placed in the *bonae litterae*—that reading and appreciating pagan, classical texts on their own terms will make readers good, that these texts could be easily applied to the lives of the readers.[31] Phillip offers that familiar and fundamental humanist idea in the Preface to his play:

---

[29] *The. xv. bookes of P. Ouidius Naso, entytuled Metamorphosis, translated oute of Latin into English meeter, by Arthur Golding* (London, 1567) STC 18956, A2v. On Golding's interest in "assimilation" of pagan and Christian values, see Joseph Wallace, "Strong Stomachs: Arthur Golding, Ovid, and Cultural Assimilation," *Renaissance Studies* 26 (2012): 728–743. Golding, like many of his contemporaries, was influenced by medieval moralizations of classical texts, even as he struck out in new directions.

[30] Golding, A2v.

[31] Not much work has been done on this play, and most of it focuses on the topicality from a political perspective. Bliss offers a fairly comprehensive account of the difference between Phillip's and Petrarch's versions of the story, arguing that the play aligns with "commonwealth literature," as in Protestantism and social conservatism ("The Renaissance Griselda," 312–14). Potter reads the play's interest in familial relations in terms of a defense of Anne Boleyn in "Tales of Patient Griselda." Donald Beecher notes the problems with the allegory, but he ascribes it to a conflict between myth and morality ("An Obstruction to Interpretation: The Authority of Allegory in *The Comedy of Patient and Meek Grissill*," in *Tudor Theatre: Allegory in the Theatre*, ed. André Lascombes [Bern & Berlin: Peter Lang, 2000], 160–61). There are also brief discussions in Catherine Belsey, *The Subject of Tragedy: Identity and Difference in Renaissance Drama* (London: Methuen, 1985), 164–71; Bernard Spivack, *Shakespeare and the Allegory of Evil* (New York: Columbia University Press, 1958), 272–78; and Charlotte Steenbrugge, *Staging Vice: A Study of Dramatic Traditions in Medieval and Sixteenth-Century England and the Low Countries* (Ludus 13; Amsterdam: Brill/Rodopi, 2014), 196–97.

120 HUMANISM AND GOOD BOOKS IN SIXTEENTH-CENTURY ENGLAND

Let *Grissells* Pacience swaye in [direct] you, wee do you all require,
Whose Historye wee vnto you, in humble wise present,
Beseechyng God, wee alwayes maye in trouble bee content:
And learne with hir in weale and woe, the Lord our God to praise.[32]

Phillip's claims about Griselda align nicely with what Elyot has said about Homer's capacity to inflame readers. Learning about Griselda will move the audience to imitate her: they will be "swayed" to let patience have "sway" over them. Familiar as these claims are, they are, in this instance, somewhat surprising. Griselda's story is not, in fact, a "Historye," a term that implies a classical text: it is instead a popular medieval *exemplum*. At the same time, as the word "Historye," underscores, Phillip's version is not the same as the medieval *exemplum* found in Chaucer's *Canterbury Tales* or Petrarch's letter. Phillip has effectively invoked both the medieval and the humanist versions of *bonae litterae* simultaneously: the *exemplum* form and the classical legacy presented as morally useful. In this way, Phillip uses his play to reflect on the relationship between literary and moral value in his own time: both the general question—how can a story be used to teach morality?—and, more specifically about the classical legacy—how can a classical text teach Christian virtue?

Humanists answered the first question—how can a story be used to teach morality?—confidently, by directing readers (and teachers) to the classical legacy. Phillip seems to be reproducing that confidence by presenting his play as a pseudo-classical text, in a sense reversing what Chaucer does in the *Physician's Tale*, when Chaucer made a classical text into a Christian *exemplum*. Philip titles the play a "comedy," which directly links it to a classical tradition, even though it is a medieval story.[33] In addition, the Preface refers to it as a "history," thus locating it in a stable and authoritative set of moral discourses drawn from the classical tradition, such as Livy's *History of Rome*. Whereas Chaucer's Clerk refers to the Griselda story repeatedly as a "tale" in the prologue, in a sense advertising its fictionality (4.26, 40, 42, 56), the play's Preface offers it as a biography:

If case by Poets skill, or *Pallas* prudent ayd
Historians oft in Hystories, their hole delightes haue staid
To pen & paynt forth painfully, the modest liues of those,
That do in Uertues Scoole their hoap [hope], and confidence repose (1–4).

---

[32] John Phillip, *The Play of Patient Grissell* (London: Malone Society Reprints, 1909), lines 17–20. Hereafter all references will appear parenthetically.
[33] Steenbrugge, *Staging Vice*, 200. Steenbrugge further notes that there is no clear link between secularism and classicism in these plays (203–8).

The author here places Griselda's story among other "Hystories," claiming thereby that her guide is one based on the truth of her "modest life."

This humanist confidence in the capacity of classical texts to teach morality is also evident in the way in which Phillip has de-exemplumed the story, so to speak, and located stability and certainty in the story itself. Not only does he identify it as a history, and therefore true, as opposed to a tale, whose claims on the truth are more ambiguous, his version is less reliant on what Stierle has called systematic discourse—the explicit exposition of lessons. Most obviously, it is a play, with speeches spoken by actors. There is no omniscient and authoritative voice, a single teller, as in Petrarch's version of Boccaccio's story, but instead the actors' "we" in the Preface and at the end. The end of the play is, of course, the logical place for a final lesson. Here the actors only refer to the "auctor;" they do not quote him, and they refer only vaguely to the meaning of the story:

> In our auctors behalfe to you we did commend,
> This historie, wherin we haue bin bould to shoe [show]
> What virtues in *Grissell*, that Ladie did floe [flow] (2097–99).

In invoking an "auctor" and a "historie," Phillip suggests the stability of the text, a confidence about its meaning as such. This confidence does not extend to usefulness for the reader, who is not told how the lesson applies to them, as they are in both Petrarch's and Chaucer's versions. Indeed, the final statement—that Griselda has virtues—is not morally instructive for the audience; it does not indicate what they should do, think, or feel, now that they have seen this story.

Although Phillip presents himself at least in part through a familiar humanist confidence about the moral value of histories, his play also calls that confidence into question. Most obviously, there is the subject matter of the medieval *exemplum*. Indeed, the play responds to the humanist claim—that the classical texts teach noble virtues—at least in part by avoiding it. If pagan men are such great examples for schoolboys, according to Erasmus and Elyot, why does this playwright choose a medieval woman? In addition, the play demonstrates an anxiety about the effect on the reader, a sense that the narrative on its own will not generate enough morality or perhaps a digestible enough morality for its audience. That is, even though it claims certainty for the text's effects, as in Elyot's account of Homer's *Odyssey*, it also uses a technique to ensure that readers see a moral meaning. This is the set of personifications, the vices and virtues who orient the reader morally: Politic Persuasion, who is called the Vice on the title page, and Patience and Constancy, who appear as companions to Griselda and comfort her in the third and final test. The addition of personified abstractions to a story that has not required them for its morality certainly suggests that the relationship between

122   HUMANISM AND GOOD BOOKS IN SIXTEENTH-CENTURY ENGLAND

morality and narrative is being thought through in a new way.[34] And yet, the novelty and the oddness of these personifications have not been sufficiently appreciated.[35] To be sure personifications appear often in medieval literature, including in drama, and they are also often associated with "morality"—ideas about good and bad human behavior, as my discussion of *The Castle of Perseverance* (c. 1400) in the second chapter demonstrates. And yet, they do not commonly appear in *exempla*, because they are not part of the moral apparatus that distinguishes this form. As Chaucer's *Physician's Tale* indicates, the moral language of *exempla* is found most often and usually in the lesson, the explicit statement of applicability to the reader that appears at the end. Although moral abstractions, such as sin and merit, appear in both the final lesson and in the narrative of Chaucer's poem, they are not personified within it. Their appearance in *Patient Grissell* therefore suggests a desire to return to the confidence of the *exemplum*, a desire to fix the moral meaning of the story, thereby proving without a doubt that "history" can be morally useful.

By including these new figures within the narrative, the play attempts to control the moral response of the reader, clearly assigning positive or negative qualities to the characters via the figures associated with them. It is as if the author is not at all confident that the audience will grasp that Griselda's husband Gautier is unreservedly good and then persuaded to be otherwise, and that is why he names his retainers after identifiable virtues, Reason, Fidence, and Sobriety, and then introduces his Vice figure, Politic Persuasion. In this way, the viewers are pushed to see the moral meaning of the actually human characters in real time, their reactions micro-managed, so to speak. At the same time, Phillip does not treat these figures as systematic discourses, in that they do not use language that links outside the play, to other texts and institutions. Despite the familiarity of Reason, who uses the term "reasonable" to refer to his "petiscyon" (126) and speaks of justice, or acting "iustlie" (149), for the most part he sounds like one of Gautier's lords. His name, therefore, merely tells us that this lord is good, as opposed to bad. He does not give

---

[34] Beecher also notes the strangeness of inserting allegorical figures into a story "devoid" of them and attributes this addition to wanting to "resolve in this way the enigmatic motivations of the protagonists" ("An Obstruction," 160).

[35] Spivack describes this play as a "hybrid" (*Shakespeare and the Allegory of Evil*, 272–78). His claim that the allegorical figures are medieval and the real characters are new reverses the facts of the play. This story did not have allegorical figures in its medieval instances, and so the allegorical characters are, in fact, new to this story. More importantly, the Vice figure as such is new to the sixteenth century, and not just new to the Griselda story. See Peter Happé, "John Bale and Controversy: Readers and Audiences," in *The Oxford Handbook of Tudor Literature: 1485–1603*, ed. Mike Pincombe and Cathy Shrank (Oxford: Oxford University Press, 2009), 146 n 10 and Steenbrugge, *Staging Vice*, 11–13, 30–33. Jane Griffiths argues for a shift in the Vice figure in the sixteenth-century in terms of allegory, not so much in terms of morality: "Counterfet Countenance: (Mis)representation and the Challenge to Allegory in Sixteenth-Century Morality Plays," *Yearbook of English Studies* 38 (2008): 17–33. Hampton claims that "this particular struggle between ideology and representation is peculiar to the Renaissance and emerges when the alterity of antiquity meets the moralism of humanist pedagogy" (*Writing from History*, 28). This "particular struggle" seems to be associated more generally with *exempla*, even medieval *exempla*.

GOOD LITERATURE AND THE GOOD   123

a clear sense of what tradition lies behind the idea of Reason, as in Henry Medwall's earlier play, *Nature* (printed 1530), in which the figure Reason is opposed
to "Sensualyte," and tells that figure to stop being so "passyonate."[36] Even Patience
and Constancy, Griselda's allegorical companions, who certainly have an existence
external to this play, in Christian accounts of virtue, do not activate those connections strongly. They appear; define themselves briefly (on which more below); and
then depart. A compelling absence in Patience's speeches is the mention of Jesus
or any other human figure, such as a martyr, who typically provides this virtue
with its meaning.[37] The failure to direct these figures' meaning outside the play is
most apparent at the end, in the final moral lesson, in which the "postemus actor"
mentions neither patience nor constancy, but "commend[s]" Griselda's "virtues"
to the audience.

The attempt to manage the reader's moral response, to secure it as the story
unfolds is most notable in the use of the Vice figure. In medieval versions of the
story, the moral significance of Gautier (known as Walter in Chaucer's *Clerk's
Tale*) is ambiguous, and, as a result, the reader might not know what to do with
him and, potentially, with Griselda herself. Indeed, the Clerk's strange moralizing at the end of Chaucer's version underlines this ambiguity: Griselda is every
person, and she is also a wife, who has a husband. Phillip, in contrast, manages
the moral ambiguity around Walter/ Gautier by introducing a Vice to explain that
what Gautier is doing is wrong. In this way, Gautier is not truly responsible.[38] The
distance between the Vice as moral personification and conventional systematic
discourses is even larger than it is for Reason and Fidence, as indicated by the
novelty of the name: Politic Persuasion.[39] If he'd been named "Lust" or "Avarice,"
he would have embodied a conventional or recognizable moral danger, one that
can be found in many other kinds of texts. But Politic Persuasion does not seem
to fit in any specific moral philosophical or penitential set of discourses, whether
the seven sins or the "vices" that threaten the cardinal virtues, such as prodigality
or intemperance. In fact, the term "politic" could at this time have both positive
and negative moral connotations. In some cases, it seems to mean "prudent," and
is thereby affiliated with one of the cardinal virtues. For the later writer, Robert

---

[36] Henry Medwall, *Nature*, in *The Plays of Henry Medwall*, ed. Alan H. Nelson (Cambridge: D. S.
Brewer, 1980) line 247. On the sophistication of Medwall's play, see Joel Altman, *The Tudor Play of
Mind: Rhetorical Inquiry and the Development of Elizabethan Drama* (Berkeley, CA: University of
California Press, 1978), 13–18.

[37] There is a figure named Patience in Henry Medwall's *Nature*, who advises Man to "remember
how Cryst dyd in tyme of hys passyon" (line 1213). Such a correlation between Christ's suffering and
patience is ubiquitous. See, for example, Lydgate's account of Patience in the *Fall of Princes*, 9.2371–433,
in which he refers to Christ's martyrs.

[38] On the Vice and Gautier, see Belsey, *Subject of Tragedy*, 169; and Bliss, "The Renaissance Griselda,"
310–322.

[39] Steenbrugge, *Staging Vice*, 80–81.

124   HUMANISM AND GOOD BOOKS IN SIXTEENTH-CENTURY ENGLAND

Greene, for example, "polliticke" is positively associated with "good counsels."[40] In other cases, it means "scheming," and there can be no question that the Vice is giving Gautier bad advice.[41] It is worth noting that any Vice figure, named as such, let alone one with an odd name, would have been a relatively new concept, since Vices only begin to appear in drama during the sixteenth-century, despite some vague precedents in medieval plays.

The play further destabilizes the confidence in *bonae litterae*, the general moral claims made for classical texts or histories, by drawing our attention to the contradictions between classical and Christian language, which are, as suggested throughout this study, inherent in the humanist project. For all of his humanism and classicizing, Phillip ensures that the audience sees this virtue of patience as importantly Christian, explicitly directing the audience to "the Lord our God" in the Preface (20); he does not, as Elyot does, translate patience into mainly classical examples, as discussed in the previous chapter. In invoking two distinct registers of virtue, the classical and Christian, Phillip reflects on the gaps between them. The play thus takes up the fundamental claim of the humanist project—that pagan, classical texts teach virtue—and turns it into a question—can pagan, classical texts teach Christian virtue? That question had been to this point in the mid-sixteenth century (and was to be well beyond it) explicitly and implicitly answered in the affirmative. The very term *bonae litterae* insists on the alignment of the various "goods," an alignment taken for granted in the mentions of "virtue" by Elyot and Golding. Phillip's play suggests instead a more cautious approach, even a desire that educators rely on Christian texts, like the story of Griselda, when it comes to teaching virtue.

At first glance, the play seems to harmonize both classical and Christian ideas of virtue through the exemplary figure of Griselda. She is assigned attributes that are directly linked with Christianity and an idea of the good. In the song with which she introduces herself, Griselda describes herself in terms of her obedience and virginity, cataloging the ways in which she honors her aged parents and keeps herself pure. Both of these virtues are directly connected to Christ, since those who obey parents will enjoy "the place which Christ hath bought/ With his hert blood, and deadly wound" (230–31). The relationship between God's physical suffering (his "wound") and obedience is underlined in the discussion that follows between Griselda and her parents. Both her "paine" and her labor are noted (272, 282) and described as "godly behavior" (32). These aspects of Griselda are not described at this point as "virtues," the term the author uses to describe classicized virtue (on which more below), but there is no question that the audience is supposed to understand her as virtuous, within a traditional Christian rubric, one that is very similar to the innocent, virginal Virginia of the *Physician's Tale*. Although

---

[40] *The Repentance of Robert Greene* (London, 1592) STC 12306, A2r.
[41] *OED* s.v. politic.

Griselda is importantly virginal, her obedience, which receives extended attention is not gendered female; honoring parents is exactly the same kind of behavior encouraged in the grammar books written for boys and the sub-genre of morality plays called prodigal-son-plays, both of which belong to a humanist, educational environment, perhaps the same one that shaped this play.

Griselda's "virtues" as such refer to an entirely different set of dispositions all explicitly drawn from classical texts and all gendered female. Virtues emerge in Gautier's speeches, not in Griselda's family life. When Gautier first speaks of his "Ladies fame" (360), directly after the scene between Griselda and her parents, he states:

> Such vertues in a yonglings brest, is syldome seene or rare,
> A Phillis for hir costant truth, a Thisbe for her loue
> Hir arguments most pythie doe, hir vertues daylye proue (363–65).

While this praise is entirely conventional, it bears little relation to the character we have just seen, who sounds much more like the ideal Sunday-school student than a character from Ovid's *Metamorphoses*, a Phyllis or a Thisbe. This is not merely an idiosyncratic moment, because Gautier repeats almost identical praise throughout the play. The most detailed language associated with the term "virtue" is one drawn from pagan texts: in the song that Griselda and Gautier sing together about their love, after they agree to marry (840–75); in his praise of her to his courtiers (979–991); and then at the end of the play, when they are reunited (1937–54). The most important of these virtues seems to be "faithfull loue" (1941), which is certainly analogous to constancy, but retains a distinctly earthly as opposed to spiritual quality, since it is only described in terms of lovers. Phillip's approach to virtue might have been inspired by a familiarity with Chaucer's poetry, such as his pagan models of feminine virtue in the *Legend of Good Women*. Lynn Shutters has argued persuasively that these pagan models influenced Chaucer's portrayal of Griselda in Chaucer's *Clerk's Tale*.[42] And yet, for Chaucer the pagan models remain only implicit, in contrast to the specifically Christian models of virtue, the patience of the martyrs, Job, and Christ.

Patience is especially suited for exploring the relationship between classical and Christian morality precisely because it was, in the sixteenth century, an identifiably accretive virtue, discussions of which very explicitly fused classical and Christian texts.[43] Lydgate's account of patience in his poem *The Fall of*

---

[42] Lynn Shutters, "Griselda's Pagan Virtue," *Chaucer Review* 44 (2009): 61–83. Charlotte C. Morse notes that Petrarch connects Griselda to "pagan martyrs" in his writings ("The Exemplary Griselda," *Studies in the Age of Chaucer* 1 [1985]: 62).

[43] On the varieties of meanings around patience, especially its mixing of classical and Christian, see Ann Astell, "Heroic Virtue in Blessed Raymond of Capua's *Life of Catherine of Siena*," *Journal of Medieval and Early Modern Studies* 42 (2012): 35–57; Ralph Hanna, "Some Commonplaces of Late

126 HUMANISM AND GOOD BOOKS IN SIXTEENTH-CENTURY ENGLAND

Princes, discussed in the previous chapter, shows how stories from these traditions can be linked together through the virtuous suffering of an exemplary figure: Anaxarchus, the Greek philosopher who was tortured to death by a tyrant and "For suffraunce gat hym a souereyn pris [Gained an outstanding reward for his suffering]" and "Blessed Edmund," who "suffred for our feith victorious greuaunce [harm]" (9.2251 and 9. 2416–17). Chaucer's *Clerk's Tale* locates such "vertuous suffraunce" in Griselda: she, and no one else, is the person who is constant in adversity (4.1162). Despite having a Griselda at the center of his play, Phillip disperses the meanings of patience, breaking it down into various moments with various meanings—as an allegorical figure, in conversations among characters, and in appeals to the audience. Not only does Phillip abandon the unified moral statement about patience around which Griselda's meaning is built, for Petrarch and then Chaucer, he also unsettles what was an assumed even automatic link between patience and suffering. In this way, he raises a question about what precisely Griselda is an example of: is she "vertuous suffraunce," as she is in Chaucer's version, or something else, a new combination of passivity and obedience?[44]

In his own attempt at humanist fusion, of classical and Christian ideas of patience, Phillip shows that such fusion limits Christian morality. To be sure, sixteenth-century audiences were likely primed to see patience as the central point of the play, given the reputation of "Patient Griselda" generated by Chaucer's and Petrarch's tales. Nevertheless, patience is in his play weaker and vaguer than in the sources. It first emerges as an ancillary to virtue not virtue itself, and in an odd context. The Vice introduces the idea of "her patience," and in a casual observation, not as part of a praise of her virtues and, therefore, quite dissimilar from the serious tone taken by Chaucer's Walter, who commands Griselda to "Shewe now youre pacience in youre werkyng [Now show your patience in your actions]" (4.495). In the play, the Vice overhears the other lords "Praysynge her for Uertues" (920). Although he does not specify these virtues, they seem to echo Elyot's "noble virtues," that is, behavior associated with the nobility, because the Vice tells the lords that Griselda is without virtue, specifically because she lacks nobility or "noble sanguinnitie [blood]" (926). Only when the lords defend her does he mention patience: he will use "pollicie" (960) and "trye her pacience another kynde of

---

Medieval Patience Discussions: An Introduction," in *The Triumph of Patience*, ed. Gerald J. Schiffhorst (Orlando, FL: University Presses of Florida, 1978), 65–87; and Schiffhorst, "Some Prolegomena for the Study of Patience, 1480–1680," in *The Triumph of Patience*, 1–31. There is nevertheless consensus that suffering is an important part of patience. Schiffhorst notes the "new attention" to patience brought by humanist interest in classical texts ("Some Prolegomena," 1).

[44] There are six instances of the word "pacience" in the *Tale* proper and two in the envoy. Elizabeth Salter notes the repetition and observes that the word "points clearly to the 'inner' meaning of the fable" (*Chaucer: The Knight's Tale and the Clerk's Tale* [London: Edward Arnold, 1962], 44). In addition, "vertuous suffraunce" appears at 4.1162 and some version of "suffer" appears six times.

waye" (962). This phrasing that suggests patience is related to virtue in that he will test whether her virtue/ nobility is patient, but it is not virtue per se.

Similarly, the personification of patience, who appears after the final test when Gautier sends Griselda back to her father, weakens this virtue. The figure describes herself mainly as an aid to right behavior not the behavior itself. Although she does define herself as a virtue, in contrast to the Vice's description, she is not, importantly suffering itself but the comfort for it:

> I represent a vertue called Pacience,
> Uery meete and neadfull for such as suffer afflicsyon,
> I comfort the mind tossed with incouenience,
> And instruckt them humblye to suffer punission,
> I teach them paciently to duer [endure] correcsion
> So that in trouble I am a safe preseruasion (1787–92).

Readers who approach this speech from the perspective of medieval accounts of patience, will be struck by its insistence on utility, on managing suffering as opposed to feeling it or facing its consequences in the world. Instructed as she is by Patience, Griselda is here less its embodiment, or the figure through which the audience or author thinks through patience, then a good student, who can and does learn what patience is.

As Patience's speech makes clear, Phillip has weakened the link between patience and suffering, thereby minimizing its particularly Christian morality. One could say that this change is a kind of side effect of the emphasis on obedience, a virtue that is not exactly the same as patience and is highlighted as distinct on the title page: the play provides a "good example" not only of patience, but also of "the due obedience of Children" (A1r). While the new emphasis on obedience makes sense, given that the play was likely performed by children, it nevertheless disrupts a very traditional meaning of patience as suffering. In the earlier part of the play, pain, such as the pain of Christ, is assigned to obedience, namely in Griselda's initial song, which details both her obedience and the suffering of Jesus. And later in the play, Griselda's reactions to her children being taken from her are imagined as painful, but not, strangely enough, in terms of patience as they are in Chaucer's version: Politic commends her "gentill disposed mynde" (1518) that seeks to "mitigate the husbands paine" with her own (1522). Although the play does refer to patience as pain, it does so only once and not for Griselda.[45] When Griselda's daughter is reunited with her mother, she says,

---

[45] Most of the instances of the word "suffer" in the play do not refer to Griselda. There are several instances that link suffering to patience: the word "suffer" occurs twice in Patience's speech (H1r, 1788 and 1790) to Griselda, once in Griselda's account of the necessity of patience (G4v, 1706), and once in Janicle's account of his own experience (H1v, 1814). Interestingly, the latter two instances separate Patience from suffering: patience is not itself suffering; one needs it in order to suffer (endure).

128 HUMANISM AND GOOD BOOKS IN SIXTEENTH-CENTURY ENGLAND

> Ah my sweet mother, did thou suffer such payne,
> For mee thy Childe, great is thy Pacience,
> God graunt I maye kindly, reward thee agayne,
> With the perfecte fruictes, of Childlie obedience (H3r, 1959–62).

This small speech brings together suffering, patience, and the idea of virtue's reward, but under the larger idea of obedience.

The personification of patience allows Phillip to secure the moral meaning for his play, but it also limits the kind of moral complexity that informs Chaucer's tale. Indeed, Phillip forestalls the questions about Griselda's behavior that remain unanswered in Chaucer's version: whether her behavior, in sacrificing her children, is, in fact, Christian; whether her suffering is redemptive or mis-directed. In Phillip's play, Patience is only one of Griselda's and her child's virtues, activated when they need it, instead of the central virtue in her story. But as much as the allegorical figure represents an internal virtue, it also, in its very embodiment, suggests that the virtue is external to Griselda. Indeed, inserting allegorical figures into a story alongside "real" characters makes the characters more human and less suited to allegorical readings. In Chaucer's and Petrarch's versions, the moral lesson at the end forces Griselda to be a symbol—"Patient Griselda." By having Patience and Constancy appear in the play, alongside Griselda, Phillip ensures that the audience sees Griselda as a character who has patience, as opposed to a character who is patience. As such, she can also have other kinds of dispositions, and any potential contradictions between her maternal feelings and her obedience, for example, can be explained in terms of the struggle between those dispositions in a "real" person. If Griselda is, as she is in Chaucer's version, an exploration of patience, then all of those contradictions must be located within the idea of patience itself.

This simultaneous dispersal and narrowing of patience's meanings end up de-Christianizing it, at least in part. After the Vice's initial use of the term, Gautier re-assigns patience, somewhat oddly, to a list of pagan feminine virtue in his third catalogue of classical women. He calls Griselda a Dido, a Penelope, a Thisbe, and then finally a Cassandra, for whom "shee for pacyence, full aptly maye be namde [named]" (988). Such a list feminizes patience, which is not necessarily a gendered virtue in the Christian tradition. After all, Christ is the model of suffering from which all other models derive. One might look, once again, to John Lydgate's account of patience in his poem *The Fall of Princes*, in which he lists a series of male saints, whom he praises for their suffering, and he even praises Edmund for his virginity (9.2413–19). In associating this virtue with pagan women, Gautier ensures that the audience sees it as de-Christianized before it becomes Griselda's signature virtue. Moreover, this new association alters the meaning of suffering. In the Christian tradition, patience is ultimately suffering for others, whether Jesus's suffering, the suffering of saints, or the pagan philosophers who suffered at the hands of the tyrants they tried to moderate, all of which are described in Book 9 of Lydgate's *Fall*. Associating patience with women who suffered for love makes it a self-indulgent and futile virtue, one that no longer has the capacity to change the world.

A further de-Christianizing of patience occurs when Phillip separates it from one of its most conventional associations, the suffering of saints. Saints only appear in the speeches of the Vice, who unsurprisingly muddies what might be an expected relationship between saints, Griselda, suffering, and patience:

> If your wyfe be so vertuous as nowe ye import,
> Surelie, surely shee is worthy commendacion,
> Shee may be made a saynte for her good conuersacion [behavior]:
> But harke my Lorde nay nowe harken in your eare,
> Try hir that waye and by myne honestie I sweare,
> You shall see hir decline from Uertues so rife,
> And alter topsie turuie hir saintish lyfe:
> Hir pacyence quicklye shall chaunged bee,
> I warrant your honor will say it is not shee (993–1001).

While the Vice is clearly asking Gautier to test Griselda's virtue, in a scene that recalls the Book of Job, his reference to saints confuses what might otherwise be a clear-cut alignment of suffering with virtue, one that typically travels with the Griselda figure. In the Vice's speech, saints are associated with a kind of pre-test Griselda, with her good behavior, and not, as they traditionally are, with suffering. As a result, calling Griselda saint could be insincere, could call saints themselves into question. That uncertainty is reinforced by the term "saintish," which raises questions about what aspects of her life are good and worthy of imitation. The mixed message around sainthood can be attributed to the immediate Protestant context for *Patient Grissell*.[46] Even more interesting is the removal of patience from the qualities of sainthood. What makes a saint a saint, at least as far as the Vice is concerned, is not patience per se, as it would be, at least in part for Lydgate, but "good conuersacion," i.e. good behavior, and "Uertues," both of which Griselda has. Her patience is once again distinguished from both of those, as something that the Vice will change so that she abandons virtue.

Finally, the play emphasizes a much narrower meaning of patience, the endurance of inconvenience, at its beginning and ending. These are, of course, the places where one looks for an explicit moral lesson, and they do not refer to suffering at all. At the opening of the play, the Preface asks the audience to "Let *Grissills* Pacience swaye in you" so that the play might be "presented" (A2r; 17, 18). This request is very similar to the phrase "I ask for your patience," in which patience

---

[46] On the Protestantism see Bliss, "The Renaissance Griselda: A Woman for All Seasons" and Potter, "Tales of Patient Griselda."

130   HUMANISM AND GOOD BOOKS IN SIXTEENTH-CENTURY ENGLAND

has only the most attenuated link to suffering. After all, waiting for some outcome is not suffering in most cases. The lines that follow this initial request do approach the meaning of patience as suffering: the audience should ask God that the audience can "in trouble bee content" and praise God no matter the circumstances. But describing Griselda as "content in trouble," is quite different from calling her "constant in adversitee" (4.1146), the phrase Chaucer uses. The former phrase suggests that she does not, in fact, suffer from the bad things that happen to her: one could rewrite it as "untroubled by trouble" or even pleased by trouble. Chaucer's phrase, in contrast, implies that she *is* suffering from the bad things, but that she remains unchanged. While it is true that after the Preface the audience sees "Patient Griselda" suffer on stage, and this action might reinforce the association between patience and suffering, the final lines of the play, where one looks for the moral, return to the less religious meaning: the "postemus Actor," says "Besechinge you all, with vs to haue pacyence" (I1r, 2094). As an actor, he requests that the audience put up with the play.

It is worth noting that these changes to the virtue of patience do not make the play less obviously or dogmatically Christian. As the directions to the audience indicate, the play approaches right and wrong human behavior, or morality, in explicitly Christian terms: the audience is to praise God and follow Griselda in virtue. And yet, in comparison with Chaucer's version, what falls under Christian behavior has shrunk quite a bit, reduced from the immensely complicated and capacious subject of what it means to suffer like Jesus in the real world to a more limited range of domestic concerns about obedience and endurance. Moreover, the play indicates that interjecting a more classically derived rubric of virtue, focusing on "noble vertues," limits the kinds of topics that can be considered under Christian behavior. Good literature may still teach the good, but the good may no longer include patience or those aspects of patience that do not align with the sufferings of Dido.[47]

Phillip's play shows a caution about the contradictions built into humanist *bonae litterae*, even a nostalgia for the medieval *exemplum*, whose form is designed to hold those contradictions at bay. As explicitly Christian, the play also offers insight into what has long been understood as the secularizing aspect of humanism.[48] That is, secularization is a kind of byproduct of the humanist claims about the usefulness of the classical legacy, that Ovid teaches virtue and vice, as Golding indicates at the outset of his translation. Such usefulness is, of course, not always there. Given the celebration of the classical text, the end result is a weakening of the Christian message, which does not match up, does not belong to the conversation that the classical text offers. From this perspective, secularization may be

---

[47] In "Heroic Virtue," Astell notes an interesting tension between an Aristotelian "heroic virtue" required for saintliness and the patience of Catherine of Siena.

[48] My thinking on secularism is indebted to J. C. D. Clark, "Secularization and Modernization: the Failure of a 'Grand Narrative,'" *The Historical Journal* 55.1 (2012): 161–94.

less a project of rejecting or even of setting aside Christianity by embracing new classical texts, such as the noble Homer, and more a process of weakening or narrowing Christianity by considering only those aspects that match classical texts, such as Elyot's "noble vertues," or by insisting that a classical text upholds Christian values when it does not. As this play demonstrates, the secularizing narrative of humanism means that humanism is closing off as many avenues of inquiry—about human behaviors, about how people should act—as it is opening new ones or establishing independence from the church or Christianity.

6

Horatian *Dulce et Utile* as Poisonous Reading

There can be no doubt of the success of humanism in sixteenth-century England, its influence on all aspects of literary production: the kinds of texts that authors wrote; how they thought of themselves as authors; and on the idea of literature or poetry itself.[1] In so far as humanism is defined as a celebration and imitation of classical texts in the vein of an Erasmus of Rotterdam or a Sir Thomas More, many authors throughout the sixteenth century, and, of course, beyond, could still be reasonably defined as humanists. At the same time, there is an important shift over time: authors in the latter half of the sixteenth century began to define themselves against their humanist fathers, so to speak. In using the terms of generational conflict, I am, of course, referring to Richard Helgerson's important study, *The Elizabethan Prodigals*, which argued that Elizabethan writers were motivated at least in part by a rebellion against "their humanistic educations."[2] A similar perspective is found in a more recent account: Jeff Dolven's *Scenes of Instruction in Renaissance Literature*, which describes the "tide of rising dissatisfaction with humanism."[3] Rebellion against and dissatisfaction with humanism meant a waning of confidence in one of its foundational beliefs: the necessary link between literary and moral excellence, the good of the *bonae litterae*.

Elizabethan doubt in humanism led authors to search for alternatives, a search that involved, at least in part, a return to pre-humanist writings. That is, medieval

---

[1] There has been a great deal of work on the role of humanism in shaping sixteenth-century English literature. I have drawn on the following: Joel Altman, *The Tudor Play of Mind: Rhetorical Inquiry and the Development of Elizabethan Drama* (Berkeley, CA: University of California Press, 1978); Colin Burrow, "Shakespeare and Humanistic Culture," in *Shakespeare and the Classics*, ed. Charles Martindale and A. B. Taylor (Cambridge: Cambridge University Press, 2004), 9–27; Rebecca Bushnell, *A Culture of Teaching: Early Modern Humanism in Theory and Practice* (Ithaca, NY: Cornell University Press, 1996); Kent Cartwright, *Theatre and Humanism: English Drama in the Sixteenth Century* (Cambridge: Cambridge University Press, 1999); Mary Thomas Crane, *Framing Authority: Sayings, Self, and Society in Sixteenth-Century England* (Princeton, NJ: Princeton University Press, 1993); Jeff Dolven, *Scenes of Instruction in Renaissance Romance* (Chicago: University of Chicago Press, 2007); Lynn Enterline, *Shakespeare's Schoolroom: Rhetoric, Discipline, Emotion* (Philadelphia: University of Pennsylvania Press, 2012); Richard Helgerson, *The Elizabethan Prodigals* (Berkeley, CA: University of California Press, 1977); Arthur F. Kinney, *Humanist Poetics: Thought, Rhetoric, and Fiction in Sixteenth-Century England* (Amherst, MA: University of Massachusetts Press, 1986); Eugene Kintgen, *Reading in Tudor England* (Pittsburgh, PA: University of Pittsburgh Press, 1996); and Peter Mack, *Elizabethan Rhetoric: Theory and Practice* (Cambridge: Cambridge University Press, 2002).

[2] Helgerson, *Elizabethan Prodigals*, 11.

[3] Dolven *Scenes of Instruction*, 8.

Humanism and Good Books in Sixteenth-Century England. Katherine C. Little, Oxford University Press.
© Katherine C. Little (2023). DOI: 10.1093/oso/9780192883193.003.0007

texts and authors played an important role in Elizabethan authors' re-examining and replacing the certain link between moral and literary value that they inherited from the humanists. Imitation of medieval texts became a means to think about the consequences of humanist imitation and a means to preserve or recreate a pre-humanist mindset, one in which literature, even *bonae litterae*, might not be good, might even be something that one should reject or abandon. In this chapter, I take up one of the most prolific authors of this period, Robert Greene, to chart this trajectory from humanist confidence to Elizabethan doubt, that is, doubt in the goodness of literature, via medieval alternatives. Greene began his writing career by advertising himself as a humanist or at least in humanist terms: his motto between 1584 and 1590 was the Horatian tag, *Omne tulit punctum qui miscuit utile dulci* [he has won the vote who has mixed the useful and the sweet].[4] To invoke Horace at this time was to assert the moral usefulness of poetry, to offer a kind of humanist party line. And yet, near the end of his life, Greene abandoned this motto and repented of many of his writings in a series of penitential treatises.[5] One of the last of these, *Vision Written at the Instant of his death* (1592), is interestingly marked by its medievalism: it is a dream vision in which the figures of Chaucer and Gower debate the moral value of writing. In this treatise, Greene uses medieval authors to revise the Horatian, humanist idea of literature, the confidence of his earlier motto, and then abandons literature altogether in favor of theology. Where humanists saw great possibilities in the capacity of literature to instruct in virtue, Greene is filled with doubts and wants to redefine, even erase, its moral claims: reading literature, even good literature, can be bad for you.

Humanist Confidence

The humanist confidence in *bonae litterae*, what one might deem Greene's starting point as an author, at least as indicated by his motto, finds its fullest articulation in the influential and now canonical text, Sir Philip Sidney's *An Apology for Poetry*. Although printed after Greene's treatise in 1595, Sidney's treatise was written c. 1581, in response to the Puritan attack on theater and poetry in Stephen Gosson's *School of Abuse* (1579). It is entirely possible that Greene was aware of Sidney's treatise, although proving its direct influence is unnecessary for my argument. Many of Sidney's ideas were broadly available during the time Greene was writing.

---

[4] I borrow the translation from the editors to George Puttenham, *The Art of English Poesy*, ed. Frank Whigham and Wayne Rebhorn (Ithaca, NY: Cornell University Press, 2007), 36 n. 97. For Greene's use of the motto, see e.g. the title page for *Arbasto The anatomie of fortune* (London, 1589) STC 12219. On Greene's mottos, see Walter Davis, *Idea and Act in Elizabethan Fiction* (Princeton, NJ: Princeton University Press, 1969), 179.

[5] In 1591, Greene took a new motto *Sero, sed serio* [late but sincere] when he turned from writing romances to an "autobiographical model" (Sandra Clark, "Robert Greene [July 1558–3 September 1592]," in *Sixteenth-Century British Nondramatic Writers*, 3rd Series, ed. David A. Richardson [Detroit, MI: Thomson Gale, 1996], 69).

134 HUMANISM AND GOOD BOOKS IN SIXTEENTH-CENTURY ENGLAND

To a great degree, his *Apology* offers a standard account of the value humanists assigned to poetry or literature, the Horatian ideal of a combined sweetness and usefulness, although, as it is also important to note, Sidney's treatise is rich and subtle on its own terms.[6] Sidney demonstrates that the idea of poetry, indeed the value of poetry, in this period depended on agreement about and, of course, confidence in its moral usefulness, its capacity to move and instruct its readers in right actions and right dispositions. More importantly, Sidney's treatise shows how this humanist confidence is constructed, by repressing contradictions and closing down the possibility that reading good books might be bad for you. Because those moral concerns could be associated in Sidney's time with the medieval tradition, in which reading pagan books was threatening to Christian belief and practice, as discussed in Chapter 1, they emerge for Sidney around the figure of Chaucer.

Before discussing what one might call Sidney's anti-medieval novelty, I do want to underline a common value. Sidney shares with Chaucer, and with medieval authors more generally, a strong belief in the affective force of imaginative literature.[7] One of the main purposes, if not the main purpose, of reading books is to shape one's behavior, feelings about, and understanding of the world one lives in. In his account of tragedy, Sidney writes that "with stirring the affects of admiration and commiseration, [tragedy] teacheth the uncertainty of this world."[8] Such a view describes almost exactly Chaucer's approach in his poem *Troilus and Criseyde*. Chaucer understands his book as a "tragedye," and he frames the story with his narrator's emotional response to "the double sorwe of Troilus;" he is "weeping" as he writes it.[9] For both Chaucer and Sidney, the affective force of a book is always potentially moral, in that it has the capacity to change human behavior for the good.

At the same time, Sidney is far more insistent than Chaucer that good, by which he means classical or classically inspired, poetry will necessarily produce this goodness in a reader, and that it will inspire only goodness, virtue as opposed to vice. This confidence should by now be familiar, since it pervades humanist accounts of classical texts, such as Sir Thomas Elyot's *Boke of the Governour* (1531) and Erasmus's *Education of a Christian Prince* (1516). For Sidney, the primacy of poetry, its superiority to moral philosophy and history, lies precisely in its greater efficacy as a virtue-delivery device: "For conclusion, I say the philosopher

---

[6] For Sidney's debts to other thinkers, see Geoffrey Shepherd's introduction in Sir Philip Sidney, *An Apology for Poetry, or The Defence of Poesy*, ed. Geoffrey Shepherd (New York: Barnes & Noble Books, 1973), 1–91. As Shepherd writes, "the main ideas in the *Apology* were not peculiar to Sidney" (16).

[7] Wesley Trimpi, "Sir Philip Sidney's *An Apology for Poetry*," in *The Cambridge History of Literary Criticism Volume 3: The Renaissance* (hereafter *CHLC* 3), ed. Glyn P. Norton (Cambridge: Cambridge University Press, 1999), 3: 187–98.

[8] Sir Philip Sidney, *An Apology for Poetry, or The Defence of Poesy*, 3rd ed., ed. Geoffrey Shepherd and R. W. Maslen (New York: Palgrave, 2002), 98. Hereafter all references will appear parenthetically.

[9] Geoffrey Chaucer, *Troilus and Criseyde*, in *The Riverside Chaucer*, 3rd ed., ed. Larry D. Benson (Boston: Houghton Mifflin, 1987), 5.1786; 1.1–7. Hereafter all references to Chaucer's works will appear parenthetically.

teacheth, but he teacheth obscurely, so as the learned only can understand him; that is to say, he teacheth them that are already taught. But the poet is the food for the tenderest stomachs, the poet is indeed the right popular philosopher, whereof Aesop's tales give good proof; whose pretty allegories, stealing under the formal tales of beasts, make many, more beastly than beasts, begin to hear the sound of virtue from these dumb speakers" (92). Poetry makes things "better" than they are with the "prettiness" of its allegories, an improvement that is as much moral as aesthetic. Such an account is a long way from the practicalities of Horace's *Ars Poetica* and its advice to make characters to seem like "living beings." For this reason, much has been made of Sidney's idealizing, his sense that "poets only deliver a golden [world]" (85).[10]

Sidney is not entirely consistent in his "Idea" of poetry, or in his idealizing, but he is consistent in asserting that poetry is morally useful for its readers (85). Poetry teaches virtue, and, to a lesser extent, how to avoid vice, and it teaches so well because it delights. That this link between teaching and delighting is fundamental to his idea of poetry cannot be doubted. Sidney repeats a combination of some version of the words delight and teach twelve times. Indeed, the link appears so often in the treatise as to appear possibly obsessive or frantic. For example, in his description of what great poets do, Sidney claims that they "imitate both to delight and teach: and delight to move men to take that goodness in hand, which without delight they would fly as from a stranger, and teach, to make them know that goodness whereunto they are moved" (87). Delight is both a necessary aid to morality, in that it moves them to the good, and a motivator for learning, attracting men to knowledge. In repeating the same terms to describe poetry throughout the treatise, Sidney reorients the reader's perspective around these two poles to the exclusion of everything else. There only two ways to view poetry, either the embrace of the Horatian mode or its rejection. One can agree with poetry's greatness or disagree. There is no language for describing different kinds of learning, teaching, and knowledge, nor is there a language for the different kinds of virtue or vice. Nor is there a way to describe the uncomfortable situation of the reader or author who reveres Virgil but thinks that his poem is filled with "cursed" pagans and harmful or rascally behavior, to borrow Chaucer's terms for the classical legacy in *Troilus and Criseyde*. Whatever contradictions appear in this treatise, and there are certainly many, they remain largely implicit. This text is, on the face of it, a defense of poetry, a defense that Sidney did not need to write but wrote anyway.[11]

Sidney's confidence in the moral value of poetry, the value of poetry for a reader, paradoxically depends on shifting attention away from that reader with a new

---

[10] For an account of the debate over "idealist" and "non-idealist" views of poetry, see Catherine Bates, *On Not Defending Poetry: Defence and Indefensibility in Sidney's Defence of Poesy* (Oxford: Oxford University Press, 2017), e.g. vii–xii.

[11] I am referring to the essay by Joseph Campana, "On Not Defending Poetry: Spenser, Suffering, and the Energy of Affect" *PMLA* 120.1 (2005): 33–48.

136 HUMANISM AND GOOD BOOKS IN SIXTEENTH-CENTURY ENGLAND

emphasis on the poet or text. In medieval classicism, in the commentaries and translations discussed in Chapter 1, the reader had to be trained to strip the profitable kernel out of the text. Even as authors acknowledged that the kernel was there, they also imagined that some might not get it; hence all of the apparatus that circulated with the texts, the glossing and moralizing. For Sidney, the moral content is, in contrast, transparent, because it was put in there by the author. After all, the poet makes things better than they are, or golden. Sidney's celebration of the poet is certainly a familiar one—at least in the Italian, humanist tradition that influenced him. For Sidney, the poet is almost divine: "Among the Romans a poet was called *vates*, which is as much as a diviner, foreseer, or prophet, as by his conjoined words *vaticinium* and *vaticinari* is manifest: so heavenly a title did that excellent people bestow upon this heart-ravishing knowledge" (83). At the same time, his neglect of the reader is curious, because Sidney's definition of poetry requires readers.[12] If poetry is teaching and delighting, then it is teaching and delighting someone. A text can only be useful if it is useful for someone. He does not, however, consider what usefulness is or the conditions under which a text might be useful. Instead, the "heart-ravishing knowledge" is in there, available to everyone who reads.

At first glance, it might seem that Sidney's treatise is not entirely confident (and not, therefore, entirely humanist) in that he allows more concerns about the reader, more uncertainty, than, say, Erasmus. But these concerns appear only in a very limited fashion and are immediately refuted. In the penultimate section of the treatise, Sidney reinforces the stability and certainty of poetry, fencing poetry off, albeit unsuccessfully, from any bad effect on readers, from its capacity to train readers in immorality as opposed to morality. Scholars have tended to see these contradictory claims about poetry's unquestionably positive effect, its training in virtue, in terms of Sidney's own historical moment: his Protestant poetics, as does Brian Cummings, or class conflict, for Robert Matz, or the profit economy, for Catherine Bates.[13] These contradictions are not, however, new to Sidney nor are they new to his time. Rather, they are contradictions that Sidney has inherited, perhaps unconsciously, from previous literary traditions. That is, Sidney's treatise shows that other ideas of literature, ideas he associates with Chaucer, must be denied or repressed in order for his "Idea" of poetry to make sense (85). In his

---

[12] The absence of readers is noted by Gavin Alexander, "Loving and Reading in Sidney," *Studies in Philology* 114.1 (2017): 41 and Robert E. Stillman, "The Scope of Sidney's 'Defence of Poesy': The New Hermeneutic and Early Modern Poetics," *English Literary Renaissance* 32.3 (2002): 358.

[13] Sidney oscillates between a sense of poetry as divine (transcendent) and poetry as fallen and therefore sinful. See Brian Cummings, *The Literary Culture of the Reformation: Grammar and Grace* (Oxford: Oxford University Press, 2003), 264–70 and Nandra Perry, "Imitatio and Identity: Thomas Rogers, Philip Sidney, and the Protestant Self," *English Literary Renaissance* 35.3 (2005): 365–406. For Robert Matz, Sidney is reconciling Protestantism, which had bourgeois connotations, and aristocratic ideals; see his *Defending Literature in Early Modern England: Renaissance Literary Theory in Social Context* (New York: Cambridge University Press, 2000), 56–87. For Bates, Sidney is rejecting "idealism and profitability" because of "their complicity with money thought" (*On Not Defending Poetry*, viii).

third and last refutation, he takes up the familiar danger of reading—the titillations of love poetry. Repeating the Puritan attack on poetry, in response to Stephen Gosson's *School of Abuse*, Sidney describes poetry as seduction: "[people say] it is the nurse of abuse, infecting us with many pestilent desires, with a siren's sweetness drawing the mind to the serpent's tale of sinful fancy—and herein, especially, comedies give the largest field to ear (as Chaucer saith); how both in other nations and in ours, before poets did soften us, we were full of courage, given to martial exercises, the pillars of manlike liberty, and not lulled asleep in shady idleness with poets' pastimes" (102). Although Sidney appears to be primarily concerned with sexual sins, as suggested by the pun on "tale," there is at least the possibility that sexual seduction stands in for other kinds of seductions, for the pleasures of "idleness," and the wrong-thinking associated with the pun therein: idol-ness, as in idolatry. This pun subtly reminds readers that poetry can seduce them from the right path, can cause them to wander from God, as imagined by Augustine's account of idolatry, which represents it as a delight in voyages or beautiful things. Indeed, Sidney echoes Roger Ascham's, *The Scholemaster* (1570), which conflates the seductiveness of Italian romances with their corrupting religious influence: "For they, carrying the will to vanitie [waste of time], and marryng good manners, shall easily corrupt the mynde with ill opinions, and false iudgement in doctrine: first, to thinke ill of all trewe Religion, and at last to thinke nothyng of God hym selfe, one speciall pointe that is to be learned in *Italie*, and *Italian bookes*."[14] Ascham's is a very Augustinian fear, that straying into the delight of a text can be a straying away from religion and from God.

Sidney's confidence is also apparent in his humanist focus on virtue; for the most part he sets aside its corollary, sin. Indeed, the word "virtue" appears three times as frequently as "vice," and the words "sin," and "sinfulness" appear only a handful of times.[15] Reading is good for you, and for that reason there is mostly no need to consider that it might be bad for you. When he does eventually consider the possible dangers to readers, the temptation to sin, his response does not, in the words of Arthur Kinney, satisfy. He merely reasserts the humanist party line. At the same time, he hints that he knows the problem is more complicated than he has stated.[16] The sign of that complication, that sense that reading might be bad for

---

[14] Roger Ascham, *The Scholemaster*, in *English Works*, ed. William Aldis Wright (Cambridge: Cambridge University Press, 1904), 231.

[15] Virtue appears thirty times; vice appears eight times, usually in relation to virtue, and sin/ sinfulness appear four times. See Sir Philip Sidney, "The Defense of Poesy," in *English Essays: Sidney to Macaulay*, The Harvard Classics (1909–14), online at https://www.bartleby.com/27/1.html.

[16] As Arthur Kinney long ago noted, Sidney's "disagreement with Gosson was not a substantial one" and further that "Sidney fails to distinguish Gosson's crucial point, that art may move men to good or evil. When an angel and devil appear on stage, who is to say which is more appealing to the playgoer? Ultimately, Sidney begs this question (possibly by assuming a greater inherent goodness in man). All in all, the *Defense* read in light of Gosson's 'attack' is neither convincing nor especially satisfying" ("Parody and its Implications in Sydney's *Defense of Poesie*," *Studies in English Literature 1500–1900* 12.1 [1972]: 16).

138 HUMANISM AND GOOD BOOKS IN SIXTEENTH-CENTURY ENGLAND

you, is Chaucer. Sidney interjects Chaucer, apparently randomly, into his response to Gosson's charge about seduction, as quoted above. He is, of course, directly alluding to the opening of Chaucer's *Knight's Tale*: "I have, God woot, a large feeld to ere [I have, God knows, a large field to plow]" (1.886). At the same time, given the subject, sin, there is also what one might call a Chaucerian unconscious, an association between Chaucer and concerns about the sinfulness of writing, its worldly vanity, to borrow the terms used at the end of *Troilus and Criseyde*. That Chaucer was understood in this period in relation to his moralizing—around both sin and worldly vanity—is made clear in a treatise that was printed before Sidney's, a treatise that similarly responds to Gosson's attack on the theater and poetry: Thomas Lodge's *Defence of Poetry, Music, and Stage Plays* (1579). For Lodge, Chaucer "in pleasant vein can rebuke sin uncontrolled; and though he be lavish in the letter, his sense is serious."[17] Lodge links Chaucer to a classical model—his writing offers both delight ("pleasant vein") and seriousness—and he appears alongside Cicero and Ovid. At the same time, Chaucer stands out for his explicitly Christian morality—the rebuking of sin.

Sidney's parenthetical mention of Chaucer demonstrates the way in which humanist confidence has contained, even repressed, the baggy and contradictory moral approach that is characteristic of medieval classicism and literature more generally. While Chaucer has worried, in his Retraction, that his tales encourage ("sownen") readers to sin and, therefore, rejects some of them, Sidney dismisses that kind of concern out of hand. He does so by reclaiming poetry from the reader: "grant, I say, whatsoever they will have granted, that not only love, but lust, but vanity, but (if they list) scurrility, possesseth many leaves of the poets' books; yet think I, when this is granted, they will find their sentence may with good manners put the last words foremost, and not say that Poetry abuseth man's wit, but that man's wit abuseth Poetry" (104). In this response, poetry is not an idea, as it has been for so much of the treatise, but a thing, one that has a real, material existence and, therefore, can be acted upon. It is a thing because it is in the "leaves" of a book, and it contrasts with "man's wit," which, is immaterial and therefore, at this moment, less immediate. This reification allows Sidney to preserve the integrity of poetry, its unity and impermeability. As an object, it cannot act but only be acted upon, and therefore, any abuse comes from the reader, not from the poem or the author.

What Sidney's discussion sets aside is precisely what bothered Chaucer and many medieval readers of Ovid—that a good, as in culturally valuable and eloquent, poem might not be useful, might not lead the reader to a moral good. Indeed, Sidney seems at least subliminally aware that he is closing off this possibility because he invokes the author for whom it is not repressed at all: Chaucer.

---

[17] Thomas Lodge, "Defence of Poetry, Music, and Stage Plays," in *Elizabethan Critical Essays*, 2 vols., ed. George Gregory Smith (Oxford: Clarendon Press, 1904), 1:69.

Sidney's reference to Chaucer at this moment seems merely parenthetical, a meta-*occupatio*, using Chaucer, famous for the *occupatio* in the *Knight's Tale*, to stand for the discussion he does not include, about comedy. And yet Chaucer's appearance here gains significance when read against the evaluation of Chaucer that appears shortly after it. In the section that surveys poetry in English, Sidney famously describes Chaucer's *Troilus and Criseyde* as both excellent and limited: "Chaucer, undoubtedly, did excellently in his *Troilus and Criseyde*; of whom, truly, I know not whether to marvel more, either that he in that misty time could see so clearly, or that we in this clear age walk so stumblingly after him. Yet had he great wants, fit to be forgiven in so reverent antiquity" (110). Even though it is Sidney's "we" who are stumbling, they are doing so because they are following Chaucer, and so the quality of stumbling becomes associated with Chaucer. Moreover, the mistiness of Chaucer's time underlines the stumbling; in this account, Chaucer is not passing easily up the steps as his classical models did. Chaucer's lack of poetic control evokes the nervous breakdown that E. T. Donaldson so persuasively assigned to the end of Chaucer's *Troilus and Criseyde*. In sum, Chaucer's limitations, his "wants," have to do with fuzziness and aimlessness: the lack of coherence, the absence of a unified vision, the messiness of the ending. These are all as much moral as aesthetic problems, and they are moral problems that Sidney has spent his entire treatise denying, insisting instead on the coherence and unity of teaching and delighting.

Greene's Medievalism

If humanism required confidence, abandoning the uncertainty of medieval authors in favor of Horace's teaching and delighting, then reclaiming medieval authors could be a way to re-introduce doubt, to reject or redefine the Horatian mode, to challenge the kinds of claims that Sidney and earlier humanists made for poetry. That challenge is seen in Robert Greene's *Vision*. Greene's use of Chaucer and Gower in this, one of his last works, is particularly notable since his other writings do not demonstrate any sustained interest in the medieval. Known now primarily for his Shakespearean connections—he famously called Shakespeare an "upstart crow," and his romance *Pandosto* (1588) is a source for *The Winter's Tale*—his writings tend to be trendy and novel, not archaizing and old-fashioned.[18] Greene was a popular pamphleteer, who made a living from his writings. Perhaps for that reason, he does not place himself within a lineage of English authors that includes Chaucer, as did Edmund Spenser. Nor does one find

---

[18] The phrase "upstart crow" appears in *Greenes Groatsworth of Wit* (1592). See Brian Vickers, "'Upstart Crow'? The Myth of Shakespeare's Plagiarism," *The Review of English Studies* 68 (2017): 244–267. On Greene and Shakespeare, see, for example, Lori Humphrey Newcomb, *Reading Popular Romance in Early Modern England* (New York: Columbia University Press, 2002).

140 HUMANISM AND GOOD BOOKS IN SIXTEENTH-CENTURY ENGLAND

pious (if backhanded) references to Chaucer's excellence, as in Sidney's *Apology* or George Puttenham's *The Art of English Poesy* (1589).[19] And yet, Greene is the only one of these Elizabethan authors who compellingly brings Chaucer himself to life.[20]

Greene's *Vision* is not very well known today, and a brief summary may be necessary. The treatise itself is a kind of anxiety dream about Greene's youthful "follies," his earlier writings that concern love. It begins with the "I" awake and penitent. After composing an Ode about "wanton writings," Greene is filled with remorse and fear about being called to account for his works. He falls asleep, and in his dream, two figures appear to him: Chaucer and Gower. They argue over the capacity of literature to instruct in morals, and then Chaucer proposes a test. Each tells a tale about jealousy. Gower considers himself the winner, and he begins to instruct Greene on what kind of literature he should write in the future: aphoristic and explicitly philosophical. Suddenly, the figure Solomon appears and tells him to reject Gower (even as Gower has rejected Chaucer) and to turn his thoughts to theology. Greene wakes up and resolves to change his ways, to leave love and seek after the wisdom "commended" by Solomon.

As should be clear from the summary, the treatise follows a trajectory from doubt to "worldly vanity"; the dissipating of confidence in humanism results in a strong statement on the uselessness, or vanity, of all non-religious writing. This ending point is a return to the medieval, in that the final moral is the same one found in Chaucer's Retraction to the *Canterbury Tales*, in which he repents of his "enditynges of worldly vanitees [compositions of worldly vanities]" and thanks Jesus for his explicitly devotional and moral works (10.1086). Although one cannot say for certain that Greene knew Chaucer's Retraction, it is worth noting this echo. Greene follows Chaucer's moral coordinates: the wrong kind of writing is a vanity (the "vanity of wanton writings") and the right kind is explicitly Christian in its content (Theology).[21] Despite the echo, Greene's condemnation of literature is bleaker than Chaucer's. There is a comprehensive, even systematic devaluing of literature, both poetry and imaginative writing more generally, a sense that it cannot be good, as in morally useful, no matter what people say, and there is,

---

[19] See *Apology*, 82, 91, 110. See also Puttenham, *The Art of English Poesy*, 148–49.

[20] Earlier scholars, such as Helgerson and Davis, were not particularly interested in Greene's use of Chaucer and Gower; see *Elizabethan Prodigals*, 96–97 and *Idea and Act*, 180–81, respectively. A more recent scholar describes the appearance of these medieval poets as "no more than a brilliant ploy to focus on himself" (Arul Kumaran, "Robert Greene's Martinist Transformation in 1590," *Studies in Philology* 103 [2006]: 256). In contrast, three recent studies read Greene in relation to Chaucer, especially his Retraction: Megan Cook, "Nostalgic Temporalities in *Greenes Vision*," *Parergon* 33 (2016): 44; Jeremy Dimmick, "Gower, Chaucer and the Art of Repentance in Robert Greene's 'Vision,'" *The Review of English Studies* 57 (2006): 467; and Robert Maslen, "Greene and the Uses of Time," in *Writing Robert Greene: Essays on England's First Notorious Professional Writer*, ed. Kirk Melnikoff and Edward Gieskes (Aldershot, UK: Ashgate, 2008), 184.

[21] *Greenes vision vvritten at the instant of his death. Conteyning a penitent passion for the folly of his pen* (London, 1592) STC 12261, B1r, image 4. Hereafter all references will appear parenthetically with folio and image numbers.

HORATIAN *DULCE ET UTILE* AS POISONOUS READING   141

therefore, no point in writing it and a clear danger in reading it. For that reason, his repentance has been seen as self-negating or in some way incomplete.[22] As Walter Davis notes in his perceptive, if brief, account of this text: the treatise is a "sweeping denial ... of any ethical effect in literature except by the most direct and bald means."[23] Greene's nihilistic perspective distinguishes him not only from Chaucer but also from his contemporaries. Indeed, it would be fair to say that he offers a nightmarish perversion of all the claims for poetry that Sidney has famously made in his *Apology*.

Fundamental to Greene's condemnation is the shift from an explicitly humanist language for (and idea of) literature to more medieval-inflected ideas. This shift can be mapped onto the two phases of the text: the meditation before the dream, in which Greene sets up his humanist anxieties about writing, and the dream itself, in which he tries and fails to solve them with the help of the medieval authors. The meditation, the first part, is clearly indebted to the language of humanism. Most obviously, Greene presents his repentance as that of a prodigal son, who is filled with "passionat remorse" for his earlier writings (B2v, image 7); he speaks to God, listing God's merciful acts, including "[thou] killest the fat Calfe for his welcome: thou hast cryed out in the Streetes" (B4r, image 8). The story of the prodigal son was closely associated with humanism from its origins, and Greene's frequent use of this motif earned him a place as "the most popular Elizabethan representative of this type" in Richard Helgerson's study, *Elizabethan Prodigals*.[24] By repenting as a prodigal, Greene suggests not only that he has not been a good enough Christian, but also that he has not been a good enough humanist. He repents for having wasted his time writing love poetry instead of praising God or "discouering vertues" (B2v, image 7). As the mention of virtue indicates, the problem is not only that his writing is about sin but also that it leads readers to sin. It is not profitable to the reader, and Greene uses this familiar language of profit to describe his failures: "wee were borne to profit our countrie, not onely to pleasure our selves" (B3r, image 7). He further explains this profit in recognizably humanist terms: he has not persuaded "men to honest & honorable actions" (B2v, image 7). In describing his failures, Greene invokes the same language used by Elyot in his *Boke of the Governour* and Sidney in his *Apology*, only to turn it on its head to describe sin and not virtue. Elyot claimed that the reader would be "inflamed" by reading Homer, and Sidney makes the same claims for the *Aeneid*: "Who readeth Aeneas carrying old Anchises on his back, that wisheth not it were his fortune to perform

---

[22] Both Maslen and Dimmick see the text as destabilizing ("Greene and the Uses," 187 and "Chaucer, Gower," 456, respectively). Helgerson identified a "hesitancy in Greene's repentance," with which others have agreed (*Elizabethan Prodigals*, 99; Maslen, "Greene and the Uses," 187; Dimmick, "Chaucer, Gower," 465).

[23] Davis, *Idea and Act*, 181.

[24] Helgerson, *Elizabethan Prodigals*, 79. My understanding of the prodigal in this paragraph is indebted to Helgerson's discussion both in his chapter on Greene and his outline of the model itself (*Elizabethan Prodigals*, 79–104; 16–43, respectively).

142   HUMANISM AND GOOD BOOKS IN SIXTEENTH-CENTURY ENGLAND

so excellent an act?" (95).[25] Greene has not only failed to inflame his readers in virtue, he has instead inflamed them with sin.

Second, Greene explores the capacity of poetry to teach and delight, the familiar Horatian mode, famously detailed in Sidney's *Apology*. In contrast to Sidney, Greene invokes these terms only to keep them separate, as if it were impossible for him to imagine a text both delighting and teaching.[26] For Greene, literature can delight or teach, not both. His revision appears most strikingly in the Ode, with which he begins his text, a poetic insert into his prose treatise. It is a self-reflexive poem, one that surveys classical poets by organizing them around this distinction of delighting and teaching. In the first and more detailed category, of delighting, Greene puts love poetry, including Virgil's *Eclogues* and Ovid's poetry. While this category is clearly negatively inflected, since it is introduced as "the vanitie of wanton writings," it is also delightful, since Greene repeats some form of the word "pleasing" three times and "fair" twice (B1r, image 5). Condemning the love poetry of classical poets is not particularly odd or notable. After all, Ovid was a very complicated and morally ambiguous figure in both the Middle Ages and the Renaissance. As Stephen Gosson writes, near the opening of his treatise attacking poetry, *The School of Abuse*, Ovid "roved long on the seas of wantonness" before becoming a good pilot.[27] What is strange is the assignment of Virgil's *Eclogues* to this category. The *Eclogues* were thought to be both delightful and morally instructive, and they are consistently praised by humanists. For example, in his influential educational treatise, *On the Method of Study*, Erasmus claims that the *Eclogues* are filled with "songs, aphorisms, and proverbs" thus aligning the delight of song with the teaching of morality.[28] In Greene's account, in contrast, the *Eclogues* are only the wrong kind of songs, "wanton lays," and no aphorisms or proverbs are to be found. Greene's "Swaines" think that Tityrus [the figure for Virgil in the *Eclogues*] "Did Poet-like his loues discusse,/ That men might learne mickle [much] good" (B1v, image 6). But Menalcas, sitting nearby, corrects them, saying "their words were all amiss:"

> For (quoth he) such wanton laies [songs],
> Are not worthie to haue praise (B1v, image 6).

No one would deny that an author, even a great author such as Virgil, could be misused by readers: Erasmus worries that readers will see homoeroticism in Virgil's Second Eclogue in his *On the Method of Study* and Sidney "grants" that "not only

---

[25] Sir Thomas Elyot, *A Critical Edition of Sir Thomas Elyot's The Boke Named the Governour*, ed. Donald W. Rude (New York: Garland Press, 1992), 44.

[26] Davis notes the "clean rift" "between usefulness and delight" in this text (*Idea and Act*, 181).

[27] Stephen Gosson, *The School of Abuse*, ed. John Payne Collier (Oxford: Oxford University Press, 1841), 4.

[28] Erasmus, *On the Method of Study*, ed. Craig R. Thompson, trans. Brian McGregor in *Collected Works of Erasmus* (*CWE*), 84 vols. (Toronto: University of Toronto Press, 1974), Vol. 24 (1978): 689.

love, but lust, but vanity, but (if they list) scurrility, possesseth many leaves of the poets' books" (*Apology*, 104). Greene is, however, claiming that Virgil's *Eclogues* will lead readers astray in every instance, that the fault lies with the author not with the readers who "abuse" poetry or bring the wrong frame of mind.

If the first category, of delight, is morally wrong, it is also detailed, its description taking up eighty-six lines. The second, and right, category of teaching is, in stark contrast, both brief and empty, with only ten lines. The figure for the right kind of poetry is the Roman Emperor Caesar Augustus, who famously banished Ovid. He appears in order to assert that poetry can teach: "Poets quils,/Ought not for to teach men ils," because "learning is a thing of prise [value]," poets should "shew precepts to make men wise" (B2v, image 7). Greene does not reject poetry outright, in favor of philosophy or history, since learning comes specifically from "Poets' quills." And yet, such poetry does not seem to exist, since neither Augustus nor anyone else goes on to detail who these poets are or what they wrote. Given the appearance of Augustus, the omission of Virgil's *Aeneid* in this category is quite strange, even stranger than the inclusion of his *Eclogues* in the category of "wanton writings." After all, Augustus himself promoted Virgil's epic poem, and it is unilaterally praised in the writings of the humanists for moving readers to virtue. As Sidney writes in his *Apology*, "no philosopher's precepts can sooner make you an honest man than the reading of Virgil" (116). It would seem that Greene has purposefully repressed the *Aeneid*, drawing our attention to the absence of the poem that was for many, including Sidney, the source of the link between teaching and delighting, or wisdom and eloquence.

Just as Greene severs the link between delight and instruct, he also cuts *dulce* off from *utile*. For Greene *dulce* is not merely distinct from *utile*, as delighting is distinct from teaching, but its opposite, since the sweetness he describes is, in fact, poison. His fears about poisonous reading first appear when he explains the effect of reading love poetry: he confesses that he has "pestred Gentlemens eyes and mindes, with the infection of many fond passions, rather infecting them with the allurements of some inchanted *Aconiton* [poison], then tempered their thought with any honest Antidote, which consideration entered thus farre into my conscience" (B3r, image 7). Despite deploying the metaphor of infection, the sentiment resembles Chaucer's in the Retraction. Greene is worried that his writing has infected his readers with passions, and this is another way of saying that he is worried about tales that "sownen into synne [lead to sin]" to use Chaucer's phrase (Retraction, 10.1086). Such a perspective is entirely conventional: reading the wrong kinds of books can lead one astray. And yet, the metaphor is confused, and it ends up suggesting that all reading material, not just love poetry, is always already potentially poisonous. The first part of the metaphor makes sense: his claim that he has given his readers "Aconiton" translates to the statement: love poetry is poison. But the second, that he has not given them an antidote, is more difficult to translate, since it assumes that the reader has already been poisoned.

144 HUMANISM AND GOOD BOOKS IN SIXTEENTH-CENTURY ENGLAND

It would make more sense to contrast the poison of love poetry with the purity or healthfulness of the right kind of writing: good books as a pure fountain, as Erasmus does, or flowers, as Sidney does, as in the "flowers of poetry" in the *Apology* (83).[29]

Greene's concern about poisonous reading is further and compellingly illustrated by his alteration of a central humanist figure: the bee. For humanists, the bee figures forth foundational beliefs about how readers gain lessons from reading and about the relationship between wisdom and eloquence. References to bees are found throughout influential classical texts, such as Seneca's *Epistula Morales,* and then appropriated into humanist writings. Seneca writes, "We too should imitate the bees; we should separate whatever we have gathered from divers reading (for things held apart are better preserved)."[30] Although apian metaphors have been much discussed in terms of the production of texts (writing poetry), it is important to note that they also describe reading.[31] Greene's own printer makes the bee-reader relationship clear at the opening of another penitential treatise attributed to him, *The Repentance of Robert Greene* (1592), in which the reader is told to be a bee: "I doubt not but you will with regarde forget his follies, and like to the Bee gather hony out of the good counsels of him, who was wise, learned and polliticke [shrewd]."[32] In this common metaphor, the reader is a bee, collecting pollen (useful precepts) from flowers (beautiful texts) in order to make honey, which combines beauty and use. Bees are in and of themselves useful, even necessary, and, as a result, the figure naturalizes a process that is educational and ideological, or not really natural at all.

Greene's anxious musings about the effect of his writings on the reader, his poisoning of the reader with sin, transform the bee into a serpent. The serpent first appears at the beginning of the text, during Greene's repentance, as a perversion of the bee, a bad reader instead of a good one. After expressing his remorse at "abusing" his gift instead of "using" it for "profit," he describes the actions of the serpent: "the serpent is then therefore an odious creature, for that he sucketh poyson from that Odorifferous flower, from whence the painefull Bee gathers her sweete Honnie" (B2v, image 7). Here the bee and serpent are parallel, both using the flower, even as Greene insists that the actions and the products are different: sucking vs. gathering, poison vs. honey. This image is odd not least because it ends up casting doubt on the flowers. They become food for snakes, helping produce poison. In addition, the bee/ serpent images conflate readerly with writerly activity so that

---

[29] Erasmus, *On the Method of Study, CWE,* Vol. 24 (1978): 669.

[30] Seneca *Epistula Morales* 84.5–6, quoted in G. W. Pigman III, "Versions of Imitation in the Renaissance," *Renaissance Quarterly* 33 (1980): 12. See also Colin Burrow, *Imitating Authors: Plato to Futurity* (Oxford: Oxford University Press, 2019), 85–87.

[31] Pigman, "Versions," 4–7. See also the brief account in Crane, *Framing Authority,* 59.

[32] *The Repentance of Robert Greene* (London, 1592) STC 12306, A2r. Greene's authorship has been called into question, but its "style strongly resembles authentic Greene" (Clark, "Robert Greene," 64).

it is not entirely clear who is doing what to whom, who is responsible for the bad effects. Shortly after the initial image, Greene writes, "so the outward phrase is not to be measured by pleasing the eare, but the inward matter by profiting the mind: the puffing glorie of the loftie stile shadowing wanton conceipts is like to the skin of a serpent that contriues impoysoned flesh" (B3r, image 7). This passage invokes the familiar terminology of profit and pleasure and seems to be guided by an implicit contrast between the serpent, which is pleasing to look at but "empoisoned" and something else, which is pleasing to look at and profitable inside (maybe bees?). This claim simply makes no sense and not only because Greene does not identify the contrasting figure. It would be hard to find anyone whose first thought on seeing a snake is that it is beautiful. Although Greene seems to be suggesting that his writings are the serpent, the rest of the metaphor does not work. Does one eat the serpent because it is beautiful and then get poisoned? Or does one look at the serpent, admiring its beauty, and then get poisoned?

In noting his failures in the established language of humanism, Greene indicts the humanist idea of literature as much as he repents for not living up to its ideals. By the end of the opening meditation, one might share Greene's anxiety about whether a text can delight and instruct simultaneously or whether a reader can easily gain moral instruction from a text, whether a writer can control whether his reader is a bee or a serpent. It is at this moment of *aporia* that he has his dream about the medieval authors, Gower and Chaucer, who engage in a story-telling competition focused on morality. The dream explores familiar humanist ideas, about delighting and teaching, but against a backdrop of non-humanist, or rather pre-humanist, kinds of literature, the stories of Gower and Chaucer. Although Greene's dream is, in a sense, a defense of poetry, or at least of the poetry of Chaucer and Gower, it is an ironized and deeply contradictory one that ends up not being a defense at all. When Solomon appears and sets aside storytelling in favor of theology, his certainty is something of a relief.

Greene characterizes both Gower and Chaucer at least in part through their popular sixteenth-century reputations, in which they are at times ambiguously moral, in contrast to the stability and certainty that typically surrounded the *bonae litterae*. Chaucer's varied reputation is well-documented: it involved ribaldry, tall tales, as well as a more serious poetic-making that could be aligned with humanism, Protestantism, or Catholicism.[33] Greene seems most interested in the apparent contradiction, between Chaucer's humanism and its implicit morality, his status as Ascham's "English Homer," on the one hand, and his ribaldry, "wanton lays," the writing that makes him like Greene, on the other.[34] Indeed, Greene's

[33] For a survey of the different versions of Chaucer in circulation, see Helen Cooper, "Poetic Fame," in *Cultural Reformations: Medieval and Renaissance in Literary History*, ed. Brian Cummings and James Simpson (Oxford: Oxford University Press, 2010), 361–78.

[34] Roger Ascham, *Toxophilus* (London, 1545), quoted in Derek Brewer, ed., *Chaucer: The Critical Heritage*, 2 vol. (London: Routledge & Kegan Paul, 1978), 1: 100.

146 HUMANISM AND GOOD BOOKS IN SIXTEENTH-CENTURY ENGLAND

pretext for his repentance is that he's been accused of writing an imitation of the *Canterbury Tales, The Cobler of Caunterburie* (1590), which he vehemently denies having written.[35] If Chaucer's significance is that of a contradictory variety, then Gower's significance looks at first glance less ambiguous, since it is more narrowly focused around morality, for which he was widely praised, praise that begins with Chaucer himself and continues through the sixteenth century.[36] Indeed, George Puttenham echoes Chaucer's assessment, praising Gower as a "grave, moral man" in *The Art of English Poesy*.[37] Gower's morality is, on closer look, more problematic than it might appear, because it does not align easily with humanist ideas. The *Confessio Amantis* is, because of its debts to Ovid, a series of "wanton lays" or stories of "lust," to quote Gower himself, mixed with stories of "lore." Even, Puttenham, who praises Gower's "good and grave moralities," finds problems with the moral rubric of the sins in the *Confessio*: the "application" is "grossly bestowed" and "the substance of his works [does not] sufficiently answer the subtlety of his titles."[38] Despite a difference in the degree of popularity and importance, both Gower and Chaucer thus represent a similarly ambivalent relationship to humanist ideas of poetry: they do not fit into the idealizing terms Sidney has mapped out in his *Apology* and that Greene has represented in his Ode.

Greene not only invokes these familiar medieval authors, he also assigns them familiar medieval genres, the fabliau and the *exemplum*. In this way, he reintroduces some of the moral questions around writing and, maybe more importantly, reading, that have been subsumed into or set aside by humanist approaches and terminology that have dominated discussions of writing in the sixteenth century: delight and instruction, eloquence and wisdom, sweetness and usefulness. If Greene fails to justify his writing according to humanist values, perhaps he can justify his writing in terms of a pre-humanist values, those of Chaucer and Gower. It turns out that he cannot, and in the end, he retreats from all imaginative literature, around the figure of Solomon. His dream nevertheless suggests a desire for a Chaucerian alternative, not Sidney's "golden" world but a version of Chaucer's Retraction: a purposeful lack of clarity about what kind of stories are sinful and a form of repentance that is also a self-promotion.

In the dream, Greene's Chaucer is both a kind of humanist, defending writing and poetry for its eloquence and its dual role in teaching and delighting, and a version of what we might consider the real Chaucer, an author of fabliaux. In this way, Greene further undercuts humanist ideas by assigning them to an unstable, ironized voice. If Chaucer is the teller of ribald tales, stories whose moral value is

---

[35] See *The cobler of Caunterburie* (London, 1590) STC 4579. On the influence of this text, see Dimmick, "Gower, Chaucer," 457; and Maslen, "Greene and the Uses," 184.

[36] Chaucer addresses Gower in the last lines of *Troilus and Criseyde*: "O moral Gower" (*Riverside Chaucer*, 5.1856).

[37] Puttenham, *Art*, 171.

[38] Puttenham, *Art*, 150.

non-existent or questionable, then he cannot also be a sincere humanist. At first, Greene's Chaucer sounds a lot like Sidney, referring to classical authors as both "pleasant" and corrective: "Is there no meanes to cure sores, but with Corasiues? no helpe for vicers [sinners], but sharpe implasters [salves]? no salue against vice, but sowr satyres? Yes, a pleasant vaine, quips as nigh the quicke as a grauer inuectiue, and vnder a merry fable can *Esope* as wel ta[u]nt folly, as *Hesiode* correct manners in his Heroicks. I tell thee this man hath ioyned pleasure with profite, & though his Bee hath a sting, yet she makes sweet honny" (C4r, image 12). Such a defense is a familiar, perhaps the most familiar, humanist position on the value of literature: it joins pleasure and profit. And yet, oddly enough, this position has not appeared before this moment, either in Greene's account of his remorse or in his Ode, and so it appears entirely self-interested. Chaucer only voices this position after making excuses for wanton poetry, for defending love poetry such as Ovid's in terms of "invention" and "conceits." And he uses the Horatian justification right before he tells his fabliau: "it behooues a Scholler to fit his Pen to the time and persons, and to enter with a deepe insight into the humours of men, and win them by such writings as best wil content their fancies, I tell thee: *Omne tulit punctum, qui miscuit vtile dulci*" (D1v, image 14). It is as if Greene wants to ironize the position that humanists took so seriously by assigning it to a character who uses it to defend the indefensible, a story about adultery, just as the real Chaucer calls his moral lessons into question by assigning them to questionable speakers, such as the Pardoner or the Manciple.

Greene destabilizes this humanist position, the link between *dulce* and *utile* even further, when Chaucer argues for the moral value of Greene's love poetry, his "wanton lays," suggesting that Greene's writings resemble stories from Ovid's *Metamorphoses*. Chaucer provides a list of precepts, very similar to the moralizations that travelled with Ovid's stories, such as the claims made by Ovid's first English translator, Arthur Golding, that the stories teach virtues and vices.[39] Greene's Chaucer sets the precepts for Greene off in the text with a title: "Sentences Collected out of the Authors bookes" (C4v, image 14). These are twenty relentlessly misogynistic statements about problems with women or a woman (appearing C4v-D1r, images 14-15). For example, the third is as follows: "Womens faces are lures, there beauties are baites, their lokes nets, their wordes charmes, and all to bring men to ruine" (C4v, image 13). Although the final two sentences, the nineteenth and twentieth, praise women's constancy and goodness, they clearly come from the same misogynistic value system. While it is one thing to argue that reading about women's beauty is delightful, as Chaucer seems to suggest in his initial defense of Greene's pamphlets, it is quite another to say that reading about it is morally instructive. Recovering "amorous" works for morality means perverting them entirely. Delight in reading about love is not sugar to make the

---

[39] See Chapter 5.

148 HUMANISM AND GOOD BOOKS IN SIXTEENTH-CENTURY ENGLAND

medicine go down, a cover underneath which the lesson lurks, but is shown to be directly opposed to the lesson or profit: some women are bad, and sex is bad. By earnestly locating sentences in Greene's writings, Greene, through Chaucer, mocks the approach Erasmus and others took to Virgil's *Eclogues*, finding proverbs and aphorisms among the songs. This Chaucer is, in this way, very Chaucerian, since the real Chaucer similarly mocks Ovidian moralizing in the *Wife of Bath's Tale* (as discussed in Chapter 1).

If Chaucer represents the contradiction facing Greene—a desire to defend his writings while understanding that they do not fit the values associated with poetry, or *bonae litterae* in his own time—then Gower represents a retreat into easy moralizing. Gower rejects the claim that poetry has moral value, and subordinates it to more worthy writing, such as moral philosophy. On the one hand, the subordination of poetry to philosophy is unsurprisingly medieval; on the other hand, Gower was known for his poetry and his storytelling, not his philosophy, and his statements are, therefore, a bit odd or surprising. Greene's Gower offers a hierarchy of writing in which values are clear-cut, as made apparent in the metaphor of gems and flowers: "some bent to pen graue Poems, other to endite wanton fancies, both honoured and praised for the height of their capacitie: yet as the Diamond is more estimated in the Lapidaries shop than the Topace, and the Rose more valued in the Garden than Gillyflowers: So men that write of Morall precepts, or Philosophicall Aphorismes are more highly esteemed, than such as write Poems of loue, and conceits of fancie" (C3r, image 11). Such a statement is a kind of wish-fulfillment: there is no confusion in shops and gardens about what one is buying or picking, as there might be in Sidney's "golden" world, where poetry bleeds into philosophy and history. Gower's position might look humanist, in its insistence on usefulness, but he is not, in fact, interested in poetry at all. If Gower's advice were to be followed, there would be no storytelling, and no real Gower, and in this way Gower is harnessed to a position similar to that of Caesar Augustus in the Ode.

Despite Gower's self-negation, he does engage in a story-telling competition with Chaucer in the dream. Both authors tell stories with a pre-assigned moral, and in this way, Greene aligns these medieval authors with the widely held view, that imaginative writing can teach morality. And, yet the defense is very idiosyncratic, a far cry from the typical pieties around aphorisms, maxims, virtues and vices, and examples. Indeed, the defense turns out to be another form of indictment. First and foremost, the moral lesson itself is strange, and possibly immoral. Gower and Chaucer are to tell stories "for the suppressing of iealousie" (D1v, image 14). This language is far removed from recognizable moral discourses, either of humanism and its noble virtues or of the biblical, penitential, and devotional modes that appear in Chaucer's *Canterbury Tales* and in Gower's *Confessio*. Jealousy is identifiable neither as vice nor virtue; it is, rather, a concept most commonly associated with patently immoral stories of sexual behavior, the fabliaux. Being jealous may be negatively inflected, and therefore punished, as it is in Chaucer's *Miller's Tale*, when John, who holds his wife "narwe [narrow] in cage" (1.3225), is humiliated by the end of the story. It is also, however, closely correlated with an embrace of and even delight in adultery. One does not, for example, find jealousy thematized in stories about virtuous behavior: the word appears only once at the end of Chaucer's *Clerk's Tale*, in the misogynistic, jokey envoy. To read Greene's moral in light of Chaucer's *Miller's Tale* is to see that a tale suppressing jealousy is often a tale that delights in sex.

Jealousy is not the only strange part of this moral lesson, since "suppressing" is not an action commonly associated with reading a text for the moral lesson. Suppressing means stopping an action or thought, sometimes violently. It is the opposite of moving readers, to behave virtuously or to avoid vice, a quality that is one the hallmarks of poetry, in Sidney's *Apology*, and of the *bonae litterae* more generally. Even if suppressing jealousy keeps readers from sin (and whether it does so is not entirely clear), it is not the same as inciting them to the kinds of "honest & honorable actions" that should come from reading the right books (B2v). In this way, Greene's Chaucer and Gower directly oppose what Sidney and Elyot claimed for literature, its capacity to inflame in virtue.

The problem with this moral is not limited to the language of its lesson; it is also very difficult to illustrate effectively or to enact, to borrow Larry Scanlon's term for the *exemplum*.[40] How does one enact the suppression of an emotion? In both stories, the stated moral lesson, "suppressing jealousy," destroys the goal of the competition from the inside: instead of showing how literature (or, in this case, stories) can teach morality; it points out the impossibility of doing so. The first story, told by Greene's Chaucer, illustrates the moral with a fabliau, along the lines of Chaucer's *Miller's Tale*. Briefly put, a wheelwright, Tomkins, becomes jealous after his marriage to a young beautiful woman, Kate. Distressed at his behavior, she plans a trick with a student from Cambridge. This student brings Tomkins to witness Kate with another man, then gets him drunk, then brings him home. When he wakes up, Kate and his mother-in-law tell him he imagined everything as part of the insanity brought on by jealousy. As should be clear from this summary, Chaucer insists that his story can delight, here in a very sexualized sense, even as it teaches. The delight is to be found in the voyeurism and the trickery, and the teaching is to be found in that Tomkins learns his lesson—not to be jealous. But the lesson, not being jealous, does not operate as a guide for good behavior. Indeed, even as the story successfully illustrates the suppressing of jealousy, it does so only by drawing attention to the latent immorality of this lesson: suppressing jealousy means titillation and trickery. It is not a story that advertises its morality, as should be obvious from the genre, the fabliau. Surely for these reasons, Gower condemns Chaucer's story as a "fantasticall" (E1r, image 17).

---

[40] Larry Scanlon, *Narrative, Authority, and Power: The Medieval Exemplum and the Chaucerian Tradition* (Cambridge: Cambridge University Press, 1994), 34.

150 HUMANISM AND GOOD BOOKS IN SIXTEENTH-CENTURY ENGLAND

Whereas Greene has used Chaucer to dissolve the humanist link between delight and instruction from the delight side, he uses Gower to dissolve it from the instruction (or morality) side. Gower tells an *exemplum*, a recognizably moral story, initially signaling that the only reliable teaching is to be found in explicit and even excessive moralizing. His story is not very story-like since it is filled with set-pieces, such as the song of the suffering wife or the husband's list of misogynistic sentences. More importantly, it draws on familiar, moralizing characters, the virtuous and suffering wife of Chaucer's *Clerk's Tale* and a wise, old man, who sounds like the father-figures that fill humanist texts, such as George Gascoigne's play *The Glasse of Governement* (1575) or Euphuistic romances.[41] The story enacts how important it is to listen to moralizing, and, in this way, the suppression of jealousy is more important as moralizing per se than as offering knowledge about a specific sin or other behavior. The story begins with a husband, Alexander, who has been driven mad with jealousy and abandons his wife, Theodora, to poverty. After a while, the husband comes upon a wise old man who explains how bad jealousy is, and he proposes a test for the wife's constancy: Alexander, disguised, should offer to pay her. She passes the test by refusing his money, and they are reunited and live happily ever after. It is worth noting that the husband only "suppresses his jealousy" when assisted by an old man, a figure of authority, who tells him at great length that "ielousie is a canckar" (F3v, image 24) and helps him come up with a plan to prove that his jealousy is unfounded.

Despite the great differences between the stories, both operate at a meta-level, as reflections on how a story might teach morality: the suppression of jealousy inside the story figuring the suppression of jealousy outside of it. If the husbands stand in for readers, since the moral is directed at their behavior, then the message is fairly bleak: readers can only be tricked or lectured into the right behavior. There is no learning through a story, no Sidneyan/ Horatian link, since neither husband learns from his own experiences. There is only accidental learning in the fabliau, or being directly told what to do in a series of lectures in the *exemplum*. In the fabliau, the husband is made drunk and then lied to, an episode that suggests the dangers of reading the wrong kind of poetry, of being led astray. And yet, it is precisely the trickery and the drunkenness, the immorality, so to speak, that improve the husband's behavior. That improvement is done against his will, and not with his participation, as would be expected from a reader who learned about good and bad behavior from a story. In the *exemplum*, the husband is lectured, and it is the moral lesson in all of its baldness that finally moves the husband, not its fictiveness, which would be what Sidney calls its poetry. After hearing the old man tell him "a perfect description of thine own patheticall humours," the husband Alexander has a strong emotional response, indicating that he has absorbed the lesson: "Oh quoth

---

[41] Paternal authority is central to the moral model of the Elizabethan prodigal. See Helgerson, *Elizabethan Prodigals*, 16–43.

HORATIAN *DULCE ET UTILE* AS POISONOUS READING 151

Alexander, and he sat him downe with teares in his eyes, and sighes, in such sort, and so deepely straind [distressed], as his heart was ready to burst. Now Father, and neuer before now, doe I see into the depth of mine owne follies, and perceiue how infortunately this Ielowse conceit hath led me: but teach me, how shall I shake of this fiend, that so mortally haunts me?" (F3v, image 24). It is worth noting that Alexander has not reacted emotionally to any of his own experiences. What he has learned is less about jealousy than about the profitability of listening to father-figures when they tell you what to do. Surely, Alexander already knows by now that jealousy is a canker because of his own experiences, and yet, he is unable to be moved by that truth until he is told.

In so far as Gower's story is recognizably moral, whereas Chaucer's is not, Greene seems to have weighted the contest in his direction. And yet Gower's victory is not an entirely happy one; indeed, it generates a dangerous level of doubt. That is, Gower's success at illustrating a moral world in which characters act virtuously is predicated on a very real danger: the insanity described in the text. The husband in Gower's story is not just a bad, as in jealous, reader, he is incapable of making sense of reality, and he inflicts suffering on himself and on others because of that incapacity. The world of the fabliau is, in contrast, less moral, but it is also less dangerous for the people involved: they might be deceived or intoxicated or even adulterous, but they do not lose everything, including their grip on reality. This complicated perspective, in which general ideas of right and wrong, or morality, must be weighed against the needs of individuals is anticipated in the *Prologue* to Chaucer's *Miller's Tale*, when the Miller tells the Reeve that he has decided not to be jealous:

> Ther been ful goode wyves many oon,
> And evere a thousand goode ayeyns oon badde.
> That knowestow wel thyself, but if thou madde.
> Why artow angry with my tale now?
> I have a wyf, pardee, as wel as thow;
> Yet nolde I, for the oxen in my plogh,
> Take upon me moore than ynogh
> As demen of myself that I were oon;
> I wol bileve wel that I am noon

> [There are many good wives and a thousand good wives for
> every bad one. You know that yourself, unless you are crazy.
> Why are you angry with my tale now? I have a wife as well as you
> do; but I would not, for the oxen in my plough, take upon me
> more than I could handle, by considering myself a
> cuckold. I will believe that I am not.] (I.3154-62).

The Miller suppresses his jealousy because to do otherwise would be to risk his sanity, to take on more than he could handle. Deciding to be jealous or not has

152   HUMANISM AND GOOD BOOKS IN SIXTEENTH-CENTURY ENGLAND

little to do with standards of morality, the language of vices or virtues. There is no clarity of right and wrong when it comes to what one suspects, because there can be no real knowledge, moral or otherwise. In echoing Chaucer's *Miller's Tale*, Greene is directing the reader back to kind of *aporia* around knowledge that it represents, replacing with doubt Sidney's confidence about the knowledge the reader gains from reading.

Greene's rejection of humanism, its certain link between literature and morality, is complete when the figure of Solomon appears.[42] Solomon stands both for the rejection of humanism and an alternative moral model, worldly vanity. His perspective is both direct and sincere, unlike those of Chaucer and Gower: Greene should stop writing literature and turn to theology; to "abiure all other studies, seeing *Omnia sub coelo vanitas* [all under the sky is vanity], and onely giue thy selfe to Theologie: be a Deuine my Sonne, for her documents are seueritie" (H3r, image 31). Solomon was, in this period, considered an author of wisdom literature, including Ecclesiastes, which is paraphrased here in the Latin tag, and he appears here in that role, as he does at the end of Chaucer's *Manciple's Tale*, "Daun Salomon" who "teacheth well."[43] He is, in other words, an undeniably and unproblematically moral author, unlike Chaucer, Gower, or any of the pagan, classical authors who are mentioned elsewhere in Greene's treatise. This is a figure whose authority is absolute, not subject to ironizing.

For Greene, as well as for his contemporaries, Solomon's wisdom is Christian, and he thus offers a new link, between morality and Theology, all the possible meanings of wisdom generated by the brief moral lessons of Proverbs and the extended questionings of Ecclesiastes. Solomon's wisdom thus rejects the terms of the pagan, classical literature, the *dulce et utile* that have informed this debate. More importantly, in highlighting the distinctness of wisdom, Solomon interrupts more dramatically and irrevocably the Sidneyan link between teaching and delighting than the Gower and Chaucer in the dream. Solomon suggests that wisdom carries its own beauty with it, as "wisdom, without blemish" (H3r, image 31), in contrast to the claims of humanist writers that wisdom was in some important sense dependent on eloquence or at least linked to it. Solomon's wisdom does not bring virtue or show virtue; it is virtue. In Gower's tale, readers have received a foretaste of what such wisdom would look like. The patient (and beautiful) Theodora quotes The Book of Wisdom, which is, of course, associated with Solomon: "O how faire is a chast generation with vertue, the memorial thereof is immortal: for it is knowen with God & men, when it is present, men take example therat, and if it go away, yet they desire it, it is alwaies crowned and houlden in honor, & winneth the reward of the vniuersall battaile" (G3v, image 28). In this account, beauty ("fair") and "virtue" go together. Those who wish to follow this

---

[42] Dimmick also notes the strangeness of Solomon's appearance, in so far as Gower has just won the competition and Solomon rejects him ("Gower, Chaucer," 462).

[43] The attribution can be found simply everywhere in the Middle Ages and sixteenth century. See, for example, *The prouerbes of Solomon newly translated into Englyshe* (London, 1534) STC 2752 pt. 1.

HORATIAN *DULCE ET UTILE* AS POISONOUS READING   153

model do so merely by knowing it and desiring it, and those who are the exemplars and the imitators are conflated together. There is an ease here, of knowing and being, that stands in startling contrast to the labor of gathering honey, avoiding serpents, ensuring that teaching delights, and keeping delight from leading readers astray.

In invoking "*Omnia sub coelo vanitas* [All under the sky is vanity]," Greene delivers the final blow to any claim for the moral usefulness of writing, the treatise's ongoing attempt to determine that only some writings, the wanton kind, are a vanity. It is worth remembering that in his initial repentance, Greene understood that vanity not in Solomon-like, here explicitly Christian, devotional, terms, but in humanist terms: the vanity of his writing had to do with it not being profitable. What the dream has revealed is the impossibility of this claim. Solomon's appearance thus corrects the misapprehension behind Greene's initial binary of wanton writing and precepts, indicating that the true opposition is earthly vanity, on the one hand, and God on the other. From this perspective, all non-devotional writing runs the risk of being vain; there is no "security," to use Greene's term, in the humanist moral position. Solomon holds out the possibility that reading might bring profit, only to then assert its futility: "Learning hath many braunches, and teacheth her Schollers many strange things, and yet my Sonne, when thou hast waded the depth of hir knowledge, and sought into the secret of her bosome, thou shalt finde all thy labours to be vexation of minde and vanitie" (H3r, image 31). One could hardly imagine a more defeatist dream for an author—an authoritative figure appears to tell him that all of his writings have been a waste of time.

Although Greene's retreat from writing sounds a lot like Chaucer's, in his Retraction and at the end of his *Troilus and Criseyde*, it is far more radical and signals thereby the irreversible effects of humanism, at least as far as Greene is concerned. Chaucer's Retraction only rejects some of his writings, even if they are the ones that later readers like the most. He was certainly able to lay claim to being a moral writer, as the translator of Boethius's *Consolation of Philosophy* in *Boece* or the author of the *Tale of Melibee*. Theology would, however, be a new mode for Greene, and it is, therefore a surprising choice, and one that scholars have understood as a posture. Greene was a prolific author, with a wide range, but he did not write anything before this date that one could remotely call religious. The absence of any religious writings does not mean that we should discount the sentiment entirely, especially given the slipperiness of all the claims in this treatise.[44] Regardless of Greene's own aims, the category of theology is for Greene entirely non-descriptive, one that holds no particular content. It lacks the detail given in Chaucer's Retraction, to the writing he does not regret, the homilies and saints' lives, and the devotional tone, of what he holds on to and why. It is as if

---

[44] In an essay on another of Greene's penitential treatises, Newcomb suggests that readers take his devotional goals seriously. See "A Looking Glass for Readers," in *Writing Robert Greene*, 133–56.

154 HUMANISM AND GOOD BOOKS IN SIXTEENTH-CENTURY ENGLAND

Greene chose theology precisely because he has not written any. From this absence one could speculate that Greene is not so much interested in the content of the theology as the fantasy of stability that it offers. One thing that we know about theology is that reading it is good for you! It cannot lead the reader to sin, and its usefulness is built into the genre.

Greene ends his life, according to this text, repentant for having led readers astray with the wrong kind of writing, for having infected or poisoned them with sin. His attempts to sort out the available arguments for the morality or immorality of his writing quickly find the limits of humanist ideas about poetry famously popularized and defended by Sidney in his *Apology*. Greene's dark imaginings of human behavior, the jealousy and cruelty depicted in the stories, are almost the exact opposite of Sidney's "golden" world, and yet they are drawn from much of the same material, the Chaucer and Gower that Sidney and other humanists celebrated. In a slow and painful retreat from writing, Greene sketches the outline of an absence, an absence that needs to be filled by something else—another kind of literature or a shift in how one thinks about literature. This new approach is not possible for Greene himself, and yet it may have been made possible by him.[45] For Greene, the medieval, his use of Chaucer and Gower, paradoxically shows that there is no going back.

---

[45] Davis writes, "Greene's reactions against fiction had the paradoxical effect of opening up new areas to it" (*Idea and Act*, 188). Maslen also underlines Greene's role in inventing prose as well as his status as outlier: Greene had "an obsession with those aspects of human experience that resist categorization or control" ("Robert Greene," in *The Oxford Handbook of English Prose, 1500–1640*, ed. Andrew Hadfield [Oxford: Oxford University Press, 2013], 191; see further 188–203).

7
Worldly Vanity and George Gascoigne

To invoke "worldly vanity" is to condemn attachment to this world, the love of "earthly thing[s]" that the character Everyman learns to abandon in the early sixteenth-century play *Everyman*.[1] As importantly, "worldly vanity" can be used to assert the futility of all human endeavors, including, perhaps surprisingly, the writing of poetry. When Chaucer ends his *Troilus and Criseyde* with the command to "Repeyreth [return] hom fro worldly vanyte," that "return" is a turn away from "poesye" in the classical tradition of Virgil, Ovid, Homer, Lucan, and Statius, who pass up the steps before Chaucer.[2] Similarly, when Robert Greene claims that all under the sky is vanity [*Omnia sub coelo vanitas*] at the end of his penitential treatise, *Vision Written at the Instant of his death* (1592), he turns away from all non-theological writing, including the greats of the classical tradition.[3] Such bleak counterpoints to the confidence and celebration, the *bonae* of *bonae litterae*, that animate many humanist texts, are not uncommon in the sixteenth century. They appear in the writings of some of the most influential Elizabethan authors: even before Robert Greene included Solomon's pessimism at the end of his *Vision*, George Gascoigne had published a treatise, entitled "The View of Worldly Vanities" (1576), and Edmund Spenser had published his poetry collection known as *Complaints* (1591) as "meditations of the world's vanity."[4] Despite its ubiquity as a framing idea in writings of this period, worldly vanity has been largely neglected. It has been described only briefly, as evidence of these authors' moral interests, implicitly distinct from their more identifiably literary achievements, their experimentations in poetry and prose.[5] And yet, for each of these

---

[1] *Everyman and its Dutch Original, Elckerlijc*, ed. Clifford Davidson, Martin W. Walsh, and Ton J. Broos (Kalamazoo, MI: Medieval Institute Publications, 2007), line 870.

[2] Geoffrey Chaucer, *Troilus and Criseyde*, in *The Riverside Chaucer*, 3rd ed., ed. Larry D. Benson (Boston: Houghton Mifflin, 1987), 5.1837 and 5.1790. Hereafter all references to Chaucer's works will be to this edition.

[3] *Greenes vision vvritten at the instant of his death. Conteyning a penitent passion for the folly of his pen* (London, 1592) STC 12,261, H3r.

[4] *The Complaints*, in *The Yale Edition of the Shorter Poems of Edmund Spenser*, ed. William A. Oram, Einar Bjorvand, and Ronald Bond (New Haven, CT: Yale University Press, 1989), page 223.

[5] This distinction between "moral" and "literary" works is commonplace. See for example G. W. Pigman's otherwise illuminating entry "George Gascoigne," in *The Oxford Encyclopedia of British Literature*, ed. David Scott Kastan (Oxford: Oxford University Press, 2006), doi: 9780195169218. Pigman writes, "'A Discourse of the Adventures Passed by Master F. J.' is a masterpiece of Elizabethan fiction, and its racy story contrasts strikingly with the lugubrious piety of moral tracts such as *The Droomme of Doomes Day* (1576)."

Humanism and Good Books in Sixteenth-Century England. Katherine C. Little, Oxford University Press.
© Katherine C. Little (2023). DOI: 10.1093/oso/9780192883193.003.0008

156 HUMANISM AND GOOD BOOKS IN SIXTEENTH-CENTURY ENGLAND

authors, worldly vanity is in dialogue with the realm of the literary, which these authors would have understood in terms of poetry or *bonae litterae*, or works written by "commendable authors."[6] Worldly vanity is not merely an empty lament, a conventional gesture, but offers a language for thinking about writing, to reflect and meditate, from a perspective outside humanism, on whether good letters are good, whether reading certain texts is morally instructive, as I shall argue in the next two chapters.

This chapter focuses on George Gascoigne (c. 1534–77), whose works, taken together, offer what I've been calling an Elizabethan trajectory, one that is similar to that of Robert Greene, the dissipation of confidence in humanism and the establishment of an alternative model, "worldly vanity." Gascoigne, like Robert Greene, was an immensely prolific and innovative author. He wrote love poetry; prose, including what is considered to be the first novel; plays; moral treatises; and explicitly didactic poetry.[7] Gascoigne was writing before both Greene and Spenser, and he has long been understood as a transitional figure between the dedicated humanists of the early and mid-sixteenth century, such as Thomas Elyot and Roger Ascham, and the more celebrated and more ambivalent Elizabethans. As G. W. Pigman writes, "From shortly after his death until today, Gascoigne's reputation as the foremost poet of his generation and the precursor of Sir Philip Sidney, Edmund Spenser, and William Shakespeare has remained constant."[8] As transitional, his works offer insight into the logic of this Elizabethan trajectory, that is, how and why worldly vanity emerged as a response to the humanist project. Gascoigne's turn toward worldly vanity is notably a return to a medieval past, since he draws on an identifiable medieval tradition of *contemptus mundi* [contempt for the world], even a particularly Chaucerian *contemptus mundi* or "Chaucerian repentance," as Pigman describes it.[9] His debts are apparent at the opening of his popular prose narrative, *The Adventures of Master F. J.* (1573), which offers Chaucer as a moral model: "And the more pitie that amongst so many toward wittes no one hath bene hitherto encouraged to followe the trace of that worthy and famous Knight *Sir Geffrey Chaucer*, and after many pretie devises spent in youth, for the obtayning a worthles victorie, might consume and consummate his age in discribing the right pathway to perfect felicitie, with the due preservation of the same."[10] Gascoigne not only celebrates Chaucer's "right pathway," he also follows it. Like Chaucer, Gascoigne translated the late twelfth-century treatise by Lotario dei Segni

---

[6] William Painter, *The Palace of Pleasure Beautified, adorned and well furnished, with Pleasaunt Histories and excellent Nouelles, selected out of diuers good and commendable Authors* (London, 1566) STC 19121, image 1.

[7] On Gascoigne's life and works, see Richard Helgerson, *The Elizabethan Prodigals* (Berkeley, CA: University of California Press, 1977), 44–57; G. W. Pigman III, "Introduction," *George Gascoigne: A Hundreth Sundrie Flowres* (Oxford: Oxford University Press, 2000), xxiii–xliii.

[8] Pigman, "George Gascoigne."

[9] *A Hundreth Sundrie Flowres*, n. 36 p. xxxviii.

[10] *A Hundreth Sundrie Flowres*, 143.

(Pope Innocent III) *De Miseria Condicionis Humane* (c. 1195).[11] One can also assume that Gascoigne was familiar with Chaucer's *Troilus and Criseyde*, which, as noted above, describes a particular moral "pathway" at its end: a turn away from the classical legacy as part of a rejection of things of the world.[12]

Gascoigne's trajectory, or "Chaucerian repentance," is most noticeable in the explicitly moralizing texts written at the end of his life: *The Glasse of Governement* (1575), which is a prodigal-son-play; *The Steele Glas* (1576), an estates satire in the *Piers-Plowman* tradition; and a group of moral and religious treatises titled *The Droome of Doomesday* [*The Drum of Judgment Day*] (1576). Gascoigne's turn, from worldly to moral writings, is a familiar one in this period, based on the model of the prodigal son, a model that Gascoigne explicitly invokes throughout his works. In the Epistle with which he prefaces *The Steele Glas*, Gascoigne writes about his "wantonnesse" and his riotous youth.[13] Indeed, Gascoigne is the first of the "Elizabethan Prodigals" discussed by Richard Helgerson in his study of Elizabethan authors. To describe Gascoigne as a prodigal is to position him in relation to humanism: Gascoigne was educated to think that writing should be morally useful, and he rehearses the familiar convention, about the capacity of *bonae litterae* to teach the good at the opening of one of his most famous works, *The Adventures of Master F. J.*: "For who doubteth but that Poets in their most feyned fables and imaginations, have metaphorically set forth unto us the right rewardes of vertues, and the due punishments for vices?"[14] From this perspective, Gascoigne's turn to moralizing at the end of his life is an attempt to repent for not having been a good enough humanist, for having indulged himself in love poetry, for having strayed from the right path, in a manner that anticipates Robert Greene. As Helgerson writes, Gascoigne "developed a romantic and rebellious side that required decisive excision"; that "excision" is Gascoigne's repentance, which Helgerson describes as "the recital of precept, much of it translated from the works of Church Fathers ... [which] proves his submission to the severest conventional wisdom."[15]

On closer look, Gascoigne's use of the prodigal son is less an embrace of its trajectory—rebellion then repentance—than a reflection on its limitations. In so

---

[11] In the Prologue to *The Legend of Good Women*, Chaucer lists many of his works. Immediately after stating that he "hath in prose translated Boece," he claims another translation: "And of the Wreched Engendrynge of Mankynde/ As man may in Pope Innocent yfynde" (in *The Riverside Chaucer*, G413–15). The editor writes that this title refers to "a lost translation of all or part of a work by Pope Innocent III, *De miseria condicionis humane*" (*The Riverside Chaucer*, p. 1065 n. G414). Given the portion of *De miseria* that appears in the *Man of Law's Prologue*, there is good reason to take Chaucer's claim seriously.

[12] Pigman notes the parallels between Chaucer's *Troilus and Criseyde* and Gascoigne's "Adventures Passed by Master F. J." ("George Gascoigne").

[13] *The Complete Works of George Gascoigne*, 2 vols., ed. John W. Cunliffe (Cambridge: Cambridge University Press, 1910) 2: 135, 136. All references to Gascoigne will appear parenthetically hereafter.

[14] *A Hundreth Sundrie Flowres*, 143.

[15] Helgerson, *Elizabethan Prodigals*, 57, 49. Helgerson also distinguishes between Gascoigne's "literary presentation" of experience and "his repentance" as if repentance were not also an experience (49).

158   HUMANISM AND GOOD BOOKS IN SIXTEENTH-CENTURY ENGLAND

far as the prodigal model offers or encodes a humanist mindset, Gascoigne is more interested in distancing himself from it than inhabiting it. That his repentance might be a pose has, of course, long been recognized. Gascoigne deploys the prodigal model intermittently throughout his career and in various contexts. As Pigman has noted, "Gascoigne adopts the stance of a reformed prodigal, whose early errors 'might yet serve as a myrrour for unbrydled youth, to avoyde those perilles which I had passed'" in the opening to the second edition of his collection, *A Hundreth Sundrie Flowres* (1575).[16] Unlike Robert Greene, who uses the prodigal model near the end of his life to withdraw and condemn his earlier writings or, at least, to perform that withdrawal and condemnation, Gascoigne invokes it to frame his earlier writings, to offer them as already moralized or as morally useful. More importantly, his later works demonstrate less a repentance for his earlier works within the prodigal model than a turn away from that model, not so much a repentance within humanism but a repentance of humanism. First, he empties out the resources of the model, as I shall demonstrate with his prodigal-son-play, *The Glasse of Governement* (hereafter *Glass*). Then, he turns to "worldly vanity," as I shall demonstrate with the treatise he published near the end of his life, *The Droome of Doomesday* (hereafter *Drum*).

Gascoigne's Morality Play

Glass has long been understood as emerging from a humanist milieu.[17] Indeed, it is so programmatic that one scholar has read it as a kind of dramatization of the English educational treatises by Ascham, *The Scholemaster* (1570) and Elyot, *The Boke of the Governor* (1531).[18] Since it is not particularly well-known, a brief plot summary may be in order. The play dramatizes the education of two sets of brothers. Their fathers hire a schoolmaster, Gnomaticus, to fill in any gaps in their education before they leave for university. They read all the standard humanist texts: the *Colloquia* of Erasmus, Cicero, Terence's comedies, Virgil (2:16–17) and the Bible (2:17). The two older sons are said to be smarter, but they are easily led

---

[16] *A Hundreth Sundrie Flowres*, xxxviii. On Gascoigne's repentance as a stance, see also Gillian Austen, *George Gascoigne* (Cambridge: D. S. Brewer, 2008), 14–20.

[17] On this play's humanism, see Kent Cartwright, "Humanist Reading and Interpretation in Early Elizabethan Morality Drama," *Allegorica* 28 (2012): 9–31; Christopher Gaggero, "Pleasure Unreconciled to Virtue: George Gascoigne and Didactic Drama," in *Tudor Drama Before Shakespeare, 1485–1590: New Directions for Research, Criticism and Pedagogy*, ed. Lloyd Kermode, Jason Scott-Warren, and Martine van Elk (New York: Palgrave Macmillan, 2004), 167–94; Helgerson, *Elizabethan Prodigals*, 50–57; Ursula Potter, "'No Terence phrase: his tyme and myne are twaine': Erasmus, Terence, and Censorship in the Tudor Classroom," in *The Classics in the Medieval and Renaissance Classroom: The Role of Ancient Texts in the Arts Curriculum as Revealed by Surviving Manuscripts and Early Printed Books*, ed. Juanita Feros Ruys, John O. Ward, and Melanie Heyworth (Turnhout: Brepols, 2013), 365–89; and Linda Salamon, "A Face in The Glasse: Gascoigne's *Glasse of Government* Re-examined," *Studies in Philology* 71 (1974): 47–71.

[18] Salamon, "A Face in the Glasse." See also Helgerson, *Elizabethan Prodigals*, 50–57.

astray by parasites familiar from Roman comedy, a courtesan and her associates. The younger sons, in contrast, study hard. Oddly enough, the differing outcomes are never dramatized; they occur off stage, when the sons have gone to university in Douai. The fathers receive word that their younger sons have succeeded: one becomes a preacher and the other works for the Palgrave, a count of the German Empire. They hear nothing of their older sons until a faithful servant returns to tell them that one has been executed for stealing and the other whipped and banished for fornication. The play ends with the punishment of the parasites at the hands of the Markgrave (the governor or magistrate): the male servants will be whipped, and the courtesan and her aunt will be put on the "cucking stool."

This summary should demonstrate Gascoigne's debts to the arguably first and certainly most influential prodigal-son-play, *Acolastus* (1529) by Gulielmus Gnapheus (Willem de Volder), the subject of Chapter 3. Like the author of *Acolastus*, Gascoigne has fused the Roman comedy of Terence—parasites, courtesans, and trickery—with the parable of the prodigal son—fathers and sons, rebellion and obedience. This play is, in other words, recognizably a prodigal-son-play. At the same time, in its explicit focus on humanist education, the play is also self-conscious, not so much a play about a prodigal son (or sons) but a play about this kind of play. In so far as this genre was, by the time Gascoigne wrote it, closely correlated with humanist education, one of its central planks, so to speak, Gascoigne uses his play to reflect on the ideas behind such an education.

First and foremost, the play explores a (if not the) foundational tenet of humanism: that reading classical texts produces virtue in students, thereby shaping a Christian subject. Gascoigne invokes this Erasmian tradition, of subordinating classical texts to their Christian, moral usefulness, on his title page. This page first identifies the play as "a tragical comedy so entitled because therein are handled as well the rewards for virtues as also the punishment for vices" and then ensures that the reader understands vices and virtues within a Christian tradition by quoting from Psalm 128: "Blessed are they that feare the Lorde, their children shall be as the branches of Olive trees rounde about their table" (2.1). In this framing, Gascoigne echoes the familiar humanist claim: classical texts can show how vices are punished and virtue rewarded, the same statement that Golding made at the opening of Ovid's *Metamorphoses*, and that Gascoigne has used to frame his earlier poetry in *A Hundreth Sundrie Flowres*.[19] As the play goes on to demonstrate, this educational goal—reading classical texts for their morality—means finding the sentences, the guidelines for future behavior. Gascoigne's schoolmaster Gnomaticus indicates that the point of reading Cicero and Terence is to gather "precepts" and "moral instructions" with an awareness of ultimately joining them to God's word: "For although *Tully* in his book of dewtyes doth teach sundry vertuouse

---

[19] *The. xv. bookes of P. Ouidius Naso, entytuled Metamorphosis, translated oute of Latin into English meeter, by Arthur Golding* (London, 1567) STC 18956, A2v.

preceptes, and out of *Terence* may also be gathered many morall enstructions ... yet the true christian must direct his steppes by the infallible rule of God's woord" (2:17).

Gascoigne's interest in "moral instructions" operates on a meta-level, in that the play consistently draws attention to the status of precepts as precepts. He informs the reader after the Prologue and before the play proper that "this worke is compiled upon these sentences," and then he lists eight groups of three, for a total of twenty-four sentences (2:7). These are entirely conventional, having to do with duty towards God, King, parents, and so on. For example, the first group is "Feare God, for he is just; Love God, for hee is mercifull; Truste in God, for he is fayth-full" (2:7). This same list appears in similar if slightly modified forms twice in the play: when the schoolmaster explains these "wholesome lessons" at length to the four sons (2:17–23; 2:28–33) and later when the two younger sons turn them into verses (2:55, 2:56–58).

Gascoigne's moralizing—his reliance on precepts—is extreme, even for a morality play, and it serves to undermine the generic function of the play, of showing how morality works. To be sure, his precepts look, at first glance, solidly humanist. There can be no question that humanists were interested in finding moral lessons in texts. Erasmus insists on the "aphorisms, proverbs, and maxims" that students are supposed to learn in school, via the classical legacy.[20] Such a perspective is echoed throughout English humanist educational texts, which were centrally concerned with guidelines for behavior, often presented as sentences or rules. Latin grammar books are filled with "preceptes of lyuynge" and "Godly lessons for Chyldren," as has been discussed previously.[21] Gascoigne is clearly familiar with this mode and represents its rationale in Gnomaticus: "I cannot otherwyse doe but commend you to the tuition of almighty GOD, whom I beseech nowe and ever to guide you by his grace, and I exhorte you for Gods sake, that you beare well in minde *the preceptes* which I have given you, assuring my selfe that ruling your actions by that measure, you shalbe acceptable to GOD, pleasing to the world, profitable to your selves, and comfortable to your parentes" (2:64, my emphasis). As this account makes clear, the goal of gathering moral instructions from Terence, among other authors, is to internalize the rules that will then guide future behavior. Such an interest in applying books to readers explains the humanist love of the morality play as genre, because plays provide opportunities for students to inhabit good and bad behavior, to see these behaviors dramatized by others.[22]

---

[20] Erasmus, *On the Method of Study*, ed. Craig R. Thompson, trans. Brian McGregor in *Collected Works of Erasmus (CWE)*, 84 vols. (Toronto: University of Toronto Press, 1974), Vol. 24 (1978): 671.

[21] John Colet, *Ioannis Coleti theologi, olim decani diui Pauli, aeditio. una cum quibusdam G. Lilij Grammatices rudimentis, G. Lilij epigramma* (Antwerp, 1527) STC 5542, A3v. See Chapter 1.

[22] On humanist education as a training in performance, see Lynn Enterline, *Shakespeare's Schoolroom: Rhetoric, Discipline, Emotion* (Philadelphia: University of Pennsylvania Press, 2012) and Paul Sullivan, "Playing the Lord: Tudor *Vulgaria* and the Rehearsal of Ambition," *ELH* 75 (2008): 179–96.

WORLDLY VANITY AND GEORGE GASCOIGNE   161

While Gascoigne's play is certainly moral, in so far as it includes a lot of lessons, it is not particularly interested in exploring the content of that morality, in terms of the behaviors, feelings, and ideas that might be right or wrong. Despite its precepts, it does not enact how a character might internalize them or what they might mean to the audience. It will be helpful here to distinguish *Glass* from other humanist and humanist-inflected plays, plays that are also considered moral and that have been discussed previously in this study: *Everyman*, *Acolastus*, and *Play of Patient Grissell*. Despite vast differences in language, tone, and characterization, all three plays similarly possess a moral content that they then dramatize through a clear plot trajectory. *Everyman* is about how one dies a good death; *Acolastus* is about how one can stray and return; *Patient Grissell* is about maintaining patience through adversity. Each play is profoundly interested in human behavior—what does it mean to realize you will die? How can you tell a friend from a flatterer? How should you act if bad things happen to you? In addition, each of these morality plays indicates that their understanding of human behavior is consciously drawn from books. That is, each of these plays not only invokes but celebrates the textuality of morality, that books are a good way to gain knowledge about the world. Gascoigne's play, in contrast, invokes the textuality of the morality only to show the ways in which a system of morality drawn from books has little to do with actual behavior. The large number of rules in the play both distracts from and fills in for the lack of plot; Gascoigne presents a mass of guidelines with no clear path through them or with them. After all, this is a prodigal-son-play that rejects one of the most basic, if not the most important, plot elements, the return to the father (on which more below).

In insisting on moral lessons as lessons, in letting the precepts replace the plot, Gascoigne reveals humanist education to be a fantasy about control. The main humanist idea—offering classical texts as guidelines for behavior—is an attempt to control students' reading process, to make them look for the aphorisms, maxims, and proverbs, as in Erasmus, or virtue and vice, as in Golding's translation of Ovid's *Metamorphoses*, even when they are difficult to find or not there at all. Almost everything the schoolmaster Gnomaticus says in the play concerns controlling the reading process. He consistently tasks his pupils with finding the precepts in the texts: "out of *Terence* may also be gathered many morall enstructions amongst the rest of his wanton discourses" (2:17). While he acknowledges that Terence did indeed write "wanton discourses," he does not acknowledge that a reader might therefore be led astray. Instead, he insists that "moral instructions" can still be gathered.

The fantasy of control is shown to be a fantasy, most obviously because the education of the sons does not succeed uniformly. Although all the sons are educated in the right kinds of texts, the *bonae litterae*, only the younger ones end up on the right path. If the main lesson is to show vices punished and virtues rewarded,

162   HUMANISM AND GOOD BOOKS IN SIXTEENTH-CENTURY ENGLAND

as indicated on the title page, the play fails to show the second part of the lesson, about virtues rewarded. Although the younger sons are rewarded (or, rather, the audience hears that they've been rewarded), there is no discussion of their virtues. All that is dramatized is their ability to memorize and compose verses out of the rules, their slow-witted dedication to the rules. Gnomaticus explains their success as students in relation to their brothers' failure: their task "was to put in verse a briefe memoriall of the chiefe poyntes wherein I did enstruct them, and I found that [the younger sons] *Philomusus* and *Phylotimus* (whom I thought not so quicke of capacity as the other) had done the same very well: on that other side, I found [the older sons] *Phylautus* and *Phylosarchus* to have done there in nothing at all" (2:60). The absence of virtue, or even of any moral content at all, is quite significant. After all, humanists were far more focused upon virtue than they were on sin, insisting, as Elyot did, that reading the classical legacy would help readers "apprehend" noble virtues and inflame them to imitate virtue.[23] Gascoigne, in contrast, seems to be more interested in sin, and he does a better job illustrating the punishment for vices; the play dramatizes the older sons' "filthy lust" and "selfe love" (2:89) and then reveals their life of crime. And yet, the audience is left with a similar question about why their education failed. Surely, if reading classical texts necessarily produces virtue, then these sons should also have become virtuous.

More specifically, and more significantly for the Christian Terence tradition, to which the prodigal-son-play is indebted, Gascoigne reveals doubts about Terentian comedy and its capacity to teach morality.[24] Despite his obvious debts to Terence, in the courtesans and flatterers, and his assertion that he is writing a "comedy," he distances himself from Terence in a burst of negativity at the opening of the play:

> No *Terence* phrase: his tyme and myne are twaine:
> The verse that pleasde a *Romaine* rashe intent,
> Myght well offend the godly Preachers vayne (2:6).[25]

In this way, Gascoigne draws attention to the problem of Terence, which humanists tended to dance around: great as Terence's Latin may be, eloquent as he is in the language of the humanists, there is nothing explicitly moral in Terence, at least from a recognizably Christian perspective. Gascoigne's caution and negativity contrast markedly both with Ascham's certainty about Terence's moral usefulness in *The Scholemaster* and the familiar praise for Roman comedy that is found in the preface to *Acolastus*. Indeed, within Gascoigne's play, Terence is shown to

---

[23] Sir Thomas Elyot, *A Critical Edition of Sir Thomas Elyot's The Boke Named the Governour*, ed. Donald W. Rude (New York: Garland Press, 1992), 44. Elyot is discussing Homer's works.

[24] Potter also sees the play as a critique, but of Calvinism, not of humanism ("'No Terence phrase'").

[25] Helgerson also notes Gascoigne's skepticism about classical texts—he shows "how unstable the balance [of classical texts and Christian faith] really was" (*Elizabethan Prodigals*, 55; see also 56).

be not moral enough. One of the younger sons asserts the moral superiority of more "unpleasant" (presumably, more openly didactic texts): "it hath in it great reason & vertue, and though it be at the first unpleasant in comparison to *Terences* comedies and such like, yet ought we to have good regarde thereunto, since it teacheth in effect the summe of our duties" (2:34). As if to underscore the moral uselessness of Terence, those scenes that are at least tangentially imitative of his comedy are explicitly moralized for the audience. For example, Gascoigne follows the scenes drawn from Roman comedy, concerning the older sons' encounters with a courtesan, with a lament from the Chorus:

> Behold behold, O mortall men behold,
> Behold and see, how soon deceipt is wrought:
> How soone mens mindes, of harmfull thinges take hold
> How soone the good, corrupted is with nought (2: 43).

Such an overwrought comment indicates that Gascoigne does not trust his audience to "gather" the "moral instructions" on their own; the lessons that are not in Terence must be added. For Gascoigne, his play is less about instructing through delighting than about overwhelming the audience with moral umbrage.

In its attention to Terence, the play dramatizes the failure of education, the failure of the right texts to inflame readers with virtue, to borrow Elyot's language. Reading Terence does not provide moral guidelines to the characters nor does it result in the right behavior within the play. That is, the Terentian scenes should test whether the sons have learned from Terence how to withstand "lewd company," how to navigate his "wanton discourses" to gain the moral instructions. And yet, the characters do not model, for the audience, how to apply Terence or any other classical text to their own lives. The failure is obvious in the behavior of the older sons, who happily succumb to "wanton discourses," following Eccho, who is the flatterer and parasite, to the lady Lamia, the courtesan, whose name evokes a beautiful woman who seduces men and destroys them. Although they have, apparently, read Terence, they do not recognize "the sotle inticement of som lewd seruant"; they have not apprehended the moral guidelines that Roger Ascham found in Terentian comedy about avoiding lewd servants.[26] Even the younger sons, who resist temptation, do not do so because they themselves have recognized the enticements, nor because they are able to apply moral instructions learned from Terence. Instead, their resistance is more of an accident. The younger sons initially wonder what has become of their older brothers, in terms that could have been drawn from Ascham and that signal their familiarity with the usefulness typically assigned to Terence: "I wonder what is become of our brethren, I pray god they be

---

[26] Roger Ascham, *The Scholemaster*, in *English Works*, ed. William Aldis Wright (Cambridge: Cambridge University Press, 1904), 208.

not entised to some vanitie by some lewde companie" (2:44). But they themselves are never tested, or "entised." They never find their way into the Terentian scenes, because they are so preoccupied with their studies that they lose sight of their older brothers: "we were so earnest in meditating such matter as our instructer delivered unto us, that mistaking the way, & not marking which way you went, we were constreyned to return hether, and to attend your returne" (2:46). In other words, the younger sons do not decide against courtesans and lewd servants out of any moral principle; rather, they are distracted by their need to memorize rules and are thus only coincidentally excluded from the fun. In so far as this scene offers a lesson, it is not one about temptation, but one about rule following. Being busy with the rules is more effective than actually knowing them or applying them.

Just as the older sons wander around in Terence's "wanton discourses" without finding his "moral instructions," they also wander around in Virgil's poetry. Virgil inspires them to write love lyrics; reading his poetry is not at all profitable, does not lead to virtue. As Philosarchus states, "shall I tell you *Phylautus*, wherfore I desired the excellencie of *Virgil*, in compounding of a verse? not ... to convert our tedious traditions there into ... but it was to furnish me with eloquence, for the better obteyning of this heavenly dame" (2:48). Here Virgil is both "excellent" and "eloquent," as he is consistently described by the humanists, but that eloquence is at odds with morality, not joined to it. Instead, morality is part of "tedious traditions" to which Virgil must be converted. It is hard not hear a note of sympathy for the older, rebellious sons, who want Virgil for his "excellence" in writing poetry, his eloquence, as distinct from his morality. Even though their perspective is clearly marked as wrong, it is also never refuted, by an author who can be both eloquent and morally useful. Gascoigne does not, in other words, offer the Sidneyan perspective, in which a reader is moved by reading Virgil to virtuous acts, of filial piety, for example.

Finally, and most distressingly, the play does not show any return or repentance, the absorption of classical ideas into a Christian moral framework. It does not dramatize the lesson so central to the prodigal-son-play, which is explicitly invoked at the beginning of the play—that a sinner can stop straying, can always be welcomed back into the father's embrace. Indeed, Gascoigne invokes this familiar idea only to leave it as an inert sentence, a moral guideline that is mentioned but never set into motion. Early in the play the schoolmaster, Gnomaticus, describes the rule "Love God," in terms of repentance: God does not delight "in the distruction of mankind, but rather that a sinner should turne from wickedness and live" (2:19–20). Despite the fathers' clear concern for their sons, their hope that they might "turn from wickedness," the older sons do not repent, and they are harshly punished. Moreover, the one character in *Glass* who asks for mercy does not get it. At the end of the play, Ambidexter (the bad servant) appeals to the Markgrave, "Oh Sir be good unto me and pardon this offence." (2:87). The Markgrave responds, "Pardon? Nay surely thou rather deservest death" (2:87). To be sure, Gascoigne

WORLDLY VANITY AND GEORGE GASCOIGNE   165

is not the only author writing plays about prodigal sons who omits repentance and forgiveness.[27] His interest in punishment is, nevertheless, excessive, especially when read against his own use of the prodigal son motif throughout his career. As indicated above, much of his early output is framed with the assertion that readers can learn from his misspent youth, his rebellions.

If the prodigal son model, as it appeared in early humanist texts such as *Acolastus*, encodes a confidence about the relationship between the classical legacy and Christian morality, then Gascoigne's play empties out that confidence. There will be no successful assimilation, no loving embrace. The bleakness of this play could, of course, result from its Calvinism, as has been suggested by a number of critics.[28] Gascoigne seems, after all, to wear his Reformism on his sleeve, beginning his play by advocating for "reformed speech:"

> Reformed speeche doth now become us best,
> Mens wordes muste weye and tryed be by touche
> Of Gods owne worde, wherein the truth doth rest (2:6).

Gascoigne cannot, if he is "reformed," effectively illustrate his moral about virtues rewarded and vices punished, since such a lesson would reinforce or introduce the works-oriented perspective that Calvinists rejected. Instead, the sons are predestined to salvation or damnation, and the arbitrariness of their fates within the play underlines the futility of human action in the world. Gascoigne's goals certainly contradict each other—reformed speech vs. virtues and vices—in a way that would have been familiar at the time. Protestant teachers and authors tended to ignore such contradictions, insisting on both the virtue-driven reading of classical texts and teachings on grace. Setting these two goals together did not typically lead authors to draw attention to the contradictions between them or to demonstrate one side as inefficacious or to indulge in the kind of bleakness found in Gascoigne's play.[29] Moreover, when read against Gascoigne's oeuvre, the bleakness of this instance of the prodigal son is in and of itself significant. His earlier invocations of prodigality in his other works communicated optimism, the capacity to get back on the right path, to keep writing and moving forward. The lack of that optimism here indicates that he wants to highlight the contradictions between classical and

---

[27] Helgerson, *Elizabethan Prodigals*, 34–35.

[28] Arthur F. Kinney, *Humanist Poetics: Thought, Rhetoric, and Fiction in Sixteenth-century England* (Amherst, MA: University of Massachusetts Press, 1986), 114.

[29] On the potential tension between Reformation ideas of grace and classical ideas of virtue more generally in the culture, see Paul Cefalu, *Moral Identity in Early Modern English Literature* (Cambridge: Cambridge University Press, 2000), 4–7. Ian Green sees these tensions as largely absent from educational settings (*Humanism and Protestantism in Early Modern English Education* [Burlington, VT: Ashgate, 2009], 293, 361–64). On the tensions between humanism and Protestantism in this play, see Cartwright, "Humanist Reading," 11, 22–25; Kinney, *Humanist Poetics*, 113–14; and Potter, "No Terence phrase," 382–84.

166   HUMANISM AND GOOD BOOKS IN SIXTEENTH-CENTURY ENGLAND

Christian in and around humanist education, contradictions that earlier authors, such as Erasmus, largely refused to acknowledge.

To suggest the purposefulness of this emptying out of the prodigal-son genre, and, relatedly, humanist claims around *bonae litterae*, is to highlight the end of the play. Here Gascoigne retreats into a more cautious, and apparently, Chaucerian perspective on classical texts:

> We live to learne, for so Sainct Paule doth teach,
> and all that is, is doone for our availe [aid]
> Both good and bad, may be the wisemans leach [doctor],
> The good may serve, to make him beare like sayle,
> The bad to shun, the faults wherein they fayle.
> Good wyndes and bad, may serve in sundry sorte,
> To bring our barkes, into some pleasant porte (2:88).

In invoking Saint Paul, Gascoigne alludes to the most common defense of classical texts in the Middle Ages, that they can also be useful—"done for our avail"—and, whether directly or indirectly, to the moral coordinates of Chaucer's Retraction.[30] Such a defense is a lot less full-throated than that of many humanists. Gascoigne, like Chaucer before him, does not assert that some texts absolutely produce virtue in the reader; nor does either author claim to know which texts are which. Gascoigne instead offers a series of cautious "may's." The potential uncertainty—how do we know what is good or bad—is underlined by the boat. A boat can get off course; it can wander around. There is no distinct "pathway" for a boat, only the hope that it will arrive in the port eventually.

Gascoigne's turn away from humanist certainties is itself a moral turn, an attempt to make sense of the value of literature outside of humanist *bonae litterae*. As he demonstrates with *Glass*, classical comedy does not provide a model for an effective morality play and neither does the prodigal-son play, which tried to combine classical with Christian for moral effect. At the end of the play, Gascoigne suggests an alternative, one that is correlated with a native, non-classical literary tradition, the mirror:

> This christall glasse, I polisht fayre and cleene,
> For every man, that list his faultes to mend,
> This was my mind, and thus I make an end (2:90).

This passage invokes a very long tradition of describing penitential and advice writings as mirrors, as discussed in the introduction. Gascoigne is thus aligning his play with Mirrors for Princes, such as John Lydgate, whose massive poem

---

[30] See Chapter 1.

The Fall of Princes offers a "mirror to all estates/ How they shall find remedies in virtue to avoid vices" and with penitential treatises and plays, such as *Everyman*, which provides a "mirror of Everyman's salvation," [*Den Spyeghel der Salicheyt van Elckerlijc*], the Dutch title to the source for *Everyman*, and with Sir Thomas More's early sixteenth-century *The Life of Pico della Mirandola*.[31] The glass cannot do more than reflect the image within. Whether his play inflames readers to virtue or instructs and delights is entirely up to them: they are the ones who must look in the mirror and see if they must change their behavior. In this way, Gascoigne lets go of the fantasy of control that has animated humanism; his Chaucerian end is thus more hopeful than his beginning.

Gascoigne's *Contemptus*

The turn to an alternative moral model that is implied in *Glass* becomes explicit in another of Gascoigne's last works, *Drum*. This work consists of three treatises, the first of which is the translation of *De Miseria*: "The View of Worldly Vanities."[32] Although Gascoigne does not reveal his precise debts, he ensures that his readers approach this work from a pre- or non-humanist perspective, underlining the strangeness of having chosen this, identifiably Catholic, treatise to translate for his Protestant patron.[33] He does so by emphasizing its age, anonymity, and ephemerality: while he was looking through his "small Lybrary ... I chaunced to light upon a small volumne" (2:212). This "old torn Pamphlet" was "written in an old kind of Characters" and he "can not certaynly say who shuld be the Author" (2:212). These traits contrast strongly with those typically assigned to the classical legacy: their authorship, their certainty, the solidity of their value.

Such a different kind of book produces a different kind of moral usefulness, as he makes clear in the dedicatory epistle, in which the usefulness of the text is not what it contains, the lesson that can be pulled out, but in the process it generates in the author. Gascoigne writes, "I finde my self giltie of much time mispent & of greater curiositie than was convenient, in penning and endightyng [composing] sundrie toyes and trifles. So that lookyng backe (with inward griefe) towardes the beginning of my recklesse race, I fynd that both the tyme, and my duetie doe challenge in me the fruites of repentaunce" (2:211). This statement echoes his earlier

---

[31] John Lydgate, *The Fall of Princes*, 4 vols., ed. Henry Bergen (London: Oxford University Press, 1924–27), Part 1: Bk 2.24–26.

[32] The other two treatises are "The Shame of Sinne," and "The Needles Eye." Both titles are fairly self-explanatory. The second treatise deals with "the huge greatness and enormities" of sin, and the third deals with "the right rules of a true Christian life" (2:210).

[33] Austen provides an account of the context for this treatise and its contents in *George Gascoigne*, 172–76. She notes the oddity of including such an identifiably Catholic work in a treatise written for a Protestant patron (175). Gascoigne does protestantize his work by combining *De Miseria* with two treatises that are more focused on scripture and obedience, but the oddness of *De Miseria* remains.

168   HUMANISM AND GOOD BOOKS IN SIXTEENTH-CENTURY ENGLAND

references, or stances, in acknowledging his straying, in positing his writings as trivial and therefore not useful to his readers. And yet, it does not follow the logic of the prodigal son model, in which such writings, whether early or late, can be profitable, can show the "perils" that the reader must draw out and learn from the text. Rather, the writings are themselves products or signs of his own repentance. The usefulness is in the repenting, not in a particular moral message that a reader can apprehend from the text.

Instead of profitability, the text as a container of lessons that one can bear away, Gascoigne underlines uselessness: earthly pursuits are futile, and their delight is what prevents people from recognizing their futility. Such a perspective has been anticipated in *Glass*: the older sons did "delight in vanities" (2:38) and were, therefore, unable to see the dangers associated with them. Indeed, *De Miseria* allows Gascoigne to break apart the humanist defense of poetry, its combined wisdom and eloquence, its delight and instruction, by taking a hard line on earthly pleasures. He notes that his treatise "doth very eloquently (and pythily) persuade all men to contempne the pomps, excessive pleasures, and delightes of this lyfe" (2:213). The words "eloquent" and "delight" are particularly telling in this context. Gascoigne shifts eloquent away from its expected position, as aligned with the delight taken in writing (and in "this life"), toward condemnation of it. In other words, he uses the eloquence of the medieval treatises to reject the eloquence praised by humanists.

This pessimism around human action contributes to the same kind of nihilism about *bonae litterae* that is found in *Glass*, the sense that writing cannot be reliably moral. Writing is, of course, not a focus of the original treatise but is condemned when it does appear. Gascoigne writes, "Let wyse men search narrowly, let them heedely [with attention] consider the height of the heavens, the breadth of the yearth, and the depth of the Sea, let them argue and dispute every one of this, let them handle them all over, and let them always eyther learne or teach, and in so doing, what shall they fynde out of this busie toyle of our life, but traveyle and payne? that knew he by experience, which sayed: I inclyned my hart to know learninge & prudence, error, and folishnesse, and I perceyved that all was labour & afflictio of the spyrite" (2:223). Here Gascoigne echoes Solomon, who is a figure for the wisdom of worldly vanity, not a more humanist Ciceronian wisdom, by paraphrasing Ecclesiastes 1:17, "dedique cor meum ut scirem prudentiam atque doctrinam erroresque et stultitiam et agnovi quod in his quoque esset labor et adflictio spiritus [And I have given my heart to know prudence and learning and errors and folly, and I have perceived that in these also there was labour and vexation of spirit].[34] In this perspective, learning is not, as it is for humanists, a path to virtue (or even to wisdom) but a path to pain, and therefore there is no point

---

[34] Ecclesiastes 1:17, in *The Vulgate Bible: Douay-Rheims Translation*. 6 vols., ed. Swift Edgar and Angela M. Kinney (Cambridge, MA: Harvard University Press, 2010–13) 3:689.

in pursuing it. Indeed, it is impossible to learn from others' "error and folish-nesse." That position is, of course, precisely opposed to the humanist model of the prodigal son, that readers can learn from errors, even errors described in a book.

What shapes the pessimism of *De Miseria* most obviously is its overwhelming focus on sin. It is, as the title suggests, interested in misery, and there is a fair bit of wallowing about: "He shal become the fewel for fier, which alwayes bur-neth and can not be quenched, the foode of worms, which ever gnaw and feedd upon him, and the continewall masse of corruption, which alwayes stincketh, and is filthie, odious, and horrible" (2:218). The treatise never leaves sin or misery behind. That is, instead of describing a trajectory from sin to repentance, *De Miseria* mainly dwells with sin, thus strongly countering the prodigal son, the humanist model for managing the sinfulness of writing. Perhaps even more importantly, it re-introduces a sense of uncertainty about morality, through the unreadability of the world. The world might not make moral sense: virtues might not be rewarded; vices might not be punished. Instead, "often times, the innocent is condempned, and the nocent is absolved; the godly is punished and the ungodly is honored" (2:236).

Such an emphasis on the dark side of reading and writing has to do not only with the capacity of books to lead people into sin, but also with their incapacity to lead them out of it, the fact that reading might not be good for you. In highlight-ing that incapacity, Gascoigne's writings end up being strikingly at odds with the familiar humanist claims that *bonae litterae* necessarily instruct in "noble virtues." The dissipation of his confidence in humanism and his search for an alternative moral model insist, even if only implicitly, on a Chaucerian pathway, a repentance that is not a prodigal pose.

8

Edmund Spenser's *Contemptus Mundi*

Where humanist writings are characterized by a certain and uniform sense of the relationship between literature and morality, what literature should do and be for readers, the Elizabethan trajectory—of dissipating confidence and the search for alternative models—is a much more varied one. Holding on to the new value assigned to literature and, at the same time, trying to make sense of the contradictions and problems led to the hodgepodge that is Greene's *Vision* or the different genres Gascoigne tries on in his last years.[1] Such variability is nowhere more apparent than in an odd collection of poems by Edmund Spenser, *The Complaints* (1591). This collection includes translations of poems by noted humanists Joachim du Bellay and Petrarch, imitations of du Bellay's poetry, and, imitations, perhaps surprisingly, of Chaucer's poetry.[2] Even the printer underlines the diversity of the poems in his opening description: they are "smale Poemes ... disperst abroad in sundrie hands."[3] Despite or perhaps due to such variety, the printer explicitly unifies them around their moral lesson—worldly vanity.[4] The poems are "all complaints and meditations of the worlds vanitie; very grave and profitable" (223). Not only does the content of the *Complaints* suggest variety and even potential contradictions but so does the timing: this collection

---

[1] The success and relative uniformity of humanist education is widely accepted. See Ian Green, *Humanism and Protestantism in Early Modern English Education* (Burlington, VT: Ashgate, 2009), e.g. 78–86.

[2] Critics tend to focus only on one poem at a time, but for brief and insightful discussions of the collection as a whole, see Katherine A. Craik, "Spenser's Complaints and the New Poet," *Huntington Library Quarterly* 64 (2001): 63–79; Mark David Rasmussen, "Complaints and *Daphnaïda* (1591)," in *The Oxford Handbook of Edmund Spenser*, ed. Richard A. McCabe (Oxford: Oxford University Press, 2010), 218–36; and Linda Vecchi, "Spenser's *Complaints*: Is the Whole Equal to the Sum of its Parts?," in *Spenser at Kalamazoo* (Clarion, PA: Clarion University of Pennsylvania, 1984), 127–38. Richard Danson Brown's study takes up the relations between poems at greater length, arguing that they show a chronological development toward a new poetics, one that is ambivalent about the moral value of poetry (*"The New Poet": Novelty and Tradition in Spenser's "Complaints"* [Liverpool: Liverpool University Press, 1999], 9). Brown gives a persuasive account of Spenser's interest in moral value and his debts to Chaucer, but he overstates the novelty of what Spenser is doing.

[3] Spenser, "The Printer to the Reader," in *The Yale Edition of the Shorter Poems of Edmund Spenser*, ed. William A. Oram, Einar Bjorvand, and Ronald Bond (New Haven, CT: Yale University Press, 1989), 223. All references to poems in Spenser's *Complaints* will appear in the text parenthetically with abbreviated titles and line numbers.

[4] Most scholars follow Harold Stein's foundational argument for authorial purpose in his *Studies in Spenser's Complaints* (New York: Oxford University Press, 1934). Jean Brink claims, in contrast, that there is no evidence that Spenser was involved in the publication. See Brink, "Who Fashioned Edmund Spenser?: The Textual History of *Complaints*," *Studies in Philology* 88 (1991): 153–168.

Humanism and Good Books in Sixteenth-Century England. Katherine C. Little, Oxford University Press.
© Katherine C. Little (2023). DOI: 10.1093/oso/9780192883193.003.0009

EDMUND SPENSER'S *CONTEMPTUS MUNDI*   171

appeared in 1591, interrupting the two installments of Spenser's epic, *The Faerie Queene* (1590, 1596).[5]

Spenser is, as is shown in *The Complaints*, and indeed in much of his poetry, both a more committed humanist, a more conscious imitator of the classical legacy, and a more committed Chaucerian than his contemporaries. This combination is not coincidental. Spenser, unlike Gascoigne and Greene, does not view his earlier writings with regret, whether real or feigned, perhaps because they fit comfortably within the Horatian guidelines he has inherited, of profit and delight. For that reason, he does not need to repent of his failure to be a humanist, as do Gascoigne and Greene. Chaucer is, nevertheless, similarly meaningful to Spenser as a model not only for writing poetry but also for thinking through its moral value, the good to which it can lay claim. For Spenser, Chaucer provides an alternative to classical imitation, to the kind of confidence that informed humanism, and that Chaucerian alternative is imagined mainly in and around worldly vanity.

To be sure, it is easy to read Spenser's *oeuvre* in terms of humanism, as an embrace and celebration of the classical legacy. His imitations seem to conform, at first glance, to a recognizably humanist approach, in that they demonstrate a valuing of style or eloquence on its own terms. In *The Shepheardes Calender* (1579), E.K., likely a persona for Spenser himself, introduces Spenser's poetry as an imitation of a primarily classical legacy, the eclogues of Virgil:

> [Spenser is] following the example of the best and most auncient Poetes, which devised this kind of wryting, being both so base for the matter, and homely for the manner, at the first to trye their habilities; and, as young birdes, that be newly crept out of the nest, by little first to prove their tender wyngs, before they make a greater flyght. So flew Theocritus, as you may perceive he was already full fledged. So flew Virgile, as not yet well feeling his winges. So flew Mantuan, as being not full somd [full fledged]. So Petrarque. So Boccace; So Marot, Sanazarus, and also divers other excellent both Italian and French Poetes, whose foting this Author every where followeth, yet so as few, but they be well sented [have a good nose], can trace him out. So finally flieth this our new Poete, as a bird, whose principals [feathers] be scarce growen out, but yet as that in time shall be hable to keepe wing with the best.[6]

In repeating, "best" to describe the classical legacy, Spenser echoes Roger Ascham's well-known section on imitation in his treatise, *The Scholemaster* (1570), which

---

[5] A number of critics have noted the way in which the *Complaints* offers a kind of interruption or alternative to Spenser's more Virgilian career. See John D. Bernard, *Ceremonies of Innocence: Pastoralism in the Poetry of Edmund Spenser* (Cambridge: Cambridge University Press, 1989), 111–22; Craik, "Spenser's Complaints;" Rebeca Helfer, *Spenser's Ruins and the Art of Recollection* (Toronto: University of Toronto Press, 2012), 14–25; and Richard Rambuss, *Spenser's Secret Career* (Cambridge: Cambridge University Press, 1993), 62–95.

[6] "Epistle" to *The Shepheardes Calender*, in *The Yale Edition*, lines 152–67.

172   HUMANISM AND GOOD BOOKS IN SIXTEENTH-CENTURY ENGLAND

praises classical authors as "the best and wisest"[7] Like Ascham, Spenser sees imitation as a process of acquiring the "tools and instruments" used by a particular author, which he describes here as "abilities."[8] Indeed, this (self-)introduction is entirely focused on an "excellence" defined in relation to a previous author. Such a model suggests beauty and freedom, as in the bird, not the "tedious traditions" of moralizing one might find elsewhere, in other less skilled imitations, such as those described by George Gascoigne.[9] In much the same way, Spenser famously presents himself as another Virgil in the opening lines of *The Faerie Queene*, drawing attention to the way in which he has followed Virgil. He will exchange his "oaten reeds" [eclogues] for "trumpets," "fierce wars," and "faithful loves" [epic].[10] Such an awareness of Virgil's different modes, his eclogues and his epic, is a literary awareness: Spenser will try to attend to the elements that make this poem an epic.

Spenser is not, however, as consistent in his humanism, his celebration and imitation of the classical legacy, as these much remarked upon passages might indicate. After all, the poems in Spenser's *Complaints* are also imitations, strictly speaking, but they are markedly less celebratory of the classical legacy, or of the skills associated with the classical legacy, and, consequently less interested in placing Spenser in loving or humbly admiring relationship to it. Most obviously, the poems are presented as already moralized, as all containing a "profitable" message about worldly vanity. In other words, the approach here is less stereotypically humanist, in that it does not advertise the poem's stylistic achievements or eloquence, and more stereotypically medieval, in that the poems are subordinated to a recognizably Christian rubric of *contemptus mundi*. In this way, Spenser returns to a medieval perspective, in which the moral function of any kind of writing must be foregrounded and, at times, evaluated. He does not accept the imitation of valued classical texts as in and of itself already implicitly moralized, as Roger Ascham does, when he considered "those that were wisest in judgment of matters" to be the same as those "that wrote most and best in either tongue."[11] From Ascham's perspective, imitating Cicero will always be good morally as well as good for one's Latin. Nor does Spenser accept that imitation is independent of morality, encouraging secularism and ambiguity, as has been suggested by later scholars.[12]

---

[7] Roger Ascham, *The Scholemaster*, in *English Works*, ed. William Aldis Wright (Cambridge: Cambridge University Press, 1904), 264–65.

[8] Ascham, *The Scholemaster*, 264–65; 267.

[9] *The Complete Works of George Gascoigne*, 2 vols., ed. John W. Cunliffe (Cambridge: Cambridge University Press, 1910) 2: 48.

[10] *The Faerie Queene*, ed. Thomas P. Roche (New York: Penguin, 1979) 1. Prol. 4, 9. Spenser's relationship to Virgil has been well-documented. See, for example, John Watkins, *The Specter of Dido: Spenser and Virgilian Epic* (New Haven, CT: Yale University Press, 1995) and David Wilson-Okamura, "Problems in the Virgilian Career," *Spenser Studies* 26 (2011): 1–30.

[11] Ascham, *The Scholemaster*, 213.

[12] Thomas M. Greene, *The Light in Troy: Imitation and Discovery in Renaissance Poetry* (New Haven, CT: Yale University Press, 1982), 30.

EDMUND SPENSER'S CONTEMPTUS MUNDI   173

Spenser's critique of humanism and his moral reflections are somewhat diffuse in the *Complaints*, and the poems, in general, less well-known than his other work. This discussion will begin, therefore, with an overview of the poems.[13] These can be grouped into three different categories, each of which has a different relationship to classical imitation and, therefore, to humanism itself. First, there are poems that are clearly humanist. These poems imitate in order to rediscover, lament, and appreciate the classical past: *Ruines of Rome: by Bellay* and *The Visions of Bellay*, both of which are translations of poems by Joachim du Bellay; *Virgil's Gnat*, a translation of the *Culex,* which circulated with Virgil's works in a text established by Pietro Bembo; and *The Visions of Petrarch*, a translation of Petrarch's *Rime* 323 via Clément Marot.[14] Second, are the poems that reflect on humanist imitation. These are poems of Spenser's own invention that take up classical topics, such as Rome or the Muses, rendering them as complaints about worldly vanity: *The Ruines of Time*, which begins the collection; *Visions of the Worlds Vanitie*; and *The Teares of the Muses*. In the third group are the fables, also of Spenser's own invention: *Muiopotmos* and *Prosopoia: Mother Hubberd's Tale*. These poems seem to be outliers in the collection both because they have little to do with worldly vanity and because they are narratives, with plots and characters, whereas the other poems are largely static speeches by one or more characters. More importantly, the literary debts of this third group are less immediately obvious. Indeed, *Mother Hubberd's Tale* advertises its outlier status within the collection by imitating Chaucer's *Canterbury Tales* instead of contemporary humanist or classical sources. My discussion will focus on a poem from each of the last two groups: *The Ruines of Time*, as Spenser's reflection on humanist confidence in imitation, and *Mother Hubberd's Tale*, as an ambivalent, Chaucerian solution to the moral questions he has raised in the collection.

Spenser's Worldly Vanity

Spenser's focus on worldly vanity, his moral framework, is not entirely original to Spenser, but it is nevertheless worth noting the way in which he is both inventing and experimenting. One might contrast the de-centered and varied approach in his *Complaints* with his source, his collaboration with Jan van der Noot, *The Theatre of Voluptuous Worldlings* (1569). For this earlier text, Spenser supplied translations of poems by du Bellay and Petrarch, which were inserted into an extensive commentary.[15] Van der Noot explicitly links his moral lessons, rigid and bleak as they are, to the typically more positive and flexible humanist Horatian sweetness

[13] M. D. Rasmussen notes the "diffuseness" of the collection and the difficulties critics have had in approaching it as a whole ("Complaints," 220 and 221–22).

[14] On the sources of *Virgil's Gnat* and the *Visions of Petrarch*, see the editor's introductions in the *Yale Edition*, 293–96 and 451–52. du Bellay's influence will be discussed further below.

174   HUMANISM AND GOOD BOOKS IN SIXTEENTH-CENTURY ENGLAND

and usefulness. He writes, at the beginning, "And to sette the vanitie and incon-stancie of worldly and transitorie thyngs, liuelier before your eyes, I haue broughte in here twentie sightes or vysions, & caused them to be grauen, to the ende al men may see that with their eyes, whiche I go aboute to expresse by writing ... according vnto the saying of *Horace. Omne tulit punctum, qui miscuit vtile dulci.* That is to say, 'He that teacheth pleasantly and well,/ Doth in eche poynt all others excell.'"[16] In fusing, somewhat oddly, the inconstancy of the world on the one hand and delight in pleasant poetry on the other, van der Noot stays within humanism, even as he hardens its moral line. That is, he is making explicit the *contemptus* that is only implicit in the sonnet sequences of the French poet Joachim du Bellay. As Anne Lake Prescott has noted, van der Noot likely recognized the "power and useful-ness of these emblems of secular ruin" in du Bellay's poetry for his moral topic of "worldly vanity."[17]

Spenser alters this very overt moralizing frame in his *Complaints*, removing the securing interpretative framework, both the commentary and the eschatological sonnets. He also has much expanded the number and kind of poems. Such alter-ations might suggest that Spenser has freed poetry to be, in a sense, more literary and less moral.[18] On closer look, one finds that he has not so much dislodged or loosened the moral frame as internalized it. That is, Spenser invents a poetic mode around *contemptus*, which will be called here *contemptus*-complaint, thus empha-sizing that morality is not just a rubric applied to texts, as it is in van der Noot's version, but generative of writing itself. Spenser's version of *contemptus*-complaint is grounded, of course, in a recognizably medieval or pre-humanist mode—the complaint. Complaints can only be very broadly described by way of their con-tent and their affect: they are laments.[19] By the late sixteenth century, this mode

---

[16] *A theatre wherein be represented as wel the miseries & calamities that follow the voluptuous worldlings* (London, 1569) STC 18,602, F2v–F3r, image 43. Helfer describes van der Noot as a kind of Virgilian in his confident perspective (*Spenser's Ruins*, 60).

[17] Anne Lake Prescott, *French Poets and the English Renaissance* (New Haven, CT: Yale University Press, 1978), 44.

[18] On the *contemptus* frame of the *Theatre for Worldlings*, see Carl J. Rasmussen, "'Quietnesse of Minde': A *Theatre for Worldlings* as Protestant Poetics," *Spenser Studies* 1 (1980): 3–27. Leonard Barkan notes how Spenser returns du Bellay's poems to their original context in the *Complaints* (i.e. not a moral one), in essence "de-Protestantizing," them by removing the eschatological apparatus ("Ruins and Visions: Spenser, Pictures, and Rome," in *Edmund Spenser: Essays on Culture and Allegory*, ed. Jennifer Klein Morrison and Matthew Greenfield [Aldershot, UK: Ashgate, 2000], 27). Helfer makes a similar point in *Spenser's Ruins*, 23, 61–62.

[19] There have been several attempts to define complaint. An early one is that of John Peter, *Complaint and Satire in Early English Literature* (Oxford: Clarendon Press, 1956), which is mainly concerned to distinguish complaint from satire. Peter does, however, include a discussion of the close link between complaint and the *contemptus* tradition, since for Peter, complaint "concerns itself simply with Man and his perennial frailties" (59). See further *Complaint and Satire*, 14–103. Thomas J. Elliott has a more useful approach, noting that complaints are not limited to avoidance of the world, but also desire a rem-edy ("Middle English Complaints against the Times: To Contemn the World or Reform it?," *Annuale Medievale* 14[1973]: 22–34). Wendy Scase expands this idea, arguing that complaint is an "expres-sion of grievance as a means of obtaining a judicial remedy" (*Literature and Complaint in England 1272–1553* [Oxford: Oxford University Press, 2007], 1), underlining the social and political focus of

EDMUND SPENSER'S *CONTEMPTUS MUNDI*   175

included a wide range of writings, from impersonations of classical figures who lament their personal sorrows, such as Chaucer's *Complaint of Mars* (c. 1385) or George Gascoigne's *Compleynt of Philomena* (1576), to what we would now think of as satire, a lament about current social or religious conditions, such as *The prayer and complaynt of the ploweman vnto Christ* (1532).[20] As Hugh MacLean observes, these are "plaintive poems ... expressing grief or lamentation for any variety of causes: unrequited love, the speaker's affairs, or the sorrows of the human condition."[21]

Although there were many kinds of complaints in circulation at the time Spenser was writing, Spenser ties his complaint to worldly vanity; hence my term *contemptus*-complaint. That is, the sorrow in his complaints has mainly to do with the world as an idea, or worldliness and anti-worldliness, and not with love or with specific social problems, such as the greed of clergy, as one finds in the examples previously listed.[22] The seeds of such a *contemptus*-complaint are apparent in one of the foundational texts in this tradition, Lotharjo dei Segni's *De Miseria Condicionis Humane* (c. 1195), which opens with a lament. I am quoting the English from George Gascoigne's translation, *The Droomme of Doomesday* (1576), which was circulating at the time Spenser was writing, and the Latin from the useful dual language edition by Robert Lewis:

> "Wherefore came I out of my mothers womb, that I might behold sorrow and payne? and that my dayes might be consumed in confusion. Yf he whome our Lord God dyd sanctifie in his mother's womb, dyd speak thus of him selfe, what shall I then saye of my selfe whom my mother hath begotten in sinne? Ah las for me, O mother (may I well saye) wherefore hast thou begotten or conceyved me the sonne of bitter sorrow and payne?"

much complaint in this period. Neither Scase nor Peter nor Elliott is interested in lovers' complaints, which were also popular in this time, and which share little except the title of complaint with the poems of social grievance. On lovers' complaints, see Craik, who argues that Chaucer is the primary influence for Renaissance authors' love complaints ("Spenser's Complaints," 74–77) and John Kerrigan, who acknowledges the variety of this mode in his introduction to *Motives of Woe: Shakespeare and "Female Complaint": A Critical Anthology*, ed. John Kerrigan (New York: Oxford University Press, 1991), 1–83. Hugh Maclean understands complaint as a distinct genre and discusses Spenser's interest in complaint throughout his career, noting the debts to Chaucer and the "variety and range of his concerns" (Hugh Maclean, "'Restlesse anguish and unquiet paine': Spenser and the Complaint, 1579–90," in *The Practical Vision*, ed. Jane Campbell and James Doyle [Waterloo, ON: Wilfrid Laurier University Press, 1978], 29–47. Vecchi provides a survey of three kinds of complaint—*de casibus*, *contemptus*, and the social—and categorizes each of Spenser's poems accordingly ("Spenser's *Complaints*).

[20] On *The prayer and complaynt of the ploweman*, see Scase, *Literature and Complaint*, 154–56.

[21] Maclean, "'Restlesse anguish,'" 30.

[22] On worldliness and anti-worldliness, see Timothy Duffy, "'The Light of Simple Veritie': Mapping out Spenser's Cosmography in 'The Ruines of Time,'" *Studies in Philology* 111 (2014): 738–756; Laurence Goldstein, "Immortal Longings and 'The Ruines of Time,'" *Journal of English and Germanic Philology* 75 (1976): 337–51; and Thomas Hyde, "Vision, Poetry, and Authority in Spenser," *English Literary Renaissance* 13 (1983): 127–145.

176   HUMANISM AND GOOD BOOKS IN SIXTEENTH-CENTURY ENGLAND

[Quare de vulva matris mee egressus sum et viderem laborem et dolorem et consumerentur in confusione dies mei? Si talia locutus est ille de se quem Deus sanctificavit in utero, qualia loquar ego de me, quem mater mea genuit in peccato? Heu me, dixerim, mater mea, quid me genuisti, filium amaritudinis et doloris?][23]

This passage explores sorrow through a first-person speaker who exclaims and questions and makes demands on the audience. In other words, this mode requires both a detailed description to underline the urgency of the speaker's state (the horror of birth) and the direct appeal to listeners, an insistence that they empathize or sympathize with a particular persona. Jonathan Crewe offers an insightful account of the way in which the lamenter of complaint has emotional designs on the audience, through the "the passive-aggressive psychology" and the foregrounding of "the mournful, vengeful subject."[24] Complaint is, in sum, a mode that emotionally links the speaker and the audience together.

Spenser's *contemptus*-complaint models itself on the lamenting of the world that is found in *De Miseria*, but alters the meaning of the world fairly drastically in order to think through the moral value of poetry. Spenser's world in *Complaints* is not at all the physical world, of bodies and food, the "earthly things" upon which Everyman was so fixated in *Everyman* and that are imagined in *De Miseria*. It is instead a world defined by writing, not least because much of it is mediated through the sonnet sequences of du Bellay and Petrarch. Not just any writing but writing that is almost entirely determined by reference to classical texts, places, and characters. For example, Spenser uses the classical muses to catalogue the sorry state of poetry in England in *The Teares of the Muses*. Each of the muses complains in turn, after the speaking voice commands them to speak:

> Rehearse [repeat] to me ye sacred Sisters nine:
> The golden brood of great Apolloes wit,
> Those piteous plaints and sorrowfull sad tine [loss],
> Which late ye powred forth as ye did sit
> Beside the silver Springs of Helicone,
> Making your musick of hart-breaking mone (*Teares*, 1–6).[25]

The world in this poem is entirely self-referential and hermetic: the muses are figures for literary production reflecting on literary production. One might con-

---

[23] *Droome*, in *Complete Works of George Gascoigne*, 2:217 and Pope Innocent III, *De Miseria Condicionis Humane*, ed. and trans. Robert E. Lewis (Athens, GA: University of Georgia Press, 1978), 93.

[24] Jonathan Crewe, *Hidden Designs: The Critical Profession and Renaissance Literature* (New York: Methuen, 1986), 159 n. 23.

[25] M. D. Rasmussen notes the self-reflexivity of *TM* in "Spenser's Plaintive Muses," *Spenser Studies* 13 (1999): 139–64.

trast this approach with other kinds of complaints, the first person "everyman" of *De Miseria,* who laments sin, or Philomena, the raped woman who tells her story in Gascoigne's *Compleynt of Philomena.* Such laments may be highly conventional, hyperbolic, and literary in so far as they use recognizable characters drawn from earlier texts, but they nevertheless refer to experiences and sensations that actual people have. In Spenser's poem, sadness about the state of the world does not emerge from its physical reality—of being assaulted, of being born—or from the helplessness of those trying to live in such a brutalizing world, but rather from a very narrowly defined kind of writing. Sadness appears here as an inevitable byproduct of writing poetry through classical imitation: it demonstrates the failure to live up to classical models.

Spenser takes up this kind of sadness, the sadness produced by a literature understood in terms of classical imitation, at great length in his opening poem of the collection, *The Ruines of Time* (hereafter *RT*). In this poem, a first-person speaker encounters a female character, Verlame, a figure for the ancient Roman town Verulamium, who is complaining about her fall and about the death of Sir Philip Sidney.[26] The speaker then has two sets of visions. In the first, he sees a series of falls, of objects into ruin. After an authoritative and disembodied voice provides him with the moral of earthly vanity, he has a second set of visions of transcendence, of objects being taken into the heavens. Not only is Spenser imitating Joachim du Bellay's two poems about the fall of Rome, *Antiquitez* and *Songe,* he is also writing a lament for Sidney and for the Dudley-Sidney family.

In writing this poem as a *contemptus*-complaint, Spenser is not himself lamenting the fall of Rome but lamenting the lamenters. In other words, this is an intensely self-reflective poem about what it means to write a certain kind of poetry and what it means to be a poet.[27] Despite its general movement toward consolation,

---

[26] In "'How Weak Be the Passions of Woefulness': Spenser's *Ruines of Time,*" *Spenser Studies* 2 (1981): 159–81, Carl J. Rasmussen offers an insightful reading of Verlame, drawing attention to this figure as a "literary device for a meditation on mourning," whose grief draws the speaker into despair (160).

[27] Most scholars have approached this poem in terms of Spenser's meditations on poetry and the role of the poet. Older scholarship sees Spenser wholeheartedly embracing the poet's role. See, for example, A. E. B. Coldiron, "How Spenser Excavates du Bellay's *Antiquitez,* or, The Role of the Poet, Lyric Historiography, and the English Sonnet," *Journal of English and Germanic Philology* 10 (2002): 41–67; A. Leigh DeNeef, "'The Ruins of Time': Spenser's Apology for Poetry," *Studies in Philology* 76, (1979): 262–71; Anne Janowitz, *England's Ruins: Poetic Purpose and the National Landscape* (Cambridge: Blackwell, 1990), 21–30; Millar MacLure, "Spenser and the ruins of time," in *A Theatre for Spenserians*, ed. Judith M. Kennedy and James A. Reither (Toronto: University of Toronto Press, 1973), 3–18; and Phillip Schwyzer, *Archaeologies of English Renaissance Literature* (Oxford: Oxford University Press, 2007), 77. More recent works see the poem as more ambivalent or critical of the poet's role. See, for example, Brown, *"The New Poet,"* 99–132; Andrew Fichter, "'And nought of Rome in Rome perceiv'st at all': Spenser's 'Ruines of Rome,'" *Spenser Studies* 2 (1981): 183–92; Huw Griffiths, "Translated Geographies: Spenser's "Ruins of Time," *Early Modern Literary Studies* 4 (1998): 26 paragraphs; Helfer, *Spenser's Ruins,* 136–67; Andrew Hui, *The Poetics of Ruins in Renaissance Literature* (New York: Fordham University Press, 2017), 177–221; Isabel Karremann, "Edmund Spenser's *The Ruines of Time* as a Protestant Poetics of Mourning and Commemoration," in *Forms of Faith: Literary Form and Religious Conflict in Shakespeare's England*, ed. by Jonathan Baldo and Isabel Karremann (Manchester: Manchester University Press, 2017), 90–109; Hassan Melehy, "Antiquities of Britain: Spenser's 'Ruines

178 HUMANISM AND GOOD BOOKS IN SIXTEENTH-CENTURY ENGLAND

its reassurance that poetry can lead to a kind of transcendence, in the objects rising to heaven, the poem is also critical of a specifically humanist project, one that is so focused on classical models and themes, presented here in terms of the loss of Rome. The *contemptus* tradition provides Spenser a moral language, from outside humanism, to describe imitation as attachment to the world, an attachment that is unhealthy and painful. Applying the *contemptus* tradition to du Bellay's version (and vision) of Rome, Spenser re-writes the humanist recovery of the classical past, the kind of imitation so central to the humanist project and to Sidney's project, as both psychologically and morally damaging. What aids him in offering this critique of the humanist project, is his alternative model, Chaucer's poetry.

Before I turn to Spenser's lament in *RT*, I think it is worth examining his source poems for the perspective on Rome and imitation he inherits, a perspective that one might describe as loss-partial recovery, following Thomas Greene's influential account of Renaissance imitation.[28] Both of du Bellay's poems offer a meditation on the Roman past: an encounter with the physical remnants of Rome in *Antiquitez*, and a vision of the symbols long associated with that Empire in the *Songe*. These are not happy poems, focusing as they do on the fact of Rome's fall, the magnitude of what has been lost. The *Antiquitez*, which Spenser translates closely, and entitles *The Ruines of Rome: by Bellay* (hereafter *RR*), is a sequence of thirty-two sonnets, framed as the expression of a first-person speaker, who views the ruins of Rome with a kind of "brooding melancholy."[29] Focusing on ruins might seem to align this poem with the *contemptus* tradition, and it is true that du Bellay includes several comments on worldly vanity. Rome is an "earthly thing," whose power disappeared "To shew that all in th'end to nought shall fade" (*RR*, 14, 280). But the speaker does not embrace this position fully; he rejects the "common voyce" and its claim that all things are subject to decay in order to offer a more cryptic claim about some future time when everything shall "come to nought" (*RR*, 121–26). Indeed, the speaker finds consolation in his own writing; he does not find it in God or in some kind of heaven. Despite the overwhelming sense of ruin, decay, corpses, age, and destruction, *RR* is, therefore, also hopeful about the power of poetry to confer immortality, the repair and recovery after loss. At the end of the poem, the speaker juxtaposes Rome's stone monuments with his lute, suggesting that the latter may find "immortality," where the former had not:

---

of Time," *Studies in Philology* 102 (2005): 159–183; Emily Shortslef; "*The Ruines of Time* and the Virtual Collectivities of Early Modern Complaint," *Journal for Early Modern Cultural Studies* 13 (2013): 84–104; and Michael Ullyot, "Spenser and the Matter of Poetry," *Spenser Studies* 27 (2012): 77–96.

[28] This is a standard perspective on du Bellay's work, aptly described by Hui, in which poetry rebuilds ruins, "supply[ing] the emptiness of ruined matter through language" (*Poetics of Ruins*, 163). Scholars tend to disagree on whether Spenser is more or less optimistic than du Bellay about rebuilding/repairing, but that dispute is here irrelevant. See also Barkan, "*Ruins* and Visions;" Coldiron, "How Spenser Excavates;" Helfer, *Spenser's Ruins*, 62–66, 138–39; Hui, *Poetics of Ruins*, 144–76; and Melehy, "Antiquities of Britain."

[29] Editor's introduction to *Ruines of Rome*, in *The Yale Edition*, 384.

EDMUND SPENSER'S *CONTEMPTUS MUNDI*   179

> If under heaven anie endurance were,
> These moniments, which not in paper writ,
> But in Porphyre and Marble do appeare,
> Might well have hop'd to have obtained it.
> Nath'les [Nevertheless] my Lute, whom *Phoebus* deigned to give,
> Cease not to sound these old antiquities (*RR*, 437, 439–44).

Thinking about Rome's fall may be horrifying, filled with ghosts and spirits, but it is also immensely generative, leading directly to songs. For this reason, Greene has described imitation in du Bellay's poem as a "double gesture," in which the reaching into the death and decay is also a building up.[30] That is, even in its consciousness of loss, the poem insists on a kind of triumph of recovery.

The *Songe*, which Spenser translates as *The Visions of Bellay* (hereafter *VB*), also follows the loss-partial recovery model, although the recovery is somewhat less obvious. In this sequence of fifteen sonnets, Rome is described as a series of objects natural and unnatural (a river, a tree, a building, etc.), which are then destroyed through various means. The recovery is largely implicit, and certainly partial, since poetry can only outline what has been lost. Although this more totalizing focus on fall and destruction would seem to support the anti-worldliness of the *contemptus* mode, the poem hesitates to commit to that moral position entirely. To be sure, the poem begins with a clear position: "all is nought but flying vanitie" (*VB*, 11). And yet, the poem only approaches the things that are subject to decay and death symbolically. That is, no actual people die; no actual buildings are destroyed; there is no sense in which the world here is the physical world, as it is in *De Miseria*, and even somewhat more fully in the *Antiquitez*. Although the poem thus fits the fall of Rome more successfully to the moral, reminding the reader at the opening that only "God surmounts all times decay" (*VB*, 13), it does so by eliding the very real and decaying antiquities that informed the previous poem.

Spenser may have been impressed by du Bellay's focus on ruins and his sonnet-making, as many scholars have noted, but the aspect of these poems that stands out, especially to someone trained in a *contemptus* perspective, is the first-person speaker who mediates Rome.[31] That is, these are not primarily poems about Roman ruins or Roman symbols but the experience of an "I," witnessing and

---

[30] Greene, *Light in Troy*, 236, 235.

[31] Much of the scholarship on the *Complaints* has focused on ruins, which become in these readings a complex symbol of the Renaissance itself, a way to recover the classical past that recognizes its destruction and loss. See Helfer, *Spenser's Ruins*, 14–25, 136–67; Hui, *The Poetics of Ruins*, 190–94; and Janowitz, *England's Ruins*, 21–30. In this, critics are mainly following Greene's approach to ruins in *Light in Troy*, and they therefore tend to accept the Renaissance as a clearly defined concept. A potentially promising corrective is suggested by Karremann, "Edmund Spenser;" Schwyzer, *Archaeologies*, 72–107 and Tom Muir, "Specters of Spenser: Translating the 'Antiquitez,'" *Spenser Studies* 25 (2010): 327–61, all of which focus on the topicality of the poem by emphasizing monastic ruins.

180 HUMANISM AND GOOD BOOKS IN SIXTEENTH-CENTURY ENGLAND

having visions.[32] Both poems draw attention to that speaker and his emotions, although he is more of a framing consciousness than a character. In *RR*, that speaker begins with a "shreiking yell" and "sacred horror" at the "deep ruines" (8, 13, 2), and gives a brief sense of his emotional state in sonnet 7:

> My sad desires, rest therefore moderate:
> For if that time make ende of things so sure,
> It als[o] will end the paine, which I endure (*RR*, 96–98).

The speaker's intrusions into his description ensure that readers see the death and decay as personal to the speaker. The *Songe* also uses an emotional, first-person speaker, who begins by referring to the "mortall miseries" sleep brings (*VB*, 4) and then returns to his emotions again until near the end, when he describes the "visions sad" that he has "deeply gron'd" (*VB*, 183). The large number of first-person interjections register what the speaker sees as well as his wonder, amazement, and astonishment. These statements recur often, as if to indicate the overwhelming nature of the vision.

Spenser's poem on Rome, *RT*, is a *contemptus*-complaint that deepens and extends the first-person speaker, emphasizing his, and potentially the reader's, emotional relationship to Rome and drawing attention to the moral problems created by this emotional relationship.[33] While Spenser follows du Bellay in addressing the ruins of Rome both in terms of physical remnants and also visions of familiar symbols of earthly decline and destruction, he has invented a female character, Verlame with whom the first-person speaker (a persona for the poet) converses. The source of such changes is neither du Bellay, who only includes characters as hints, nor the classical legacy, but Chaucer's dream poetry.[34] There can be no doubt that Spenser knew at least the *Book of the Duchess* (*BD*); the most obvious evidence is Spenser's *Daphnaida* (1591), an imitation of *BD*, which appeared in print in the same year as the *Complaints*. Chaucer's *BD*, like *RT*, imagines a first-person speaker saddened by a conversation with a lamenting figure, the Black Knight; indeed, Chaucer's poetry is filled with emoting and reactive speakers.

Spenser uses the "I" as a figure for the poet and the other character, Verlame, as a figure for a set of ideas that he must confront and about which he evidently has somewhat mixed feelings, in this case the ruin of Rome. This confrontation draws

---

[32] On Spenser's use of a persona in *Ruines of Rome*, see Fichter, "'And nought.'" On the visionary aspect of Spenser's translations, see Hyde, "Vision, Poetry and Authority."

[33] Prescott notes, "Spenser is more explicit than du Bellay both in his open weeping and in his religious consolations" (*French Poets*, 52).

[34] Both C. J. Rasmussen and Margaret Ferguson note that Verlame is "Chaucerian," without much further discussion. See Ferguson, "'the Afflatus of Ruin': Meditations on Rome by du Bellay, Spenser, and Stevens," in *Roman Images: Selected Papers from the English Institute*, ed. Annabel Patterson (Baltimore, MD: Johns Hopkins University Press, 1984), 35 and C. J. Rasmussen, "'How Weak,'" 164, respectively.

attention to the moral value of the classical legacy for those who are imitating it. Spenser begins his poem with the encounter between the two:

> It chaunced me on day beside the shore
> Of silver streaming *Thamesis* to bee,
> Nigh [near] where the goodly *Verlame* stood of yore,
> Of which there now remaines no memory,
> Nor any little moniment to see,
> By which the travailer, that fares that way,
> This once was she, may warned be to say.
> There on the other side, I did behold
> A woman sitting sorrowfullie wailing,
> Rending her yeolow locks, like wyrie golde,
> About her shoulders carleslie downe trailing,
> And streames of teares from her faire eyes forth railing.
> In her right hand a broken rod she held,
> Which towards heaven shee seemd on high to weld (*RT*, 1–14).

This opening establishes Rome or the Roman past as entirely mediated through the inner experiences and emotions of human characters, not as an independent physical reality. The immateriality of Rome is not only a result of not having any monument associated with it, but also of the generic cues given to the reader: this might be a dream vision, since the speaker is a wanderer gazing in the water.[35]

Such a character-driven approach ensures that the reader understands the loss of Rome as both intense and personal; indeed, it is this personalized aspect, this attachment, that Spenser wishes not only to investigate in his poem but also to critique, for being psychologically harmful. The intensity of attachment is apparent in the female figure, who is not named at this point, and who is clearly mourning something, since she is performing familiar ritualized actions: wailing and rending. It is also apparent in the speaker himself, who is greatly affected by her sadness even though he does not yet understand the source:

> Much was I mooved at her piteous plaint,
> And felt my heart nigh riven in my brest
> With tender ruth to see her sore constraint,
> That shedding teares a while I still did rest
> And after did her name of her request (*RT*, 29–33).

Indeed, Spenser seems to be far more interested in the speaker's empathetic response to Verlame than in Verlame herself, giving detailed attention to the development of his empathy—he ends up "shedding tears" to match her "streames of

---

[35] On the dream vision, see Brown, "*The New Poet*," 104–8.

182   HUMANISM AND GOOD BOOKS IN SIXTEENTH-CENTURY ENGLAND

teares" (*RT*, 12), as well as in the relationship he attempts to establish with her. After seeing her "so piteouslie perplexed," the speaker "askt what her so vexed" (*RT*, 20–21) and then asks her name. The personal nature of this relationship is underlined by the hints that she is beautiful woman and he is a man. Our sense that he is in love with her, or drawn to her, is informed by the way in which we have entered the poem: through the literary traditions of both dream vision and complaint.

The first part of the poem, the dialogue between the speaker and Verlame, shows a trajectory of attachment to loss, in which the speaker is pulled down into an immersive sadness about the Roman past, one that complicates his ability to draw a moral from his experience. The trajectory of this attachment to loss is, interestingly enough, the opposite of the path charted by Chaucer's *BD*, of loss to acceptance, in which the Black Knight's laments slowly shift in focus because of his conversation with the first-person speaker.[36] First, Spenser's poem shows that Verlame cannot let go, not of the greatness of Rome but of the fact of its demise. More importantly, her own attachment requires that others mourn with her:

> Ne ought to me remaines, but to lament
> My long decay, which no man els doth mone,
> And mourne my fall with dolefull dreriment [sadness].
> Yet it is comfort in great languishment,
> To be bemoned with compassion kinde,
> And mitigates the anguish of the minde (*RT*, 156–61).

Given that Verlame is a figure for a town and, more generally, for the Roman past, one can read this appeal to the speaker allegorically: that the Roman past demands a particular kind of attachment from the poet, one that is predicated on deep sadness. That is, the attachment the poem explores does not concern people or even places or things, but ideas, and particularly literary ideas at that, about the eternity of Rome. Such sadness infects the speaker, and after Verlame finishes her speech, the speaker is overcome with emotion:

> Thus having ended all her piteous plaint
> With dolefull shrikes shee vanished away,
> That I through inward sorrowe wexen [grew] faint,
> And all astonished with deepe dismay
> For her departure, had no word to say;
> But sate long time in sencelesse sad affright [state of terror],
> Looking still, if I might of her have sight (*RT*, 470–76).

---

[36] Like many readers of *Book of the Duchess*, I have been influenced by Louise Fradenburg, "'Voice Memorial': Loss and Reparation in Chaucer's Poetry," *Exemplaria* 2 (1990): 169–202.

The speaker then expands on this state of mind by describing his "troubled braine" (*RT*, 481), "anguish" (*RT*, 482), "groning brest" (*RT*, 484), until he sees the "strange sights" (*RT*, 489), the first set of visions. This account demonstrates the depth of the speaker's attachment to Verlame: he simply cannot let her or her words go. He looks for her, and when he cannot find her, he internalizes her words and then her speech. Such attachment produces the same pain that she seems to have felt: he is grieving and groaning and horrified. At this point, he has no way to resolve or move beyond this attachment to a perspective outside of it, one that would enable him to see it impersonally. Such is her influence that the speaker has visions that reproduce her understanding—the horror and sadness of the fall of a "statelie Towre" (*RT*, 505), for example.

This immersive sadness, this attachment to loss, is shown to incapacitate morality, to prevent the speaker, who is, importantly, here a reader, from learning anything useful from this figure, the lesson about the transitoriness of the world that he should apply to his own life.[37] First Verlame and then the speaker misrepresent the familiar moral of *contemptus* in ways that keep them focused on the world instead of enabling them to leave it behind. Most obviously, Verlame herself alters the moral of *contemptus*, which traditionally has some combination of the following elements: 1. all worldly things pass; 2. earthly things should be hated or abandoned; 3. only God is constant. This multi-part moral would, of course, have been very familiar to Spenser. Chaucer uses a version of it at the end of *Troilus and Criseyde*, when he directs his readers to turn away from the world to God because the world will fade, like flowers.[38] Spenser himself includes another version at the end of his translation, *The Visions of Petrarch*: "Loath this base world, and thinke of heavens bliss" (96). And yet, in *RT*, Verlame offers only the first part of the moral—on the transitoriness of the world. After identifying herself to the speaker at the beginning of the poem, she states,

> O vaine world's glorie, and unstedfast state
> Of all that lives, on face of sinfull earth,
> Which from their first until their utmost date
> Tast no one hower of happines or merth
> But like at the ingate of their berth,
> They crying creep out of their mother's woomb
> So wailing backe go to their wofull toomb (*RT*, 43–49).

---

[37] Ruth Kaplan has also noted the problematic relationship between pity and moral learning in this poem. Although she describes the first-person speaker as a "Chaucerian narrator," she is more interested in the influence of classical rhetoric ("The Problem of Pity in Spenser's *Ruines of Time* and *Amoretti*," *Spenser Studies* 29 [2014]: 270).

[38] Geoffrey Chaucer, *Troilus and Criseyde* in *The Riverside Chaucer*, 3rd ed., ed. Larry D. Benson (Boston: Houghton Mifflin, 1987), 5.1837–41.

184   HUMANISM AND GOOD BOOKS IN SIXTEENTH-CENTURY ENGLAND

At first glance, this looks like a conventional version of *contemptus*; its mention of birth and the womb evoke *De Miseria*. Such an echo reminds the reader of the goal of *contemptus*, as it was described by van der Noot in the preface to his *Theatre*: it is "profitable" for readers to think about the "inconstancy" of the world as well as its sinfulness, disgustingness, and sorrow. It is difficult, however, to see how thinking about the world's problems is profitable for Verlame. Her thoughts do not lead her to hate the world for its baseness or sin. Indeed, she continues to speak of her world admiringly, its "princelie pallaces" (*RT*, 93), "high steeples" (*RT*, 127), and "winged ships" (*RT*, 148). By focusing on the loss of those worldly things, she paradoxically keeps that world alive.

Even more importantly, Verlame uses *contemptus* to resist accepting loss, losses that include Rome and then deaths in the Dudley family, namely Sir Philip Sidney. Verlame describes the death of Sidney in terms familiar from *contemptus*:

> His blessed spirite full of power divine
> And influence of all celestiall grace,
> Loathing this sinfull earth and earthlie slime,
> Fled back too soone unto his native place,
> Too soone for all that did his love embrace,
> Too soone for all this wretched world, whom he
> Robd of all right and true nobilitie (*RT*, 288–94).

The world is here sinful, wretched, and slimy, and Sidney is, in contrast, heavenly, and yet, Verlame wants to keep him in the world. The world is poorer without him, and that is made clear in the use of the word "robbed" (294). Despite the use of *contemptus* details, this account does not fit with *contemptus*, because of the loss-orientation. While *contemptus* certainly insists that everyone dies, as in the play *Everyman*, death is not understood as loss. In fact, conceiving objects as lost would be precisely the kind of attachment to the world that *contemptus* is designed to address. Everyman has to learn that nothing belongs to him, and he must therefore lose all things without thinking of them as lost. The logic of *contemptus* is that the transitoriness of the world means letting all of it go, no matter how much one has loved it.

Spenser thus uses Verlame to transform *contemptus* from a self-examining mode (why was I born into sin?) into a self-aggrandizing mode (what about me and my sadness?). The potential for wallowing is, of course, there in the original, but wallowing has a purpose in that it frames the question to which there is an obvious answer: God. Knowing that everyone dies, knowing that decay and sin are inescapable, should lead one to turn questions upon oneself about how to be saved. Hence the question at the opening of *De Miseria*: "Why was I born?" One could see how such self-examining questions relate to the sacrament of penance, and it should come as no surprise that the author of *De Miseria* was

EDMUND SPENSER'S *CONTEMPTUS MUNDI*   185

also the authority behind the Constitutions of Lateran IV (1215), including a decree that required annual auricular confession for the first time.[39] Verlame's self-indulgent grief indicates that the problem with the moral lesson in the poem is Verlame herself, not the moral as such. She has altered it to suit her own conditions instead of using it to lead her outside of them to universally accepted truths about the relationship between humans and God, their need for him. For all of her claims about universalism (the address to "all"), the moral comes across as deeply personal. At the end of her speech, before her disappearance, she states

> And who so els that sits in highest seate
> Of this worlds glorie, worshipped of all,
> Ne feareth change of time, nor fortunes threate,
> Let him behold the horror of my fall,
> And his owne end unto remembrance call;
> That of like ruine he may warned bee,
> And in himself be moov'd to pittie me (*RT*, 463–69).

The moral lesson she offers begins perfectly conventionally: look at me and see that everyone who is high on Fortune's wheel might fall! Then, it takes a surprising turn since the desired goal is not that the listener turn away from the world, but that he turn toward it with greater attachment. What Verlame wants is pity for herself not that others be warned by her example not to be so sorrowful.

In using Verlame as an untrustworthy character, who points out the self-interestedness of a moral that, in other contexts, is well-regarded and perceived as true, Spenser is imitating a very Chaucerian technique. Indeed, Verlame's relationship to "worldly vanity" raises the same kinds of questions as the moral of Chaucer's *Monk's Tale*, which is also concerned with the fall of great men, and which is similarly based in a version of humanism, that is, an attachment to pagan, classical texts. Chaucer's Monk offers his monolithic moral early in his *Tale*: "Lat no man truste on blynd prosperitee [Let no man trust in blind prosperity]."[40] The Monk is not wrong, but his moral is partial: his condemnation of the world provides no redemption, as the happy ending of the *Nun's Priest's Tale* makes abundantly clear. Ironizing established morals is one of Chaucer's favored forms of critique, and in the *Monk's* Tale, Chaucer's failed *contemptus* moral functions as a critique of the clergy: what is the Monk doing if he is thinking about tragedies and their paganism and not about Jesus?

---

[39] On Innocent III, see the entry, "Innocent III," in the *Oxford Encyclopedia of the Middle Ages*, ed. Andrew Vauchez (Oxford, 2005), doi: 9780227679319. For an account of confession, see my *Confession and Resistance: Defining the Self in Late Medieval England* (Notre Dame, IN: University of Notre Dame Press, 2006), 1–15.

[40] Chaucer, *The Monk's Tale*, 7.1997.

186   HUMANISM AND GOOD BOOKS IN SIXTEENTH-CENTURY ENGLAND

In Spenser, Verlame's failed moral suggests a similar, if less institutional, critique—of humanist imitation from a Christian perspective. That is, as Verlame makes clear, humanist imitation encodes within it too much of the wrong kind of worldliness, too much paganism and not enough Christianity. The potential contradiction, between classical texts and Christian morality, is nowhere clearer than in her discussions of immortality. That is, classical texts and, therefore, humanist imitation, encourage a pagan idea of immortality: the eternity of poetic fame. Verlame describes this eternity through a contrast between monuments and the heavens:

> All such vaine moniments of earthly masse
> Devour'd of Time, in time to nought doo passe
> But fame with golden wings aloft doth flie,
> Above the reach of ruinous decay,
> And with brave plumes doth beate the azure skie,
> Admir'd of base-borne men from farre away:
> Then who so will with vertuous deeds assay
> To mount to heaven, on *Pegasus* must ride,
> And with sweete Poets verse be glorifide (*RT*, 421–27).

This passage seems to map this familiar, classical idea about fame onto the Christian morality of worldly vanity: buildings are "vain," because earthly, but fame and poetry are spiritual, associated with the "sky" and a "heaven." Even as Verlame ensures that poetry is moralized, since it describes "virtuous deeds," she indicates that classical ideas of poetry (maybe even classical poetry) and Christian morality do not align. Her version of fame is still worldly, even if not exactly earthly, as in on earth. Much as the sky might connote heaven, in this passage it is actually connected to the world, since it is visible to men, whose earthliness is underlined here by "base-born." Moreover, heaven here seems more of a synonym for sky ("the heavens") than a specific Christian and, therefore, spiritual location, given that the pagan Pegasus is the means of approach.

Although the poem does eventually reach an explicitly moral, and Christian, conclusion by activating the full *contemptus* moral in the two sets of visions at the end, Spenser shows how difficult that moral has become. In the first set of visions, Verlame's influence, the pull of humanist attachment, is so powerful, that it undermines the speaker's attempts to reach a moral for himself. After hearing her speak, he reproduces her version of *contemptus* in the first set of visions, immersing himself in loss and sadness by imagining the destruction of earthly things. The speaker sees an image fall to ashes (*RT*, 502) a tower fall to dust (*RT*, 517); a garden "wasted" (*RT*, 529); a giant fall into an abyss (*RT*, 545); a bridge fall (*RT*, 558); and finally two bears crushed by their cave (*RT*, 571–72). Almost all of these visions have the same impact on the speaker: he is overwhelmed with sorrow, in much the same manner he had been in his conversations with Verlame. The last lines describing each vision, except one, the vision of the Giant, underline his sadness: he laments (*RT*, 504); then his heart is almost about to burst with grief (*RT*, 518); he cries (*RT*, 532); grief pains his spirit (*RT*, 560); and he hates the "worlds felicitie" (*RT*, 574).

Only after this first set of visions, does the real moral appear. The speaker hears a voice "loudly" calling to him (*RT*, 580) and that voice, unlike Verlame, is disembodied, and it provides the *contemptus* moral, now recognizably complete:

> Behold (said it) and by ensample see,
> That all is vanitie and griefe of minde,
> Ne other comfort in this world can be,
> But hope of heaven, and heart to God inclinde;
> For all the rest must needs be left behinde (*RT*, 582–86).

This is the first time in the poem that the possibility of comfort for grief has appeared, and the mention of God finally moves the speaker away from his sorrow. In other words, the complete moral, the inclusion of God, works for the speaker whereas Verlame's version, with no Christianity and no God, did not. The second set of visions reinforces that the poem has now shifted to an identifiably Christian moral perspective on the world: turning away from it. All the visions depict transcendence and stellification: the speaker sees a swan, harp, coffin, bed, knight, and an ark, all carried away to heaven. Finally, the last words of the poem, in the envoy, reinforce this Christianized position:

> So unto heaven let your high minde aspire,
> And loath this drosse of sinfull worlds desire (*RT*, 685–86).

This moral clarity is offered to the reader, and in its familiarity, it echoes Chaucer's, at the end of *Troilus and Criseyde*: to "repeyreth hom fro worldly vanyte [return home from worldly vanity]" and look "to thilke God that after his ymage/ Yow made [to the same God that made you in his image]."[41]

As with Chaucer's poem, the explicit statement of a moral does not tie everything up, and one cannot forget what comes before moral. Indeed, this ending, taken as a whole, is not as satisfyingly complete as the final words of the poem might suggest.[42] Focused as they are on heaven, the second set of visions still con-

---

[41] Chaucer, *Troilus and Criseyde*, 5.1837; 1839–40.

[42] Scholars are mixed on how successfully Spenser resolves the contradiction between immortality and transitoriness. See for example, Brown, "*The New Poet*," 199–132 and C. J. Rasmussen, "'How Weak,'" who find him entirely successful in shifting to a Christian immortality. Those who find him more ambivalent are Hui, *The Poetics of Ruins*, 190–94 and Shortslef, "*The Ruines of Time* and the Virtual Collectivities," 87. Helfer claims that Spenser finds resolution in an immortality in remembering ruins, one that is neither the humanist immortality nor the Christian one (*Spenser's Ruins*, 137–40).

tains hints that the speaker cannot fully leave attachment to loss behind. Poetry in imitation of and response to the classical legacy keeps him fixated on the world even as he seeks a Christian consolation. To be sure, the second, obviously more authoritative, set of visions seems to correct the worldliness of the first set: they are more clearly biblical and, therefore, Christian objects, and their movement is reversed, in that they now go up not down. They do not, however, correct the mood of the speaker. Indeed, the poem retains its elegiac character, its focus on loss, in this case the loss of Sidney, who is memorialized in each of the visions. The concluding lines for each vision in this set recall the last lines of the first set, focusing on speaker's sadness. They are not so uniform in their sorrow, but the final reaction reaches almost the extremity of the lines in the first set: "And I for dole was almost like to die" (*RT*, 672). Such expressions return us to the perspective closely associated with Verlame, that sadness at earthly loss hinders an understanding of the other parts of the *contemptus* moral.

As importantly, the objects themselves do not unilaterally point away from the world, toward God. Indeed, some of the objects point the reader back to earlier parts of the poem and the earthly concerns articulated there. The swan and the harp, which connote classical poetry, Apollo and Orpheus, respectively, belong to the same world as the golden statue of Zeus and the bridge over the Hellespont, described in the first, grief-stricken, set of visions, when the speaker cannot get over his sadness; they are not different kinds of objects. Even more problematically, Verlame has already framed this later encounter with some of the objects. Verlame first mentions both Orpheus and Pegasus in her discussion of immortality earlier in the poem, when she insists upon the importance of singing and its capacity to grant "eternitie" (*RT*, 367): Orpheus is mentioned twice, as someone already singing in the afterlife (*RT*, 333) and as someone with the power to sing Eurydice back from the afterlife (*RT*, 391). Riding Pegasus is set parallel with poetry: whoever wants to "mount to heaven, on *Pegasus* must ride,/ And with sweete Poets verse be glorifide" (*RT*, 426–27). When Sidney is compared to Orpheus (*RT*, 607) or a Knight riding Pegasus (*RT*, 646–47) in the second set of visions, then, the reader cannot help but think of his poetry on earth as somehow guaranteeing him Christian immortality, even though that would expressly go against the final moral: to look only to heaven and hate the world. Spenser makes this contradiction clear in the treatment of Sidney's remains. In the final vision, an ark, symbolizing Sidney, appears, and it is brought to heaven by Mercury (*RT*, 670), not by a more obviously Christian means, such as the angels who carry the coffer to heaven (*RT*, 625) in a previous vision. Even more importantly, the speaker notes that "the heavens with the earth did disagree,/ Whether should of those ashes keeper bee" (*RT*, 664–65). Due to his fame, Sidney is as immortal on earth as he is in heaven. What then is the point of Christian immortality or even the *contemptus* model?

EDMUND SPENSER'S *CONTEMPTUS MUNDI*   189

Spenser's Chaucerian Morality

For Spenser, humanism with its idea of literature, its attachment to classical texts, can be morally dangerous. Humanism can even pervert or defang the anti-worldliness of *contemptus*, a conventional moral perspective that should be outside of it, that should allow a repentance of all the kinds of earthly attachments one might have, including humanism itself. That is how worldly vanity functions in the work of a Robert Greene or a George Gascoigne. Just as these contemporaries of Spenser turned to a Chaucerian alternative when they were faced with the limits of humanist thinking about literary value, of the good of poetry, so does Spenser. This alternative is Spenser's *Mother Hubberd's Tale* (hereafter *MHT*), which the editor of the Yale edition calls "Spenser's most Chaucerian work."[43] *MHT* marks a turn away from the humanism in the *Complaints*—the influences of du Bellay and Petrarch—which is also a return to Chaucerian influences and a Chaucerian moral ambiguity. As a complicated beast fable, one that undercuts the moral clarity and explicitness that readers expect, the tale echoes Chaucer's *Nun's Priest's Tale*. Also like the *Nun's Priest's Tale*, Spenser's is a moral tale that alludes to contemporary people and events, in Spenser's case, William Cecil, Lord Burghley.[44] What these events are specifically is unimportant; it is enough for my argument to note that readers are led to think about the contemporary world in terms of morality, about how one should or should not behave. That contemporary world is, of course, either absent in the other poems, which occupy a visionary space, or entirely mediated through the focus on Rome and classical imitation, such as in *The Teares of the Muses*. As a result, *MHT* offers an implicit critique of humanist discourses: their attachment to classical imitation and the classical legacy has prevented or forestalled a literature that would speak with moral authority to the contemporary moment. With its mixture of genres and insistence on the present, *MHT* reminds the reader that there is an actual world that may be largely untouched by humanist concerns and that poetry has a kind of duty to represent that world in all of its moral complexity.

A brief summary may be in order so that the moral complications can be clear. *MHT* is a beast fable about corruption. A Fox and an Ape travel through the estates, which are here presented as rural labor, the priesthood, the court, and the monarchy, and as they travel, they cheat and steal their way to the top. Their social mobility contrasts starkly with the traditional estate structure, represented here

---

[43] Editor's introduction to *Mother Hubberd's Tale* in *The Yale Edition*, 329.

[44] For the most comprehensive account of how to read the allegory topically, see Stein, *Studies*, 78–100. General agreement is that the fox is William Cecil, Lord Burghley. For more nuanced discussions of the political interests in *MHT*, see Annabel Patterson, *Fables of Power: Aesopian Writing and Political History* (Durham, NC: Duke University Press, 1991), 64–67; Rambuss, *Spenser's Secret Career*, 81–84; Lauren Silberman, "Aesopian *Prosopopoia*: Making Faces and Playing Chicken in *Mother Hubberds Tale*," *Spenser Studies* 27 (2012): 221–247.

190 HUMANISM AND GOOD BOOKS IN SIXTEENTH-CENTURY ENGLAND

by the husbandman and priest, whom they meet first and who are conventional figures in estates satire. The Ape and Fox, in contrast, are not only animals, whereas the husbandman and priest are not, they also disguise themselves: first as beggars (ex-soldiers), then shepherds, priests, courtiers, and finally as king and counselor. Their outrages as rulers make Jove angry, and he sends Mercury to find the Lion (whom they have displaced) and urge him to take back his throne. The Lion returns, punishes the Fox and Ape, and the story ends rather abruptly.

From the very opening of the poem, Spenser ensures that this story is understood as Chaucerian, a Chaucerian-ness that emerges in opposition to classical influences. He writes, "No Muses aide me needes heretoo to call;/ Base is the style, and matter meane withall" (*MHT*, 43–44). Spenser here alludes to Chaucer's famous disclaimer in the *General Prologue* to the *Canterbury Tales*:

> Whoso shal telle a tale after a man,
> He moot reherce as ny as evere he kan
> Everich a word, if it be in his charge,
> Al speke he never so rudeliche and large

[Whoever repeats a story that has been told by another man must tell it again as closely as he can to the original, every word, if it is in his power, even if he must speak rudely and freely].[45]

Spenser is following Chaucer, not only repeating a story he heard from someone else, but also providing the same disclaimer, in a kind of double imitation. In Spenser as in Chaucer, the reference to the baseness of the tale similarly asserts a truth or accuracy in representation. Moreover, that baseness directly contrasts with the Muses and perhaps functions as a corrective to it. After all, classical imitation, associated with the Muses, does not repeat stories told by "a man" but translates and adapts what has already been written in books.

Spenser's Chaucerian imitation fuses two modes or genres that are recognizably moral: the beast fable and estates satire. Both modes, despite very different provenance and structure, are concerned with outlining right and wrong behavior and, as a result, with shaping their readers. Both modes assume a shared sense of the good among their readers and often a shared language for describing it, whether that sense is drawn from commonplaces—do not listen to flattery—or Christian social theory—God has determined that everyone should work for others in a particular estate. Perhaps more importantly, both modes emphasize individuals acting in social relations, not individuals acting in isolation, as in *contemptus*.

Spenser's odd fusion demonstrates both the difficulty of establishing clear morals, in the changes to beast fable, and the possible moral correctives, in the

---

[45] Chaucer, *General Prologue*, 1.731–34.

EDMUND SPENSER'S *CONTEMPTUS MUNDI*   191

use of estates satire. Given that Spenser is not indebted to any particular beast fable, his version alludes more generally to the form of beast fables, and, therefore, the expectation of a lesson, since medieval beast fables tend to circulate with such lessons.[46] In including a fox, Spenser gestures toward an Aesopian tradition, which was ubiquitous. Versions of Aesop's *Fables* were printed in England about eighteen times between William Caxton's first printing in 1484 and the time Spenser was writing. More importantly, Chaucer offers his own version of an Aesopian fable in the *Nun's Priest's Tale*.[47] Chaucer is typically evasive, but the Nun's Priest's words at the end of his tale indicate that readers would look to the end of such a story for an explicit moral:

> Lo, swich it is for to be recchelees
> And necligent, and truste on flaterye.
> But ye that holden this tale a folye,
> As of a fox, or of a cok and hen,
> Taketh the moralite, goode men.

[Lo, this is what happens when one is careless and negligent and trusts in flattery. But those of you who consider this story to be foolishness about a fox, or about a rooster and hen, take the moral lesson, good men].[48]

The Nun's Priest provides a concluding comment to his audience that functions as a moral about flattery, which is signaled with a "Lo," and resembles the moral that circulates with a popular beast fable, Aesop's tale of the Fox and the Raven (Crow): "And this fable teaches us how men ought not to be glad nor take rejoicing in the words of caitiff [wicked] folk nor also to believe flattery nor vainglory."[49] Chaucer's Nun's Priest does not dwell with the Aesopian moral but instead moves on to offer a kind of meta-moral, that all stories can offer morals.

Spenser does not activate the moral aspects of his beast fable, even problematically or ironically, in this way suggesting that the beast fable cannot contain, as in represent and moralize, the problems of the world.[50] Although the Fox and Ape are discovered and punished, both when they act as courtiers and when they act as rulers, their punishment does not seem to have any effect. There is no real sense of comeuppance within the story, nor is the lesson made available to the reader. As the editor of the Yale editions notes, "the plot of the poem would seem to suggest

---

[46] On the moral aspects of the Aesopic beast fable, see Jill Mann, *From Aesop to Reynard: Beast Literature in Medieval Britain* (Oxford: Oxford University Press, 2009), 2–16.

[47] An EEBO search for Aesop revealed 18 entries for the period in question, the beginning of printing to 1591, the date of *The Complaints*.

[48] Chaucer, *Nun's Priest's Tale*, 7.3436–40.

[49] William Caxton, *Caxton's Aesop*, ed. R. T. Lenaghan (Cambridge, MA: Harvard University Press, 1967), 84.

[50] See Brown, "*The New Poet*," 173, and further 169–212.

192 HUMANISM AND GOOD BOOKS IN SIXTEENTH-CENTURY ENGLAND

a conservative moral: that while earthly evil may triumph temporarily, it will be overcome in the long run," and yet "the view of evil that the poem offers is more ambivalent. The very fact of the repeated cycle reminds us that the companions are not stopped: they possess a demonic energy which may enable them to continue in their metamorphic career long after the poem has ended."[51] Even more importantly, the narrator does not provide a moral; she merely ends the story:

> So Mother *Hubberd* her discourse did end:
> Which pardon me, if I amisse have pend,
> For weake was my remembrance it to hold,
> And bad her tongue that it so bluntly tolde (*MHT*, 1385–88).

This looks like a moral story, but it does not act like one. The point of breakdown is not within the story, which has represented both Ape and Fox as bad. After all, those animals are by definition morally problematic. The point of breakdown is in its application to the world outside the text. No one has digested the moral and made it available. As a result, readers have no way of applying it to their own experience. Do not trust the socially mobile? Beware of a weak monarch?

Although Spenser has denied the reader a clear moral lesson around the beast fable, his tale is not entirely without moral guidance: it offers the more implicit and reader-oriented corrective of estates satire.[52] Estates satire, as Spenser likely understood it, was a traditional and highly conventionalized mode for describing the job duties of a particular class or occupation and, often, the failure of those within that class or occupation to live up to the ideal.[53] Despite or maybe because of its essential conservativism, estates satire is reformist and therefore corrective: calling out for people to return to the right way of being in their estates. John Gower's Prologue to his *Confessio Amantis* (1390) is typical:

> It is that men now clepe and calle,
> And sein the regnes ben divided:
> In stede of love is hate guided,
> The werre wol no pes purchace,
> And lawe hath take hire double face,

> [Men now cry out and say that the realms are divided. Hate is the guide instead of love. Wars will not purchase peace, and law is two-faced].[54]

---

[51] Editor's introduction to *Mother Hubberd's Tale* in *The Yale Edition*, 331–32.

[52] On the way in which the figuration shifts, see Kent T. Van den Berg, "'The Counterfeit in Personation': Spenser's *Prosopopoia*, or *Mother Hubberds Tale*," in *The Author in his Work: Essays on a Problem in Criticism*, ed. Louis L. Martz and Aubrey Williams (New Haven, CT: Yale University Press, 1978), 85–102; and Silberman, "Aesopian *Prosopopoia*."

[53] Jill Mann, *Chaucer and Medieval Estates Satire: The Literature of Social Classes and the General Prologue to the Canterbury Tales* (Cambridge: Cambridge University Press, 1973).

[54] John Gower, *Confessio Amantis*, 3 vols. ed. Russell A. Peck with Latin Translations by Andrew Galloway (Kalamazoo, MI: Medieval Institute Publications, 2005–13), 1: Prol. 126–30.

EDMUND SPENSER'S *CONTEMPTUS MUNDI*   193

Even if one does not take this complaint seriously, even if one does not see it as a sincere demand for change, it certainly performs concern about the state of the world and indicates how that state might be fixed.

Spenser's version of estates satire is, in contrast, strikingly inconsistent, not only in that there is movement across estates, but also in that the animals interact as humans within them. His poem begins with two typical and human estate representatives: the husbandman and the priest, the first of which is virtuous and the second corrupt. And then the stereotyping becomes confused. The court and its nobility are not represented by one person, whom the Ape and the Fox deceive, as were the other estates, but are instead referred to throughout as some version of "Court," and the other members are likely animals, since the Ape and Fox meet a Mule on the way to Court. Once the Fox and Ape become rulers, the estates satire is largely abandoned: the focus is not on the corruption already in the estates but on the corruption generated by the Fox and the Ape. The insertion of beast fable into estates satire underlines the precariousness of the ties that hold the estates together and keep social order. After all, the Fox and the Ape are animals, who disrupt the social order of the estates with their rapacity and deceit.

At the same time, Spenser maintains the moral and corrective focus of the estates satire. He does so by focusing attention on the sheep, the animal, or symbol, that links the two modes—beast fable and estates satire—together, consistently reminding the reader of the right behavior in the world outside the poem: to care for the sheep.[55] The first sheep to appear are mainly literal, in that they belong to the husbandman, but they also are figurative, in that they allude to a literary tradition of virtuous rural labor. Indeed, the husbandman is indebted to Chaucer's Plowman in *The General Prologue* to *The Canterbury Tales*, William Langland's *Piers Plowman*, and the *Piers Plowman*-tradition. As a rural laborer, he is unquestionably good; the only character in the entire poem who is charitable, offering aid to the Fox and Ape. The description underlines both his "honest" nature and the details of his labor, when he lists the kind of work required in "husbandrie:" "To plough, to plant, to reap, to rake, to sowe/ To hedge, to ditch, to thrash, to thetch, to mowe" (*MHT*, 259, 262, 263–64). Because the Fox and Ape cannot do manual labor, a refusal that signals their lack of virtue to the reader, although not, unfortunately, to the husbandman, the husbandman gives them his sheep to tend. Fox and Ape then utterly destroy the flocks:

> And that same evening, when all shrowded were
> In careles sleep, they without care or feare
> Cruelly fell upon their flock in folde,
> And of them slew at pleasure what they wolde (*MHT*, 333–36).

---

[55] The pastoral aspect of this tale is briefly noted by Helen Cooper, *Pastoral: Mediaeval to Renaissance* (Cambridge: D. S. Brewer, 1977), 161. Van den Berg also notes the "metaphoric" connections between "false shepherds," "false pastors," the "slaughter of a flock," and the "exploitation of a congregation" ("'The Counterfeit in Personation,'" 88).

194   HUMANISM AND GOOD BOOKS IN SIXTEENTH-CENTURY ENGLAND

The play on "careless" drives the meaning home: the sheep should be sleeping without fear—carelessly or more appropriately in modern English, in a carefree manner—and, at precisely that moment, the shepherds attack them without care, carelessly. Their violence is both actual and linguistic: they slaughter the sheep and thereby pervert the language of shepherdly care.

Spenser's second use of sheep appears within and invokes the moral coordinates of ecclesiastical pastoral. Ecclesiastical pastoral, sometimes called biblical pastoral, appears frequently within late medieval and sixteenth-century estates satire to describe priests' duties or priests' failures to perform their duties. Based on Jesus's statement, "I am the good shepherd" (John 10:11), it represents priests as shepherds and their congregations as sheep.[56] Chaucer's Parson in the *General Prologue* of the *Canterbury Tales*, is a "shepherde" who does not leave "his sheep encombred in the myre," but helps them instead.[57] It's fair to say that part of the power of this figurative language in Chaucer's time, and likely Spenser's as well, is the strength of its connection to the literal level. In a culture in which many people owned livestock, including sheep, a shepherd's care for his flock was not merely a figure of speech but a lived reality.

The transition from the virtuous husbandman to the bad priest has a moral logic generated by the readers' knowledge of this familiar mode: the Fox and Ape are literally bad shepherds and, as a result, they meet a corrupt priest, who is, therefore, a figurative bad shepherd, and become his associates. The Priest explicitly invokes ecclesiastical pastoral in his conversation, "He is the Shepheard, and the Priest is hee" (*MHT*, 443), and then he goes on to describe how little he works in his position:

> And all his care was, his service well to saine [say],
> And to read Homelies upon holidayes:
> When that was done, he might attend his playes;
> An easie life, and fit high God to please (*MHT*, 392–95).

The phrase "all his care" underlines his limitations: he does not do the kind of work Chaucer's Parson does, such as riding around, preaching and teaching, and helping his parishioners. Instead, Spenser's shepherd only says the service and reads the Homilies. In addition, he rejects the Ape's statement that his "charge" is onerous, saying that he does not need to "feed mens soules" (*MHT*, 432). This new version of ecclesiastical pastoral empties out the labor and care of shepherding, the feeding and watching over the sheep. Priesthood is instead a life of ease.

These moral associations, lent by estates satire and ecclesiastical pastoral, shape the reader's encounter with the final sheep, borrowed from beast fable, who

---

[56] *The Geneva Bible: A Facsimile of the 1560 Edition* (Madison, WI: University of Wisconsin Press, 1969), 48r of the New Testament.

[57] Chaucer, *General Prologue*, 1.508.

EDMUND SPENSER'S *CONTEMPTUS MUNDI*   195

appears near the end of the poem. The Fox and Ape become the king's royal advisor and the king, respectively, and the humans of the estates satire have been left entirely behind. Sheep, who is a mother, appears at court to petition the king because her Lamb has been killed "most cruellie" by the Wolf (*MHT*, 1210). The Fox sends her away, claiming that she seeks to "slaunder" the Wolf's name, and "So went the Sheepe away with heavie hart" (*MHT*, 1219, 1222). This is a mini-fable of the helplessness of those who live under authoritarian regimes, "a nightmare image of the political world inhabited by the reader," as Silberman has argued.[58] In this nightmare, there is no shepherd to watch over the sheep. The incidents in *MHT* all underline the failure of the shepherd, of authoritative care for the vulnerable, as well as the failure of the language of shepherding within the tale. Surely, everyone should recognize that lambs (or sheep) are innocents in need of care? This kind of language is conventional, and yet not a single character in the tale follows the moral dictates inherent in that language: Sheep is entirely alone.

Instead of providing an explicit moral lesson based in the fable, Spenser offers more of a moral lens, a language of virtuous labor or Christian action through which one should read the behavior of individuals.[59] From this perspective, the tale is not only a meditation on the precariousness of the language that ensures a shared morality but also an insistence that the social world might still be corrected and might be corrected through the right kind of poetry. Hints of a Chaucerian poetry's reformist potential can be found in the one place within *MHT* that resonates with the other poems in Spenser's *Complaints*, *contemptus*-complaint. When the Fox and the Ape first encounter the husbandman, there is a brief reference to worldly vanity and complaint. The Ape appeals to the husbandman, saying,

> This yron world (that same he weeping sayes)
> Brings downe the stowtest hearts to lowest state:
> For miserie doth bravest mindes abate,
> And make them seeke for that they wont to scorne,
> Of fortune and of hope at once forlorne.
> The honest man, that heard him thus complaine,
> Was griev'd, as he had felt part of his paine;
> And well disposd him some reliefe to showe
> Askt if in husbandrie he ought did knowe (*MHT*, 254–62).

[58] Silberman, "Aesopian *Prosopopoia*," 241.

[59] In his discussion of this poem, Crewe notes the incompletion at the end, one that at least gestures toward some solution: "Both completion and a saving difference await the finally imaginable if not representable 'return' of the shepherd/ pastor/ poet, an exemplary figure now absent from the poem, but whose space remains and whose absence continues forever to be marked" (*Hidden Designs*, 64). For a blunter and more confident account of repair or healing that happens in the tale itself, see Kenneth John Atchity, "Spenser's *Mother Hubberds Tale*: Three Themes of Order," *Philological Quarterly* 52 [1973]: 161–72).

196   HUMANISM AND GOOD BOOKS IN SIXTEENTH-CENTURY ENGLAND

The Ape's lament sounds a lot like Verlame's, with his weeping and reference to fortune, except that he is mourning his own descent into poverty. The husbandman's
empathy (he feels part of the Ape's pain) is thus a response to an actual social and
economic condition and not the fall of Rome and the loss of a classical heritage.
His empathy is neither overwhelming nor incapacitating, as it is for the speaker in
RT, and, although he may be too trusting, it would be a mistake to suggest that he is
in some way being critiqued for foolishness.[60] He has no way of knowing that the
Ape is lying. More importantly, the Christian virtue with which he is associated
both here and through the literary tradition of the plowman requires him to love
his neighbor as himself, as Chaucer makes clear in the plowman-portrait in the
General Prologue:

> God loved he best with al his hoole herte
> At alle tymes, thogh him gamed or smerte,
> And thanne his neighebor right as hymselve

[He loved God best, with his whole heart at all times, whether it pleased or pained
him, and then his neighbor as himself].[61]

His charity, what might now be called empathy, drives him to offer "relief" to someone who seems to need it. Here morality is made material. Instead of indulging in
emotion, there is action, and the hint of an alternative. As Annabel Patterson has
noted in her perceptive reading of this tale, Spenser here "provides the model for
an alternative metaphor for monarchy. The caring, if too incautious husbandman,
owner of the sheep farm."[62]

Chaucerian imitation produces a poetry fundamentally intertwined with
morality, one that is also a conscious alternative to the humanist idea of poetry.
Part of *MHT*'s distinctiveness has to do with its content in its context: it does not
share its characters or concerns with any of the other poems in the *Complaints*,
thus offering itself as an alternative moral perspective. In addition, the tale itself
represents humanist poetry as entirely ineffectual. Humanist poetry first appears
in the idealized portrait of the "brave Courtier" (*MHT*, 717), who "withdrawes"
himself "unto the Muses" (*MHT*, 760), and after conferring with them "he kindleth
his ambitious sprights/ To like desire and praise of noble fame" (*MHT*, 768–69).[63]
This passage alludes to the idea, familiar from Sidney's *Apology for Poetry* and Sir
Thomas Elyot's *Boke of the Governor*, that reading poetry inflames people to noble
deeds. This ideal poet does not, however, have any effect on what one might call
the real-world problems presented by the Ape: he does not interact with the Ape,

---

[60] Patterson describes the husbandman as "incautious" (*Fables of Power*, 103). Rambuss claims that
the poem "casts doubts" on the husbandman, who "responds foolishly" (*Spenser's Secret Career*, 89).

[61] Chaucer, *General Prologue*, I. 533–35.

[62] Patterson, *Fables of Power*, 103. See also Crewe, *Hidden Designs*, 62–65.

[63] For a more optimistic perspective on the courtier, see Van den Berg, "'The Counterfeit in
Personation,'" 93, 95.

and he therefore has no power to correct him. Spenser underlines this incapacity by grouping praise of the Courtier in the same couplet with a description of the Ape: "Such is the rightfull Courtier in his kinde:/ But unto such the Ape lent not his minde" (*MHT*, 793–94). Their link in the couplet shows, paradoxically, that they do not occupy the same space.

Even more distressingly, humanist poetry is shown to be complicit in the corruption. The Ape appropriates the kind of poetry associated with that courtier, turning poetry that generates virtue and vice in the reader into poetry that leads readers astray:

> Thereto he could fine loving verses frame,
> And play the Poet oft. But ah, for shame
> Let not sweete Poets praise, whose onely pride
> Is vertue to advaunce, and vice deride,
> Be with the worke of losels [scoundrels'] wit defamed,
> Ne let such verses Poetrie be named:
> Yet he the name on him would rashly take,
> Maugre [in spite of] the sacred Muses, and it make
> A servant to the vile affection
> Of such, as he depended most upon (*MHT*, 809–18).

The Ape's poetry unsurprisingly "apes" good, that is, humanist, poetry, given the reference to the "sacred Muses." Despite his verses not being concerned with virtue and vice, but with a scoundrel's wit, the speaker acknowledges it as "poetry" and the ape as "poet." Because of the resemblance to the right kind of poetry, his poetry leads listeners astray, feeding "vaine humours" with "fruitles follies, and unsound delights" (*MHT*, 822–23). There is here an acknowledgment of the humanist claim that good poetry inculcates virtue, only to show its failure. After all, the Ape's poetry sounds good ("fine"), but it produces nothing good, perhaps nothing at all (it is "fruitless"). Similarly, poetry that really is good does not lead to good actions:

> And whenso love of letters did inspire
> Their gentle wits, and kindly wise desire,
> That chieflie doth each noble mind adorne,
> Then would he scoffe at learning and eke scorne (*MHT*, 829–32).

In this episode, the Ape prevents poetry from having the right effect, which would be "inspiring" readers in gentle and kindly ways of thinking. Indeed, the account calls that conventional idea into question, not only because the Ape prevents the virtue that is supposed to be inspired, by scoffing at learning, but also because it suggests that virtue derived from books is only a decoration, an adornment, and

198 HUMANISM AND GOOD BOOKS IN SIXTEENTH-CENTURY ENGLAND

does not lead anywhere substantial, only to an ambiguous nobility held entirely on the inside in "gentle wits" and "noble mind."

Read against the other poems in the *Complaints*, *MHT* offers a critique of any poetry oriented around immortality and the classical legacy. The Ape with his courtly poetry directly opposes the husbandman and the poetic tradition to which he is indebted, the tradition of both Chaucer and Langland. If the Ape is to be defeated, in the world outside the poem, there must be a return to the poetry of social corrective. To alter W. H. Auden's famous line slightly, poetry dedicated to the "sacred Muses" makes nothing happen, but a Chaucerian poetry dedicated to baseness might still have a chance.[64]

For Spenser, Chaucer is a living resource, a storehouse of characters, archaic language, and plotlines, and, even more importantly, an idea of what poetry should be and do. Chaucer's Alcyone and Black Knight show Spenser how to imagine a literary lament; his self-aggrandizing pilgrims in the *Canterbury Tales* show Spenser how to negotiate a particular kind of moral ambiguity. Chaucerian ambiguity is not the impossibility of morality, the ambiguity so prized by literary scholars, but the ambiguity that arises when people want to be moral but cannot. This is the kind of ambiguity found in the speaker's nervous breakdown at the end of *Troilus and Criseyde* or the speaker's response to Verlame in *RT*. Chaucerian ambiguity is also the kind that arises when people think that they are moral but are not, as in the Monk in Chaucer's *Monk's Tale* or the priest in Spenser's *MHT*. Chaucer is not, for Spenser, standing on the other side of a divide, barely visible in some "misty time," as he seems to be for Sidney.[65] He is, instead, a means to think about what is valued, whether Rome or poetry itself, and, through poetry, to imagine correctives to that world in which he lives, to "moralize" a song.[66]

---

[64] "For poetry makes nothing happen" but "it survives/ A way of happening, a mouth" (W. H. Auden, "In Memory of W. B. Yeats," in *The Norton Anthology of Poetry*, Shorter 5th ed., ed. Margaret Ferguson, Mary Jo Salter, and Jon Stallworthy [New York: W. W. Norton & Co., 2005] lines 36 & 40–41).

[65] Sir Philip Sidney, *An Apology for Poetry, or The Defence of Poesy*, 3rd ed., ed. Geoffrey Shepherd, rev. R. W. Maslen (New York: Manchester University Press, 2002), 110.

[66] I am quoting the last line of the first stanza of *The Faerie Queene*: "Fierce warres and faithfull loues shall moralize my song" (1.1.9).

Afterword
Confidence and Doubt

The humanist rediscovery of the classical legacy can be told as a story about a new confidence in the value of literature. Reading classical texts, the "study of humanity," is an honorable pursuit and worthy of praise, to borrow the terms that Thomas More uses in his biography of the famous Italian humanist, Pico della Mirandola.[1] Indeed, the phrase frequently used to refer to the classical legacy—*bonae litterae*—similarly claims that these texts are inherently good.

The goodness, or value, of "*litterae* [letters]" for the humanists is, as this study has demonstrated, an importantly moral one. Indeed, the term "excellent" is used by More to describe Pico della Mirandola's learning and his virtue, as if these two attributes were indistinguishable.[2] From this perspective, literature is good not only because it is well-written or filled with knowledge about the world but also because it is good for you: it teaches you how to behave, think, and feel. Such praise was not empty, as far as the humanists were concerned; morality was not merely an extra benefit associated with or added onto a text's literary greatness. Rather, humanists used morality to help articulate the value of classical texts, to ensure that their value was seen as clear and unassailable. Morality was thus fundamental to an idea of literature, a category of specially valued writings, that humanists made their own and widely promoted.

In theorizing literature in this way, coherently around morality, humanists redefined the space in which authors might invent themselves. After humanism, authors who wanted to position their own writings as *bonae litterae*, in the tradition of the greats, aligned themselves with moral goodness as well as literary greatness. Edmund Spenser, writing at the end of the sixteenth century, opens his epic-romance, *The Faerie Queene*, with a nod to the Roman poet Virgil: "Lo I the man, whose Muse whylome did maske,/ As time her taught, in lowly Shephards weeds."[3] As importantly, he claims for his text the same kind of positive moral effect that *bonae litterae*, such as Virgil's *Aeneid*, were thought to have on their readers. In the dedicatory letter to Sir Walter Ralegh, Spenser famously states that he has written the poem with an explicit moral purpose: "the generall end therefore of

---

[1] Pico della Mirandola, *Here is conteyned the lyfe of Iohan Picus erle of Myrandula a grete lorde of Italy an excellent connynge man in all sciences, and verteous of lyuynge* (London, 1525) STC 19898, A3r.
[2] Mirandola, *Lyfe*, A7v, A3v.
[3] Edmund Spenser, *The Faerie Queene*, ed. Thomas P. Roche, Jr. (New York: Penguin, 1978), Book 1, Proem, lines 1–2.

Humanism and Good Books in Sixteenth-Century England. Katherine C. Little, Oxford University Press.
© Katherine C. Little (2023). DOI: 10.1093/oso/9780192883193.003.0010

all the booke is to fashion a gentleman or noble person in vertuous and gentle discipline."[4] For Spenser, the value of his poem rests, in great part, on its capacity to shape its reader for the good.

At the same time, it is easy to see that humanist confidence in the moral value of literature added a burden that writings could not carry consistently or effectively. That is, in linking the value of literature so firmly to its morality—its impact on readers and the wisdom it contained—humanists posited the security and stability, even the predictability, of those impacts and that wisdom. As any teacher knows, what readers gain from a text is rarely uniform and can at times be surprising. Even if responses to and interpretations of a text converge or overlap, readers do not necessarily apply texts to their lives in the same ways, nor do they find texts similarly relevant or meaningful. For this reason, humanist confidence in the new way of seeing and valuing literature inevitably dissipated or led to questions. Doubt in the moral impact of reading poetry haunts even the most obviously confident formulations. The bold and simple statement in the dedicatory letter of *The Faerie Queene* indicates that Spenser knows what virtue is and how readers will apprehend it. But generations of readers of that poem have not found that same confidence in the poem. As the editors of the recent collection *Edmund Spenser's Poetry* (2014) indicate, "recent work on Spenser has tended to stress the degree to which his epic is not so much illustrative of the virtues in action as it is interrogative and exploratory, interested in demonstrating the complexity and limitations of the virtue in question."[5] Similarly, Sir Philip Sidney's *Apology for Poetry* argues that poetry breeds virtue, that it is, in a sense always useful, but at the same time he must acknowledge at least the possibility that it will be abused.[6]

From the perspective of the Middle Ages, a time when writers were far less certain in predicting the effects of reading or in seeing the text as a stable container of value, humanist confidence certainly gave writers a new gift—the unquestioned value of something called literature. Calling classical poetry honorable, good, and excellent elevates not only the classics, but also poetry and indeed fiction more generally, or at least poetry and fiction that attempts to align with the classics, as Sidney's *Apology* indicates. This new gift, inspiring as it was, also came with a cost; writers were tasked with a very large requirement, that delight always be linked to instruction, to borrow Sidney's phrasing. In other words, writers in the generation after humanism, that is, the Elizabethans, may have been inspired by the possibilities of imitating Virgil, as was Spenser, but they may have also felt trapped by the requirement to provide moral goodness. There were new freedoms, to be sure, but the freedom to have doubts or to retain an untheorized bagginess of different and potentially contradictory kinds of goods was not one of them.

---

[4] Spenser, *The Faerie Queene*, 714.

[5] Edmund Spenser, *Edmund Spenser's Poetry*, 4th ed., ed. Anne Lake Prescott and Andrew D. Hadfield (New York: W. W. Norton and Co., 2014), x.

[6] Sir Philip Sidney, *An Apology for Poetry, or The Defence of Poesy*, 3rd ed., ed. Geoffrey Shepherd and R. W. Maslen (New York: Palgrave, 2002), 102.

From the perspective of the twenty-first century, we are still living within some of the framework that the humanists built.[7] Indeed, the humanities, which were central to the emergence of the modern university, bear some resemblance to the study of humanity that sixteenth-century humanists outlined; there is still a discipline called literature, which in its very existence proves that humanists secured its cultural and educational importance. Their success in securing that place was, to a certain degree, a result of claiming literature for morality, of asserting its value in shaping character. After humanism, few would deny that literature could and should fashion readers. Indeed, the rationale of the mid-twentieth century "Great Books of the Western World," an American, post-war series of influential books, or *bonae litterae*, is that reading will make readers better, not only more educated, but nobler. Those who read through the fifty-four volumes of what the editors considered "classics," which include some of the same texts on the sixteenth-century humanist syllabus, were engaging in the "noble work of self-improvement."[8] In the twenty-first-century, literature is still thought to be more valuable than other kinds of writing for related reasons: its superior capacity in shaping readers in right thinking or feeling. For example, a recent experiment found evidence for the moral greatness of the great books: reading good books, or literary fiction, made readers more empathetic than reading either popular fiction or non-fiction. These were the findings of David Comer Kidd and Emanuele Castano in their social-psychological study, "Reading Literary Fiction Improves Theory of Mind."[9]

At the same time, as Elizabethan reactions to humanism make clear, any assertion that literature not only contains moral lessons but also has a positive moral impact on readers, that it instructs in virtue, will always generate doubts about the efficacy of such a project. Such a tension, between confidence and doubt in the goodness (virtue) of the *bonae litterae* was thus built into the idea of literature itself. Insofar as education still depends on an idea of literature inherited from the humanists, about a greatness that is not only aesthetic, not only cultural, but also personally applicable, as in moral, that tension has persisted. And it will likely do so as long as literature, not only the books themselves but the idea of literature as good or great books, is part of educational programs and other kinds of self-fashioning. Indeed, twenty-first century defenses of "Great Books" courses, of familiar canonical texts, explicitly invoke the realm of the moral: great books are a means of teaching "self-knowledge." These defenses inevitably and immediately

---

[7] See Anthony Grafton and Lisa Jardine, *From Humanism to the Humanities: Education and the Liberal Arts in Fifteenth- and Sixteenth-Century Europe* (Cambridge, MA: Harvard University Press, 1986) and Jennifer Summit, "Renaissance Humanism and the Future of the Humanities," *Literature Compass* 9.10 (2012): 665–78.

[8] "History of Great Books Foundation," Northwest Great Books, accessed March 3, 2022, https://nwgreatbooks.com/about/history/. For the history of the Great Books, see Joan Rubin, *The Making of Middle Brow Culture* (Chapel Hill: University of North Carolina Press, 1992), 148–97.

[9] David Comer Kidd and Emanuele Castano, "Reading Literary Fiction Improves Theory of Mind," *Science* 342.6156 (2013): 377–80, doi: 10.1126/science.1239918.

202 HUMANISM AND GOOD BOOKS IN SIXTEENTH-CENTURY ENGLAND

lead to the counter-charge that literature has no higher moral claim than other disciplines, that readers are not necessarily worse or better for having read particular books.[10]

The tensions around the moral greatness of the "Great Books" should suggest that humanist confidence in the certainty of literature's moral lessons was always and continues to be misplaced. What is, perhaps, less easy to see is the other side of the coin, that it is impossible to separate literature from moral questions. While one cannot be confident that reading is morally useful, one cannot also disregard morality entirely in favor of some other realm of literature's value, such as the aesthetic or the cultural or the political or the economic. For most readers, the value of literature is inarguably moral, by which I mean that it necessarily raises questions about whether behavior, thoughts, or feelings are right or wrong, whether within the confines of the text or when applied to the life of the reader. In his introductory guide to poetry, *How to Read a Poem*, Terry Eagleton defines poetry at least in part in terms of a moral realm, using the word moral to refer to "a qualitative and evaluative view of human conduct and experience."[11] For Eagleton, the moral contrasts with the aesthetic as well as with other lenses on human experience such as the political; these different values cannot be conflated nor can they be translated into each other. The inescapability of moral value is, perhaps unwittingly, underlined by John Guillory's account of the canon debates of the 1980s, *Cultural Capital: The Problem of Literary Canon Formation*. In that study Guillory shows how both sides, the canon-busters and the canon-preservers, shared a belief that the books are "repositories" of value, including "moral values."[12] From this perspective, debates about the canon that pretended to be political, such as those about representation and exclusion, were more concerned with "moral judgment."[13] For Guillory, the pervasiveness of morality is a problem; it has distracted everyone from a true understanding of what literature (or the canon) has been historically or should be. It is perhaps for that reason that morality does not factor at all in the reform he proposes at the end of his study. What is needed instead is a proper understanding of the aesthetic value of literature and the way in which evaluative judgements, about what books are and are not great, are informed by "the means of production and consumption."[14]

---

[10] Louis Menand, "What's so Great about Great Books Courses," *The New Yorker*, December 13, 2021, https://www.newyorker.com/magazine/2021/12/20/whats-so-great-about-great-books-courses-roosevelt-montas-rescuing-socrates.

[11] Terry Eagleton, *How to Read a Poem* (Malden, MA: Wiley-Blackwell, 2007), 28.

[12] John Guillory, *Cultural Capital: The Problem of Literary Canon Formation* (Chicago: University of Chicago Press, 1993), 22, 25.

[13] Guillory, *Cultural Capital*, 25–26.

[14] Guillory, *Cultural Capital*, 340. Guillory writes that "the point is not to make judgment disappear but to reform the conditions of its practice. If there is no way out of the game of culture, then, even when cultural capital is the only kind of capital, there may be another kind of game, with less dire consequences for the losers, an *aesthetic* game. Socializing the means of production and consumption

That these canon debates have not ended, whether on Guillory's terms or on any others, is due at least in part to the intractability and persistence of moral questions, how or whether to lay claim to a moral value for literature.[15] That is, the new crisis of the humanities that characterizes the twenty-first century American university has raised the same questions about moral greatness again. For some, the rapidly declining enrollments in English departments are an urgent sign that literature must return to the canon, the great books or *bonae litterae*, not only for the eloquence of the writing but also for moral teachings.[16] For others, moral claims made for the canon, the twinned greatness of the great books, ring false; these claims are, simply put, unsustainable in the multicultural and economically fraught world of the twenty-first century.[17] The crisis has also, and more helpfully, generated a broader perspective on moral value by turning attention away from the greatness of specific texts, the canon, and toward the impact of writing, whether great or not so great, on readers. Rita Felski's recent manifesto, *The Uses of Literature*, argues boldly that the value of literature is to be found in its capacity to affect its readers, through recognition, enchantment, knowledge, and shock.[18] None of these characteristics belongs exclusively to the canon, nor to works traditionally defined as literature or literary, and they are all recognizably connected to values that would have been familiar to medieval and Renaissance authors, at the origin of writing in English.

Re-situating humanism in its proper context, between medieval bagginess and Elizabethan doubt, underlines its transitional, as opposed to originary, status. Humanist certainty in the twinned goods of the *bonae litterae* is the product of a particular moment, and, as historically situated, shows both continuity and change across this period. As such, humanism, in its sixteenth-century form, can remind us not only that moral values cannot and will not remain stable, but that the study of literature nevertheless requires us to ask about them. We may be no closer to determining the value of books for readers in shaping our behavior, thoughts, and feelings, but as long as we are readers, we cannot let the question go.

---

would be the condition of an aestheticism unbound, not its overcoming. But of course, this is only a thought experiment" (340).

[15] On the legacy of the canon wars, see Viet Thanh Nguyen, "Canon Fodder," *The Washington Post*, May 3, 2018, https://www.washingtonpost.com/news/posteverything/wp/2018/05/03/feature/books-by-immigrants-foreigners-and-minorities-dont-diminish-the-classic-curriculum/.

[16] See Menand, "What's so Great."

[17] See Menand, "What's so Great" and Nguyen, "Canon Fodder."

[18] Rita Felski, *Uses of Literature* (Malden, MA: Wiley-Blackwell, 2008), 21.

Works Cited

Primary Sources

Aesop. *Caxton's Aesop*. Edited by R. T. Lenaghan. Cambridge, MA: Harvard University Press, 1967.

Aesop. *Here begynneth the book of the subtyl historyes and fables of Esope whiche were translated out of Frensshe in to Englysshe by wylliam Caxton at westmynstre in the yere of oure Lorde M. CCCC. Lxxxiij*. London, 1484. STC 175.

Alighieri, Dante. *Dante's Convivio*. Translated by William Walrond Jackson. Oxford: Clarendon Press, 1909.

Aristotle. *The ethiques of Aristotle, that is to saye, preceptes of good behauoute*. London, 1547. STC 754.

Aristotle. *The Nicomachean Ethics*. Translated by David Ross. Revised by Lesley Brown. New York: Oxford, 2009.

Ascham, Roger. *English Works*. Edited by William Aldis Wright. Cambridge: Cambridge University Press, 1904.

Ashley, Kathleen and Gerard NeCastro, eds. *Mankind*. Kalamazoo, MI: Medieval Institute Publications, 2010.

Auden, W. H. "In Memory of W.B. Yeats." In *The Norton Anthology of Poetry*, Shorter 5th Edition, edited by Margaret Ferguson, Mary Jo Salter, and Jon Stallworthy, 939–940. New York: W. W. Norton & Co., 2005.

Augustine, Saint. *On Christian Doctrine*. Translated by D. W. Robertson, Jr. New York: Macmillan, 1958.

Baldwin, William. *A treatise of morall phylosophie contaynyng the sayinges of the wyse. Gathered and Englyshed by Wylliam Baldwyn*. London, 1547. STC 1253.

Bale, John. *A mysterye of inyquyte contayned within the heretycall genealogye of Ponce Pantolabus*. London, 1545. STC 1303.

Bevington, David, ed. *Medieval Drama*. Boston: Houghton Mifflin, 1975.

Chance, Jane, ed. *The Assembly of the Gods*. Kalamazoo, MI: Medieval Institute, 1999.

Chaucer, Geoffrey. *The Riverside Chaucer*. 3rd edition. Edited by Larry D. Benson. Boston: Houghton Mifflin, 1987.

Chaucer, Geoffrey. *Troilus and Criseyde with Facing-page Il Filostrato*. Edited by Stephen A. Barney. New York: W. W. Norton & Co., 2006.

Chaucer, Geoffrey. *The workes of Geffray Chaucer newly printed*. London, 1532. STC 5068.

Cicero. *Marcus Tullius Ciceroes thre bokes of duties to Marcus his sonne, turned out of latine into english, by Nicholas Grimalde*. London, 1556. STC 5281.

Cicero. *Marcus Tullius Ciceroes thre bokes of duties to Marcus his sonne, turned out of latine into english, by Nicholas Grimalde*. London, 1558. STC 5281.8.

Cicero. *The thre bookes of Tyllyes offyces both in latyne tonge [et] in englysshe, lately translated by Roberte Whytinton poete laureate*. London, 1534. STC 5278.

Cicero. *The thre bookes of Tyllyes offyces both in latyne tonge [et] in englysshe, lately translated by Roberte Whytinton poete laureate*. London, 1540. STC 5279.

WORKS CITED   205

Colet, John. *Ioannis Coleti theologi, olim decani diui Pauli, aeditio. una cum quibusdam G. Lilij Grammatices rudimentis, G. Lilij epigramma.* Antwerp, 1527. STC 5542.

Davidson, Clifford and Peter Happé, eds. *The Worlde and the Chylde.* Kalamazoo, MI: Medieval Institute Publications, 1999.

Davidson, Clifford, Martin W. Walsh, and Ton J. Broos, eds. *Everyman and its Dutch Original, Elckerlijc.* Kalamazoo, MI: Medieval Institute Publications, 2007.

Edgar, Swift and Angela M. Kinney, eds. *The Vulgate Bible: Douay-Rheims Translation.* 6 vols. Cambridge, MA: Harvard University Press, 2010–13.

Elyot, Thomas. *A Critical Edition of Sir Thomas Elyot's The Boke Named the Governour.* Edited by Donald W. Rude. New York: Garland Press, 1992.

Erasmus of Rotterdam. *Bellum Erasmi.* London, 1534. STC 10449.

Erasmus of Rotterdam. *Collected Works of Erasmus.* 72 vols. Toronto: University of Toronto Press, 1974 –.

Erasmus of Rotterdam. *The complaint of peace. Wryten in Latyn, by the famous clerke, Erasimus Roterodamus. And nuely translated into Englyshe by Thomas Paynell.* London, 1559. STC 10466.

Erasmus of Rotterdam. *An exhortation to the diligent studye of scripture, made by Erasmus Roterodamus. And translated in to inglissh.* London, 1529. STC 10493.

Erasmus of Rotterdam. *Opera Omnia,* 9 vols. Amsterdam: North Holland, 1969–.

Erasmus of Rotterdam. *The praise of folie.* London, 1549. STC 10500.

Fisher, John. *English Works of John Fisher, Bishop of Rochester: Sermons and Other Writings 1520 to 1535.* Edited by Cecilia A. Hatt. Oxford: Oxford University Press, 2002.

Fisher, John. *A sermon had at Paulis,* London, 1526. STC 10892.

Fowler, David C., Charles F. Briggs, and Paul G. Remley, eds. *The Governance of Kings and Princes: John Trevisa's Middle English Translation of the De Regimine Principum of Aegidius Romanus.* London: Routledge, 1997.

Foxe, John. *The Unabridged Acts and Monuments Online or TAMO.* The Digital Humanities Institute, Sheffield, 2011. http//www.dhi.ac.uk/foxe.

Furnivall, Frederick James, ed. *Hymns to the Virgin and Christ.* London: Kegan Paul, Trench, Trübner, 1867.

Gascoigne, George. *The Complete Works of George Gascoigne.* 2 vols. Edited by John W. Cunliffe. Cambridge: Cambridge University Press, 1910.

Gascoigne, George. *A Hundreth Sundrie Flowres.* Edited by G. W. Pigman III. Oxford: Oxford University Press, 2000.

The Geneva Bible: A Facsimile of the 1560 Edition. Madison, WI: University of Wisconsin Press, 1969.

Gesta romanorum. London, 1510. STC 21286.3.

Gnapheus, Gulielmus (Willem de Volder). *Acolastus: A Latin Play of the Sixteenth Century.* Edited and translated by W. E. D. Atkinson. London, ONT: Humanities Departments of the University of Western Ontario, 1964.

Gnapheus, Gulielmus (Willem de Volder). *The Comedy of Acolastus, Translated from the Latin of Fullonius by John Palsgrave.* Edited by P. L. Carver. London: Humphrey Milford, 1937.

Gosson, Stephen. *The School of Abuse.* Edited by John Payne Collier. Oxford: Oxford University Press, 1841.

Gower, John. *Confessio Amantis.* 3 vols. Edited by Russell A. Peck with Latin Translations by Andrew Galloway. Kalamazoo, MI: Medieval Institute Publications, 2004–13.

Greene, Robert. *Arbasto The anatomie of fortune.* London, 1589. STC 12219.

Greene, Robert. *The Cobler of Caunterburie.* London, 1590. STC 4579.

Greene, Robert. *Greenes, groats-worth of witte, bought with a million of repentance.* London 1592. STC 12245.

206 WORKS CITED

Greene, Robert. *Greenes vision vvritten at the instant of his death. Conteyning a penitent passion for the folly of his pen.* London, 1592. STC 12261.

Greene, Robert. *The Repentance of Robert Greene.* London, 1592. STC 12306.

Herrtage, Sidney J. H., ed. *The Early English Versions of the Gesta Romanorum.* Early English Text Society Extra Series 33. London: N. Trübner & Co., 1879; repr. 1962.

Horace. *Ars Poetica.* Los Altos, CA: Packard Humanities Institute, 1991. https://latin.packhum.org/loc/893/6/0#0.

Horace. *Horace his arte of poetry, pistles, and satyrs.* London, 1567. STC 13797.

Horace. *Satires. Epistles. The Art of Poetry.* Edited and translated by H. Rushton Fairclough. Loeb Classical Library 194. Cambridge, MA: Harvard University Press, 1926.

John of Salisbury. *John of Salisbury: Policraticus.* Edited and translated by Cary J. Nederman. Cambridge: Cambridge University Press, 1990.

Klausner, David., ed. *Two Moral Interludes: The Pride of Life and Wisdom.* Kalamazoo, MI: Medieval Institute Publications, 2008.

Langland, William. *The Vision of Piers Plowman: A Complete Edition of the B-Text.* Edited by A. V. C. Schmidt. London: J. M. Dent & Sons, 1987.

Lester, G. A., ed. *Three Late Medieval Morality Plays: Mankind, Everyman, Mundus et Infans.* New York: W. W. Norton & Co., 1981.

Lily, William. *Lily's Grammar of Latin in English: An Introduction of the Eyght Partes of Speche and the Construction of the Same.* Edited by Hedwig Gwosdek. Oxford: Oxford University Press, 2013.

Lily, William and John Colet. *A Short Introduction of Grammar, 1549.* Menston, UK: Scolar Press, 1970.

Lodge, Thomas. "Defense of Poetry, Music, and Stage Plays." In *Elizabethan Critical Essays.* Edited by George Gregory Smith, 1: 63–86. Oxford: Clarendon Press, 1904.

Lothario dei Segni (Pope Innocent III). *De Miseria Condicionis Humane.* Edited and translated by Robert E. Lewis. Athens, GA: University of Georgia Press, 1978.

Lydgate, John. *The Fall of Princes.* 4 vols. Edited by Henry Bergen. Early English Text Society Extra Series 121, 122, 123, 124. London: Oxford University Press, 1924–27.

Mannyng, Robert. *Handlyng Synne.* Edited by Idelle Sullens. Binghamton, NY: Center for Medieval and Renaissance Texts and Studies, 1983.

Medwall, Henry. *The Plays of Henry Medwall.* Edited by Alan H. Nelson. Cambridge: D. S. Brewer, 1980.

Minnis, A. J. and A. B. Scott, eds. *Medieval Literary Theory and Criticism, c. 1100–c. 1375, The Commentary Tradition.* New York: Oxford University Press, 1988.

More, Thomas. *The Complete Works of St. Thomas More.* 15 vols. New Haven, CT: Yale University Press, 1963–97.

Morison, Richard. *A remedy for sedition vvherin are conteyned many thynges, concernyng the true and loyall obeysance, that commens owe vnto their prince and soueraygne lorde the Kynge.* London 1536. STC 20877.

Mubashshir Ibn Fatik, Abu al-Wafa. *Here endeth the book named the dictes or sayengis of the philosophres.* London, 1477. STC 6826.

Ovid. *The Book of Ovyde Named Methamorphose.* Translated by William Caxton. Edited by Richard Moll. Toronto: PIMS, 2013.

Ovid. *The Metamorphoses.* Translated by A. S. Kline. Charlottesville: University of Virginia Electronic Text Center, 2000.

Ovid. *The. xv. bookes of P. Ouidius Naso, entytuled Metamorphosis, translated oute of Latin into English meeter, by Arthur Golding.* London, 1567. STC 18956.

Painter, William. *The Palace of Pleasure Beautified, adorned and well furnished, with Pleasaunt Histories and excellent Nouelles, selected out of diuers good and commendable Authors.* London, 1566. STC 19121.

WORKS CITED   207

Phillip, John. *The Play of Patient Grissell.* London: Malone Society Reprints, 1909.

Pico della Mirandola. *Here is conteyned the lyfe of Iohan Picus erle of Myrandula a grete lorde of Italy an excellent connynge man in all sciences, and verteous of lyuynge.* London, 1525. STC 19898.

The prouerbes of Solomon newly translated into Englyshe. London, 1534. STC 2752.

Puttenham, George. *The Art of English Poesy.* Edited by Frank Whigham and Wayne Rebhorn. Ithaca, NY: Cornell University Press, 2007.

Schonaeus, Cornelis. *Terentius Christianus, sive Comoediae duae.* London, 1595. STC 21821.

Sidney, Philip. *An Apology for Poetry, or The Defence of Poesy.* Edited by Geoffrey Shepherd. New York: Barnes & Noble Books, 1973.

Sidney, Philip. *An Apology for Poetry, or The Defence of Poesy.* 3rd edition. Edited by Geoffrey Shepherd and R. W. Maslen. New York: Palgrave, 2002.

Sidney, Philip. "The Defense of Poesy." In *English Essays: Sidney to Macaulay.* The Harvard Classics (1909–14). https://www.bartleby.com/27/1.html.

Spenser, Edmund. *Edmund Spenser's Poetry.* 4th edition. Edited by Anne Lake Prescott and Andrew D. Hadfield. New York: W. W. Norton & Co., 2014.

Spenser, Edmund. *The Faerie Queene.* Edited by Thomas P. Roche, Jr. New York: Penguin, 1978.

Spenser, Edmund. *The Yale Edition of the Shorter Poems of Edmund Spenser.* Edited by William A. Oram, Einar Bjorvand, and Ronald Bond. New Haven, CT: Yale University Press, 1989.

Terence. *Floures for Latine spekynge selected and gathered oute of Terence.* Translated by Nicholas Udall. London, 1534. STC 23899.

Terence. *Terence in English: An Early Sixteenth-Century Translation of The Andria.* Edited by Meg Twycross. Lancaster, UK: Dept. of English Language and Medieval Literature, University of Lancaster, 1987.

Terence. *Terence I: The Woman of Andros. The Self-Tormentor. The Eunuch.* Edited and translated by John Barsby. Loeb Classical Library 22. Cambridge, MA: Harvard University Press, 2001.

Terence. *Terence II: Phormio, the Mother-in-Law, the Brothers.* Edited and translated by John Barsby. Loeb Classical Library 23. Cambridge, MA: Harvard University Press, 2001.

Terence. *Terens in englysh.* Paris, 1520. STC 23894.

Tyndale, William. *A path way into the holy scripture,* London, 1536. STC 2443

Tyndale, William. *William Tyndale's New Testament.* Edited by David Daniell. New Haven, CT: Yale University Press, 1996

Van der Noot, Jan. *A theatre wherein be represented as wel the miseries & calamities that follow the voluptuous worldlings.* London, 1569. STC 18602.

Waldis, Burkardt. *De parabell vam vorlorn Szohn.* Riga, 1527.

Secondary Sources

Alexander, Gavin. "Loving and Reading in Sidney." *Studies in Philology* 114.1 (2017): 39–66.

Allen, Elizabeth. *False Fables and Exemplary Truth in Later Middle English Literature.* New York: Palgrave Macmillan, 2005.

Allen, Judson Boyce. *The Ethical Poetic of the Later Middle Ages: A Decorum of Convenient Distinction.* Toronto: University of Toronto Press, 1982.

208 WORKS CITED

Als, Hilton. "Ghosts in the House" (2003). *The New Yorker*, July 27, 2020, 30–39.

Altman, Joel. *The Tudor Play of Mind: Rhetorical Inquiry and the Development of Elizabethan Drama*. Berkeley, CA: University of California Press, 1978.

Astell, Ann. "Heroic Virtue in Blessed Raymond of Capua's *Life of Catherine of Siena*." *Journal of Medieval and Early Modern Studies* 42 (2012): 35–57.

Atchity, Kenneth John. "Spenser's *Mother Hubberds Tale*: Three Themes of Order." *Philological Quarterly* 52 (1973): 161–172.

Austen, Gillian. *George Gascoigne*. Cambridge: D.S. Brewer, 2008.

Baker, David. *Divulging Utopia: Radical Humanism in Sixteenth-Century England*. Amherst, MA: University of Massachusetts Press, 1999.

Baldwin, T. W. *William Shakspere's Smalle Latin and Lesse Greeke*. Urbana, IL: University of Illinois Press, 1944.

Barkan, Leonard. "Ruins and Visions: Spenser, Pictures, and Rome." In *Edmund Spenser: Essays on Culture and Allegory*, edited by Jennifer Klein Morrison and Matthew Greenfield, 9–36. Aldershot, UK: Ashgate, 2000.

Bates, Catherine. *On Not Defending Poetry: Defence and Indefensibility in Sidney's Defence of Poesy*. Oxford: Oxford University Press, 2017.

Beck, Ervin. "Terence Improved: The Paradigm of the Prodigal Son in English Renaissance Comedy." *Renaissance Drama* 6 (1973): 107–122.

Beckwith, Sarah. "Language Goes on Holiday: English Allegorical Drama and the Virtue Tradition." *Journal of Medieval and Early Modern Studies* 42 (2012): 107–130.

Beecher, Donald. "An Obstruction to Interpretation: The Authority of Allegory in *The Comedy of Patient and Meek Grissill*." In *Tudor Theatre: Allegory in the Theatre*, edited by André Lascombes, 157–66. Collection THETA Vol. 5. Bern & Berlin: Peter Lang, 2000.

Belsey, Catherine. *The Subject of Tragedy: Identity and Difference in Renaissance Drama*. London: Methuen, 1985.

Bernard, John D. *Ceremonies of Innocence: Pastoralism in the Poetry of Edmund Spenser*. Cambridge: Cambridge University Press, 1989.

Betteridge, Thomas. "'When Lyberte Ruled': Tudor Drama 1485–1603." In *The Oxford Handbook of Tudor Drama*, edited by Betteridge and Greg Walker, 1–18. Oxford: Oxford University Press, 2012.

Betteridge, Thomas. "William Tyndale and Religious Debate." *Journal of Medieval and Early Modern Studies* 40 (2010): 439–461.

Bevington, David, *From Mankind to Marlowe: Growth of Structure in the Popular Drama of Tudor England*. Cambridge, MA: Harvard University Press, 1962.

Blamires, Alcuin. *Chaucer, Ethics, and Gender*. Oxford: Oxford University Press, 2006.

Bliss, Lee. "The Renaissance Griselda: A Woman for All Seasons." *Viator* 23 (1992): 301–343.

Bloemendal, Jan. "Religion and Latin Drama in the Early Modern Low Countries." *Renaissance Studies* 30 (2016): 542–561.

Brantley, Jessica. "Middle English Drama Beyond the Cycle Plays." *Literature Compass* 10.4 (2013): 331–342.

Brantley, Jessica. *Reading in the Wilderness: Private Devotion and Public Performances in Late Medieval England*. Chicago: University of Chicago Press, 2007.

Briggs, Charles F. "Moral Philosophy and Wisdom Literature." In *The Oxford History of Classical Reception in English Literature: Volume 1: 800–1558*, edited by Rita Copeland, 299–321. Oxford: Oxford University Press, 2016.

Brink, Jean. "Who Fashioned Edmund Spenser? The Textual History of *Complaints*." *Studies in Philology* 88 (1991): 153–168.

Brown, Richard Danson. *"The New Poet"*: *Novelty and Tradition in Spenser's Complaints*. Liverpool: Liverpool University Press, 1999.

Buehler, Curt F. "A Survival from the Middle Ages: William Baldwin's Use of the 'Dictes and Sayings.'" *Speculum* 23 (1948): 76–80.

Burckhardt, Jacob. *Civilization of the Renaissance in Italy*. Translated by S. G. C. Middlemore. London: Sonnenschein, 1904.

Burrow, Colin. *Imitating Authors: Plato to Futurity*. Oxford: Oxford University Press, 2019.

Burrow, Colin. "Shakespeare and Humanistic Culture." In *Shakespeare and the Classics*, edited by Charles Martindale and A. B. Taylor, 9–27. Cambridge: Cambridge University Press, 2004.

Bushnell, Rebecca. *A Culture of Teaching: Early Modern Humanism in Theory and Practice*. Ithaca, NY: Cornell University Press, 1996.

Campana, Joseph. "On Not Defending Poetry: Spenser, Suffering, and the Energy of Affect." *PMLA* 120.1 (2005): 33–48.

Campion, Edmund. "Defences of Classical Learning in St. Augustine's *De Doctrina Christiana* and Erasmus's *Antibarbari*." *History of European Ideas* 4.4 (1983): 467–471.

Cannon, Christopher. *The Grounds of English Literature*. Oxford: Oxford University Press, 2005.

Cannon, Christopher. "Reading Knowledge." *PMLA* 30.3 (2015): 711–717.

Carley, James P. and Ágnes Juhász-Ormsby. "Survey of Henrician Humanism." In *The Oxford History of Classical Reception in English Literature: Volume 1: 800–1558*, edited by Rita Copeland, 515–540. Oxford: Oxford University Press, 2016.

Cartwright, John. "The Morality Play: Dead End or Main Street?" *Medieval English Theatre* 18 (1996): 3–14.

Cartwright, Kent. "Humanist Reading and Interpretation in Early Elizabethan Morality Drama." *Allegorica* 28 (2012): 9–31.

Cartwright, Kent. *Theatre and Humanism: English Drama in the Sixteenth Century*. Cambridge: Cambridge University Press, 1999.

Caspari, Fritz. *Humanism and the Social Order in Tudor England*. Chicago: University of Chicago Press, 1954.

Cefalu, Paul. *Moral Identity in Early Modern English Literature*. Cambridge: Cambridge University Press, 2000.

Clark, J. C. D. "Secularization and Modernization: The Failure of a 'Grand Narrative.'" *The Historical Journal* 55.1 (2012): 161–194.

Clark, Sandra. "Robert Greene [July 1558–3 September 1592]." In *Sixteenth-Century British Nondramatic Writers*, edited by David A. Richardson, 87–102. 3rd Series. Detroit, MI: Thomson Gale, 1996.

Clebsch, William. *England's Earliest Protestants 1520–1535*. New Haven, CT: Yale University Press, 1964.

Clopper, Lawrence M. *Drama, Play, and Game: English Festive Culture in the Medieval and Early Modern Period*. Chicago: University of Chicago Press, 2001.

Coldewey, John. "Morality Plays." In *The Oxford Encyclopedia of British Literature*. Edited by David Scott Kastan. Oxford: Oxford University Press, 2006. DOI: 9780195169218.

Coldewey, John. "Plays and Play." *Research Opportunities in Renaissance Drama* 28 (1985): 181–188.

Coldiron, A. E. B. "How Spenser Excavates Du Bellay's *Antiquitez*, or, The Role of the Poet, Lyric Historiography, and the English Sonnet." *Journal of English and Germanic Philology* 10 (2002): 41–67.

Conley, John. "The Doctrine of Friendship in *Everyman*." *Speculum* 44 (1969): 374–382.

210 WORKS CITED

Cook, Megan. "Nostalgic Temporalities in *Greenes Vision.*" *Parergon* 33 (2016): 39–56.

Cook, Megan. *The Poet and the Antiquaries: Chaucerian Scholarship and the Rise of Literary History, 1532–1635*. Philadelphia: University of Pennsylvania Press, 2019.

Cooper, Helen. *Pastoral: Mediaeval to Renaissance*. Cambridge: D. S. Brewer, 1977.

Cooper, Helen. "Poetic Fame." In *Cultural Reformations: Medieval and Renaissance in Literary History*, edited by Brian Cummings and James Simpson, 361–378. Oxford: Oxford University Press, 2010.

Copeland, Rita. "Arts of Poetry." In *The Cambridge History of Literary Criticism, Volume 2: The Middle Ages*, edited by A. J. Minnis and Ian Johnson, 2:42–67. Cambridge: Cambridge University Press, 2005.

Copeland, Rita. "Horace's *Ars poetica* in the Medieval Classroom and Beyond: The Horizons of Ancient Precept." In *Answerable Style: The Idea of the Literary in Medieval England*, edited by Andrew Galloway and Frank Grady, 15–33. Columbus: Ohio State University Press, 2013.

Copeland, Rita. "Introduction." In *The Oxford History of Classical Reception in English Literature: Volume 1: 800–1558*, edited by Copeland, 3–18. Oxford: Oxford University Press, 2016.

Craik, Katherine A. "Spenser's Complaints and the New Poet." *Huntington Library Quarterly* 64 (2001): 63–79.

Crane, Mary Thomas. *Framing Authority: Sayings, Self, and Society in Sixteenth-Century England*. Princeton, NJ: Princeton University Press, 1993.

Crewe, Jonathan. *Hidden Designs: The Critical Profession and Renaissance Literature*. New York: Methuen, 1986.

Cronk, Nicholas. "Aristotle, Horace, and Longinus: The Conception of Reader Response." In *The Cambridge History of Literary Criticism, Volume 3: The Renaissance*, edited by Glyn P. Norton, 3:199–204. Cambridge: Cambridge University Press, 1999.

Cummings, Brian. "Erasmus and the Invention of Literature." *Erasmus Yearbook* 33 (2013): 22–54.

Cummings, Brian. *The Literary Culture of the Reformation: Grammar and Grace*. Oxford: Oxford University Press, 2002.

Cummings, Robert. "The Province of Verse: Sir Thomas More's Twelve Rules of John Picus Earle of Mirandula." In *Elizabethan Translation and Literary Culture*, edited by Gabriela Schmidt, 201–226. Berlin: Walter de Gruyter, 2013.

D'Andrade, Roy. *The Development of Cognitive Anthropology*. Cambridge: Cambridge University Press, 1995.

Dagenais, John. *The Ethics of Reading in Manuscript Culture: Glossing the "Libro de buen amor."* Princeton, NJ: Princeton University Press, 1994.

Daniell, David. *William Tyndale: A Biography*. New Haven, CT: Yale University Press, 2001.

Davidson, Clifford. *Visualizing the Moral Life: Medieval Iconography and the Macro Morality Plays*. New York: AMS Press, 1989.

Davies, Tony. *Humanism*. 2nd edition. London: Routledge, 2008.

Davis, Nicholas. "The Meaning of the Word 'Interlude.'" *Medieval English Theatre* 6 (1984): 5–15.

Davis, Walter R. *Idea and Act in Elizabethan Fiction*. Princeton, NJ: Princeton University Press, 1969.

Debax, Jean-Paul. "Complicity and Hierarchy: A Tentative Definition of the Interlude Genus." In *Interludes and Early Modern Society: Studies in Gender, Power and Theatricality*, edited by Peter Happé and Wim Hüsken, 23–42. Leiden: Brill, 2007.

WORKS CITED   211

Delcorno, Pietro. *In the Mirror of the Prodigal Son: The Pastoral Uses of a Biblical Narrative (c. 1200–1550)*. Leiden: Brill, 2017.

DeNeef, A. Leigh. "'The Ruins of Time': Spenser's Apology for Poetry." *Studies in Philology* 76 (1979): 262–271.

Dickens, A. G. and Whitney R. D. Jones. *Erasmus the Reformer*. London: Reed International Books, 1994.

Dimmick, Jeremy. "Gower, Chaucer and the Art of Repentance in Robert Greene's 'Vision.'" *The Review of English Studies* 57 (2006): 456–473.

Dolven, Jeff. *Scenes of Instruction in Renaissance Romance*. Chicago: University of Chicago Press, 2007.

Donaldson, E. T. *Speaking of Chaucer*. New York: W. W. Norton, 1970.

Dowling, Maria. *Humanism in the Age of Henry VIII*. London: Croom Helm, 1986.

Duffy, Timothy. "'The Light of Simple Veritie': Mapping out Spenser's Cosmography in 'The Ruines of Time.'" *Studies in Philology* 111 (2014): 738–756.

Eagleton, Terry. *How to Read a Poem*. Malden, MA: Wiley-Blackwell, 2007.

Elliot, Thomas J. "Middle English Complaints against the Times: To Contemn the World or Reform it?" *Annuale Medievale* 14 (1973): 22–34.

Enterline, Lynn. *Shakespeare's Schoolroom: Rhetoric, Discipline, Emotion*. Philadelphia: University of Pennsylvania Press, 2012.

Felski, Rita. *Uses of Literature*. Malden, MA: Wiley-Blackwell, 2008.

Ferguson, Arthur. *The Articulate Citizen and the English Renaissance*. Durham, NC: Duke University Press, 1965.

Ferguson, Margaret. "'The Afflatus of Ruin': Meditations on Rome by Du Bellay, Spenser, and Stevens." In *Roman Images: Selected Papers from the English Institute*, edited by Annabel Patterson, 23–52. Baltimore, MD: Johns Hopkins University Press, 1984.

Fichte, Joerg O. "New Wine in Old Bottles: The Protestant Adaptation of the Morality Play." *Anglia: Zeitschrift fur Englische Philologie* 110 (1992): 65–84.

Fichter, Andrew. "'And nought of Rome in Rome perceiv'st at all': Spenser's 'Ruines of Rome.'" *Spenser Studies*, 2 (1981):183–192.

Fish, Stanley. *Self-Consuming Artifacts: The Experience of Seventeenth-Century Literature*. Berkeley, CA: University of California Press, 1972.

Fowler, Alastair. *Kinds of Literature: An Introduction to the Theory of Genres and Modes*. Cambridge, MA: Harvard University Press, 1982.

Fox, Alistair and John Guy. *Reassessing the Henrician Age: Humanism, Politics and Reform, 1500–1550*. Oxford: Basil Blackwell, 1986.

Fradenburg, Louise. "Voice Memorial: Loss and Reparation in Chaucer's Poetry." *Exemplaria* 2 (1990): 169–202.

Freccero, John. "The Fig Tree and the Laurel: Petrarch's Poetics." *Diacritics* 5.1 (1975): 34–40.

Freedman, Paul. *Images of the Medieval Peasant*. Stanford, CA: Stanford University Press, 1999.

Frow, John. *Genre*. 2nd edition. New York: Routledge, 2015.

Frow, John. "'Reproducibles, Rubrics, and Everything You Need': Genre Theory Today." *PMLA* 122.5 (2007): 1626–1634.

Fumo, Jamie. C. *The Legacy of Apollo: Antiquity, Authority, and Chaucerian Poetics*. Toronto: University of Toronto Press, 2010.

Gaggero, Christopher. "Pleasure Unreconciled to Virtue: George Gascoigne and Didactic Drama." In *Tudor Drama Before Shakespeare, 1485–1590: New Directions for Research,*

212 WORKS CITED

Criticism and Pedagogy, edited by Lloyd Kermode, Jason Scott-Warren, and Martine van Elk, 167–194. New York: Palgrave Macmillan, 2004.

Gelley, Alexander. *Unruly Examples: On the Rhetoric of Exemplarity*. Stanford, CA: Stanford University Press, 1995.

Giancarlo, Matthew. "Mirror, Mirror: Princely Hermeneutics, Practical Constitutionalism, and the Genres of the English *Fürstenspiegel.*" *Exemplaria* 27.1–2 (2015), 35–54.

Gibson, Gail McMurray. *The Theater of Devotion: East Anglian Drama and Society in the Late Middle Ages*. Chicago: University of Chicago Press, 1989.

Gillespie, Alexandra. *Print Culture and the Medieval Author: Chaucer, Lydgate, and their Books, 1473–1557*. Oxford: Oxford University Press, 2006.

Gillespie, Vincent. "The Study of Classical Authors." In *The Cambridge History of Literary Criticism, Volume 2: The Middle Ages*, edited by A. J. Minnis and Ian Johnson, 2: 162–169. Cambridge: Cambridge University Press, 2005.

Glossarial Concordance to Middle English: The Works of Geoffrey Chaucer and the English Works of John Gower, Johns Hopkins University, Sheridan Libraries, 2021, https://middleenglish.library.jhu.edu.

Goldstein, Laurence. "Immortal Longings and 'The Ruines of Time.'" *Journal of English and Germanic Philology* 75 (1976): 337–351.

Grabes, Herbert. *The Mutable Glass: Mirror-imagery in Titles and Texts of the Middle Ages and English Renaissance*. Translated by Gordon Collier. Cambridge: Cambridge University Press, 1982.

Grafton, Anthony, and Lisa Jardine. *From Humanism to the Humanities: Education and the Liberal Arts in Fifteenth- and Sixteenth-Century Europe*. Cambridge, MA: Harvard University Press, 1986.

Green, D. H. *The Beginnings of Medieval Romance: Fact and Fiction, 1150–1220*. Cambridge: Cambridge University Press, 2008.

Green, Ian. *Humanism and Protestantism in Early Modern English Education*. Burlington, VT: Ashgate, 2009.

Greenblatt, Stephen. *Renaissance Self-Fashioning: From More to Shakespeare*. Chicago: University of Chicago Press, 1980.

Greene, Thomas. *The Light in Troy: Imitation and Discovery in Renaissance Poetry*. New Haven, CT: Yale University Press, 1982.

Griffiths, Huw. "Translated Geographies: Spenser's 'Ruins of Time.'" *Early Modern Literary Studies* 4 (1998): 26 paragraphs.

Griffiths, Jane. "Counterfeit Countenance: (Mis)representation and the Challenge to Allegory in Sixteenth-century Morality Plays." *Yearbook of English Studies* 38 (2008): 17–33.

Griffiths, Jane. "Lusty Juventus." In *The Oxford Handbook of Tudor Drama*, edited by Thomas Betteridge and Greg Walker, 262–75. Oxford: Oxford University Press, 2012.

Guillory, John. *Cultural Capital: The Problem of Literary Canon Formation*. Chicago: University of Chicago Press, 1993.

Guillory, John. "The Location of Literature." In *A Companion to Literary Theory*, edited by David H. Richter, 151–164. Malden, MA: Wiley-Blackwell, 2018.

Hadfield, Andrew. "Edmund Spenser's Translations of Du Bellay in Jan van der Noot's *A Theatre for Voluptuous Worldlings.*" In *Tudor Translation*, edited by Fred Schurink, 143–160. New York: Palgrave Macmillan, 2011.

Hadfield, Andrew. "The Summoning of *Everyman.*" In *The Oxford Handbook of Tudor Drama*, edited by Thomas Betteridge and Greg Walker, 93–106. Oxford: Oxford University Press, 2012.

WORKS CITED 213

Halpern, Richard. *The Poetics of Primitive Accumulation: English Renaissance Culture and the Genealogy of Capital*. Ithaca, NY: Cornell University Press, 1991.

Hampton, Timothy. *Writing from History: The Rhetoric of Exemplarity in Renaissance Literature*. Ithaca, NY: Cornell University Press, 1989.

Hanna, Ralph. "Some Commonplaces of Late Medieval Patience Discussions: An Introduction." In *The Triumph of Patience*, edited by Gerald Schiffhorst, 65–87. Orlando: University Presses of Florida, 1978.

Happé, Peter. "John Bale and Controversy: Readers and Audiences." In *The Oxford Handbook of Tudor Literature: 1485–1603*, edited by Mike Pincombe and Cathy Shrank, 138–153. Oxford: Oxford University Press, 2009.

Happé, Peter. "'Pullyshyd and Fresshe is your Ornacy': Madness and the Fall of Skelton's *Magnyfycence*." In *The Oxford Handbook of Tudor Drama*, edited by Thomas Betteridge and Greg Walker, 482–98. Oxford: Oxford University Press, 2012.

Harbage, Alfred. *Annals of English Drama: 975–1700*. Revised by Samuel Schoenbaum. London: Methuen & Co., 1964.

Hardin, Richard F. "The Literary Conventions of Erasmus' *Education of a Christian Prince*: Advice and Aphorism." *Renaissance Quarterly* 35 (1982): 151–163.

Helfer, Rebecca. *Spenser's Ruins and the Art of Recollection*. Toronto: University of Toronto Press, 2012.

Helgerson, Richard. *The Elizabethan Prodigals*. Berkeley, CA: University of California Press, 1977.

Herdt, Jennifer. "Introduction." *Journal of Medieval and Early Modern Studies* 42 (2012): 1–12.

Herdt, Jennifer. *Putting on Virtue: The Legacy of the Splendid Vices*. Chicago: University of Chicago Press, 2008.

Herford, Charles. *Studies in the Literary Relations of England and Germany in the Sixteenth Century*. London: Frank Cass and Co, Ltd., 1966.

Hexter, J. H. "The Education of the Aristocracy in the Renaissance." *Journal of Modern History* 22 (1950): 1–20.

Hirsch, E. D., Jr., "Two Traditions of Literary Evaluation." In *Literary Theory and Criticism: Festschrift Presented to René Wellek in Honor of his Eightieth Birthday*, edited by Joseph P. Strelka, 283–298. New York: Peter Lang, 1984.

Hogrefe, Pearl. *The Life and Times of Sir Thomas Elyot, Englishman*. Ames, IA: Iowa State University Press, 1967.

Holstun, James. "The Spider, the Fly, and the Commonwealth: Merrie John Heywood and Agrarian Class Struggle." *ELH* 71.1(2004): 53–88.

Horbury, Ezra. "Performing Repentance: (In)sincerity in Prodigal Son Drama and the Henry IVs." *Renaissance Studies* 32.4 (2017): 583–601.

Hui, Andrew. *The Poetics of Ruins in Renaissance Literature*. New York: Fordham University Press, 2017.

Hunter, G. K. "Elizabethan Drama on the High Wire." *The Sewanee Review* 88.1 (1980): 100–105.

Hyde, Thomas. "Vision, Poetry, and Authority in Spenser." *English Literary Renaissance* 13 (1983): 127–145.

Janowitz, Anne. *England's Ruins: Poetic Purpose and the National Landscape*. Cambridge: Blackwell, 1990.

Jauss, Hans Robert. *Toward an Aesthetic of Reception*. Translated by Timothy Bahti. Minneapolis, MN: University of Minnesota Press, 1982.

214 WORKS CITED

Jeffrey, David Lyle, ed. *A Dictionary of Biblical Tradition*. Grand Rapids, MI: W. B. Eerdmans, 1992.

Johnson, Eleanor. *Practicing Literary Theory in the Middle Ages: Ethics and the Mixed Form in Chaucer, Gower, Usk, and Hoccleve*. Chicago: University of Chicago Press, 2013.

Juhász-Ormsby, Ágnes. "Dramatic Texts in the Tudor Curriculum: John Palsgrave and the Henrician Educational Reforms." *Renaissance Studies* 30.4 (2016): 526–541.

Juhász-Ormsby, Ágnes. "Nicholas Udall's *Floures for Latin Spekynge*: An Erasmian Textbook." *Humanistica Lovaniensia: Journal of Neo-Latin Studies* 52(2003): 137–158.

Kahn, Victoria. *Rhetoric, Prudence, and Skepticism in the Renaissance*. Ithaca, NY: Cornell University Press, 1985.

Kaplan, Ruth. "The Problem of Pity in Spenser's *Ruines of Time* and *Amoretti*." *Spenser Studies* 29 (2014): 263–294.

Karremann, Isabel. "Edmund Spenser's *The Ruines of Time* as a Protestant Poetics of Mourning and Commemoration." In *Forms of Faith: Literary Form and Religious Conflict in Shakespeare's England*, edited by Jonathan Baldo and Isabel Karremann, 90–110. Manchester: Manchester University Press, 2017.

Kerrigan, John, ed. *Motives of Woe: Shakespeare and 'Female Complaint': A Critical Anthology*. New York: Oxford University Press, 1991.

Kidd, David Comer and Emanuele Castano, "Reading Literary Fiction Improves Theory of Mind." *Science* 342.6156 (2013): 377–380. DOI: 10.1126/science.1239918.

King, Pamela M. "Morality Plays." In *The Cambridge Companion to Medieval English Theatre*, edited by Richard Beadle, 235–262. Cambridge: Cambridge University Press, 1994.

Kinney, Arthur F. *Humanist Poetics: Thought, Rhetoric, and Fiction in Sixteenth-century England*. Amherst, MA: University of Massachusetts Press, 1986.

Kinney, Arthur F. "Parody and Its Implications in Sydney's Defense of Poesie." *Studies in English Literature 1500–1900* 12.1 (1972): 1–19.

Kintgen, Eugene. *Reading in Tudor England*. Pittsburgh, PA: University of Pittsburgh Press, 1996.

Kolve, V.A. "*Everyman* and the Parable of the Talents." In *The Medieval Drama*, edited by Sandro Sticca, 69–97. Albany, NY: SUNY Press, 1972.

Kristeller, Paul Oskar. *The Classics and Renaissance Thought*. Cambridge, MA: Harvard University Press, for Oberlin College, 1955.

Kristeller, Paul Oskar. "Humanism and Moral Philosophy." In *Renaissance Humanism: Foundations, Forms and Legacy*, 3 vols., edited by Albert Rabil, Jr., 3: 271–309. Philadelphia: University of Pennsylvania Press, 1988.

Kumaran, Arul. "Robert Greene's Martinist Transformation in 1590." *Studies in Philology* 103 (2006): 243–263.

Kuskin, William. *Symbolic Caxton: Literary Culture and Print Capitalism*. Notre Dame, IN: University of Notre Dame Press, 2008.

Lazarus, Micha. "The Dramatic Prologues of Alexander Nowell: Accommodating the Classics at 1540s Westminster." *The Review of English Studies* 69. 288 (2017): 32–55.

Lehmberg, Stanford. *Sir Thomas Elyot: Tudor Humanist*. Austin, TX: University of Texas Press, 1960.

Lewalski, Barbara Kiefer. "How Poetry Moves Readers: Sidney, Spenser, and Milton." *University of Toronto Quarterly* 80.3 (2011): 756–768.

Lewis, C. S. *Oxford History of English Literature Volume 3: English Literature in the Sixteenth Century: Excluding Drama*. Oxford: Clarendon Press, 1965.

WORKS CITED 215

Little, Katherine C. *Confession and Resistance: Defining the Self in Late Medieval England*. Notre Dame, IN: University of Notre Dame Press, 2006.

Little, Katherine C. *Transforming Work: Early Modern Pastoral and Late Medieval Poetry*. Notre Dame, IN: University of Notre Dame Press, 2013.

Little, Katherine C. "What Spenser Took from Chaucer: Worldly Vanity in *The Ruines of Time* and *Troilus and Criseyde*." *ELH* 83 (2016): 431–455.

Lupton, Joseph Hirst. *A Life of John Colet: With an Appendix of Some of his English Writings*. London: George Bell and Sons, 1887.

Lyons, John D. *Exemplum: The Rhetoric of Example in Early Modern France*. Princeton, NJ: Princeton University, 1990.

MacCracken, Henry Noble. "A Source of *Mundus Et Infans*." *PMLA* 23 (1908): 486–496.

MacIntyre, Alasdair. *After Virtue*. 2nd edition. Notre Dame, IN: University of Notre Dame Press, 1984.

Mack, Peter. *Elizabethan Rhetoric: Theory and Practice*. Cambridge: Cambridge University Press, 2002.

Maclean, Hugh. "'Restlesse anguish and unquiet paine': Spenser and the Complaint, 1579–90." In *The Practical Vision*, edited by Jane Campbell and James Doyle, 29–48. Waterloo, ON: Wilfrid Laurier University Press, 1978.

MacLure, Millar. "Spenser and the ruins of time." In *A Theatre for Spenserians*, edited by Judith M. Kennedy and James A. Reither, 3–18. Toronto: University of Toronto Press, 1973.

Major, John. *Sir Thomas Elyot and Renaissance Humanism*. Lincoln, NE: University of Nebraska Press, 1964.

Mann, Jill. *Chaucer and Medieval Estates Satire: The Literature of Social Classes and the General Prologue to the Canterbury Tales*. Cambridge: Cambridge University Press, 1973.

Mann, Jill. *From Aesop to Reynard: Beast Literature in Medieval Britain*. Oxford: Oxford University Press, 2009.

Marenbon, John. *Pagans and Philosophers: The Problem of Paganism from Augustine to Leibniz*. Princeton, NJ: Princeton University Press, 2015.

Marshall, Peter and Alec Ryrie, eds. *The Beginnings of English Protestantism*. Cambridge: Cambridge University Press, 2002.

Maslen, Robert. "Greene and the Uses of Time." In *Writing Robert Greene: Essays on England's First Notorious Professional Writer*, edited by Kirk Melnikoff and Edward Gieskes, 157–188. Aldershot, UK: Ashgate, 2008.

Maslen, Robert. "Robert Greene." In *The Oxford Handbook of English Prose, 1500–1640*, edited by Andrew Hadfield, 188–204. Oxford: Oxford University Press, 2013.

Maslen, Robert. "William Baldwin and the Tudor Imagination." In *The Oxford Handbook of Tudor Literature: 1485–1603*, edited by Mike Pincombe and Cathy Shrank, 291–306. Oxford: Oxford University Press, 2009.

Matz, Robert. *Defending Literature in Early Modern England*. Cambridge: Cambridge University Press, 2000.

McConica, James. *English Humanists and Reformation Politics under Henry VIII and Edward VI*. Oxford: Clarendon Press, 1965.

Melehy, Hassan. "Antiquities of Britain: Spenser's 'Ruines of Time.'" *Studies in Philology* 102 (2005): 159–183.

Menand, Louis. "What's so Great about Great Books Courses." *The New Yorker*, December 13, 2021, https://www.newyorker.com/magazine/2021/12/20/whats-so-great-about-great-books-courses-roosevelt-montas-rescuing-socrates.

216 WORKS CITED

Middleton, Anne. "The Physician's Tale and Love's Martyrs: 'Ensamples Mo Than Ten' as a Method in the *Canterbury Tales.*" *Chaucer Review* 8 (1973): 9–32.

Miller, Mark. "Displaced Souls, Idle Talk, Spectacular Scenes: *Handlyng Synne* and the Perspective of Agency." *Speculum* 71 (1996): 606–632.

Mills, David. "Anglo-Dutch Theatre: Problems and Possibilities." *Medieval English Theatre* 18 (1996): 85–98.

Mills, David. "The Theaters of *Everyman.*" In *From Page to Performance: Essays in Early English Drama*, edited by John A. Alford, 127–149. East Lansing:, MI: Michigan State University Press, 1995.

Mineo, Bernard, ed. *A Companion to Livy*. Malden, MA: Wiley-Blackwell, 2015.

Minnis, A. J. *Chaucer and Pagan Antiquity*. Cambridge: D. S. Brewer, 1982.

Minnis, A. J. *Medieval Theory of Authorship: Scholastic Literary Attitudes in the Later Middle Ages*. London: Scholar Press, 1984.

Minnis, Alastair and Ian Johnson. "Introduction." In *The Cambridge History of Literary Criticism, Volume 2: The Middle Ages*, edited by Minnis and Johnson, 1-12. Cambridge: Cambridge University Press, 2005.

Miola, Robert S. *Shakespeare and Classical Comedy: The Influence of Plautus and Terence*. Oxford: Clarendon Press, 1994.

Mitchell, J. Allan. *Ethics and Exemplary Narrative in Chaucer and Gower*. Woodbridge, UK: Boydell and Brewer, 2004.

Morse, Charlotte C. "The Exemplary Griselda." *Studies in the Age of Chaucer* 1 (1985): 51–86.

Moss, Ann. "Humanist Education." In *The Cambridge History of Literary Criticism, Volume 3: The Renaissance*, edited by Glyn P. Norton, 3:145–154. Cambridge: Cambridge University Press, 1999.

Moss, Ann. *Printed Commonplace Books and the Structuring of Renaissance Thought*. Oxford: Clarendon Press, 1996.

Muir, Tom. "Specters of Spenser: Translating the Antiquitez." *Spenser Studies* 25 (2010): 327–361.

Munson, William. "Knowing and Doing in *Everyman.*" *Chaucer Review* 19 (1985): 252–271.

Murakami, Ineke. *Moral Play and Counterpublic: Transformations in Moral Drama, 1465–1599*. New York: Routledge, 2011.

Nauert, Charles G. "Rethinking 'Christian Humanism.'" In *Interpretations of Renaissance Humanism*, edited by Angelo Mazzoco, 155–180. Leiden: Brill, 2006.

Newcomb, Lori Humphrey. "A Looking Glass for Readers." In *Writing Robert Greene: Essays on England's First Notorious Professional Writer*, edited by Kirk Melnikoff and Edward Gieskes, 133–156. Aldershot, UK: Ashgate, 2008.

Newcomb, Lori Humphrey. *Reading Popular Romance in Early Modern England*. New York: Columbia University Press, 2002.

Nguyen, Viet Thanh. "Canon Fodder," *The Washington Post*, May 3, 2018. https://www.washingtonpost.com/news/posteverything/wp/2018/05/03/feature/books-by-immigrants-foreigners-and-minorities-dont-diminish-the-classic-curriculum/.

Norbrook, David. *Poetry and Politics in the English Renaissance*. London: Routledge, 1984.

Norbrook, David. "Rehearsing the Plebeians: *Coriolanus* and the Reading of Roman History." In *Shakespeare and the Politics of Commoners: Digesting the New Social History*, edited by Chris Fitter, chapter 9. Oxford: Oxford University Press, 2017. DOI: 9780198806899.

WORKS CITED 217

Norland, Howard B. *Drama in Early Tudor Britain*. Lincoln, NE: University of Nebraska Press, 1995.

Normington, Katie. *Medieval English Drama: Performance and Spectatorship*. Cambridge: Polity Press, 2009.

Northwest Great Books. "History of Great Books Foundation." Accessed March 3, 2022. https://nwgreatbooks.com/about/history/.

Norton, Glyn P. "Introduction." In *The Cambridge History of Literary Criticism, Volume 3: The Renaissance*, edited by Norton, 3:1–22. Cambridge: Cambridge University Press, 1999.

Olson, Glending. *Literature as Recreation in the Later Middle Ages*. Ithaca, NY: Cornell University Press, 1982.

Orme, Nicholas. *Education and Society in Medieval and Renaissance England*. London: Hambledon Press, 1989.

Palmer, Ada. "Humanist Lives of Classical Philosophers and the Idea of Renaissance Secularization: Virtue, Rhetoric, and the Orthodox Sources of Unbelief." *Renaissance Quarterly* 70 (2017): 935–976.

Parente, James A., Jr., "Drama." In *The Encyclopedia of the Reformation*, edited by Hans J. Hillebrand. Oxford: Oxford University Press, 1996. DOI: 9780195064933.

Parker, Patricia. "Shakespeare and the Bible: *The Comedy of Errors*." *Recherches Sémiotiques/Semiotic Inquiry* 13.3 (1993): 47–72.

Patterson, Annabel. *Fables of Power: Aesopian Writing and Political History*. Durham, NC: Duke University Press, 1991.

Patterson, Lee. *Chaucer and the Subject of History*. Madison, WI: University of Wisconsin Press, 1991.

Pearsall, Derek. *The Routledge History of English Poetry: Volume 1: Old English and Middle English Poetry*. London: Routledge & Kegan Paul, 1977.

Peltonen, Markku. "Virtues in Elizabethan and Early Stuart Grammar Schools." *Journal of Medieval and Early Modern Studies* 42 (2012): 157–179.

Perry, Nandra. "Imitatio and Identity: Thomas Rogers, Philip Sidney, and the Protestant Self." *English Literary Renaissance* 35.3 (2005): 365–406.

Peter, John. *Complaint and Satire in Early English Literature*. Oxford: Clarendon Press, 1956.

Peterson, Joyce E. "The Paradox of Disintegrating Form in *Mundus et Infans*." *English Literary Renaissance* 7 (1977): 3–16.

Phillips, Margaret Mann. *The "Adages" of Erasmus: A Study with Translations*. Cambridge: Cambridge University Press, 1964.

Pigman, G. W. III. "George Gascoigne." In *The Oxford Encyclopedia of British Literature*, edited by David Scott Kastan. Oxford: Oxford University Press, 2006. DOI: 9780195169218.

Pigman, G. W. III. "Versions of Imitation in the Renaissance." *Renaissance Quarterly* 33 (1980): 1–32.

Potter, Robert. *The English Morality Play: Origins, History and Influence of a Dramatic Tradition*. London: Routledge & Kegan Paul, 1975.

Potter, Ursula. "'No Terence phrase: his tyme and myne are twaine': Erasmus, Terence, and Censorship in the Tudor Classroom." In *The Classics in the Medieval and Renaissance Classroom: The Role of Ancient Texts in the Arts Curriculum as Revealed by Surviving Manuscripts and Early Printed Books*, edited by Juanita Feros Ruys, John O. Ward, and Melanie Heyworth, 365–389. Turnhout: Brepols, 2013.

Potter, Ursula. "Tales of Patient Griselda and Henry VIII." *Early Theater* 5 (2002): 11–28.

218 WORKS CITED

Prescott, Anne Lake. *French Poets and the English Renaissance*. New Haven, CT: Yale University Press, 1978.

Quinn, Naomi. "The History of the Cultural Models School Reconsidered: A Paradigm Shift in Cognitive Anthropology." In *A Companion to Cognitive Anthropology*, edited by David B. Kronenfeld et al, 30–46. Malden, MA: Wiley-Blackwell, 2011.

Rädle, Fidel. "*Acolastus* – Der Verlorene Sohn: Zwei lateinische Bibeldramen des 16. Jahrhunderts." In *Gattungsinnovation und Motivstruktur*, Teil II, edited by Theodor Wolpers, 15–34. Göttingen: Vandenhoeck & Ruprecht, 1992.

Rambuss, Richard. *Spenser's Secret Career*. Cambridge: Cambridge University Press, 1993.

Rasmussen, Carl J. "'How Weak Be the Passions of Woefulness': Spenser's *Ruines of Time*." *Spenser Studies* 2 (1981): 159–81.

Rasmussen, Carl J. "'Quietnesse of Minde': A *Theatre for Worldlings* as Protestant Poetics." *Spenser Studies* 1 (1980): 3–27.

Rasmussen, Mark David. "Complaints and *Daphnaida* (1591)." In *The Oxford Handbook of Edmund Spenser*, edited by Richard A. McCabe, 218–231. Oxford: Oxford University Press, 2010.

Rasmussen, Mark David. "Spenser's Plaintive Muses." *Spenser Studies* 13 (1999): 139–164.

Reeve, Michael D. "Classical Scholarship." In *The Cambridge Companion to Renaissance Humanism*, edited by Jill Kraye, 20–46. Cambridge: Cambridge University Press, 2004.

Robertson, D. W. *A Preface to Chaucer: Studies in Medieval Perspectives*. Princeton, NJ: Princeton University Press, 1962.

Rubin, Joan. *The Making of Middle Brow Culture*. Chapel Hill, NC: University of North Carolina Press, 1992.

Rycroft, Eleanor. "Morality, Theatricality, and Masculinity in *The Interlude of Youth* and *Hick Scorner*." In *The Oxford Handbook of Tudor Drama*, edited by Thomas Betteridge and Greg Walker, 465–81. Oxford: Oxford University Press, 2012.

Salamon, Linda. "A Face in The Glasse: Gascoigne's *Glasse of Government* Re-examined." *Studies in Philology* 71 (1974): 47–71.

Salman, Phillip. "Instruction and Delight in Medieval and Renaissance Criticism." *Renaissance Quarterly* 32 (1979) 303–332.

Salter, Elizabeth. *Chaucer: The Knight's Tale and the Clerk's Tale*. London: Edward Arnold, 1962.

Scanlon, Larry. *Narrative, Authority, and Power: The Medieval Exemplum and the Chaucerian Tradition*. Cambridge: Cambridge University Press, 1994.

Scase, Wendy. *Literature and Complaint in England 1272–1553*. Oxford: Oxford University Press, 2007.

Schiffhorst, Gerald. "Some Prolegomena for the Study of Patience, 1480–1680." In *The Triumph of Patience*, edited by Schiffhorst, 1–31. Orlando, FL: University Presses of Florida, 1978.

Schwyzer, Philip. *Archaeologies of English Renaissance Literature*. Oxford: Oxford University Press, 2007.

Shagan, Ethan. *Popular Politics and the English Reformation*. Cambridge: Cambridge University Press, 2003.

Shortslef, Emily. "*The Ruines of Time* and the Virtual Collectivities of Early Modern Complaint." *Journal for Early Modern Cultural Studies* 13 (2013): 84–104.

Shrank, Cathy. "Sir Thomas Elyot and the Bonds of Community." In *The Oxford Handbook of Tudor Literature: 1485–1603*, edited by Mike Pincombe and Shrank, 154–168. Oxford: Oxford University Press, 2009.

Shutters, Lynn. "Griselda's Pagan Virtue." *Chaucer Review* 44 (2009): 61–83.

WORKS CITED 219

Siebers, Tobin. *Morals and Stories*. New York: Columbia University Press, 1992.

Silberman, Lauren. "Aesopian *Prosopopoia*: Making Faces and Playing Chicken in *Mother Hubberds Tale*." *Spenser Studies* 27 (2012): 221–247.

Simon, Joan. *Education and Society in Tudor England*. Cambridge: Cambridge University Press, 1966.

Simpson, James. *Burning to Read: English Fundamentalism and its Reformation Opponents*. Cambridge MA: Belknap Press of Harvard University Press, 2007.

Simpson, James. *The Oxford English Literary History, Volume 2, 1350–1547: Reform and Cultural Revolution*. Oxford: Oxford University Press, 2002.

Skinner, Quentin. *The Foundations of Modern Political Thought, Volume 1: The Renaissance*. Cambridge: Cambridge University Press, 1978.

Spivack, Bernard. *Shakespeare and the Allegory of Evil*. New York: Columbia University Press, 1958.

Sponsler, Claire. *Drama and Resistance: Bodies, Goods, and Theatricality in Late Medieval England*. Minneapolis, MN: University of Minnesota Press, 1997.

Steenbrugge, Charlotte. *Staging Vice: A Study of Dramatic Traditions in Medieval and Sixteenth-Century England and the Low Countries*. Ludus 13; Amsterdam: Brill/Rodopi, 2014.

Stein, Harold. *Studies in Spenser's Complaints*. New York: Oxford University Press, 1934.

Stierle, Karl-Heinz. "Story as Exemplum, Exemplum as Story: On the Pragmatics and Poetics of Narrative Texts." In *New Perspectives in German Literary Criticism: A Collection of Essays*, edited by Richard E. Lange and Victor Amacher. Translated by David Henry Wilson, 389–417. Princeton, NJ: Princeton University Press, 1979.

Stillman, Robert E. "The Scope of Sidney's 'Defence of Poesy': The New Hermeneutic and Early Modern Poetics." *English Literary Renaissance* Vol. 32.3 (2002): 355–385.

Strier, Richard. *The Unrepentant Renaissance: From Petrarch to Shakespeare to Milton*. Chicago: University of Chicago Press, 2011.

Sullivan, Paul. "Playing the Lord: Tudor *Vulgaria* and the Rehearsal of Ambition." *ELH* 75 (2008): 181–182.

Summit, Jennifer. *Memory's Library: Medieval Books in Early Modern England*. Chicago: University of Chicago Press, 2008.

Summit, Jennifer. "Renaissance Humanism and the Future of the Humanities." *Literature Compass* 9.10 (2012): 665–678.

Swanson, Jenny. *John of Wales: A Study of the Works and Ideas of a Thirteenth-Century Friar*. New York: Cambridge University Press, 1989.

Trimpi, Wesley. "Sir Philip Sidney's *An Apology for Poetry*." In *The Cambridge History of Literary Criticism, Volume 3: The Renaissance*, edited by Glyn P. Norton, 3:187–198. Cambridge: Cambridge University Press, 1999.

Trousdale, Marion. "A Possible Renaissance View of Form." *ELH* 40 (1973): 179–204.

Ullyot, Michael. "Spenser and the Matter of Poetry." *Spenser Studies* 27 (2012): 77–96.

Van den Berg, Kent. "'The Counterfeit in Personation:' Spenser's *Prosopopoia*, or *Mother Hubberds Tale*." In *The Author in his Work: Essays on a Problem in Criticism*, edited by Louis L. Martz and Aubrey Williams, 85–102. New Haven, CT: Yale University Press, 1978.

van Elk, Martine. "'Thou shalt present me as an eunuch to him': Terence in Early Modern England." In *A Companion to Terence*, edited by Antonios Augoustakis and Ariana Traill, 410–428. Hoboken, NJ: Blackwell, 2013.

Vauchez, André, ed. *Oxford Encyclopedia of the Middle Ages*. Oxford: James Clarke & Co., 2005. DOI: 9780227679319.

220 WORKS CITED

Vecchi, Linda. "Spenser's *Complaints*: Is the Whole Equal to the Sum of its Parts?" In *Spenser at Kalamazoo*, edited by Francis G. Greco, 127–138. Clarion, PA: Clarion University of Pennsylvania, 1984.

Vickers, Brian. "'Upstart Crow'? The Myth of Shakespeare's Plagiarism." *The Review of English Studies* 68 (2017): 244–267.

Wabuda, Susan. "'A day after doomsday': Cranmer and the Bible Translations of the 1530s." In *The Oxford Handbook of the Bible in Early Modern England, c. 1530–1700*, edited by Kevin Killeen, Helen Smith, and Rachel Willie, Chapter 1. Oxford: Oxford University Press, 2015. DOI: 9780199686971.

Wailes, Stephen L. "Is Gnapheus' *Acolastus* a Lutheran Play?" In *Semper Idem et Novus: Festschrift for Frank Banta*, edited by Francis Gentry, 345–357. Göppingen: Kümmerle, 1988.

Wailes, Stephen L. *Medieval Allegories of Jesus' Parables*. Berkeley, CA: University of California Press, 1987.

Walker, Greg. *Writing under Tyranny: English Literature and the Henrician Reformation*. Oxford: Oxford University Press, 2005.

Wallace, John. "'Examples Are Best Precepts': Readers and Meanings in Seventeenth-Century Poetry." *Critical Inquiry* 1 (1974): 273–290.

Wallace, Joseph. "Strong Stomachs: Arthur Golding, Ovid, and Cultural Assimilation." *Renaissance Studies* 26 (2012): 728–743.

Wasson, John. "The End of an Era: Parish Drama in England from 1520 to the Dissolution." *Research Opportunities in Renaissance Drama* 31 (1992): 70–78.

Wasson, John. "The Morality Play: Ancestor of Elizabethan Drama?" *Comparative Drama* 13 (1979): 210–222.

Watkins, John. "The Allegorical Theatre: Moralities, Interludes, and Protestant Drama." In *The Cambridge History of Medieval English Literature*, edited by David Wallace, 767–792. Cambridge: Cambridge University Press, 1999.

Watkins, John. *The Specter of Dido: Spenser and Virgilian Epic*. New Haven, CT: Yale University Press, 1995.

Weinberg, Bernard. *A History of Literary Criticism in the Italian Renaissance*. 2 vols. Chicago: University of Chicago Press, 1961.

Welter, Jean-Thiébaut. *L' Exemplum dans la litterature religieuse et didactique du moyen age*. Paris: Occitania, 1927, rept. New York: AMS Press, 1973.

White, Helen C. *Social Criticism in Popular Religious Literature of the Sixteenth Century*. New York: The Macmillan Company, 1944.

Whiting, B. J. *Proverbs in the Earlier English Drama: With Illustrations from Contemporary French Plays*. Cambridge, MA: Harvard University Press, 1938.

Wilson, John Dover. "*Euphues* and the Prodigal Son." *The Library* 10.40 (1909): 337–361.

Wilson-Okamura, David. "Problems in the Virgilian Career." *Spenser Studies* 26 (2011): 1–30.

Young, Alan R. *The English Prodigal Son Plays: A Theatrical Fashion of the Sixteenth and Seventeenth Centuries*. Salzburg: Universität Salzburg, 1979.

Index

Acolastus 10–11, 69–87, 109, 159–163
Adam and Eve 103, 106–107
Advice to Princes *see* Mirrors for Princes
Aesop 6, 23–24, 134–135, 190–191
Alexander, Gavin 135–136 n.12
Aligheri, Dante 99
Allen, Elizabeth 113–114 n.14
Allen, Judson Boyce 20–21 n.19, 114
Als, Hilton 22–23
Altman, Joel 15–16 n.6, 37–38, 46–47 n. 27,
    50–51 n. 47, 72–73 n.23, 122–123 n.36,
    132n. 1
Anabaptists 11, 92–93, 95–96, 101–102,
    106–107 n. 46
Aristotle 6–7, 21 n. 23, 31–33, 89–90
  Nicomachean Ethics 4–8, 20–21, 31, 78–79,
    104–105 n. 44
Ascham, Roger 8–9, 34–36, 68–69, 72, 74,
    136–137, 145–146, 156–159, 162–164,
    171–172
The Assembly of the Gods 60 n.71
Astell, Ann 125–126 n.43, 130 n. 47
Atchity, Kenneth John 195 n. 59
Atkinson, W. E. D. 69 n.6, 69–70 n.9, 70–71
    n.15, 75–76 n. 39, 78 n. 44, 78–79 n. 46,
    81 n.56, 84–85 n. 64
Auden, W. H. 198
Augustine 6–7, 24–25, 28–29, 31, 33–34,
    136–137
Austen, Gillian 157–158 n.16, 167 n.33

Baker, David Weil 92–93 n.14, 96–97 n.27,
    106–107 n. 46
Baldwin, T. W. 115–116 n.19
Baldwin, William 7–8
Bale, John 95
Barclay, Alexander 64
Barkan, Leonard 174–175 n.18, 178 n.28
Bates, Catherine 5 n.16, 134–135 n.10, 136–137
beast fable 189
  see also Aesop
Beck, Ervin 69 n.6, 69–70 n.11, 78 n.44
Beckwith, Sarah 37–38 n.5
Beecher, Donald 119 n.31, 121–122 n. 34
Belsey, Catherine 61–62 n. 75, 119 n. 31,
    123–124 n. 38

Bernard Silvestris 19–20
Bernard, John D. 170–171 n.5
Betteridge, Thomas 38–39 n.6, 94–95 n.19
Bevington, David 37–41, 52 n. 58
Bible 6–7, 80, 93–94, 97, 117–118
  access to 92
  Ecclesiastes 53, 152–153, 168–169
  Exodus 24, 34
  Good Shepherd (John 10:11) 117–118, 194
  Job 129
  parable of the prodigal son (Luke 15) 70–71,
    79–80, 85–86
  Proverbs 3–4, 117
  Romans 18–19, 27–28
  Wisdom Literature 48–49, 152–153
Blamires, Alcuin 27–28 n.48
Bliss, Lee 110 n. 3, 119 n. 31, 123–124 n. 38, 129
    n.46
Bloemendal, Jan 69–70 n.10, 70–71 n. 15, 75–76
    n. 39
Boccaccio, Giovanni 35–36
  Decameron 109, 112–114, 121
  Il Filostrato 27 n.45
body politic 100–101
books as mirrors 1–3, 56, 59, 115–116, 166–167
  see also "The Mirror of the Periods of Man's
    Life" and Mirrors for Princes
Brant, Sebastian 64
Brantley, Jessica 40 n.12, 45–46 n. 26
Briggs, Charles 6–7 n.21, 20–21 n. 20, 112–113
    n.9
Brink, Jean 170–171 n.4
Brown, Richard Danson 170–171 n.2, 177–178
    n.27, 181 n.35, 187–188 n.42, 191–192
    n.50
Buehler, Curt F. 7–8 n.25
Burckhardt, Jacob 10–11
Burrow, Colin 68–69 n.1, n.4, 132.n.1, 144 n.30
Bushnell, Rebecca 47 n.28, 47–48 n.32, n.34

Campana, Joseph 135 n.11
Campion, Edmund 24 n.39
Cannon, Christopher 3–4 n. 11, 17–18
canon 5 n. 17, 22–23, 201–203
Carley, James P. 33–34 n. 69
Cartwright, John 41–42

222 INDEX

Cartwright, Kent 37–38, 50 n. 43, 54 n.62, 132 n.1

Caspari, Fritz 88–89 n.5, 90 n.7, 98–99 n.30

Castano, Emanuele 201

Castle of Perseverance 39–44, 50–51, 58–59, 66, 67

Caxton, William 6, 18–19 n. 13, 190–191

Cefalu, Paul 8–9 n. 29, 165–166 n. 29

Chaucer, Geoffrey 12–13, 15–16, 74, 109, 136–137

  as a fictional character 145–150

  Boece 28–29, 153–154

  The Book of the Duchess 180

  The Canterbury Tales 12–13, 23–24, 114–117, 120, 145–146, 148–149, 172–173, 198

    Clerk's Tale 107, 109–110, 114–117, 120, 123–127, 148–150

    General Prologue 23–24, 103–104, 117–118, 190, 193–194, 196

    Knight's Tale 136–139

    Man of Law's Prologue 156–157 n.11

    Manciple's Tale 3–5, 114, 146–147, 152

    Miller's Tale 23–24, 151–152

    Monk's Tale 185

    Nun's Priest's Tale 42, 189, 190–191

    Pardoner's Tale 23–24, 80, 114–117, 146–147

    Parson's Tale 6–9, 66–67, 116–117

    Physician's Tale 115–119, 121–122

    Retraction to the *Canterbury Tales* 27–29, 35–36, 138, 140–141, 143–144, 146, 153–154, 166

    Tale of Melibee 5 n.15

    Wife of Bath's Tale 21–22, 99

  The Legend of Good Women 125, 156–157 n.11

  Troilus and Criseyde 25–28, 35–36, 134, 135, 138–139, 145–146 n.36, 155–157, 183, 187

Christian Terence 10, 13, 69–71, 75–76, 84–85

Cicero 1–2, 7, 31–32, 54, 56–57, 68–69, 76–77

  De Officiis 4, 6, 104–105

Clark, J. C. D. 130–131 n. 48

Clark, Sandra 132–133 n. 5, 144 n. 32

classical legacy 1–3, 199–201

  medieval approach to 17, 110–118

  paganism of 6–8, 20–21, 24–27, 31, 34

  humanist approach to 10–11, 30, 48, 72, 96, 118–119

  in Edmund Spenser's work 171–173

Clebsch, William 94–95 n.19

The Cobler of Caunterburie 145–146

Clopper, Lawrence M. 39–40 n. 11, 51 nn. 53–54

Coldewey, John 40 n. 15, 41–42 n. 20, 50–51 nn. 8– 9, 51–52 n. 53

Coldiron, A. E. B. 177–178 n. 27, n. 28

Colet, John 33–34

  Aeditio 48–49, 61–62, 160

comedy 120

  Roman comedy 69–71, 74–79, 86, 158–159, 162–163, 166

commonplace books 47–48

complaint 174–178, 180, 181–182, 193, 195

confession 45–46, 66, 184–185

Conley, John 56–57 n.63

Conrad of Hirsau 23–24 n. 34

contemptus mundi see worldly vanity

Cook, Megan 109 n.1, 139–140 n.20

Cooper, Helen 145–146 n. 33, 193 n.55

Copeland, Rita 17–18 n.10, 23–24 n.31, n.32, 25, 27–28 n.49, 33

copia 47–48

Craik, Katherine 170–171n.2, n.5, 174–175 n.19

Crane, Mary Thomas 47 nn. 28–29, 47–48 n.32, n.35, 132 n.1, 144 n.31

Crewe, Jonathan 176, 195 n. 59, 196 n. 62

crisis of the humanities 203

Cronk, Nicholas 35 n. 74

cultural model 70–71, 75, 84

Cummings, Brian 4 n.14, 8–9 n.29, 136–137

Cummings, Robert 1–2 n.3

D'Andrade, Roy 71

Dagenais, John 15–16 n.5

Daniell, David 94 n.16, 94–95 n.19

Davidson, Clifford 39–40 n.10, 45–46 n.26, 50–51 n.44, n. 46, 59–60 n. 69

Davies, Tony 1–2 n.4

Davis, Nicholas 51–52 n.54

Davis, Walter 132–133 n.4, 139–140 n.20, 140–141, 142 n.26, 154 n.45

De Miseria Condicionis Humane (Lotario dei Segni) 13, 156–157, 167–169, 175, 176, 179, 184–185

Debax, Jean-Paul 51–52 n.54, n.55

Delcorno, Pietro 80 nn.49–50, 81 n.58

Deneef, A. Leigh 177–178 n.27

Dickens, A. G. 57 n.66, 94–95 n.20

Dimmick, Jeremy 139–140 n.20, 140–141 n.22, 145–146 n.35, 152 n.42

Dolven, Jeff 2–3 n.10, 11–12 n.38, 47 n.28, 132

Donaldson, E. Talbot 26–27, 138–139

Dowling, Maria 98–99 n.30

du Bellay, Joachim 77–78, 170–174, 177–180, 189

Duffy, Timothy 175 n.22

dulce et utile 12, 23, 31–33, 143–144, 147–148,
    152–153, 173–174
    see also Horace

Eagleton, Terry 202
ecclesiastical pastoral 194–195
education 2–3, 7, 8–10, 30, 33–34, 46, 68–69,
    72–73, 75–76, 92, 98–100, 110, 114,
    124–125, 158, 199–203
egalitarianism 11, 90, 92, 99, 101–104, 106–107
Elliott, Thomas J. 174–175 n.19
Elyot, Thomas 156–157
    Boke of the Governor 11, 47–48, 88–92,
        96, 118–122, 124, 126–127, 130–131,
        134–135, 141–142, 149, 158–159,
        163–164, 196–197
English Protestantism 92, 129, 136–137, 167
Enterline, Lynn 49–50 n.42, 132 n.1, 160 n.22
Erasmian humanism 8–9, 33–35, 46, 72–73, 78,
    88–89, 159–160
Erasmus of Rotterdam 8–9, 11–12, 57, 74–75,
    94–95, 121–122
    Adages 30–31, 47
    Apothegms 115–116
    Complaint of Peace 4
    Education of a Christian Prince 7, 11, 47–48
        n.31, 72, 89, 100–101, 106–107, 134–135
    On the Method of Study 33, 47–48, 55, 72–75,
        142–144, 147–148, 160, 161
    Praise of Folly 64
estate/ social class 99–104
estates satire 189–195
Euphues/ euphuism 69–70, 149–150
Everyman 1–2 n.8, 9–10, 38–40, 50, 67, 70–73,
    155–156, 160–161, 166–167, 176, 184
exempla 11, 103–104, 109, 110, 146, 149–151

fabliau(x) 146–151
Felski, Rita 16–18, 203
Ferguson, Arthur 88 n. 2, 95 n.22
Ferguson, Margaret 180 n.34
Fichte, Joerg O. 37–38 n.5, 40 n.15
Fichter, Andrew 177–178 n.27, 179–180 n.32
Fish, Stanley 67 n.80
Fisher, John 95–96
Fowler, Alastair 56–57
florilegia 48, 72–73
Fox, Alistair 88–89 n.3, n.5, 90 n.7
Foxe, John 94
Fradenburg, Louise 182 n. 36
Freccero, John 15–16 n.1
Freedman, Paul 103 n.42
Frow, John 71 n.19
Fumo, Jamie C. 27 n.46

Gaggero, Christopher 158–159 n.17
Gardiner, Stephen 94–95
Gascoigne, George 12–13, 155–157, 170–171,
    189
    The Adventures of Master F. J 156–157
    The Compleynt of Philomena 174–177
    A Hundreth Sundrie Flowres 157–158
    The Droome of Doomesday 13, 157, 167,
        175–176
    The Glasse of Governement 13, 149–150, 157,
        158, 171–172
    The Steele Glas 157
Gelley, Alexander 113–114 n.14
Gesta Romanorum 111–113
Gibson, Gail McMurray 45–46 n.26
Giancarlo, Matthew 91 n.9
Giles of Rome 20–21, 31
Gillespie, Alexandra 109 n.1, 114–115 n.18
Gillespie, Vincent 17–18 n.10, 20–21, 23–24
    n.31
Gnapheus, Gulielmus (Willem de
    Volder) 69–87, 159
Golden Age 103
Goldstein, Laurence 175 n.22
Golding, Arthur 118–119, 124, 130–131,
    147–148, 159–161
Gosson, Stephen 133–134, 136–138, 142
Gower, John 12, 21–22, 26–27, 35–36, 74
    as a fictional character 132–133, 139–140,
        145–154
    Confessio Amantis 18–20, 23–25, 27–29,
        117–118
Grabes, Herbert 1–2 n.8
Grafton, Anthony 2–3 n.10, 4 n.14, 7 n.23,
    31–32, 47 n.29, 74–75 n.35, 88–89 n.4,
    201 n.7
grammar books 48–50, 72, 110, 124–125, 160
Great Books 201–202
Green, D. H. 17–18 n.10, 23–24 n.31, n.33
Green, Ian 2–3 n.10, 30–31 n.54, 98–99 n.30,
    115–116 n.19, 165–166 n.29, 170–171 n.1
Greenblatt, Stephen 1–2 n.1, 3–4 n.11, 10–11
    n.35
Greene, Robert 12–13, 123–124, 132, 156–158,
    189
    Arbasto The anatomie of fortune 132–133 n.4
    Greenes Groatsworth of Wit 139–140 n. 18
    The Repentance of Robert Greene 123–124
        n.40, 144
    Vision Written at the Instant of his death 139,
        155–156, 170–171
Greene, Thomas 15–16, 20–21 n. 21, n.25, 30
    n.52, 68–69 n.1, n.4, 71–72 n.20, 77–78
    n.42, 84, 172 n. 12, 178–179

224 INDEX

Griffiths, Huw 177–178 n.27
Griffiths, Jane 38–39 n.6, 59–60 n. 69, 65 n.77,
 121–122 n.35
Guillory, John 5 n. 17, 15–16 n.5, 202–203
Guy, John 88–89 n.3, n.5, 90 n.7

Hadfield, Andrew 38–39 n.6, 39–40 n.8, n.10, 57
 n. 65
Halpern, Richard 5 n.16, 30 n.53, 49–50 n.40,
 98–99 n.31
Hampton, Timothy 90, 113–114 n.14, 121–122
 n.34
Hanna, Ralph 107 n.47, 125–126 n.43
Happé, Peter 50–51 n. 47, 54 n.62, 59–60 n.69,
 121–122n.35
Harbage Alfred 37–38, 39–40 n.11, 50–51 n.45,
 59–60 n.69
Hardin, Richard 90 n.7
Helfer, Rebeca 170–171 n.5, 173–174 n.16,
 174–175 n.18, 177–178 n.27, n.28, 179
 n.31, 187–188 n.42
Helgerson, Richard 11–12, 50 n.43, 69 n. 6,
 n.8, 69–70, 81 n.58, 132, 139–140 n.20,
 140–141 n.22, 141–142, 149–150 n.41,
 156–157 n.7, 157, 158–159 n.17, n.18,
 162 n.25, 164–165 n.27
Henry VIII 69–70, 94–97, 101–102
Herdt, Jennifer 6–7 n.21
Herford, Charles 69–70 n.69, 75–76 n.40,
 86 n.6
Hexter, J. H. 98–99 n.30
Heywood, John 54 n.62
Higden, Ranulph 27–28 n.49
Hirsch, E. D., Jr. 15–16 n.5, 22–23 n.28
Hogrefe, Pearl 96–97 n.27, 99 n. 32,
 104–105 n.44
Holstun, James 101, 103
Homer 118–122
Horace 12, 47–48, 76–77, 85–86, 132–133
 Ars Poetica 17–18, 23–24, 31–33, 134–135
 See also dulce et utile
Horbury, Ezra 69 n.8, 69–70 n.11
Hui, Andrew 77–78 n.42, 177–178 n.27, n.28,
 179–180 n.31, 187–188 n.42
humanities 201–203
Hunter, G. K. 15–16 n.6
Hyde, Thomas 175 n.22, 179–180 n. 32

imitation 10, 13, 26, 49–50, 68–87, 132–133,
 170–173, 176–180, 186, 189–190,
 196–197
Innocent III see Lothario dei Segni
interlude 37–39, 51–52
Interludium de Clerico et Puella 51–52

Janowitz, Anne 177–178 n.27, 179–180 n.31
Jardine, Lisa 2–3 n.10, 4 n.14, 7 n.23, 31–32, 47
 n.29, 74–75 n.35, 88–89 n.4, 201 n.7
Jauss, Hans Robert 71
Jeffrey, David Lyle 24n. 39
Jerome 80–81
John of Salisbury 91, 100–101 n.36
John of Wales 112–113 n.9
Johnson, Eleanor 20–21 n.19, 23–24 n.31
Jones, R. D. 57 n.66, 94–95 n.20
Jonson, Ben 69
Juhász–Ormsby, Ágnes 33–34 n. 69, 69–70 n.10,
 72–73 n.24

Kahn, Victoria 34–35 n. 72, 90 n.7
Kaplan, Ruth 183 n.37
Karreman, Isabel 177–178 n.27, 179–180 n.31
Kerrigan, John 174–175 n.19
Kidd, David Comer 201
King, Pamela 37–38 n.2, 40
Kinney, Arthur 1–2 n.4, 16–17 n.75, 49–50 n.42,
 132 n.1, 137–138, 165 n.28
Kintgen, Eugene 47 n.28, 132 n.1
Kolve, V. A. 57 n.67
Kristeller, Paul Oskar 1–2 n.6, 6, 10, 47 n.29,
 68–69
Kumaran, Arul 139–140 n.20
Kuskin, William 39–40 n.10, 50–51 n.44

lament see complaint
Langland, William 29–30, 35, 62–63, 103–104,
 193, 198
Lazarus, Micha 72–73 n.23, 74 n.29
Lehmberg, Stanford 1–2 n.3, 88–89 n.3, 97,
 101–102 n.39, 104–105 n.44
Lester, G. A. 54 n.61, 59–60 n.69
Lewalski, Barbar Kiefer 17–18 n.9
Lewis, C. S. 47 n.28,
Lily's Grammar of Latin in English 8–9, 48–49,
 110
literary criticism 15–17, 112–113, 116–117
 See also Philip Sidney, An Apology for Poetry
Livy 35–36, 115–116, 119, 120
Lodge, Thomas 8–9, 11–12, 137–138
Lotario dei Segni see De Miseria
Luther, Martin 93–96
Lydgate, John 60 n. 72, 74, 109
 The Fall of Princes 1–2, 91–92, 97, 99–103,
 107–108, 111, 122–123 n.37, 125–126,
 128–129, 166–167
Lyons, John D. 113–114 n.14

MacCracken, Henry Noble 60–62
MacIntyre, Alasdair 6–7 n.21

INDEX   225

Mack, Peter 47 n.28, 49–50 n.42, 132 n.1
MacLean, Hugh 174–175
MacLure, Millar 177–178 n.27
Macropedius, George 75–76 n.40
Major, John 88–89 n.3, 91 n.9, 96–97 n.27, 99
    n.32, 104–105 n.44
Mankind 39–42, 44–45, 50–51, 54 n.62,
Mann, Jill 190–191 n.46, 192 n.53
Mannyng, Robert 110, 114–115
Marenbon, John 6–7 n.21, 21, 24 n.38
Marot, Clément 172–173
Maslen, R. W. 7–8 n.25, 139–140 n.20, 140–141
    n.22, 145–146 n.35, 154 n.45
Matz, Robert 5 n.16, 31–32 n.59, 88 n.1, n.2, 97
    n.29, 98–99 n.31, n.32, 136–137
Melanchthon, Philipp 30–31 n.54
McConica, James 33–34 n. 69, 57 n. 66, 88–89
    n.5, 90 n.7
Medwall, Henry 38–39
    Fulgens and Lucrece 37–38, 41–43, 46–47
    Nature 41–42, 46–47, 50–51, 60 n.71,
    122–123
Melehy, Hassan 177–178 n.27, n.28
Menand, Louis 201–202 n.10, 203 n.16, n.17
Middleton, Anne 116–117
Miller, Mark 114 n.16
Mills, David 39–40 n.10, 51 n.49
Minnis, A. J. 19–20 n.16, 20–21 n.19, 27 n.46,
    27–28 n.49
Miola, Robert S. 72–73 n.23, 75–76 n.40
mirrors *See* books as mirrors
"The Mirror of the Periods of Man's Life" 59–60,
    62–63
Mirrors for Princes (*Fürstenspiegel*) 91, 98–99,
    103, 104–105, 110
Mitchell, J. Allan 114 n.16
monarchy 90–92, 97, 98–99, 101–102
morality plays 9–10, 37–46, 158–159, 166–167
moral philosophy 6–8, 20–21, 30–31, 81,
    134–135, 148
More, Thomas 1–2, 31, 32–34, 132, 199
    The Life of Pico della Mirandola 1–3, 5–6, 56,
    83–84, 87, 166–167
    Utopia 92–93 n.12, 96–97 n.27
Morison, Richard 95–96, 101
Morrison, Toni 22–23
Morse, Charlotte C. 125 n.42
Moss, Ann 10–11 n.34, 47 n.29, 48 nn.34–.35
Mubashshir ibn Fatik, Abu al-Wafa 7–8 n.27
Muir, Tom 179–180 n.31
Mundus et Infans 9–10, 38–40, 51–52, 59, 72–73
Munson, William 57 n.67
Murakami, Ineke 37–38 n.5

Nauert, Charles 74–75 n.35
Nelson, Alan 40, 60 n.71
Newcomb, Lori Humphrey 139–140 n.18,
    153–154 n.44
Nguyen, Viet Thanh 203 n.15, n.17
nobility 97–100, 108, 126–127
Norbrook, David 1–2 n.1, 92–93 n.12, 102–103
    n.40
Norland, Howard 37–38 n.2, 40 n.15
Normington, Katie 51 n.52
Norton, Glyn P. 30 n.52, 68–69 n.1

Olson, Glending 17–18 n.10, 23–24 n.31, n.34,
    n.37
Orme, Nicholas 8–9 n.30, 48–49 n.35
Ovid 22, 130–131, 142, 143, 145–146
    Metamorphoses 18–19, 21–22, 35, 118–119,
    125, 146–148, 159–161

Painter, William 35–36, 155–156 n.6
Palmer, Ada 31 n.58, 88 n.2
Palsgrave, John 10, 69–70, 82–83, 86
    De Parabell vam vorlorn Szohn 85–86
Parente, James A., Jr. 75–76 n.40
Parker, Patricia 70–71 n.14
patience, as virtue 11, 104–105, 107–108,
    122–131, 160–161
Patterson, Annabel 189 n.44, 196 n.60, 196
Patterson, Lee 27–28 n.47
Pearsall, Derek 91 n.11
Peltonen, Markku 34–35 n.72
penitential discourse 1–3, 6–9, 38–39, 41–43,
    45–46, 54,57–58, 62–63, 66–67, 80,
    82–84, 110–115, 132–133, 144, 166–167
Percy, Thomas 40–41
Perry, Nandra 136–137 n.13
personification allegory 121–124, 128
Peter, John 174–175 n.19
Peterson, Joyce 64 n.75
Petrarch, Francesco 1–2, 15–16 n.1, 77–78,
    109–110, 112–114, 120, 121, 125–128,
    170–173, 176, 189
Phillip, John *see The Play of Patient Grissell*
Phillips, Margaret Mann 30–31 n.55
Pico della Mirandola 1–3, 5–6, 56, 83–84, 87,
    166–167, 199
Piers Plowman-tradition 103–104, 157, 193
Pigman, G. W., III 68–69 n.1, n.4, 144 nn.30–31,
    155–156 n.5, 156–157, 156–157 n.12,
    157–158
The Play of Patient Grissell 11, 109, 119, 160–161
plowmen 93–94, 103–104, 107, 196
Potter, Robert 52 n.58, 59–60 n.69

226 INDEX

Potter, Ursula 72–73 n.23, 110 n.3, 119 n.31, 129 n.46, 158–159 n.17, 162 n.24, 165–166 n.29
Prayer and Complaynt of the Plowman 174–175
precepts 4, 23–25, 38–39, 48–50, 54–67, 81, 105–106, 143, 144, 147–148, 153, 159–161
Prescott, Anne Lake 173–174, 180 n.33
Pride of Life 39–40, 42, 50–51
prodigal son 10, 69, 80, 85–87, 141–142, 167–169
  prodigal-son-plays 69–70, 75–76 n.40, 85–86, 124–125, 157–167
The prouverbes of Solomon newly translated 152 n.43
proverbs 30–31, 47, 54, 56–57, 142, 147–148
Puttenham, George 139–140, 145–146

Quinn, Naomi 71

Rädle, Fidel 70–71 n.15
Rambuss, Richard 170–171 n.5, 189 n.44, 196 n.60
Rasmussen, Carl J. 170–171 n.5, 189 n.44, 196 n.60
Rasmussen, Mark 170–171 n.2, 172–173 n.13, 176 n.25
Reeve, Michael D. 1–2 n.2
Reformation 11, 40, 88–89, 92
  Calvinism 165
  Radical Reformation 95–96
repentance *see* penitential discourse
rhetoric 31–32, 34–35
Robertson, D. W. 24 n.40
Roman de la Rose 115–116
Roman comedy *see* comedy
Rome (ancient) 101–104, 177–182
Roye, William 93–94
Rubin, Joan 202 n.8
Rycroft, Eleanor 38–39 n.6

Salamon, Linda 158–159 nn.17–18
Salman, Phillip 118–119 n.27
Salter, Elizabeth 125–126 n.44
Scanlon, Larry 111–112 n.6, 113–114, 149
Scase, Wendy 174–175 nn. 19–20
Schiffhorst, Gerald J. 125–126 n.43
Schonaeus, Cornelis 71 n.5
Schwyzer, Phillip 177–178 n.27, 179–180 n.31
Scott, A. B. 19–20 n.16
secularism/ secularization 9–10, 31, 46–47, 67, 69, 88–89, 97, 104–105, 108, 130–131, 172
Seneca 144

sententiae [sentences] *see* precepts
Shagan, Ethan 92–93 n.13
Shakespeare, William 37–38, 67, 69, 139–140, 156–157
Shepherd, Geoffrey 31–32 n.59, 133–134 n.6
Shortslef, Emily 177–178 n.27, 187–188 n.42
Shrank, Cathy 88–89 n.3
Shutters, Lynn 125
Siebers, Tobin 16 n.8, 113–114 n.14
Sidney, Philip 78, 84, 150–152, 156–157, 164, 177–178, 184, 187–188
  An Apology for Poetry 11–13, 15–17, 133, 139–146, 149, 154, 196–198, 200
Silberman, Lauren 189 n.44, 193 n. 52, 194–195
Silvester, Bernard 19–20
Simon, Joan 8–9 n.30, 33–34 n. 69, n.70, 88–89 n.5, 95 n.21, 98–99 n.30
Simpson, James 2–3n.9, 93–94
Sir Gawain and the Green Knight 50–51
Skelton, John 50–51, 54 n. 62
Skinner, Quentin 1–2n.6
Solomon (biblical King and author) 3–4, 45, 89–90, 140, 145–146, 152–153, 155–156, 168–169
Spenser, Edmund 12–13, 77–78, 84, 139–140, 156–157, 171
  The Complaints 13, 155–156, 170–173
    Mother Hubberd's Tale 189
    Muiopotmos 172–173
    Ruines of Rome 178–179
    Ruines of Time 177–188
    Teares of the Muses 176–177
    Virgil's Gnat 172–173
    Visions of Bellay 179–180
    Visions of Petrarch 183
  Daphnaida 180
  The Faerie Queene 170–172, 198, 199–200
  The Shepheardes Calender 171–172
Spivack, Bernard 38–39 n.6, 119 n.31, 121–122 n.35
Sponsler, Claire 37–38 n.5
Den Spyeghel der Salicheyt van Elckerlijc 1–2 n.8, 56, 166–167
Steenbrugge, Charlotte 119 n.31, 120 n.33, 121–122 n.35, 123–124 n.39
Stein, Harold 170–171 n.4, 189 n.44
Stierle, Karl-Heinz 112–113, 121
Stillman, Robert E. 135–136 n.12
Strier, Richard 10–11 n.35
studia humanitatis 1–2
Sturm, Johannes 30–31 n.54
Sullivan, Paul 37–38 n.42, 160 n.22

Summit, Jennifer 1–2 n.4, 100–101 n.36,
  201 n.7
Terence 4, 33–34, 68–69, 78–79, 159–160,
  162–164
  Adelphoe 78–79 n.48
  Andria 72–75, 81, 84–85
Terens in English 74, 85
tragedy 26, 75–78, 81–83, 85–86, 134
Trevisa, John 20–21
Trimpi, Wesley 134 n.7
Trousdale, Marion 118–119 n. 27
Twain, Mark 22–23
Tyndale, William 80, 85–86, 94–95

Udall, Nicholas 72–75
Ullyot, Michael 177–178 n.27

van den Berg, Kent T. 192 n. 52, 193 n.55,
  196–197 n.63
van der Noot, Jan 173–175, 184
van Elk, Martine 72–73 n.23
Vecchi, Linda 170–171 n.2, 174–175 n.19
Vice figure 121–124, 126–127, 129
Vickers, Brian 139–140 n.18
Virgil 33–34, 164, 171–172
  Aeneid 4–5, 19–20, 141–143, 199–200

Eclogues 74–75, 142–143, 147–148, 171

Wabuda, Susan 95–96 n.25
Wailes, Stephen L. 70–71 n.15, 80 n.50
Waldis, Burkardt 85–86n.69
Walker, Greg 38–39 n.6, 88–89 n.3, 91 n.9
Wallace, John 118–119 n.27
Wallace, Joseph 118–119 n.29
Wasson, John 39–40 n.11
Watkins, John 37–38, 39–40 n. 8, 52 n.58,
  171–172 n.10
Weinberg, Bernard 15–16, 31–32 n.60, 33,
  68–69, 112–113 n.13
Welter, Jean–Thiébaut 112–113
White, Helen C. 95 nn. 21–22
Whiting, B. J. 54 nn. 61–62
Wilson, John Dover 69 nn.6–8, 75–76
Wilson–Okamura, David 171–172 n.10
Wisdom 39–42, 45
worldly vanity 12–13, 53, 137–138, 140–141,
  152–153, 155–157, 167, 170–173, 190,
  195
  see also De Miseria

Young, Alan R. 69 n. 6, 75–76 n.39, 78 nn.
  43–44, 78–79 nn. 45–46, 80 n.49